THE CHANCE OF SALVATION

The
Chance of Salvation

✠✠✠✠✠✠✠✠✠✠✠✠✠✠✠✠✠✠✠✠✠✠✠✠✠✠✠✠✠✠✠✠

A HISTORY OF CONVERSION
IN AMERICA

Lincoln A. Mullen

Harvard University Press

Cambridge, Massachusetts
London, England
2017

First printing

Cataloging-in-Publication Data available from the Library of Congress
ISBN: 978-0-674-97562-0 (alk. paper)

For Grandmom

Contents

Preface

ALL MY LIFE, people have been telling me stories about how they came to their faith. The Baptist church in Massachusetts where I grew up asked people to give an account of their conversions before they were baptized and accepted for church membership. Men, women, and teenagers stood in front of the congregation to describe how they had been born again and saved from their sins. Their speech was often halting as they tried to explain an experience that they had felt deeply but never before put into words. Later, those same people would give testimonies of what Jesus had done for them, often recounting their conversion narratives. As they grew accustomed to retelling their conversions and learned the conventional vocabulary, their accounts became more fluent but no less fervent. "I love to tell the story,/for those who know it best/seem hungering and thirsting/to hear it like the rest" were words to a gospel song that might have been applied to people's conversion stories.

When I was young, I assumed that only Baptists of our particular stripe told stories to explain their faith. After all, if telling a conversion narrative was what made you a Baptist, then only Baptists could tell conversion narratives. Of course, I was wrong. I have since heard Christians from nearly every kind of background relate histories of their life and faith. People in the Anglican tradition that I now count as my own tell such stories as frequently as the Baptists of my childhood. Nor were such accounts limited to Christians. I have since heard conversion accounts of a different sort from people who became Jews or Muslims or Buddhists. Certain stories stuck out: two drug addicts who became Pentecostal street evangelists; the pastor whose conversion account was featured on the *Unshackled* radio program; the former student at a Christian college who led the call to prayer at a mosque I visited. Perhaps the most common kind of story that I have heard—often told in a sentence, sometimes told at great length—is the narrative of people who grew up with some kind of religious faith or commitment and then stepped away from it as an adult.

And then there were books. Augustine's *Confessions* was perhaps the first such book that I read, followed by the narratives of Sarah Pierpont Edwards and David Brainerd, John Wesley and Jarena Lee, but also Thomas Merton's *The Seven Storey Mountain*, Bertrand Russell's *Why I Am Not a Christian*, and the like. Somewhere I read the conversion relations of Congregationalists in New England towns in the seventeenth century. When compared to the relations of my Massachusetts Baptists, they were as different as a great-grandparent and a child, yet they bore a family resemblance.

As I listened to and compared these stories, it became apparent that they fell into patterns. However much the details might vary, Baptist conversion narratives all had to hit the main beats of repentance and faith to count as part of the genre. But there were other, more striking patterns. If someone had been born again as a child, then it was almost certain that they would be born again for a second time, or at least experience an "assurance of faith," as a teenager or young adult. People who had grown up Catholic were likely to say that they had never been asked to appropriate the gospel for themselves until they read the Bible. On the other hand, the narratives of people who had left religion were, if anything, even more uniform, almost invariably mentioning a distaste for "organized religion," political or moral differences, or the evidence of science.

When people told their stories, they usually framed them as a religious choice. Yet those same people seemed unable to tell stories that differed from the general patterns. Their apparent autonomy was curiously constrained. And so I came to ask a few questions: What kinds of patterns was it possible for people to experience? And how did those patterns change over time? I formed these questions at first because of my own experiences. But for reasons that I explain in the introduction to this book, those questions are far more than

personal. They get to the heart of the way many Americans have experienced religion as a matter of choice, but as a choice that they are
obligated to make. This book is an attempt to do justice to some of
the bewildering varieties of conversion experiences. But even more,
it is an attempt to explain not simply what people believed, but what
it was possible for them to believe in the first place.

Few things can spark a conversation among historians quite like
the difficulties of relying on autobiographical evidence such as narratives of conversion. To what extent do autobiographical materials
accurately show what people actually experienced, and to what extent do they merely reflect how people have arranged their narratives to fit existing conventions? As I mentioned, even insiders who
begin to compare accounts start to notice their similarities. All historians (whose job is to make comparisons) share a certain wariness
about these kinds of sources. In religious studies, the tendency to assume a critical posture toward the "data" that religious actors offer
is even stronger. For my own part, having worked with a wide variety of materials on conversion from several centuries, I share that
hermeneutic of suspicion. These sources are difficult for scholars to
parse, and I think that nobody can in any meaningful sense speak
outside the constraints on thought and language imposed by their
own time.

Yet this book is animated by a sympathy for the people whose stories I tell. John Henry Newman described writing his *Apologia Pro
Vita Sua* (a justification of his conversion from the Church of England
to Roman Catholicism) as "a cruel operation, the ripping up of old
griefs." In many of the conversion narratives in this book, the note of
loss is sounded as often as the note of gain. In my estimation, we can
learn more from historical empathy than from a rigid posture of
critical distance, by taking people on their own terms rather than by
imposing a scholarly vocabulary upon them. But the empathy of the
historian does not consist simply in retelling other people's stories
for them. They can do that well enough for themselves. Rather, it
consists in going beneath individual accounts to reveal deeper patterns of thought, word, and deed, in demonstrating to people that
though they may have acted of their own will yet they have acted
within historically conditioned constraints. The empathy lies in

demonstrating what it was possible for people to say so that they can better understand what they have said.

While told through the stories of many converts, this book is more a history of how the idea of conversion shaped and became central to American religious life. I am telling a different story than most converts would tell themselves about agency or choice. Yet I hope that this larger story of conversion is one that will help illuminate the experiences of the many people, living and dead, who took the time to tell their stories.

Religion is a *forced* option, so far as that good goes. We cannot escape the issue by remaining sceptical and waiting for more light, because, although we do avoid error in that way *if religion be untrue*, we lose the good, *if it be true*, just as certainly as if we positively chose to disbelieve. . . .

Indeed we *may* wait if we will,—I hope you do not think that I am denying that,—but if we do so, we do so at our peril as much as if we believed. In either case we *act*, taking our life into our hands.

—William James, *"The Will to Believe"*

Introduction

RELIGION AS CHOICE

Samuel Hill had not always been an infidel. Hill was born in Maine in 1777, to a father who died when Hill was eight and to a godly Christian mother. His mother "used all the means in her power, according to her best judgment, in educating her children in the Fear of God, & in respect for his ordinances." He absorbed Christianity at the village school, where "the books mostly in use were Bibles & Testaments," as well as Isaac Watts's hymns and John Milton's *Paradise Lost*. But Hill's inherited Christianity did not go unchallenged. He read "immoral books" while a youth, and found more potent stuff in Thomas Paine's *The Age of Reason*. Paine's attack on institutional Christianity and the Bible turned American Christians against the revolutionary pamphleteer and author of *Common Sense*. But for the small group of Deists who flourished briefly in the postrevolutionary United States, Paine's form of skepticism provided an alternative to Christianity.[1]

When he was seventeen, Hill went to sea and worked his way up to captain. During his seafaring career, Hill became a confirmed unbeliever. From fellow sailors he learned a habit of "profane allusion to Religion or Scripture," and once, after attending a Methodist meeting, he "retired immediately afterwards with my companions

1

to amuse ourselves by turning to contemptuous Ridicule all that we could remember of the service." Just as important, he was thoroughly read in anti-Christian literature, both ancient and contemporary. In a foreign port he bought Voltaire's *Philosophical Dictionary*, which he considered "an invaluable acquisition, as it furnished me with new ideas & arguments, to Ridicule the Religion of Jesus, as also its teachers." He found justification for his views in Lucretius's *On the Nature of Things.* Hill even tried to convince his wife that "the System of Christianity was founded in falsehood."[2]

The turning point in Hill's life came in Canton (Guangzhou) during the winter of 1818–1819. There he met Robert Morrison, an Anglican priest and the first Protestant missionary to China. It was no coincidence that a man as traveled as Hill should encounter a missionary, for Protestants in Britain and the United States had begun to send thousands of missionaries both around the world and to the interior of North America. Hill might just as easily have encountered mission Christianity in the port of Salem, Massachusetts, from which he had sailed on the China trade and from which the missionaries of the American Board of Commissioners for Foreign Missions embarked. The Rev. Dr. Morrison was well equipped with the stock-in-trade of missions: books and Bibles. He gave Hill copies of David Bogue's *Essay on the Divine Authority of the New Testament*, Philip Doddridge's widely distributed *Rise and Progress of Religion in the Soul*, and his own works on the Chinese language, along with a book of sermons he had preached.[3]

During the long voyage from Canton to Valparaiso, Chile, Hill "employed most of my leisure in the study of the books received from Dr. Morrison." First he read Bogue's defense of the New Testament, and "before I had got through the book my former doubts had vanished." He "became thoroughly convinced of the truth & Reality of the Divine Mission of Jesus Christ." Next he turned to Doddridge's explanation of how to experience an evangelical conversion: "Here I found the Situation of a person under the bondage of sin so strongly & clearly described." He felt "the urgent necessity, as well as [the] reasonableness & Propriety of falling in with the terms offered by the Gospel of Christ." Hill studied the Bible for several weeks, after which he resolved to be baptized and to join a church. But Hill judged these resolutions insufficient to mark his conversion from infidelity to Christianity. So while the ship *Packet* rolled in the Pacific Ocean "in Latd. 33 deg north, Longd. 179 deg. East from Greenwich," Hill copied a prayer of conversion from *The Rise and Progress of Religion in the Soul* onto eight pages of his journal as the act by which he converted to Christianity:

> Trembling may justly take hold on me when I, a sinful worm, presume to lift up my head to thee, presume to appear in thy majestic presence on such an occasion as this. To thee, therefore do I now come, invited by the name of thy son, and trusting in his righteousness and grace, laying myself at thy feet with shame and confusion of face, and smiting upon my breast, I say, with the humble publican, God be merciful to me, a Sinner; I acknowledge, O Lord, that I have been a great transgressor.[4]

Reading Hill's handwriting is as close as anyone can come to actually observing a historical religious conversion in progress, because Hill wrote down what he was thinking as he converted. Though his experience was unique in being recorded with the meticulousness of a ship's log, in many ways it typified conversions in his day. Hill marked his conversion with a sinner's prayer, a form that developed in the nineteenth century from older evangelical practices and from biblical models. Hill, like many others, learned that form of conversion from evangelistic literature widely distributed through print. His conversion was part of a widespread effort at Christianizing the world—including the United States—that began in earnest during the nineteenth century. Hill converted from complete unbelief to Christianity; many other people considered themselves complete unbelievers before their conversion.

But the most important point about Hill's experience was that his religion ceased to be an identity that he had inherited and became an identity he had chosen. In his childhood, Christianity was instilled in him by his family and education; in his youth, he rejected it for skepticism and irreligion; in middle age, he consciously adopted Christianity for himself. Hill's conversion offers us a starting place for considering how religion shifted from being an identity that nineteenth-century Americans could inherit to being an identity that they were obligated to choose for themselves.

⊹

When it comes to religious identity, the United States today is the product of religious conversions like Hill's. Compared to most of Europe, the United States is famously religious. By virtually every measure—including rates of affiliation, attendance at services, and personal practices such as prayer—Americans engage in religion more than Europeans.[5] Americans also change their religions—a lot. According to a 2009 Pew Research Center report, some 46 percent of Americans have changed their religious affiliation from the faith in which they had been raised as children. Former Catholics made up 9 percent of the population; half of them had become Protestants. Protestants who had become unaffiliated were 7 percent of the population. Fifteen percent of Americans had changed from one Protestant denomination to another. Four percent of Americans had been raised without any particular religious affiliation and then joined a religion; put another way, 54 percent of the people raised without a religion went on to join one, most becoming Protestant.

Of the 54 percent of Americans in 2009 who remained in the religion or denomination of their childhood, 16 percent (that is, 9 percent of all Americans) had at one time left their childhood faith only to return to it. Many Americans change religious traditions more than once. Slightly more than half of Protestants who had switched denominations changed two or more times. And Protestants were surprisingly the most stable group: for every religion or denomination, between 51 and 70 percent of the people who had changed religions did so twice or more. In this nationwide religious shuffle, the biggest losses have been to non-Latino Catholics, the biggest gains to the unaffiliated (a group distinct from atheists), who are growing rapidly among young adults. But even among those who became unaffiliated, some 33 percent of former Roman Catholics and some 38 percent of former Protestants explained that they "just have not found the right religion for them yet."[6] The result is that many denominations are composed in large part of converts. "By 1978," for example, "an estimated 48 percent of adult Episcopalians had been raised in other traditions."[7]

Americans tend to choose their religious identity even when they wish to retain a cultural identity that they have inherited. Consider the case of American Catholics. According to a 2015 Pew Research Center report, some two out of ten Americans claim Roman Catholicism "as their current religion," and another one out of ten "were raised in the faith and have now fallen away." But a third group—comprising some 9 percent of all Americans—consider themselves "indelibly Catholic by culture, ancestry, ethnicity, or family tradition" yet do not claim Catholicism as their religion. In fact, many of these "cultural Catholics," to use Pew's term, claim Protestantism as their religion or are agnostics or atheists.[8] We can note a similar phenomenon among American Jews, some 22 percent of whom think of themselves as Jewish—but not by religion.[9] Mormons are unusually likely to retain members who grew up in the LDS church, but they too have a contingent of "cultural Mormons."[10] These people are making the straightforward claim that they have inherited an identity as Catholics or Jews from their families and upbringings. Yet there is also an unspoken assumption that the religious part of their identity can be chosen at will. They feel they have inherited a Catholic or Jewish identity but have made a conscious choice not to embrace Catholicism or Judaism as their religion. This means that *religious* denotes the part of their identity that can be chosen, while *cultural* denotes the part that is inherited.[11]

The prevalence of religion as choice instead of religion as inheritance is distinctively (though not uniquely) American. A team of sociologists has investigated the prevalence of conversion in forty countries around the world. They found that in many countries, the rate of conversion is negligible. Countries such as Greece, Italy, Ireland, Spain, or Russia had conversion rates of 1 percent or lower; the average country had a rate of conversion in the 4 to 5 percent range. The only countries with conversion rates of more than 10 percent were the United States, Canada, Chile, and New Zealand, and people in the United States converted most often.[12]

When asked why they convert and switch and drift away, most Americans offer reasons that they would classify as religious. To be sure, life events such as marriage are the reason for many conversions, and some switching is the result of people migrating to places without their preferred denomination. A conservative Baptist might join a conservative "Bible" church, while a mainline member of the United Church of Christ might attend a mainline Presbyterian church. But most conversions are driven by reasons such as interpretations of the Bible or doctrine, disagreements over morality, or finding a religious group that meets spiritual needs better. Other life cycle events, such as the death of parents or the birth of a child, provide opportunities for people to act on their unexpressed religious convictions. Becoming unaffiliated is for most people a process of drifting away; becoming affiliated is for most a conscious choice. Even people who remain in the religion of their birth feel the obligation to respond to other possible religions, or the possibility of no religion. By maintaining their identity unchanged, they are in effect choosing to reject other possibilities.

The religion scholar Thomas Tweed has proposed a theory in which religion can be understood in terms of "crossing" and "dwelling."[13] If that is the case, then Americans are in the habit of crossing. These religious crossings are important for what they imply about how religion functions in the United States. The movement of people from one religious group to another is not simply a characteristic of religion: the system itself is set up to be a perpetual motion machine. Religious mobility is, in one sense, a freedom that Americans have. They can change their religion, and so they do. But in the United States, people not only *may* pick their religion, they *must*. One's religious affiliation is a form of identity, and if the polls are to be believed, it is an identity that many people regard as central. But it is not a form of identity that one can in any simple sense inherit from one's parents or community. Religious identity in the United States is profoundly a matter of individual choice.

✠

The history of how Americans came by this religious mobility is curiously foreshortened, because it is usually ascribed to two relatively brief periods. Two stories attempt to explain its origin.

According to the first story, usually told by historians, disestablishment set the character of American religion. In the aftermath of the Revolution, Congress declared in the Northwest Ordinance that "no person, demeaning himself in a peaceable and orderly manner, shall ever be molested on account of his mode of worship or religious sentiments," and the federal Constitution guaranteed that "Congress shall make no law respecting an establishment of religion, or prohibiting the free exercise thereof."[14] Eventually, all of the states also disestablished religion, albeit sometimes slowly, and the Congregationalist churches in New England and the Anglican churches in the South lost their state-sponsored privileges. Americans were free to choose their own religions, so the story goes, and they did so in ever greater numbers, founding their own new religions when none of the old would do.

Disestablishment really did open up religious choice. The paradox of disestablishment—that people affiliated with religion more readily the less the state encouraged them to do so—was embraced by people like the minister Lyman Beecher. Beecher at first strongly opposed disestablishment, but he came to realize that it was "the best thing that ever happened to the State of Connecticut. It cut the churches loose from dependence on state support. . . . They say ministers have lost their influence; the fact is, they have gained. By voluntary efforts, societies, missions, and revivals, they exert a deeper influence."[15]

Furthermore, disestablishment, whose rationale was expressed in the 1786 Virginia Statute for Religious Freedom, established the ground rule that religious groups had to persuade their adherents.[16] In the statute, Thomas Jefferson articulated a psychology of religious belief. When governments established a particular denomination, people might seem to choose the favored denomination to avoid "temporal punishments or . . . civil incapacitations," but the mind was free even when the body was coerced because "the opinions and belief of men depend not on their own will, but follow involuntarily the evidence proposed to their minds." In other words, religious coercion simply could not work, because one could not arbitrarily will oneself to believe this or that. Thus the statute guaranteed freedom not just "to profess" but also "by argument to maintain, their opinion in matters of religion."[17] State governments no longer financed churches or required attendance at services, but they did protect the attempt to persuade others of the truth of one's religion. Disestablishment turned American religion into a system where arguments were propounded—in the public square and at home, in the press, and as popular entertainment—and belief followed or not.[18]

According to the second story, often told by sociologists of religion, after World War II (and especially after immigration reform in 1965) the United States became more meaningfully diverse and thus more religiously plural. David Yamane, for instance, argues that "moderate denominational pluralism" became a "seemingly unlimited diversity of religious options" after World War II. Religion came to be "centered on *personal autonomy*, 'meaning . . . an enlarged arena of voluntary choice.'"[19] In this view, a number of contributing factors, including the revolutions in individualism fostered by the 1960s and '70s, along with increased immigration from non-European countries, changed the shape of American religion. The classic statement is found in Robert Bellah's *Habits of the Heart*, in which "Sheila Larson" describes her own brand of religion: "My faith has carried me a long way. It's Sheilaism. Just my own little voice." Religion for Sheila and others like her thus became something individual, defined by oneself, and uncoupled from community, doctrine, or tradition.[20] Sociologists of American religion tend to take the 1950s as a baseline because their disciplinary practice and sociological data go back to that decade. The 1950s, though, were an exceptional decade that witnessed trends such as the growth of religious affiliations and the increasing suburbanization of religious institutions, and thus make a poor baseline.

Both of these common narratives have much to recommend them, and both observe that the most noteworthy features of American religion are its constant flux and individualism. Yet each compresses the origins of religious choice to an influential decade. This work offers a longer history of how Americans came to constantly switch religious affiliations, and of what those changes mean. While disestablishment was indeed a fundamental change, the meaning of religious identity changed for over a century following disestablishment, and that change was due to conversions and pressures to convert. Yet in distinction to the post–World War II origin thesis, the fundamental characteristics of an unstable religious identity had already been set by the beginning of the twentieth century.

✠

This book is a history of conversions between religious traditions in the nineteenth-century United States. It uncovers how Americans moved between different religions, such as Christianity, Judaism, and unbelief, as well as between major traditions within Christianity, such as evangelical Protestantism, Catholicism, African American Protestantism, and Mormonism. It describes the development of a new form of conversion experience by evangelicals; the missionary effort to convert Native Americans in the southeastern United States; the conversions of enslaved and free African Americans in the period surrounding Emancipation; the growth of Mormonism through persistent proselytizing; attempts to evangelize Jews and Jews' efforts to resist evangelism while winning their own converts; and converts who rejected the system of religious choice by converting to Catholicism.

The chapters proceed roughly chronologically. They begin with the Protestant awakenings and missions in the first half of the century, continue with the experiences of African Americans and Mormons in the middle of the century, and conclude with the experience of Catholics and Jews at the end of the century. The introduction considers Hannah Adams's experience after the American Revolution, and the conclusion ends in 1902, the year that psychologist and philosopher William James published *The Varieties of Religious Experience*. It is thus bounded on the one hand by a deep change in social structures as experienced by one of the United States' first scholars of religion, and on the other by James's attempt to describe religion in terms of the experiences of his day.

The central tension in this book is between the many varieties of conversion that Americans have experienced, on the one hand, and the way that those conversions have created a common understanding of religion as choice, on the other. The book attempts to depict the extraordinary range of conversion in meaning and practice. A single comparison: there is a gulf between the evangelical, interior conversion of Samuel Hill, described earlier, and the 1848 conversion of Abraham Kirkas, who, though he thought of himself as a Jew and had been born to a Jewish mother in Syria, presented himself before a rabbinical court in New York in order to be circumcised and converted to Judaism according to the *halakhah* (Jewish law).[21]

The varieties of conversion, however, produced a shared understanding about religion. Over the nineteenth century, Americans came to think of religion as an identity that one could and must choose for oneself. This common understanding developed not despite, but because of, the many and varied ways of converting, all of which presented themselves as options to be decided on while undermining the ability to inherit religion. This was the origin of religious choice in the United States—or more precisely, the origin of religion as choice.

The history of conversion thus provides a synthetic view of American religion in the nineteenth century. It pulls together many of the extraordinarily disparate pieces of American religious history into a coherent narrative that shows what was common to them all, and thus what made them different.[22] Sidney Mead attempted this kind of analysis in *The Lively Experiment* (1963), in which he traced the history of religious freedom, the denominational system, and democracy to distill the essence of American religious life.[23] The most comprehensive attempt at synthesis, though, came from Sydney Ahlstrom. The publication of his *Religious History of the American People* in 1972 was a watershed moment for the field because it tried to encompass, in a single history, every kind of religion or denomination and not just the Protestant mainstream. Ahlstrom's book was followed by a four-decade-long flourishing of the field as historians turned their attention to religious groups of every kind.[24]

Our understanding of American religious history is much richer for this scholarly turn, but it has also left behind the task of synthesizing American religious history. As one book on the state of the field puts it, "Religious history is simultaneously rich in its diversity of interests and methods and rudderless in its overall direction or sense of professional priorities."[25] What is striking about Ahlstrom's book is not the gaps exposed in his synthetic, *longue durée* treatment by the historiography since 1972, but that scholars who have all the benefit of that new historiography have not written such a synthesis, and indeed seem mostly to have given up on the attempt. The synthesis that the field needs will be like Mead in its attempt to find the commonalities of American religion and like Ahlstrom in bringing many religious groups within a single purview, at the same time that it borrows from the past several decades' worth of writing the history of every kind of religious group.

Conversion is one starting point for a synthesis of religious history, because conversion offers the chance to both compare religious groups and to observe their interactions. Conversions are where different religious traditions recognize one another, speak to or past one another, and define the conditions of religious identity in terms of rituals, membership, practices, and beliefs. The history of conversion reveals a fundamental change in religious identity; it is a basso continuo beneath the ever-changing counterpoint of American religion. Conversion was one of the ever-present themes of nineteenth-century American religion, but for it to become ubiquitous, Americans had to discover that it was a possibility, as Hannah Adams did in her books.

✠

Hannah Adams was born in 1755 in Medfield, Massachusetts, to a family of declining means. Adams at first contributed to the household economy with her needle, then with her pen. Reading widely in the history of religions around the world, she published her first book, *An Alphabetical Compendium of the Various Sects*, in 1784. Adams's volume listed all the religions and denominations she knew. When she learned of more, she published an expanded edition in 1791, *A View of Religions*, which sold very well. A final 1817 edition titled *A Dictionary of All Religions and Religious Denominations* also included information about religious denominations in the United States. The book was an Enlightenment project in the way it classified and cataloged knowledge, creating a category of religion into which widely disparate groups and institutions, beliefs, and practices were classified under a single rubric.[26]

Writing her *Dictionary* profoundly destabilized Hannah Adams's own religious identity. In her memoir, she recalled how, "stimulated by an ardent curiosity, I entered into the vast field of religious controversy, for which my early reading had ill prepared me." In doing the research for the first edition, "I perused all the controversial works I could possibly obtain, with the utmost attention, in order to abridge what appeared to me the most plausible arguments for every denomination." Becoming aware of the options, Adams stumbled: "I suffered extremely from mental indecision, while perusing the various and contradictory arguments adduced by men of piety and learning in defense of their respective religious systems." The confusion about religion in general narrowed to a decision about the Unitarian controversy in Boston, the dispute in the early decades between Trinitarian Congregationalists who believed in the deity of Jesus and Unitarian Congregationalists who denied it.[27] Adams became a Unitarian, though she "deeply felt the difficulties upon both sides of the question" and "never arrived to that degree of decision that some have attained on that subject."[28]

In her memoir, Adams attributed her "indecision" and "perplexity" to being a woman, since "reading much religious controversy must be extremely trying to a female, whose mind . . . is debilitated by reading romances and novels."[29] One suspects that the gendered excuse meant the opposite of what it said. Adams was not given to reading romances and novels, but theologies and histories, and to writing them too. Describing what was expected of a woman cleverly played up Adams's success as a scholar, as did mentioning how Boston's best-known clergymen consulted her and patronized her writing. Furthermore, "the perplexity and embarrassment of my mind, while writing my *View of Religions*," she explained, was also felt by others who were troubled by the Unitarian controversy.[30]

In her perplexity, Adams was at the leading edge of a new experience of religious doubt and destabilization.[31] Adams felt the presence of many religious groups through her reading, and she felt obligated to sort them out. To her, only some of the choices, like Unitarian Christianity or orthodox Congregationalism, seemed like possibilities. Adams by no means thought that all religions offered salvation and truth. In fact, she came to increasing "convictions of the truth of that religion, to the examination of which I had devoted so much of my time." Most notably, she was a leader behind the first organization in the early republic that aimed at converting Jews, the Female Society of Boston and the Vicinity for Promoting Christianity amongst the Jews, and her two-volume *History of the Jews* was a call to the evangelism of the Jews.[32] Adams's reading had destabilized her faith, which she found again through argument.

The destabilization Adams felt was increasingly experienced by other Americans as well. That is to say, what for Adams was a rare situation of contemplating other religious possibilities brought about by her vocation as a scholar became a dilemma common to many people who met neighbors of other faiths, read their polemics, or passed by their meetinghouses. Recounting how this type of experience diffused throughout the nineteenth-century United States, and how varying traditions dealt with it, is the theme of this present work. Consider how a few experiences, each varied in its own way, resonate with Adams's.

Early in the century, Stephen Blythe was determined to sort out the many religious groups he met in his travels. Blythe was a Bostonian who tried the Episcopal, Moravian, Universalist, and Swedenborgian churches, spoke with Tom Paine in France about Deism, and even sent a letter to a Turkish ambassador to Britain inquiring about Islam; he then converted to Catholicism in Boston. As he wrote in 1815, "In this chaos of creeds—amid this anarchy of sects and opinions, it is true with mathematical certainty that all cannot have truth on their side."[33]

When Joseph Smith gave an account in 1832 of the origins of Mormonism, he told a narrative very like Protestant conversion accounts of his time. He reported that in 1820 he went out into the woods of Palmyra, New York, and had a vision. He had read the Bible, but his "intimate acquaintance with those of differant denominations led me to marvel excedingly" that "there was no society or denomination that built upon the gospel of Jesus Christ."[34] In another account, Smith emphasized that when he had his first vision, he was "wrought up in my mind, respecting the subject of religion and looking at the different systems taught the children of men, I knew not who was right or who was wrong."[35] Smith, and other visionaries like the Shakers, received new revelations that settled the problem for themselves, even as they went on to provoke new choices among those who encountered their message.[36]

When the English novelist Anthony Trollope traveled in the United States in the early 1860s, he noted how easily and frequently Americans discussed religion. Trollope observed that "it is not a common thing to meet an American who belongs to no denomination of Christian worship and who cannot tell you why he belongs to that which he has chosen." Trollope thought that the consequence of all this discussion and choosing of religion was that "everybody is bound to have a religion" and—speaking as a supporter of the established English church—he feared "it does not much matter what it is." Trollope reacted with some horror to the American idea that "they are willing to have religion, as they are willing to have laws; but they choose to make it for themselves."[37]

The *New-York Freeman's Journal and Catholic Register* offered a vignette of how one convert dealt with these pressures:

> Jonah Smith, a distinguished merchant of this city, connected with the Baptist church, became, some years since, dissatisfied with the grounds upon which the peculiar tenets of that sect are attempted to be sustained. After some years spent in investigation of the claims set forth by the various religions denominations, he ultimately recognized the truths of the Catholic church, and was received into its communion. Having once embraced the truth, he laboured earnestly in an effort to communicate it to those still enveloped in the darkness of error.[38]

The elements of the pattern are clear: dissatisfaction with the truths of one's own religion or denomination, perhaps through encountering the polemics or at least the presence of another group; investigation into the truth of the matter; conversion, sometimes multiple times; and finally the attempt to convert others and present them with the same dilemma. This pattern marked the emergence of a new kind of religious choice and, with it, a new meaning for religious identity.

✠

Conversions—actual and potential—changed the terms under which one could hold a religious identity. Over the course of the nineteenth century, religious identity in the United States became something that one had to warrant to oneself and justify to others. In the face of widespread conversions and opportunities to convert, one could not simply assume that one held a particular identity by default. The experience of religion moved on the spectrum from being inherited to being chosen. The explicit choices of the minority of Americans who converted obligated most Americans to make an implicit choice. The United States became a society where nearly everyone had to choose between religions, no less a forced choice for the fact that most chose to stay in the religion of their birth. Even people who remained in their childhood religion had to explain that choice to others and to themselves in face of the pressure to join another group or the option of having no religious affiliation at all. The history of conversion thus explains how the United States became at once more religious (in terms of how many people claimed a religious affiliation) and at the same time more secular (in terms of whether religion could be considered an unwarranted default). As religion became voluntary, more people chose religion, but fewer could be religious without a choice.

The possibility of converting as much as actual conversions changed the nature of religious identity. American religions expended an enormous amount of effort presenting their faiths to other people. This is not to say that everyone to whom an alternative faith was propounded found that faith appealing. The antimissionary publications by Jews, the apologetic theology published by Catholics, the polemical denunciations of Mormons by Protestants, the squabbling between Protestant groups such as the Baptists and Methodists, and especially the attacks on religion from atheists and agnostics and the rebuttals by every kind of religious group all demonstrate that each group had a stake in cutting down the array of religious options that kept springing up.[39] But the options were there nonetheless, and not merely there, but made present through the repeatedly demonstrated possibility of crossing religious boundaries. Even if one wished to reject the entreaty to convert, one increasingly had to provide reasons for doing so, to oneself as much as to others. Disestablishment created a religious free-for-all where the idea that a religion naturally pertained to any particular group was repeatedly under siege. For example, by the very beginning of the twentieth century, the Episcopal clergyman Charles Comfort Tiffany, hardly an evangelical of the hotter sort, thought that the basis of his formerly established denomination was choice. While he wished that the Episcopal Church would be "the church of the nation," he hoped for that end "not as an enforced ecclesiastical establishment, but as the chosen religious home of willing souls, convinced of the truth which it proclaims, and intent on the life which it incites."[40] Religion still had an undeniable relationship to ethnicity, but just as American pluralism eroded ethnic boundaries, so it eroded the connection between religion and ethnicity. Asking the question about religious identity mattered as much as the answer that people gave, because it created a forced choice.

Religious choice was in no simple sense a new kind of freedom; it is better understood as an obligation. Conversions were accompanied by a sense of loss—the loss of the simplicity of an inherited religious faith uncomplicated by the pull of other options. Converts made visible the ubiquitous cross-pressures of religious options by leaving a record of how they crossed boundaries. Rarely did converts write about their conversion in terms of taking advantage of a religious freedom, though that is often the mode in which scholars write about religious choice. Almost all converts described themselves as compelled to convert. Next to no one thought they were making a choice in the simplistic, consumer sense that our culture and economy fetishize. Almost everyone who converted felt that his or her options had narrowed until only one choice was left. The freedom more likely to be celebrated was the freedom not to convert: the rabbi Max Lilienthal, for example, contrasted the freedom that American Jews had to remain in their religion with the way that czarist Russia drafted Jews into the army and forced them to convert.[41] Less corrosive than state persecution, the American obligation to make a choice was a real loss for the stability of religious identity, and it was a choice that many people did not wish to make. Clergy tried to keep their congregations from straying; parents feared that their children would choose to convert. Many groups attempted to isolate their members to avoid the destabilization of obligatory choice. Some groups and some individuals managed to avoid the obligation more than others.

The degree to which people felt the pressure to convert and were free to act on that pressure varied with personal circumstance. Take the family of Orestes Brownson, a journalist who repeatedly converted between a series of Protestant and Transcendentalist groups before finally becoming in 1844 a vigorous and outspoken Catholic. Brownson led the way by changing his religions in a very public manner. Both Brownson and his son Henry insisted that Sally Healy Brownson, Orestes's wife, also converted out of conviction, but we do not have her testimony on the matter. What is certain is that within a few months of Orestes's conversion, she and six of her seven (at that time) children had been received into the Catholic church as well. Orestes Brownson Jr., the eldest son, waited several months before he too became a Catholic. We have here a range of choices: from intellectual agency, to the power of infant baptism, to the mixed agency of a spouse, to the agency of a child. This is not to suggest that in every case of intermarriage the wife had less say in the family religion. Women frequently exercised a great deal of control over their own religions and especially the religion of children, since the home was marked as a religious sphere.[42]

There were several competitors to the idea of religion as choice. Universalism strongly challenged the notion that one's choice of religion settled the question of salvation—though of course Universalism was such a strong challenger because it converted so many to its movement. Universalism affirmed that all would be saved, and so it denied that one's choice of religion affected one's eternal destiny. Another option was religious liberalism, which argued that all religions were essentially the same. In *The Sympathy of Religions*, for example, Thomas Wentworth Higginson argued that all religions "show similar aims, symbols, forms, weaknesses, and aspirations. Looking at these points of unity, we might say that under many forms there is but one religion, whose essential creed is the Fatherhood of God, and the Brotherhood of Man." The liberal religion of Higginson and others did increasingly become an option in the latter half of the century, though it appealed mostly to the circles of the Free Religious Association and like organizations.[43] Higginson's idea that religions were essentially the same effectively declared that no choice had to be made. Against his cosmopolitanism, most liberal

Protestants continued efforts to Christianize the United States that were rooted in their earlier evangelical tradition, even as they revised that tradition in accordance with what they saw as the needs of the times. These "liberal evangelicals" continued to preach the need for conversion alongside social reform.[44]

Universalism and liberalism certainly had many adherents. Yet Universalists had difficulty convincing Americans who were obsessed with the possibility of hell and damnation.[45] The pamphlets of the American Tract Society and other Protestant publishers inveighed against liberal Christianity and infidelity, two categories into which they placed Universalism.[46] Roman Catholics offered similar confutations of those who believed there was no choice to be made. Catholics used the term "indifferentism" to describe the indifference both of the irreligious and of the entire Protestant denominational system. "Indifferentism" was the false idea that if one "is known for a faithful husband, a good father, a just master, a loyal citizen, it is unimportant . . . what creed he holds. Be he Catholic or Baptist, Quaker or Unitarian, let him call himself by the name of any one of the myriad sects that spring up, mushroom-like, around him, his salvation is in every case secure, because all these religions are equally pleasing to God."[47] As one historian has put it, "Much of the history of religion in America has been written to emphasize the triumph of pluralism. Perhaps rightly so. That has meant, however, that those who have never conceded the premise that all or most religions, or even most Christian denominations, are more or less equal, have not been taken as seriously in our histories as they might." The acceptance of religious pluralism was not so much in competition with, as parallel and complementary to, religion as choice.[48]

✠

This historical argument about a shift from religion as a default to religion as a choice is indebted to two much-discussed philosophers of religion, Charles Taylor and William James.[49] Since James published his *Varieties of Religious Experience* in 1902, within the chronological scope of this book, he appears in the conclusion as a historical actor more than a theorist. James thought religious options could be described as "living," "forced," and "momentous."[50] A live choice was one in which the possibilities had a plausible and not merely hypothetical appeal. A forced choice was an unavoidable choice, where even a refusal to choose had the effect of making a choice. And a momentous choice was one where the choosing mattered. This way of speaking about choice and specifically religious choices was not a timeless philosophy but James's own response to the pressures of his day.

Taylor, though, is a contemporary whose book *A Secular Age* attempts to explain what it means to be secular through a genealogy (not a history) of the lived experience of belief and disbelief from the year 1500 to the present. Taylor provides a way of thinking about secularity that helps us see the meanings implied in religious choice. He distinguishes between kinds of secularity. The first is defined "in terms of public spaces" that "have been allegedly emptied of God." Public life, especially in the political but also in the economic or social sphere, can be undertaken without explicit reference to God.[51] The second kind of secularity is the extent to which people participate in religious belief and practice: the percentage of adherents to religion, the frequency of prayer, and so forth. It is well known that the United States differs from Western Europe in the way it has combined these two ideas of secularity: as Taylor puts it, though the United States was "one of the earliest societies to separate Church and State, it is also the Western society with the highest statistics for religious belief and practice."[52] That seemingly paradoxical combination is why the United States is the rock on which many theories of secularity have foundered.

Taylor's work is useful for his third concept of secularity: "a move from a society where belief in God is unchallenged and indeed, unproblematic, to one in which it is understood to be one option among others, and frequently not the easiest to embrace."[53] This fresh approach to the problem of secularity offers a way forward in the context of high religious belief or the presence of highly developed rituals and symbols of civil religion, both of which are characteristic of the United States. Taylor's definition of secularization, like James's account of the relationship between the will and belief, centers on options.[54] Both Taylor and James are thus useful in uncovering

the changed meanings of religion as religious options proliferated
through conversions.

Taylor's own idea of conversion is mostly focused on interior, even
mystical experiences of "fullness," a focus chosen because for Taylor
the self has become "buffered," meaning "not open and porous and
vulnerable to a world of spirits and powers."[55] One implication of the
buffered self is "that the depths which were previously located in
the cosmos, the enchanted world, are now more readily placed within"
the human psyche. We can see something of this turn in, for example, the way that psychologists like William James looked for
religious experience within human interiority.[56] Though the book
focuses mostly on outward conversions between religions or major
religious traditions, Taylor's concepts are useful for thinking through
the many accounts of conversion and the self, especially his idea
that switching between faiths could change the meaning of religious identity. Conversion changes not just an individual's affiliation but the nature of how identity is formed because "conversion,
breaking out into the broader field, normally makes one aware of how
much we are always shutting out."[57] The widespread conversions of
the nineteenth century made it impossible for many people to ignore
the broader field, the array of religious options available to people,
and thus made them more secular. In short, conversions between
religions removed the possibility that people could be "free of all
doubt, untroubled by some objection—by some experience which
won't fit, some lives which exhibit fullness on another basis, some
alternative mode of fullness which sometimes draws me," because
more and more people had to acknowledge alternative frames.[58]

⊹

To the extent that histories of religion have focused on Protestantism,
and in particular evangelicalism and revivalism, they have often dealt
with the topic of conversion. Conversion is both the central theological question and the defining practice for evangelicals, but
scholars have recently questioned whether the category is useful for
studying other groups.[59] One might justly wonder whether in discussing conversion one is using a Christian, and perhaps specifically

evangelical Protestant, category, and pressing other religions and religious traditions into its mold.

There are at least three primary meanings of the word *conversion*.[60] The first kind of conversion is interior, of the sort that evangelicals define as being "born again," that Taylor more generically describes as a moment of "fullness," and that William James "arbitrarily" circumscribed as "the feelings, acts, and experiences of individual men in their solitude, so far as they apprehend themselves to stand in relation to whatever they may consider the divine."[61] This kind of conversion is particular to evangelicalism, but because its more abstract forms have been seen as universal, it is the type of conversion with which we have to take the most care to avoid seeing other religious traditions through borrowed lenses. This kind of conversion is found in histories of evangelicalism and revivalism, but also of ecstatic religious experiences.

A second kind of conversion involves moving within groups that are relatively close to one another—for example, transferring membership from a Congregationalist to a Presbyterian church. Sociologists usually call this kind of conversion "switching." This type of conversion figures prominently in studies of the religious marketplace. The third kind of conversion is moving between different religious traditions. Distinguishing between denominational switching and conversion between religions is inexact. Conversions between entirely distinct faiths such as Judaism and Christianity obviously count as conversions between religions. But conversions between different Christian traditions where there was much animosity, such as Protestantism and Catholicism for most of U.S. history, are likewise conversions between religions rather than switching. A liturgical rule of thumb is that switching between denominations can be handled by bureaucratic procedures, such as transferring a letter of membership, or may not be formalized at all; conversion between religions is often marked by a ritual, such as baptism, confirmation, or circumcision. A social rule of thumb is that a conversion between religions is one that would upset one's parents—though that is of course an ambiguous category indeed. Many religions, even if strongly tied to ethnicity, have a point of entrance to outsiders, often with regular, formal procedures.

This book looks primarily at movement between religious traditions, while taking the other two kinds of conversion into account. All three kinds of conversion are linked in that the rituals of conversion and the experiences of conversion often went hand in hand. Consider the conversions of Ammi Ruhamah Bradbury, who was likely baptized as a Congregationalist when an infant, yet who considered himself an unbeliever until he experienced a heart conversion while in college under the ministry of a Congregationalist pastor. He was then baptized in a Free Will Baptist Church (which practiced open communion) rather than a Calvinist Baptist church so that he could take communion with Congregationalists.[62] Was this conversion regeneration (being born again), switching (from Congregationalist to Free Will Baptist), or conversion as movement across religions (from unbelief to belief)? Any given conversion might involve aspects of any or all of these concepts. But the aim of looking at these many kinds of conversions is to identify the fault lines in nineteenth-century American religion and to learn how people crossed them. The benefit of bringing together the study of these kinds of conversion is that we can see what connected religious experience across religious traditions. They were connected when the Protestant model of internal choice became a live, genuine, forced option for many Americans, albeit always refracted through the practices and beliefs of different groups.

On their own, the chapters that follow capture something of the varieties of religious conversions available to nineteenth-century Americans, the seemingly inexhaustible array of options from which converts had to select.[63] Together, they uncover the shared experience of obligatory religious choice. The nineteenth-century United States saw the expansion of a regime of choice in many spheres, and the realm of religion came to be defined as a choice. The people who joined religions, left them, and returned to them saw new possibilities, new freedoms that they might or might not take, new options shaped by the particular experiences of the religious traditions in which they were born and the faiths that appealed to them. These possibilities, though, added up to a burden to choose one's religion: the defining feature of what American religions had in common.

1

Prayer

PROTESTANT CONVERTS AND
THE SINNER'S PRAYER

*F*ROM 1826 TO THE end of the nineteenth century, the Presbyterians in the United States weathered their share of changes. They split into two denominations in 1837, then split again during the Civil War, only to be reunited in the 1870s. They were rocked by disputes over slavery, Darwinian evolution, and theological liberalism, but for the most part Presbyterians maintained a remarkable stability thanks to their mode of church governance and their reading of the Bible within the confines of the Westminster Confession.[1] Their numbers grew enormously: in 1826, there were 127,440 members of 1,819 Presbyterian churches; in 1900, there were 1,007,689 members of 7,750 Presbyterian churches. But then, there was more of everything in a rapidly growing United States, and the Presbyterians grew from 1.1 percent of the population to only 1.3 percent.[2] The most meaningful change for the Presbyterians lay below the surface. It would not have been apparent to a visitor to any particular church, though its effects were recorded in the baptismal registers of every congregation, aggregated in the minutes of the General Assembly, and printed by the denomination's own publishing house. The change lay in how people came to think of themselves as Presbyterians in the first place. By 1900, members were far less likely to have become Presbyterian through infant baptism.

Baptizing infants expressed in practice the theological idea that the children of Christians could inherit membership in the church through the administration of the sacrament, backed by God's eternal

23

decree of election. But that doctrine increasingly conflicted with another theological idea, the idea that to be saved all people—regardless of whether they had been baptized as children—had to undergo a conversion experience in which they repented and believed for themselves. Baptists had long resolved the tension by holding that baptism was valid only for believers. The declining rates of infant baptism among Presbyterians were a sign that they too felt the tension between those ideas. There were two main ways that one could become a Presbyterian.[3] One could choose to become a member as an adult by having a conversion experience and then being baptized. If someone converted as an adult and had already been baptized as a child, then he or she might be received as a member by examination. In other words, infant baptism was a sign of inherited religion, and adult baptism was a sign of religion as choice.[4] The two ideas about religious belonging expressed themselves in two different rituals.

The interplay between inheriting a religion and choosing it can be seen in the sharp dip in the percentage of infant baptisms in 1832–1833 (Figure 1.1). In 1832, more infants were baptized than the year before, but the percentage dropped so rapidly because there were twice as many adult baptisms that year as the year before. It was in 1832 that Charles Finney, a lawyer turned revivalist, moved to New York and introduced revivalism to Manhattan.[5] That year, more people became Presbyterians because they were converted and then baptized or transferred membership than became Presbyterians through infant baptism. Such revivals remained "seasons" of grace—unusual, brief, and unpredictable. But the change in how people affiliated themselves with a Protestant denomination eventually became permanent.

The denominational history of Presbyterians provides an insight into the meaning of this trend. In 1837, the Presbyterians split into two denominations: Old School Presbyterians and New School Presbyterians. The reasons for the schism were complex, including divisions over slavery and difficulties in interpreting the 1801 Plan of Union with Congregationalists in what was then the northwest of the United States. Old School ministers such as Charles Hodge, Ashbel Green, and William Buell Sprague held to a more tradition-

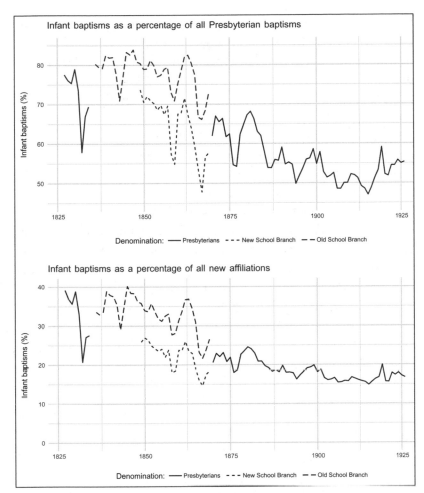

FIGURE 1.1 Declining rates of infant baptism among Presbyterians, 1826–1926. Data: Herman Carl Weber, *Presbyterian Statistics through One Hundred Years, 1826–1926* (Philadelphia: Presbyterian Church in the U.S.A., 1927).

alist understanding of the Westminster Confession, while New School ministers such as Albert Barnes and Lyman Beecher favored the New England theology that was revising the Calvinism.[6] But the most significant disagreement was over revivalism. The Old School was suspicious of the revivalists and their techniques; the New School embraced them, and many of the New School ministers were revivalists. The New School Presbyterians had lower levels of infant baptism in every year because they placed more emphasis on a conscious conversion. The Old School Presbyterians, on the other hand, continued to emphasize the inheritance of the faith. In terms of the rate of infant baptism, by the end of the nineteenth century all Presbyterians were like New School Presbyterians in the middle of the nineteenth century.

By 1900, then, the significance of religion as an inheritance had declined sharply, and the significance of religion as a choice had been established. These records of baptisms show a deep change in religious identity. This change was not confined to Presbyterians; it had an impact on Methodists, Congregationalists, and evangelical Episcopalians as well. Conversion had always been important for evangelicals, but beginning in the 1830s it began to replace rather than coexist with theological ideas and practices about the inheritance of religion.[7] Charles Finney and other revivalists disrupted older patterns of conversion but created new patterns that were codified and distributed in the pamphlets published by the American Tract Society. These tracts then trained generations of Protestants to have a conversion experience according to the norms set in the 1830s.

The characteristic ritual of the new pattern of Protestant conversion, as in the conversion of Samuel Hill, was the sinner's prayer, and its characteristic meaning was conversion away from infidelity, or "nominal Christianity."[8] Protestants usually experienced conversion as an intensification of, rather than the switching of, affiliation; in other words, rather than changing from one religion to another, they usually moved from a weak connection with a religious group to a firmer, fuller commitment with the same group. But theologically speaking, evangelicals increasingly thought of their conversions not as fulfilling an earlier commitment but as a renunciation of infidelity. Because of the theological demand that everyone experience heart conversion, regardless of whether they had been baptized or were members of the church, Christianity could not be meaningfully inherited. Children of Christian parents proved to be a difficult case. But over time evangelical parents came to think of their children as needing evangelism as much as catechesis.

And if religion could not be inherited, how could one know whether he or she was saved? Sometimes the sky was rent and the world shaken in ecstatic conversion experiences, but only the most extreme would insist that such experiences were necessary for all.

What was needed was a more accessible ritual. Since Protestants were generally suspicious of formalism, the antithesis of heart religion, that ritual needed to be informal and individual. And so the nineteenth century saw the modification of the Puritan conversion narrative into the sinner's prayer. The sinner's prayer was a way of acknowledging sin and asking for God's mercy in a formulaic, yet spontaneous, prayer. Puritan or early evangelical conversions tended to be gradual: their success was determined by the judgment of the congregation, and their results were found in moving from the promise of the sacrament of baptism to the fullness of participation in the sacrament of the Lord's Table. The nineteenth-century ritual was more immediate, at least in theory: its success was determined by the individual convert, and its customary form was not sacramental but experiential. By the time the sinner's prayer had fully developed, Protestant conversions were matters of choice and individual initiative; being defined against unbelief or irreligion, they were a kind of conversion between religions.

Evangelical Protestants did not fall into this pattern of conversion spontaneously. The form developed gradually, thanks to the preaching of revivalists and the distribution of millions of tracts that explained how to have a heart conversion. This change came about because evangelicals developed a system focused on conversion. And the most controversial of the system builders was a lawyer turned revivalist, with a prominent pulpit in New York.

☩

In the fall and winter of 1834, a congregation gathered at Chatham Street Chapel in New York City to hear a series of lectures by their pastor, Charles Grandison Finney. Tall and gaunt, with sunken cheeks but an imposing brow, his body still recovering from cholera and general ill health, Finney nevertheless held his audiences captive as he explained the system behind his revivals.[9]

No preacher believed in the power of a system to convert sinners as much as Finney did. He had been practicing his technique since

his own conversion experience in 1821, when he gave up his law practice to fulfill his "retainer for Jesus Christ" as a Presbyterian minister.[10] Finney continued in the ministry for over fifty years, but even
by 1834 the greatest movings of the Spirit were behind him. By then
Finney had preached scores of revivals in the "burned over district"
of Western New York, most successfully in Rochester in 1830–1831,
but also throughout New England, Pennsylvania, and New York.[11]
The wealthy merchants Arthur and Lewis Tappan set up Finney
in the Chatham Street Chapel in New York City, where Finney became the pastor. New York at that time was in the midst of a great
expansion in evangelicalism. A historian of evangelicals in New York
conservatively estimates that "the percentage of New Yorkers who
had a conversion experience and joined an evangelical church increased steadily from 4 percent of the city's adult population in 1790
to 15 percent in 1855," not counting people who experienced an evangelical conversion but did not affiliate with an identifiably evangelical
church.[12] The kind of conversion experience that Finney encouraged
was thus touching the lives of many more people in New York, even
though Finney himself remained in the city for only a year, soon
moving on to Ohio to teach at the abolitionist Oberlin College.

The task before him in giving his 1834 lectures on revivals of religion was to define and defend a system of revivalism. These lectures were not revival preaching; they were a discourse about revival
preaching. With a theological mind trained by experience rather
than education, Finney was offering a systematization of his life's
work. Finney's great change—like all great changes, a long time in
coming and a long time in working out its effects—had already been
brought about by his preaching and the preaching of scores of other
ministers, not to mention the conversions of thousands through his
kind of evangelical experience of the new birth.

Before Finney built his own system, he announced the demolition
of another. Finney did not regard his "new measures" as being entirely new, but he did see them as a radical modification of what had
come before. In his lectures, he often cited Jonathan Edwards's 1742
book, *Some Thoughts Concerning the Present Revival of Religion in New
England*. Nevertheless, Finney aimed his lectures directly at established patterns of conversion experience, and the means that previous

generations had used to bring them about. In the lecture teaching other people how to bring sinners to conversion, he told his audience that sinners would never be converted in the way that they expected: "Sinners often lay out a plan of the way they expect to feel, and how they expect to be converted, and in fact lay out the work for God, determined that they will go in that path or not at all. Tell them this is all wrong, they must not lay out any such path beforehand, but let God lead them as he sees to be best."[13]

The sinners who were being converted in Finney's revivals were not blank slates but, as Finney well knew, people who had been trained to have definite ideas about how they should be converted in a particular set of steps. They anticipated that conversion would come when sinners realized the enormity of their sin, acknowledged God's justice in damning them, then apprehended the gospel by faith and attained a knowledge of their salvation. Even in its later, simpler forms, this well-entrenched method of conversion offered a gradual process. While they waited for conversion, potential converts were expected to use the means of grace—prayer, attendance at meeting, Scripture reading, wise counsel, and other devotional practices—to move their souls along, subject always to the mysterious, miraculous movings of the sovereign God, until they converted and were admitted to the Lord's Table.[14]

In his lectures, Finney announced that the process of gradual conversion would be replaced by the direct, instantaneous experience of conversion. The moment when sinners felt the movement of the Spirit (or the new measures) was the moment when they could be converted or not: "anxious sinners" were "in a very *solemn and critical state.* They have in fact come to a turning point," where "their destiny is *settled.*"[15] Finney was speaking to a congregation of "professors of religion." Sometimes that term meant people who were "hopefully converted," but it could also mean people who participated in Christianity without actually being converted—outwardly pious, inwardly infidel.[16] For Finney, it was absurd to think that a "careless sinner" might be an "intellectual believer"; such a sinner was only "an infidel, let his professions be what they may." This idea depended on a definition of faith not as an "intellectual conviction" but as "trust, or confidence, in the scriptures."[17] He warned those potentially unregenerate listeners that there could be no delay: "To-night it will be told in hell, and told in heaven, and echoed from the ends of the universe, what you decide to do. This very hour may seal your eternal destiny. Will you submit to God to-night—NOW?"[18]

Finney's emphasis on immediacy was an out-and-out attack on earlier Calvinist understandings of conversion. The means of grace, Finney said, were false comforts given to people who were "anxious" about conversion but who had not actually converted. Key among these false comforts was to "tell awakened sinners that 'Conversion is a progressive work,' and in this way ease their anxiety." People sometimes warned potential converts against "*sudden* conversions," advising them that "you must wait and let it work, and by and by you will get comfort." But Finney condemned this approach as only delaying salvation, since "regeneration, or conversion, is *not* a progressive work. . . . It is the first act of genuine obedience to God—the first voluntary action of the mind that is what God approves, or that can be regarded as obedience to God. That is conversion. When persons talk about conversion as a progressive work, it is absurd."[19]

For Finney, there were no stages and no preparation, only an immediate conversion, with sanctification to follow. Most of all, he urged his audience not to be "afraid of sudden conversions." He testified that "some of the best Christians of my acquaintance were convicted and converted in the space of a few minutes." And "in one quarter of the time that I have been speaking, many of them were awakened, and came right out on the Lord's side."[20] The only duty of sinners was to repent before God, and there was no psychological or theological reason why they could not simply exercise their wills to do so. For Finney, the bottom line was that if God commanded sinners to repent, then there was nothing that stood in their way from immediately exercising their will: "God commands you to do it, expects you to do it, and if it ever is done, you must do it."[21]

Having removed people's expectations for how they might be converted, and having undercut the means of grace to prepare for conversion, Finney offered only the slightest of systems in its place. His oft-discussed "new measures" were a system for starting revivals, not a systematic explanation of conversion. Still, Finney needed to explain what demarcated the sinner from the saved. Finney thought the anxious bench—the place where sinners considering conversion might sit during a revival meeting—was chiefly responsible for separating out the people who were willing to actually move toward salvation and those who were not. He did not equate going to the anxious bench with faith itself, though he did equate *not* going to the anxious bench with infidelity. Rather, he thought it symbolized the inward motion of the heart in repentance. The anxious bench functioned like baptism, a shocking substitute for the sacrament. Conversion experiences in the eighteenth century were usually connected to the sacrament of baptism or the Lord's Supper; the backwoods revivals of the Second Great Awakening were often connected to sacramental "Holy Fairs."[22] But Finney decoupled conversion from the sacrament and replaced baptism with the anxious bench. The anxious bench, he claimed, "uncovers the delusion of the human heart," exposing people who feel like they are Christians but are "not willing to do so small a thing" as come to the anxious seat. In the days of the apostles, Finney believed, baptism held "the precise place that the anxious bench does now, as a public manifestation of their determination to be Christians."[23]

In place of the sacrament, Finney offered prayer. He believed in what he called "effectual prayer," that is, prayer that, through its earnestness, actually brought about what was requested of God. Through prayer, congregations could bring about revivals; through prayer, individuals could exercise their wills toward faith.[24] Finney thought prayer could bring about immediate results. His emphasis on conversion through prayer stands in contrast to the idea expressed several generations earlier in Jonathan Edwards's *Life of David Brainerd*, a book that was widely circulated and read among evangelicals: "I saw that there was no necessary connection between my prayers and the bestowment of divine mercy; that they laid not the least obligation upon God to bestow his grace upon me."[25]

But Finney's theological prescriptions actually became descriptions of how many Protestants experienced conversion, through the power of imitation and of the press. In 1835–1836, the revivalist preacher Jedidiah Burchard, to take an extreme example, held revivals in Vermont, earning the ire of opponents who condemned

"Burchardism." Characteristic of Burchard's methods were the importance of prayer for sinners and especially the claim that he could win conversions in minutes—two minutes by some accounts, five minutes by others. Accompanying Burchard's promise of quick conversions was his threat that delaying conversion might bring damnation. He (reportedly) told a parable about a man who delayed converting long enough "to write a receipt for two dollars" and was "just *one minute too late!*"[26] Finney's conviction that prayer was the central act of conversion was shared by other revivalists such as Presbyterian minister Samuel Irenaeus Prime. In his books about the revivals of 1858 titled *The Power of Prayer* and *Five Years of Prayer, with the Answers,* Prime gave scores of examples of people who converted because other people prayed for them and brought about revival. In such revivals a common practice was to have sinners who were seeking conversion stand for prayer.[27]

The lectures that Finney gave in 1834 and 1835 propounded a system, and his prominence gave the lectures as wide a hearing as a set of public addresses could have. But Finney also harnessed his message to the power of print. The lectures had been scheduled in the first place as an attempt to keep afloat the *New York Evangelist,* a newspaper published by a friend. Finney's lectures were first published in that paper and then gathered into book form as *Lectures on Revivals of Religion.*[28] Finney's ideas about conversion were soon distributed through the instrument that had the greatest reach among American Christians: the religious press.

✠

The Protestant publisher with the greatest reach was the American Tract Society (ATS). The ATS was founded in 1825 from the merger of the New-York Religious Tract Society and the Boston-based American Tract Society (formerly the New England Religious Tract Society).[29] It was at the forefront of the benevolence movement that united Protestants of many denominations in an attempt to reform the morals and evangelize the souls of the United States.[30] Thanks to the volume of its imprints and the extent of their distribution, if any institution had the power to produce a deep change in the experience of Protestant religion, it was the ATS. In hundreds of tracts printed in millions and millions of impressions, the American Tract Society and its counterparts in denominational publishing houses codified and popularized the kind of conversion experience that Finney had described in his preaching.[31]

The decade between 1825 and 1835 was the critical period for the American Tract Society, because it was during these early years that it ramped up the publication of its tracts. By 1835, the ATS had produced the first edition of most of its tracts, which it then reprinted for the next several decades. Of the 440 or so tracts published during this time period, about 200 were primarily about conversion, and conversion was a prominent theme in about 150 more. Many of these early pamphlets were reprints from British tract societies, such as the Religious Tract Society of London, founded in 1799. As was the case with most evangelical institutions of this period, the British had a head start, and evangelicalism was an Anglophone movement with debts to German, French, and Swiss Protestants.[32] The ATS republished works from proven British authors, such as Legh Richmond and Hannah More, and occasionally tracts from other European authors. After the initial borrowing, the ATS began to publish more original tracts. The society built its list of publications during the period when Charles Finney was most active as a revivalist, and these tracts then got out the message for the rest of the nineteenth century. The ATS published these tracts in very large quantities: at least four million impressions for its most successful tract, *The Dairyman's Daughter*, and usually tens of thousands of impressions for its other titles.[33]

Though the original publication date of ATS tracts came from a relatively constrained time period, the content was taken from a much wider chronological range. Many of the ATS publications were written specifically as tracts, but the ATS excerpted many others from classic works of evangelical piety and doctrine. The ATS borrowed from Puritan divines such as John Flavel, John Owen, and Richard Baxter, but also from revivalists and evangelicals such as the theologian Jonathan Edwards, the hymn writer Isaac Watts, and most frequently the nonconformist pastor Philip Doddridge. The tracts thus had their roots in the long evangelical tradition of heart religion and vital piety, centered on conversion. In a sense, the developments of the early nineteenth century were extensions of that earlier tradition; in another sense, those developments transformed the tradition into something new. The ATS selected these materials and put them in new contexts that changed the significance and meaning of the older texts. When the ATS shortened much longer works by Edwards, Baxter, and Doddridge, their tracts placed an emphasis on immediacy that did not appear in the originals.

These tracts touched on nearly every part of the Christian life. The ATS thought it had a dual mission to educate Christians and to convert non-Christians, and so its tracts covered many different topics. But some topics recurred far more often than others. The most common topic was conversion, as tracts dealt with salvation, repentance, future punishment, and the life stories of real, fictional, and semifictional converts. A second set of topics involved family life: the education of children and the running of the home. But these tracts, too, often touched on conversion, since they were about the duty of parents to prepare their children for salvation. (A different genre of children's tracts spoke directly to children about preparing for conversion.) These tracts about raising children spoke to a deep-seated need to impart faith to the next generation, but the way for parents to pass on their faith was to prepare children for conversion.[34] Most of the rest of the tracts were instructions in doctrine and the means of grace. Even these tracts related to conversion, since they often encouraged readers to consider whether they had been soundly converted.

As it published this large corpus of widely distributed texts in the 1830s and 1840s, the American Tract Society developed a new kind of sinner's prayer. The sinner's prayer was a pattern of converting in which a sinner prayed for salvation and then felt that he or she had received it. The defining feature was the form more than the exact words of the prayer, which often (but not necessarily) might be repeated from a prayer published in a tract or devotional book. The prayer contained an acknowledgment of sin and a plea for God's mercy. It might be as brief as the biblical phrase, "God be merciful to me, a sinner," or theologically elaborate enough to fill several paragraphs.[35] The sinner's prayer was not formally labeled as a ritual. Nevertheless it functioned as a ritual, in that it was a practice with a prescribed set of procedures (even if those procedures were intended to be somewhat spontaneous) whose result was an inner sense of having converted and been justified by God. The ritual was powerful because it was a way of expressing faith that counted as "justifying faith"—that is, faith that brought about justification. The ritual was an attempt to solve the longstanding evangelical problem of knowing when and how someone was justified: the ritual pointed out the method and the moment. The sinner's prayer thus made conversion more punctual; that is, it tended to collapse the process to one point.

The ATS did not develop the sinner's prayer intentionally, though the form fit naturally with the brevity of the tracts and the calls for punctiliar experiences by revivalists like Finney. Rather, the form developed out of the felt needs of preparing effective tracts, and especially from biblical prayers of repentance and penitence used as models in early tracts. The ATS recognized that tracts "must be simple, serious, and practical. They must be intelligible to the 'wayfaring man,' and the tenant of the cottage" and those who "otherwise would scarcely read any thing." And so "learned criticism, discussions in polemic theology, and even articles of religious intelligence [i.e., doctrine], unless comprised in a few sentences, can have no place in these little pamphlets."[36] Especially in its earliest publications, the ATS did not always practice this rule of simplicity, publishing some very lengthy tracts. Over time, the ATS got better at simplicity. It learned to emphasize urgency and a turning point. The evangelical tract itself became a centerpiece of the ritual, because the tracts included many stories of conversions where tracts were the instruments of conversion.

The tracts framed the ever-pressing question of conversion against the possibility of infidelity. Many of the tracts warned against atheism and liberal religion; others warned of future eternal punishment because Universalists denied that doctrine. Still other tracts were written against Unitarians. Deists, infidels, Unitarians, and Universalists were mentioned far more often than Roman Catholics, who are often cited by historians as the bugaboo of nineteenth-century

Protestants. What drove the message of these tracts was a concern with infidelity: both a concern for the many unconverted members of society and a worry about the possibility of infidelity lurking in the soul of the reader, who might already be "hopefully converted."[37]

When the ATS tracts are read in order of publication, the pattern of instantaneous conversion emerges slowly, developing in four stages.[38] First, the earliest tracts cited prayers from the Bible that were often examples of repentance and faith in a moment. Second, the fictionalized characters in the tracts came to adopt the prayers as their own. Third, the tracts repeated biblical injunctions about immediacy in repentance, so that the steady drumbeat of "today is the day of salvation" and "today, if you will hear his voice" became the hallmark of the tracts. Finally, the tracts subtly redefined the means of grace. Prayer and Scripture reading became the moment of grace, not just the means to grace. In its earliest publications, the ATS was willing to distinguish between converts who recognized their conversions instantly, and those who recognized them gradually, though in both cases the conversion itself (viewed as God's act of justifying the sinner) happened in a moment. Thomas Goodwin wrote in *Growth in Grace* that "there are, among christians, two sorts of converts; those who, at the time of conversion, are sensible of the change wrought in their minds; and those to whom the change is not, at the time, perceptible."[39] Such nuance was gradually dropped from the tracts as the sinner's prayer came to define a normative conversion. The tracts, not unlike the small engravings that decorated their paper wrappers, were a highly simplified representation of conversions.

The earliest sinner's prayers in the ATS tracts were quotations from the Bible. Those biblical prayers appeared at prominent places in the narrative, especially at the end. That evangelicals used biblical prayers as models for their tracts is unsurprising, since evangelicals tried to base all of their practices on biblical models. Because evangelicals regarded conversion as a scriptural requirement for salvation, they sought scriptural patterns for what conversions should look like.

The most quoted biblical prayers came from the Gospels, though the prayer of repentance in Psalm 51 was also commonly used. One common passage was the parable that Jesus told comparing a publican (tax collector) and a Pharisee. While the Pharisee's prayer mentioned his obedience to the law, the publican prayed, "God be merciful to me a sinner." The message of the parable, in Jesus's own interpretation, was, "This man went down to his house justified rather than the other." The tracts used this text to make a distinction between righteousness based on "the deeds of the law" and righteousness based on justification by grace through faith. The publican's prayer of repentance and faith thus brought about justification.[40]

The second most frequently quoted text came from Jesus's exchange on the cross with one of the "malefactors" crucified next to him, who said, "Lord, remember me when thou comest into thy kingdom." Jesus replied, "To day, shalt thou be with me in paradise."[41] The malefactor's prayer was a model of repentance at the end of life, and evangelicals took Jesus's response as a promise that anyone who turned to Christ in faith could be saved in a moment. The accounts of both the publican and the malefactor offered a compelling narrative in which a simple prayer defined the moment of salvation, a moment in which a sinner was offered justification and salvation. The same biblical texts that offered a theology of justification also offered a simple model for practice (Figure 1.2).

The ATS tracts put these biblical prayers to use in relating accounts of conversion. In *The African Servant*, written by Legh Richmond, William, the servant of a British naval officer, asked to be baptized because "me believe that Jesus died for poor negro. What would become of poor wicked negro, if Christ no die for him. But he died for the chief of sinners, and that make my heart sometime quite glad." When the officer asked what part of the Bible he was reading, William replied that he had made the words of the malefactor his own: "Me read how the man on the cross spoke to Christ and Christ spoke to him. Now that man's prayer just do for me. 'Lord, remember me'; Lord, remember poor negro sinner."[42] The officer, who like many characters in the tracts was the mouthpiece for evangelical doctrine, assured him that "the Lord hears that prayer. He pardoned and accepted the thief upon the cross, and he will not reject you; he will in no wise cast out any that come to him." Despite the stilted dialect attributed to William (the tract on the

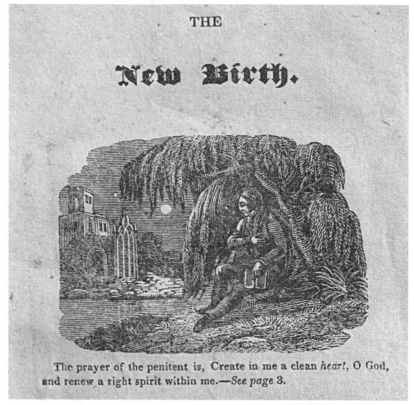

THE

New Birth.

The prayer of the penitent is, Create in me a clean *heart*, O God, and renew a right spirit within me.—*See page* 3.

FIGURE 1.2 Illustration from the cover of a tract about regeneration. In this illustration, a man prays in solitude at night. He is holding a small book, perhaps a Bible but more likely a tract. The caption points out that he is praying Psalm 51, one of the biblical sinner's prayers. From *The New Birth* (New York: American Tract Society, between 1827 and 1830). Image courtesy American Antiquarian Society.

whole was mildly antislavery), the reader was supposed to identify with him and adopt the prayer of the sinner.

The use of biblical prayers was pervasive. *A Voice from Heaven* was simply a collection of biblical texts on conversion, judged sufficient to get someone to convert without interpretation. It quoted both the publican's prayer and the malefactor's prayer, along with prayers of repentance from the Psalms.[43] Most tracts were more explicit in their interpretations of Scripture. *Solemn Inquiries, and Counsel to Careless Sinners* offered the advice "to receive and rest upon Christ alone for salvation, as he is freely offered in the Gospel." It exhorted readers to put that advice into practice: "Let me beseech you, then, to go to Christ with the publican's humble prayer, 'God be merciful to me a sinner.'"[44] *The Dairyman* (sequel to *The Dairyman's Daughter*) was published with Isaac Watts's metrical adaptation of Psalm 51 on its wrapper. The title—"The Penitent's Supplication"—was a clue to how the psalm was supposed to be used: the repentant sinner was to make King David's prayer of confession his or her own. The first stanza of the prayer asked God to forget sins, and the second asked God to regenerate the sinner's nature:

> O Thou that hear'st when sinners cry!
> Though all my crimes before thee lie,
> Behold them not with angry look,
> But blot their memory from thy book.
>
> Create my nature pure within,
> And form my soul averse to sin;
> Let thy good Spirit ne'er depart.
> Nor hide thy presence from my heart.[45]

Among the early ATS publications, the tract *The One Thing Needful* made the most striking use of a biblical sinner's prayer to undercut the idea that someone could have an inherited religion. This tract featured a dialogue between a "traveler," a stock character who represented the person who handed out the tract, and the recipient of the tract, unsubtly labeled "you." The traveler called into question whether the reader could inherit religion from community or kin:

TR.   Of what religion are you?

YOU.   Of what religion, Sir? the same as my neighbors.

TR.   And pray what religion is that?

YOU.   Why the same as our fathers' before us.

TR.   I should be glad to know what that was?

YOU.   You ask very odd questions. I never thought much about religion. I go to church now and then, and pay every man his own. That's all I know about it.

Having undermined the ideas that someone could have an unchosen religion, the tract urged the reader to enter into faith through the exercise of the will. "You," the reader, was encouraged to pray for salvation using another quotation from the Gospels: "O hesitate no longer. Say heartily, 'I cannot live without God, without Christ, without hope.' '*Lord I believe; help thou mine unbelief.*' "[46]

Already in *The One Thing Needful*, the sinner's prayer was positioned at the end of the tract as the decisive moment in which willingness to pray determined whether the reader would convert. The sinner's prayer developed as a technique for providing a clear turning point in the narrative. Many of the tracts featured two main characters: a knowledgeable, evangelistic Christian, and a person who should convert by the end of the tract. These characters presumably mirrored the way the tracts were intended to be used in real life, with an evangelistic Christian handing them out to potential converts, as depicted in the artwork on the tracts. But in these dialogues, the potential convert was as passive as a Socratic interlocutor, offering only replies that gave the main character permission to keep explaining the truth. While this literary technique worked for conveying doctrine, it did not allow readers to turn in faith.

The tracts thus hit upon the solution of elaborating on the biblical sinner's prayers in order to give the potential convert a guide to an appropriate response. The tract *Children of the Forest*, which purported to recount a revival "at the headwaters of the Delaware" in western New York or Pennsylvania, contains an example of the form. In the tract an impious husband and wife are visited by a clergyman, and both of them pray sinner's prayers. According to the narrator, the father prayed "in substance" as follows:

Oh Lord, for Christ's sake have mercy upon me [Ps. 51:1] and upon my wife and children. Pour down thy good Spirit upon us [Isa. 44:3], and take away our hard and stony hearts, and give us hearts of flesh [Ezek. 36:36]; send out the arrows of conviction, and give me unfeigned penitence for sin; let the great deep of sin be broken up in my soul, and show me all the abominations of my heart [Prov. 26:25] before it is too late. Help me to work out my salvation with fear and trembling [Phil. 2:12]; and let the man of sin [2 Thess. 2:3] be slain in me by the power of the Holy

Ghost; give me a spirit of prayer and supplication [Eph. 6:18], and help me from this day forward to erect and maintain an altar for thy service in my house. Lord help my wife and children to call upon thee aright, and give them likewise of thy grace to spend the rest of their days in thy service. Give us all hearts to believe on the Lord Jesus Christ to the saving of our souls [Acts 16:31], and let us all be thoroughly cleansed from all pollution in the fountain of his blood [Rev. 1:5, 7:14].[47]

That prayer could not have been uttered by the actual converts of the real revival, since moments earlier in the tract they had been protesting their ignorance of the Scriptures and presumably of the common phrases of Protestant Christianity ("unfeigned penitence," "great deep of sin," "arrows of conviction," an "altar" of family prayer). The editors of the text did not intend that this elaborate sinner's prayer should be taken as an accurate report from the western revival. It was intended to be a model that the sinner reading the tract could pray. The words of the tract might be fiction, but the reader was invited to make them fact.

Having offered these sinner's prayers modeled on biblical prayers, the ATS tracts insisted that sinners convert immediately. Among the most frequently quoted biblical passages came from the Epistle to the Hebrews: "To day if ye will hear his voice, harden not your hearts."[48] Another oft-quoted verse was "Behold, now is the accepted time; behold, now is the day of salvation."[49] One tract was excerpted from a Richard Baxter sermon titled *Now or Never* and edited to make that message even more plain. Where the original sermon emphasized that hearers should immediately begin using the means of grace to prepare for conversion, the shortened version in the tract emphasized that they should move straight on to converting.[50]

The tracts were filled with people who delayed converting and were damned because of it. In *Convictions Stifled*, the potential convert died at a tragically young age because he or she was mired in sinful habits and lacked the time to truly repent.[51] In *Lydia Sturtevant*, a young woman resolved to repent but died because she "could not be pardoned—it was too late—too late."[52] *The Almost Christian* (its title taken from the account in Acts of the failed conversion of

Agrippa) emphasized that salvation came in a moment. It warned that "millions are lost by this kind of delay: they perish, because there is no period at which they are ready solemnly to vow before God, 'NOW, from THIS MOMENT, I will, in dependence on divine grace, seek supremely the honor of Christ in the salvation of my soul.' "[53] Often the failed converts insisted that they could not pray, because they lacked the words. Such tracts warned readers not to wait to convert, but they also recognized that potential converts had a genuine difficulty in finding the right words to express faith and be converted. *The Danger of Delay*, which drove home its point with an engraving of a carriage carrying one young woman over a cliff as it ran over two other people, was full of dire stories, warning readers to "consider that the present favourable opportunities of securing salvation, may, if neglected, pass away, never to return."[54]

Over time, the tracts became increasingly insistent that not only *should* the sinner convert immediately, but he or she *could* convert immediately. In the tract *What Must I Do* (its title taken from the account in Acts of the conversion of the Philippian jailer), the reader was told that there was a simple way to be saved: "The connection between believing and being saved is certain and infallible. Believe and thou shalt be saved. There is no peradventure here. Thou shalt be saved."[55] Prayer went from being the preparation for faith to being the act of faith itself. In some ATS tracts such as *The Ring-Leader*, converts attributed their conversion not to a sinner's prayer but to the secret intercessory prayer of Christians (another theme of Finney's).[56] But the tract *Some Memorials of Edward Lee* combined both the sinner's prayer and secret prayer. Lee cried out in the prayer of the publican and the prayer of the apostle Peter:

> At length one night, amidst the agony of his convictions, he resolved to throw himself upon the mercy of his Savior. He arose from his bed, determined that, if he must perish, it should be pleading at the feet of Jesus, and crying out in the deepest abasement, "Lord save me, I perish." "God be merciful to me a sinner."

Crying out in the words of that biblical sinner's prayer led Lee in that moment to a sense of salvation: "He had no sooner done this, than he found peace, even while upon his knees in prayer: . . . despair . . . was ended in the praises of his Redeemer."[57]

Finally, some tracts included model prayers. *The Danger of Delay* included this "Prayer of a Repenting Sinner" as its last page:

O gracious Redeemer! I have already neglected thee too long. I have crucified thee afresh by my guilt and impenitence, as if I had taken pleasure in putting thee to an open shame [Heb. 6:6]; but my heart now bows itself before thee in humble, unfeigned submission. I would be entirely thine. Teach me, O Lord, what thou wouldst have me to do [Acts 9:6]; for I desire to learn the lesson, and to learn it that I may practise it. If it be more than my feeble powers can answer, thou wilt, I hope, give me more strength, and in that strength I will serve thee. O receive a soul which thou hast made willing to be thine! Permit me to come and throw myself at thy feet, like a helpless outcast, that hath no shelter but in thy compassion: like one pursued by "the avenger of blood," and seeking earnestly an admittance into "the city of refuge" [Deut. 19].

I wait for the Lord, my soul doth wait; and in thy word do I hope that thou wilt receive me graciously [Ps. 130:5]. My soul confides in thy goodness, and adores it. I adore the patience which has borne with me so long, and the grace that now makes me heartily willing to be thine, to be thine on thine own terms, thine on any terms. O secure this treacherous heart [Jer. 17:9] to thyself. O, unite me to thee in such inseparable bonds, that none of the allurements of flesh and blood, none of the vanities of an ensnaring world, none of the solicitations of sinful companions, may draw me back from thee, and plunge me into new guilt and ruin! Be surety, O Lord, for thy servant for good [Ps. 119:122]; that I may still keep my hold on thee [Gen. 32:24–32], and so on eternal life; till at length I know more fully, by joyful and everlasting experience, how complete a Saviour thou art! AMEN.[58]

A pastiche of biblical quotations formed the backbone of the prayer, and many of the remaining phrases are biblical in origin. The first quotation came from Hebrews 6, a passage commonly used to warn

that someone who heard the gospel and rejected it was in effect crucifying Jesus for the second time. The second quotation came at the
moment in the prayer where the sinner turns (converts) from his sin
to faith. The words were taken from the account of the apostle Paul's
conversion on the road to Damascus, a passage used to justify instantaneous conversion. The quotation from Psalm 130 rested on
God's word as the basis of faith. The prayer described even repentance as a grace, where God first moved the heart, which was treacherous or depraved. An allusion to the passage in Genesis where Jacob
wrestles with God thus stood for the struggles of the soul to obtain
conversion.

This sinner's prayer, presented without attribution in the tract as
a means for the sinner to use to convert, was taken from chapter 10
("The Sinner Seriously Urged and Entreated to Accept of Salvation
This Way") of the English Nonconformist minister Philip Doddridge's *The Rise and Progress of Religion in the Soul*, the same book
from which Samuel Hill had selected his shipboard prayer of conversion. That book was frequently excerpted by the American Tract
Society and distributed in its entirety by publishers such as the American Bible Society. It was a mainstay of evangelical publishing and
thus of the gospel of conversion. Excerpting the prayer of a repenting
sinner from the sermon kept the spirit of Doddridge's message. But
Doddridge's book contained thirty chapters intended to take a person
from his or her first encounter with religion through the Christian
life up till death, and each of those chapters ended with a "devout
meditation, or prayer."[59] By separating out the prayer from the chapter,
isolating it at the end of an appeal to convert, and reproducing it thousands of times, the ATS turned the prayer into a means of conversion
that could itself be replicated in the lives of many converts.

✠

The ATS tracts developed the sinner's prayer, but how did people
use the tracts in the following decades? To state the question another
way, did people actually use these tracts and convert in the way that
the tracts tried to train them?[60] A full answer is difficult since the
most likely sources are conversion narratives, which are themselves

constructed literary texts, subject to the same changes in genre. Nevertheless, Kyle Roberts points out that "evangelicals believed a tract could effect the conversion of its reader, or . . . its listener. It could transform a person reading a tract aloud into a minister exhorting the unconverted."[61] There is evidence that people acted on that belief and actually enacted the conversions described in the tracts.

Nevertheless, the tracts themselves cannot be regarded as reliable sources for how people actually converted. Most tracts were fictionalized to some degree, usually in a way that the reader could not mistake. Following the conventions of fiction, many of the names of individuals and places were replaced with initials.[62] Characters fit into ideal types—the infidel, the Universalist, the pious Christian, the anxious sinner, the delaying sinner—stock characters who were supposed to represent the categories and stages of conversion. This is not to say that the tracts had no basis in fact. Authors like the Anglican minister Legh Richmond had real parishioners who stood behind the composite sketches in *The Dairyman's Daughter* and *The Dairyman*.[63] These underlying characters were sufficiently real to readers that Clarence Walworth's aunt, who rightly suspected that her nephew had not experienced an evangelical conversion, took him to the American Bible Society in New York. There they saw a "large arm-chair," and she insisted that Walworth sit in "the very chair that the 'Dairyman's Daughter' died in."[64]

Some of the tracts, though, bear evidence of how their readers used them. A woman named Anna Johnson recorded the power of the tracts in her copy of *The Work of the Holy Spirit:* "Anna C. Johnsons Book/God gave her grace hear in to look/And wen the bell for her doth toll/Then may the lord presear[v]e her soul."[65] Precisely what Johnson's experience was is unknowable, but the main lines are clear: she read the tract, was converted, and expected to be saved after death.

Millions of ATS tracts were actually put into the hands of readers, thanks to two distribution channels. First, beyond donations from wealthy contributors such as the Tappans, the main funding for the ATS came from evangelistic Christians who bought tracts from the ATS and distributed them to people who were not converted. Some cities, like New York, were divided into "tract districts" to organize the distribution. Just as the American Bible Society sold

FIGURE 1.3 A middle-class family of Christians handing out tracts from a basket to poorer city dwellers. From *The Address of the Executive Committee of the American Tract Society, to the Christian Public* (New York: American Tract Society, 1825). Image courtesy American Antiquarian Society.

well-bound, high-quality Bibles to Christians in order to finance distribution of mass-market Bibles to unbelievers, so the ATS sold "premium tracts" such as booklets of doctrine and small hymnbooks to be kept by contributors. These sales underwrote the cost of printing evangelistic tracts for distribution.[66] The ATS, like most other benevolent and reform movements, also undertook distribution through local auxiliaries (Figure 1.3).

The other distributors of the ATS were hundreds of colporteurs (book and tract peddlers).[67] These colporteurs were often seminarians who worked for the ATS during the summer. Surviving reports from these colporteurs describe how far they penetrated into the country's literal wilderness, as well as into the spiritual wilderness of the un-Christianized pockets of the country. A particularly rich collection of reports remains from colporteurs who traveled through the pine barrens of New Jersey, where they went from house to house distributing tracts and Bibles, selling them when the person could afford it, but mostly giving them away.[68] These colporteurs emphasized that people had "grown up in sin and ignorance, [and] so are stupid and indifferent about their souls." The colporteurs were accurate in reporting that large proportions of the country had no religious affiliation. They commonly told stories about children who had never heard of Jesus or, more frequently, who had heard his name but knew nothing about him. The Mormons seem to have had at least as great a reach into the pine barrens as traditional Protestantism. But often people asked for tracts: "One lady asked for the 'Dairyman's Daughter,' saying it was blessed to the conversion of her brother. A gentlemen, who is now a Baptist minister, told us that he was first seriously awakened by reading the tract 'My Spirit Shall not always Strive.'" One Methodist man "traces his conversion to the reading of the 'Dairyman's Daughter.'" The colporteurs (who were often doing double duty with the American Bible Society) gave away those tracts and others, along with books such as Richard Baxter's *Call to the Un-converted* and Joseph Alleine's *An Alarm to the Unconverted*. They kept careful records of whom they gave the tracts to:

> To a colored fam. The father a professor of religion, but of doubtful state. The mother ignorant & degraded. . . .
> To four interesting [i.e., interested] families with no religious books, able but entirely out of money. . . .
> To an irrelig. family without relig. books & unable to purchases.[69]

The ATS may have had the most far-flung distribution network of any organization besides the U.S. Post Office in the antebellum United States, reporting that its colporteurs "visited the numerous islands along our coast, the lumber districts of the East; the frontiers of the North; the mountainous area dividing the East from the West; the barren pines stretching down for 1000 miles to the Gulf; the bayous and hammocks of the South, and along the borders of the lakes and prairies of the West." Extravagant language aside, the ATS was right.

The ATS annual reports relayed scores of anecdotes about people who had been converted by reading the tracts.[70] Though the anecdotes cannot be taken at face value, they are evidence that the tracts did have an effect. The reports claimed, for example, that Legh Richmond "is said to have received information of *three hundred conversions*" on account of *The Dairyman's Daughter*, and one local committee of the ATS heard of "more than twenty instances of conversion by the instrumentality of Tracts."[71] Even if the home office tended to publish only the best reports, the colporteurs themselves were not always given to exaggeration. One reported that "we cannot point out as many clear instances of conversion effected through the instrumentality of our agency as we could desire." Yet "by inquiry it was ascertained that the tracts had been universally read and a considerable portion of their contents remembered; and some, at least, who then had no hope, have since professed to be followers of Jesus." Another reported that "we have not been able it is true after much inquiry, to learn that there were any cases of conversion to be traced to some of the vols as the means of awakening serious conviction & reflection." But he also noted that the area he had visited last year near Goshen, New Jersey, had experienced a revival, and so "there is reason to trust that they have been, there at least, instruments of good."[72]

The sinner's prayer in the ATS tracts changed later conversion narratives. Conversion, especially for Protestants, often functioned like a typology in which one figure stood as an allegory or model for another. Protestants held forth certain people as models of genuine conversions to be imitated by others. Jonathan Edwards produced two such types, with his anonymous account of Sarah Edwards's conversion in *Some Thoughts concerning the Present Revival of Religion* and with his *Life of David Brainerd*.[73] Another commonly reprinted and excerpted conversion narrative was that of John Newton, the slave trader turned Anglican priest and hymn writer.[74] Evangelicals relied on these conversion narratives, which they read in print and which were held up as examples in countless sermons, to know how they should be converted themselves.

After the ATS developed the form of the sinner's prayer, it started to appear in other conversion narratives.[75] One such account was the narrative of Max Rossvally. Rossvally was born a Jew, became a skeptic while in the Union Army, and married a Catholic woman. After the Civil War, he attended a revival meeting at a Congregational Church in Washington, DC, after an evangelist had told him he would be converted when he reached that city. Rossvally wanted to leave the revival meeting, which he attended on a whim, but he was arrested by the tune "Jesus of Nazareth Passeth By" and by a woman who wanted to talk to him. Rossvally, an alcoholic, hoped to drown his memories of the service with brandy, but "a strange restraining power" kept him from the saloon. During a night of agony, he prayed a kind of sinner's prayer:

> Oh! Lord Jesus Christ, if thou art the Messiah that I am looking for—if thou are the Saviour of mankind—reveal thyself to me this night. Take away this darkness and enlighten my mind, and let me feel that peace and consolation that thy children feel. Take away this terrible appetite and evil passion, and I will serve thee while I live. Hear my prayer, oh! Lord, Jesus, and cleanse my soul from sin, for thy dear name's sake.[76]

The words of Rossvally's prayer were his own, but the form was the same as the sinner's prayers in the ATS tracts.

✠

Changes in the pattern of conversion also registered in the relations that converts gave privately within their churches. In 1856 and again in 1858, the Congregationalist church in Pawtucket, Rhode Island, experienced revivals. Among the many converts in that church were eighty-seven people who wrote out their relations as a speech or a letter.[77] These people presented evidence of their conversions during the revival in order to be admitted to church membership and the privilege of participating in the Lord's Supper, a practice inherited from seventeenth- and eighteenth-century Congregationalism. Over 80 percent of the Pawtucket narratives were written by women or girls; the remaining relations with male names were mostly by children. Women converted more frequently than men, but this proportion seems unusually high. It is more likely that women and children did not speak in church, so their relations were written down and read publicly or privately by the minister. Whatever the specific policies that caused these relations to be written down while others went unrecorded, they offer an unusual opportunity to read relations written for a congregation rather than for the press.

The Pawtucket conversion relations were in many respects deeply conservative: they bore an unmistakable family resemblance to the centuries-old Congregational tradition from which they came. The most important continuity with the tradition of relations was that converts were applying to gain admission to the "duty and privilege" of the Lord's Supper. The most important change from the tradition involved the striking absence of baptism in the narrative. Only a few people mentioned that they had been baptized, though many emphasized that they had been educated in Christianity in their youth. Though many if not most of the narrators had been baptized as children, none of the narrators harkened back to their baptism as the start of a covenant with God that they had to fulfill by being admitted to the Lord's Table, which was one of the commonplaces of older Congregational narratives. Rather, they universally regarded themselves as converting not from one stage of Christianity to the next, but as converting from unbelief or merely nominal Christianity to true belief. Though most of the Pawtucket converts were participants in Christianity, even if somewhat sporadically, they asked to become "Christians," and they described their earlier training in religion to illustrate how unbelieving they had been. This change in terminology was even enforced, presumably by the minister, who crossed out terms such as "professing Christian" or "hopeful Christian" to be just "Christian." Thus Louisa Jerauld confessed, "I must find my self a greater sinner in the sight of God before I could be a Christian."

Most of the Pawtucket narrators converted with a sense of urgency exacerbated by their own delay.[78] Their pastor preached that "indecision is an aggravated sin." The converts' worries about delay, especially their fear that the Holy Spirit might not move them to conversion again, were the same concerns expressed in the ATS tracts. Even as a child, Frederick Bates experienced the pull several times: "God has sent this Holy Spirit to strive with me several times, once on the conversion of my sister, and again on the death of my father, but each time I resisted and thought I would put it off a little longer." Charles E. Davis had felt many times that he needed religion, but he "made business and the cares of the world an excuse for delay in seeking untill some future time." Many feared that the Holy Spirit would pass them by if they delayed any further. Frances A. Carpenter decided not to "trifell with the Holy Spirit any longer." Addie L. Bliss was moved to awakening by hearing the text "now is the accepted time, now is the day of salvation." Harriet Bliss resisted the immediacy of conversion, saying, "I do not know as anything in particular first awakened me. I alwa[y]s wanted to become a Christian, ever since I began to know good from evil." But even she was likely moved to make her conversion definitive that winter because her sister and others in the congregation were doing so. Jennie F. Clapp, a school-aged girl, was converted for that reason: "As I daily heard of the conversion of my young friends it made me sad when I thought of the difference between them and me." Some of the converts expressly disclaimed the use of the means of grace for conversion. Mary Holmes thought that when she used the means she was "trying to prepare myself to be a Christian. I was trying to understand it as I would a sum in Arithmetic," instead of having faith.

Though the conversions were urgent, they were not ecstatic. As re-vivals go, the revival in Pawtucket seems fairly staid. Several converts said they had heard of more ecstatic conversions but did not experi-ence them. As Rachel M. Bosworth wrote, "I did not feel that ex-tatic joy which I have heard some speak of but a peace within that I cannot describe a trust in the Redeemer." Bosworth's experience of peace and rest was much more common, and it often came after hearing the "still, small voice" of the Holy Spirit calling them to con-version. Addie Bliss wrote, "I found no rest until I came humbly to the foot of the cross." Adelaide Fish liked the prayer meetings because they told her what she had to do to be saved, and then "I began to feel the blessed assurance that my sins were forgiven."

These experiences of peace and joy often came after prayer. Prayer meetings were frequently mentioned as a sign that people had been Christians, as in Elizabeth E. Burns's narrative. Sylvia Wheaton Bowen experienced conversion after days of prayer:

I resolved that I would become a Christian & for this I prayed & prayed, for the Lord to have mercy on me. after A few days light and peace broke in upon my Soul. I felt that God had for-given my sins And now I am happy in the Lord, I love God & I feel that He loves me. I love the Bible, I love Christians, as I never loved before.

Jennie Clapp felt that she was converted after praying at home. When the pastor and his wife visited her, the pastor's wife "told me how willing Jesus was to be my Saviour if I would only trust and believe in Him." Clapp prayed after they left, and she felt that Jesus had brought her case before God. She did have doubts as to whether her conversion through prayer was enough: "It was very hard for me to believe that I had really experienced the change for which I had always longed. It did not seem change enough. But I think I have since been blessed with a feeling of perfect security." Her doubts show that Clapp expected peace and salvation to follow prayer, even if that pattern was hard to put into practice. Catherine Cashen likewise was converted by praying alone in her room after having gone to a meeting in the vestry. William Metcalf was converted when he "knelt in Prayer for the first time." Cynthia Maria Miller resolved not to pray out of fear that God would not hear her, but she felt compelled to pray and so "determined" to be a Christian. Almira S. Pratt came to feel "the importance of an immediate decision to love and serve God." Mary Elizabeth Rhodes prayed in silence at her pastor's home. The prayer of conversion did not always have the desired effect. Several of the converts felt like S. A. Ryder, who at times read the Bible and prayed more, "but did not feel as I thought I ought to feel." But Ryder and the others were waiting for the effective prayer of conversion.

Among many influences, Pawtucket converts read tracts published by the American Tract Society. Horace Carpenter had gone to Sabbath school since childhood, but he "tried to puzzle my teacher with hard questions, rather than to know and obey the truth." Starting in the fall of 1858, he wrote, a companion "gave me some tracts which I read carefully," including *Come to Jesus* and *The Cause and Cure of Infidelity*. Mary A. Pervear was given *The Anxious Enquirer after Salvation*. The converts were also pointed to the biblical passages that contained sinner's prayers. Minerva Ingraham, after being "considerably awakened to a sense of my own danger by the conversion of friends," was encouraged to read Psalm 51. As she did, a voice said,

"Now is the accepted time, now is the day of salvation." The simplified world of the tracts could not be perfectly imitated in the spiritual lives of converts. But converts did read them and tried to experience conversion in the way the tracts trained them to expect it.

✠

By the middle of the nineteenth century, the new pattern of conversion called for by Finney, defined by the American Tract Society, and put into practice by converts was a central element of American evangelicalism. This change was controversial and not without ambiguities that had to be resolved. The ATS tracts were often excerpted liberally from systematic works written by theologians and pastors. But the tracts in turn modified later generations of writing on revivalism and theology, which focused on conversion and offered theological justifications for the experiences that Protestants were having. Although there were always dissenters from this type of conversion, the practice nonetheless had widespread theological ramifications.

One difficulty centered on whether conversions were instantaneous or gradual. In 1857–1858, a "businessmen's revival" broke out in New York, Boston, and other cities, as people stopped their work at noon to meet for prayer. In response to criticisms of the revival, the Congregationalist pastor Nehemiah Adams, minister of the Essex Street Church in Boston, offered an explanation of the doctrine of conversion, titled *Instantaneous Conversion*. The critics of the revival argued that true Christians needed to be changed into the pattern described in the Sermon on the Mount, and that change took time. One could no more "get religion" than one could "get" an education. Adams instead advanced a doctrine of justification that he termed "instantaneous regeneration." He argued that "we have learned from the Bible and experience that there is a certain way of beginning a religious life, and without this there is, for us, no true religion." Adams defended this doctrine out of the Scriptures, but most importantly, he argued on the basis of experience: "We speak the experience of multitudes without number when we say, that there is a wonderful power in the atonement by Christ to satisfy the conscience at once." This experience of "sudden and great joy which accompanies conversion" came when the convert "is fully aware that he has exercised saving faith." In other words, Adams recognized that the conversion had to have a decisive moment, and that the experiences of conversion had shaped the doctrine of conversion.[79]

In 1858, the journalist William C. Conant wrote a history of the businessmen's revival that served as an important collection of conversion narratives. In addition to summarizing newspaper reports of the revival, Conant gathered accounts of conversion from the entirety of Protestant history, from "the day of Pentecost to the great awakening in the last century," as the title put it. The book was thus an argument for the universality of a particular kind of conversion experience. An introduction written by the celebrity pastor of Plymouth Church in Brooklyn, Henry Ward Beecher, made clear what brought those accounts together: "that there is an instantaneous influx of spiritual influence upon the hearts of men . . . cannot reasonably be doubted by those who take the pains to examine the facts of actual life." Conant provided those facts of life in a set of narratives that borrowed their style and their brevity from the genre of the tract, as well as from their emphasis on converting prayer. A sailor who was converted in a Plymouth church "began to pray, and to pray earnestly for my salvation." In a report of an 1830 conversion, the narrator told an old man that he must "repent of his sins, and give himself up to Christ," which the man agreed to do in prayer: "I knelt by his side, and united with him in prayer. When he arose he was full of joy and peace." In another account, a woman named Nancy acknowledged that she was in rebellion against God; the narrator told her "this acknowledgment turned into a prayer would be a good one": "Go and say, O Lord, I am a desperate sinner. . . . *Lord save; I perish.*" A convert at a prayer meeting in Boston said that "he had been reading infidel books for the last few years; but that, during the previous night, on his bended knees, alone, he was enabled to make a complete surrender of himself to God, and found peace."[80]

Another problem was how to reconcile God's grace and sovereignty with the convert's actions. The Baptist minister Augustus Hopkins Strong wrote a *Systematic Theology*, which became a definitive theological work for Baptists of the Calvinist persuasion. Not only was the book a theological text in its own right, it was also a "compendium and commonplace-book" of other Calvinist theological works. Strong thus explicitly gathered the theological reflections of the past century and made them available to students. In many ways, Strong's views of conversion were unremarkable. Like most Calvinists, he denied that human beings had any ability to respond to God in a way that could merit salvation.

Still, Strong found a way to reconcile God's sovereignty with immediate human action. He wrote that "much confusion and error have arisen from conceiving of these [regeneration, conversion, and justification] as occurring in chronological order. The order is logical, not chronological." In other words, for Strong there was no reason why a conversion had to have a long intervening time while someone waited for God's work before responding to the gospel. For Strong, the logic of salvation implied that there might be no chronological distinction whatsoever. On the basis of scriptural texts like Romans 8:40 ("whom he did predestinate, them he also called: and whom he called, them he also justified: and whom he justified, them he also glorified"), it was inconceivable that God could regenerate someone who did not respond in conversion with repentance and faith and thus receive justification. Regeneration—and thus conversion—happened in an instant. Humans might never be able to parse out precisely when that instant was, because for Calvinists God rather than man was the first mover. There might therefore be a long train of human experience and preparation and work in the conversion experience, but conversion, the theological concept, was immediate.[81]

✠

The most serious challenge to the theology and practice of Protestant conversions as choice was children. Did a child have to be converted, just like an adult, to be saved and considered a Christian, or were the children of Christian parents also Christians, since they were raised within the faith and baptized as children? Were the children of Christian parents to be catechized or evangelized? Early nineteenth-century evangelicalism insisted on the need for everyone

to be converted, and in a number of instances they included children
in that *everyone*. Evangelical parents and pastors never relinquished
the desire to transmit their religion to their children; if anything, they
felt that need all the more keenly. But for some evangelicals, the primary means shifted from catechesis to preparation for evangelism.[82]

The ambiguity between nurturing and converting children had
been a long time in the making for American Protestants who emphasized heart religion. For evangelicals, conversion became decoupled from the life cycle during the eighteenth-century revivals. New
England Puritans in the seventeenth century had usually experienced
conversion and applied for admission to the Lord's Supper after marriage or the birth of a child, as part as a "family strategy" of en-
suring their children's access to baptism.[83] In the evangelical revivals
of the eighteenth century, however, spiritual awakening could come
at any age. For example, people who were awakened in East Windsor,
Connecticut, were in their early teens, while at Northampton, Massachusetts, Jonathan Edwards's congregation had people awakened
in both youth and old age.[84] Before the awakenings, the conversion
of children was seldom expected; after the awakenings, it was a genuine possibility.

Tracts from the ATS and denominational publishers, including
those aimed at people who were already Christians, urged evangelicals to think of their relatives and their children as unconverted.[85]
In *All in the Ark*, Nehemiah Adams warned that "the children of some
of the best of christians are yet unconverted, and are entering upon
life impenitent." Even a pious Christian who bought pamphlets to
give to others might be a "formal Christian" and a heart atheist.[86]
In a tract that defended infant baptism, Adams saw no inconsistency
between the need for children to convert and their infant baptisms.
He addressed baptized children, saying, "It may be, that my young
friend is not yet a Christian. You have never acknowledged the con-
secration which your parents made of you when you were baptized."
The way to acknowledge that baptism was to "call upon Him in
prayer." He invited baptized children to "give yourself away to God
in some such words as these" and offered them a prayer not unlike
the sinner's prayers described above.[87] Tracts insisted that parents
had the duty to prepare their children for conversion.[88] A Presbyte-

rian tract addressed to parents written in 1872 began bluntly: "The early conversion of all the children of the Church should be intensely desired and incessantly prayed for."[89]

The need for children to convert was a matter of justifiable concern for parents. Consider this poem, titled "The Anxiety of Pious Parents for Their Children":

> Though parents may in covenant be,
> And have their heaven in view,
> They are unhappy, till they see
> Their children happy too.
> . . .
>
> Till they can see victorious grace
> Their children's souls possess,
> The sparking wit, the smiling face,
> But adds to their distress.

These few lines understand the parent to be "pious" and "in covenant," yet that covenant did not extend to children until "they can see victorious grace."[90] Parents had reason to be anxious, then, until their children were converted. As another tract put it, they had to "earnestly seek for that conversion of the soul which consists in being born again, in being born of the spirit of God."[91]

Tract publishers and denominational authorities had special reason to fear that children might become irreligious if unconverted. A commission of the Presbyterian church in 1840 "doubted whether there is a body of people at this time on the earth, so orthodox in their creed, and at the same time so deplorably delinquent in the religious education of their children." The effect of a "neglect of a religious education" was that "our young people may be expected, in such a case, to depart from the church of their fathers, and either stray into communions of the most corrupt character, or become totally regardless of religion in any form." The fear then was that children might become infidels, or what was practically the same thing, Unitarians or Universalists. Uneducated children were "little better than heathen in fact, though Christian in name." This pamphlet did not

regard baptized and educated Christian children as wholly unconverted, and in fact enjoined ministers to make a special effort to educate baptized children. However, it did anticipate "the hopeful
conversion of children in catechetical and Bible classes."[92]

In a period of very high infant and child mortality, the conversion
of children was a matter of life and death.[93] William S. Plumer, a
leader of the Old School Presbyterians, reminded his readers that "it
ought never to be forgotten that children may die" and that "all
who die when young . . . go either to heaven or to hell." Infants and
children of believers have "very strong hopes" to salvation, but
children "who are old enough to understand God's revealed will in
the moral law and the plan of salvation" must have a "regeneration
whose fruits shall be manifest to man." Caveats about infants aside,
"if [children] have not early piety, they have no piety for ever and
ever." Children were not just to be educated in morals and character,
but "they and all men are wholly depraved" and needed "that great
work to be wrought in them, Regeneration." One should not think
that parents who followed this advice were utterly dour: parents were
instructed to teach doctrine with stories, to avoid corporal punishment as much as possible, to be cheerful, and to "let love reign in
all your intercourse with your children." Plumer did not claim that
children had to be converted at the earliest possible age, but he did
think that because children were susceptible to impressions parents
could very strongly dispose their children to conversion and regeneration. While admitting there were few "examples of undoubted
piety" at the earliest ages, he argued that God could "renew and save
one whose mind had advanced to the first grades of intellectual and
rational exercise." He went on to give examples of early piety from
both the Bible and children of his own acquaintance—including one
only four years old—who gave evidence of being a "child of grace."
Mary Frances Huntington, for example, had been baptized as an infant but experienced conversion and "the hope of having become a
Christian" before her death at the age of ten.[94]

The question of whether children must be converted depended on
whether or not they could be converted. To answer that question,
parents had to couple theological ideas with observations of their
own children. Theologically, there was reason to doubt whether a child

was capable of responding with his or her own will—a problem that became more acute the more one's theology depended on the freedom of the will (Arminianism) instead of God's sovereign choice (Calvinism). Then, too, children often reverted to their childlike ways after sober experiences of faith, not least since "serious impressions" were difficult for children to maintain. One admonition to parents laid the responsibility for children's backsliding on parents, since "children are so constituted by the Author of their being, that they are no more capable of taking care of their souls themselves, than their bodies." Nevertheless the same author insisted that "very many of those children who, after appearing to be Christians for a time, lose their impressions, become light and vain, and in outward appearance much they were before, have been the subjects of genuine conversion."[95]

Optimism that children could be converted came from the bedrock evangelical idea that God's grace could touch every person, which necessarily included children. Parents noted that children could experience what were obviously sincere religious experiences. A historian of American Sunday schools points out that the early part of the nineteenth century saw a shift in the psychological views of children, who were no longer "considered capable merely of receiving religious information; they were candidates for evangelization, perhaps even conversion." Children were " 'pliable . . . tender, and capable of impressions.' "[96]

There were two primary means by which parents and Christian workers set about converting children: the publication of tracts and other children's literature, and the Sunday school. The same publishers who created conversion literature for adults also produced thousands of children's tracts, as well as children's periodicals and Sunday school literature. These tracts addressed children directly, aimed to convert them, and in some instances, encouraged children to work for the conversion of their parents.[97] *The Glory of Israel*, for instance, was a tract aimed at Jewish children, on the supposition that they were more likely to be converted in their youth than after being educated as Jews. They in turn were supposed to evangelize their parents.[98]

The Sunday school was an even more effective means than tracts of bringing evangelism to children. Like tract societies, Sunday schools were the invention of British Anglicans. Robert Raikes, an Anglican layman, started what was likely the first Sunday school in Gloucester, England, in 1780, teaching children the Bible and catechism. Sunday schools spread on both sides of the Atlantic in the 1780s and 1790s. In the newly founded United States, these "First Day schools" aimed to teach children of the poor basic morality and literacy.[99] A few of these early Sunday schools were evangelistic, such as Robert May's services for children in Philadelphia in 1811.[100]

By the 1830s, evangelicals had started a new type of school that aimed to convert students rather than educate them. These new schools aimed not only at the education of the poor and unchurched children, but included children who might previously have attended only catechesis classes. The Sunday school provided a place and a set of techniques for converting children, or at least preparing them for conversion, and conversion became "a key theme in weekly lessons." The curriculum was designed to gradually lead children to conversion as adolescents.[101] Sunday schools became widespread in many denominations. Anne Boylan estimates that in 1825, only 2.2 percent of the eligible children in the country were participants in Sunday schools, but by 1832 those numbers had climbed to 7.9 percent. Sunday schools were far more common in cities, and in places like Philadelphia approximately 27.9 percent of the children of the targeted age were members of Sunday schools in 1832.[102]

As they became institutionalized, particularly through the American Sunday School Union (ASSU), Sunday schools formalized practices of evangelizing children. The announced aims of the organization were to "instruct the ignorant, awaken the careless, and guide the inquiring" as well as to "convert to God the soul of man."[103] In the last quarter of the nineteenth century, ASSU missionaries formalized the practice of holding evangelistic efforts in the winters, paying special attention to unchurched children, and missionaries correspondingly reported more conversions.[104] Sunday schools occasionally reported revivals. The Sabbath School in Hatfield, Vermont, reported that sixty-five members "were hopefully converted during the first three months of the present year." The report noted that only children who participated in the Sunday school experienced these conversions. Munson, Vermont, reported 110 children who had become "interested" (meaning seriously awakened and on the road to conversion). The report went on to note that "about seventy of the 110 were baptized in infancy," highlighting the importance of conversion over the sacrament.[105]

When the historian of the American Sunday School Union summed up what the organization had accomplished, he claimed that the "evangelical Union schools are among the richest tributaries to the strength of American churches." In tallying conversions in the years 1905 to 1915, he found "98,556 who confessed Christ through their mission work, besides others not counted in many schools." The schools were effective, he claimed, because "the chief teaching in the Union Sunday-schools is the Bible doctrines that are essential to salvation—a teaching never in vain."[106] One need not take these statistics at face value—though they do suggest something of the magnitude of the evangelistic efforts of the schools—as much as note that children had become a mission field and that much evangelistic and institutional effort was expended to convert them.

The idea that children had to be converted did not go unchallenged. Its best known opponent was Horace Bushnell, who advanced instead the idea of "Christian nurture." In Bushnell's theology, "a child is to grow up a Christian. In other word, the aim, effort and expectation should be not, as is commonly assumed, that the child is to grow up in sin, to be converted after he comes to a mature age, but that he is to open on the world as one that is spiritually renewed, not remembering the time when he went through a technical [conversion] experience, but seeming rather to have loved what is good from his earliest years."[107] Bushnell's objection, however, did not persuade everyone. In Boylan's assessment, "it would be erroneous to assume . . . that Christian nurture quickly displaced conversion as the main goal of Sunday school instruction. The two goals existed side by side for some time and many religious educators remained profoundly skeptical of the implications of Christian nurture theory."[108]

In sum, the question of whether children should be converted was one of the primary challenges to the notion of religion as a matter of choice. But while parents never completely abandoned theological or commonsense views of children as inheritors of their religion, evangelicals increasingly laid stress on the need for children to be prepared for and to actually experience conversion, even as they deemphasized the importance of the infant baptisms that they continued to perform.[109] For many children, then, the inheritance of religion came to be couched in terms of religious conversion and choice.

✝

Even as the new pattern of conversion was reflected in Protestant theologies, Protestants themselves were being secularized by their message of conversion.[110] The ATS tracts brought secularism—meaning the obligation to choose religion—in two ways. Earnest Christians distributing tracts and colporteurs selling them or giving them away forced people to make a choice. Like the reader of *The One Thing Needful*, the ATS tracts confronted people with religious choices they otherwise would not have been exposed to, people who might otherwise have been content to follow the same religion as their neighbors. The tracts also secularized people who thought they were already Christians, in the sense that the tracts obligated them to consider whether they might actually be unbelievers. In *The New Birth*, the author urged everyone, including those who had ties to religion, "to set apart some time for the duty of self-examination. Let every one, without exception, take up or renew this grand inquiry, 'Am I in Christ? That is, Am I a new creature, or not? Am I a child of God? or do I still continue an heir of hell?' "[111] And while parents never gave up on passing down their religion to their children, for many families the means by which it was passed down were not primarily the sacrament of baptism, or a religious education, but rather preparation for conversion.

The development of the sinner's prayer was uneven, and of course it represents only part of the variety of Protestant religious experience. But given the importance of conversion to liberal and evangelical Protestants alike, the earliest stages of a newly codified form of experience represented a widespread change in American religious life.[112] Many experienced what John Newton captured in a hymn:

Once a sinner, near despair,
Sought thy mercy-seat by prayer;
Mercy heard and set him free—
Lord, that mercy came to me.[113]

Most important was the way that the sinner's prayer redefined the religious identity of American Protestants. The publications of the evangelical benevolence movement convinced many that they could not have inherited their religious identity through baptism or religious education. Lyman Beecher estimated that in 1833 the world's population contained 200 million "nominal" and 10 million "real" Christians; American Christians came to think of nominal Christians as no kind of Christian at all.[114] The tracts' emphasis on the need to pass on faith to children was a timeless concern made all the more relevant because evangelicals were themselves calling the inheritance of faith into question, but the tracts also provided a new ritual by which people might enact their choice to be converted.

2

Gift

CHEROKEE CONVERTS AND THE
RECEPTION OF MISSIONS

O<small>N A</small> S<small>ATURDAY</small> <small>NIGHT</small> sometime in the 1830s, Daniel Butrick and John Huss gathered a congregation in the Cherokee Nation for two days of religious exercises. The religious experiences were a way for the congregation to experience their piety as a group by practicing the most important rituals of their evangelical Presbyterian faith. From Saturday night to Sunday morning, the congregation fasted and prayed while listening to sermons in preparation for five baptisms and the celebration of the Lord's Supper.

"About 150 persons (Cherokees)" were present on Saturday night for Huss's preaching and for the "night prayer meeting," wrote Butrick, though many of them were not members of the congregation and observed "mostly from a distance." On Sunday morning, Huss preached two more times, at 9 A.M. and again at 10:30. Butrick spent the morning sessions "conversing with five persons who wished to unite with the church." Butrick gave his weary fellow preacher a break and preached at noon from Jesus's parable of the importunate widow. The text was an encouragement "that men ought always to pray, and not to faint," but Cherokee listeners threatened with removal from their land would not have made a great leap in finding a political meaning in the parable's "unjust judge" who "feared not God, neither regarded man" or in Jesus's promise, "Will not God give justice to his elect, who cry to him day and night?"

Preaching was but prologue to the most important work of the day. After the noon sermon, Butrick and Huss together baptized five people: Levi Woodward, John Ashhopper, Betsy Ashhopper, Nancy Partridge, and Suky Burns. To covenant with the church, these baptismal candidates almost certainly had to answer a series of questions about their beliefs, and they had to be admitted by a vote of the congregation. Following the baptism, a Cherokee Christian, "Br[other] Le-ni-ta . . . confessed his fault for intemperate drinking," and the congregation readmitted him to fellowship. That act of reconciliation complete, the congregation partook of the Lord's Supper, the symbol of Christian unity reserved only for full members of the church, all of whom had given relations of their conversions. The day ended in the glow of a candlelight meeting at the mission house.[1]

This event could be read as a story of how some Cherokee came to adopt the Christianity offered to them by white missionaries. Indeed, the practices described in Butrick's notes differ hardly at all from descriptions of entirely white congregations. Fasting, prayer, preaching, baptism, Communion, and church discipline were common practices among Congregationalists and Presbyterians influenced by the eighteenth-century awakenings, as were revival meetings centered on particular congregations. However, the interactions between Cherokee and missionaries were more complex. Daniel Butrick was a white missionary from New England in the service of the American Board of Commissioners for Foreign Missions (ABCFM). But his fellow minister, John Huss, was a Cherokee convert. In 1833, Huss had been ordained at the Creek Path mission station in Tennessee by a council of ministers, and then he had preached the customary ordination sermon. But Huss spoke only Cherokee. At his ordination council, the sermon and charge of the white ministers who ordained Huss were translated from English to Cherokee by Elias Boudinot, and Huss's own sermon that day was translated from Cherokee to English by Stephen Foreman. Both translators were Cherokee converts.[2] Huss preached in the primary language of Cherokee Christians, who comprised the majority of a congregation that exercised the power to admit and discipline members and to administer the sacraments.

The interaction between converts and missionaries at that meeting points to the importance of considering the terms in which Christianity was received by Cherokee converts. At first glance, the history of missions to the Cherokee might seem like a typical example of the free market in religion. Several denominations sought to expand by opening up untapped (even colonial) markets. Missionaries, along with other white settlers, literally brought market capitalism to the Cherokee lands, building mills, establishing stores, and constructing roads. The denominations competed for adherents, though they tried to coordinate with one another to allocate the market.

But while the kinds of options that the missionaries presented mattered, what mattered more was how Cherokees who converted to Christianity shaped the Christianity that they received.[3] Though the Cherokee were far less powerful than the federal and state governments that took their lands, when it came to deciding whether to accept Christianity, the balance of power was in their hands. In their day-to-day interactions with missionaries, they put their own conditions on the encounter with Christianity. Though the form of the Christianity that they received was in many respects like the Christianity that the missionaries brought, the Cherokee controlled the terms on which they received it. They tended to receive Christianity in their own language, translating the Bible and rituals of Christianity into their own idiom. They gained control over their own churches, both in the preaching and in the reception of new converts. In particular, they preferred to receive Christianity as a gift—that is, as a relationship of mutual obligation. In the end, a few of the missionaries fulfilled their reciprocal obligation by joining the Cherokee on the Trail of Tears. As the United States expanded through the power of the state and market, Cherokee converts encountered a new religious option and turned it into a gift.

☩

In the early decades of the nineteenth century, the United States relentlessly expanded west. Expansion had to reckon with Spanish and French possessions to the south and British possessions to the north, but also the indigenous nations that hemmed in the United States: in the Southeast, the Seminole, Choctaw, Chickasaw, Creek, and Cherokee. The political boundaries of the United States were roughly the boundaries of Protestantism in North America. An 1856 map of the world from a Protestant perspective, colored according to the religious affiliations of its inhabitants, showed the expanding United States and part of Canada as blue for Protestant, with Catholicism to the south. Most of North America was shaded green: the color of "other pagans." Yet the map showed Protestant mission stations among the Indian nations, outposts of the expansion of Christianity. The earliest missions, starting with the American Board of Commissioners for Foreign Missions in 1812, went overseas to India and Burma.[4] But first the Moravians, then the ABCFM, and finally Baptist and Methodist missionary boards also undertook missions to the Native American nations on the periphery of the United States. The ABCFM alone undertook missions to fifteen tribes, with the earliest mission to the Cherokee beginning in 1817 and the last continuing mission to the Dakota ending in 1883.[5] These missions to expand Christianity began outside the formal political boundaries of the United States, though in the case of the southeastern nations, never outside the power of American treaties, the U.S. War Department, and the economy of white settlers. The attempt at Christianizing the continent proceeded in an uneasy, sometimes antagonistic, relationship with the political expansion of the United States.

Christianity was planted among the Cherokee by missionaries. Near the end of the roughly four decades that white missionaries had a presence in the Cherokees' ancestral lands in Georgia, Alabama, Tennessee, and North Carolina, perhaps 8 percent of Cherokees became Christians. Yet Christianity also became an indigenous Cherokee religion. The shock of being removed across the Mississippi by the United States government disrupted the power of both Christian missions and traditional Cherokee cosmology. After a rapid but brief decline in the number of Cherokee affiliated with Christianity, the rate of Cherokee adherence to Christianity doubled from its pre-removal peak to a new high of perhaps 15 percent in the decade or two after removal. Cherokee converts translated their new religion into the Cherokee language and Cherokee idioms. The result was that Christianity became as much a Cherokee religion as was traditional Cherokee cosmology.

✠

Their encounter with Christianity in the early nineteenth century presented the Cherokee with a number of choices. Some of the decisions to be made were as old as their encounter with Europeans beginning in the sixteenth century—how to trade, how to protect their land—but they received new forms and urgencies as the Cherokee Nation negotiated with the United States from the presidencies of Washington to Jackson. Other questions were raised as the missionaries entered Cherokee territories, including the question of whether to adopt Christianity.

The choice a Cherokee made about one question was inextricably tied to the choices made about the others. For the Cherokee who were asked to choose between conversion to Christianity and renewed zeal for Cherokee cosmology, the choice was bound up with other choices—whether to acculturate, whether to adopt American-style agriculture and market trade, whether to enter into treaties, whom to fight in the War of 1812. To choose conversion had different religious meanings over time, but it also had different political, economic, and social meanings.[6]

Viable combinations of choice changed over time, as hunting and traditional agriculture became less feasible and as the U.S. government, missionaries, and other white settlers permeated the Cherokee Nation with roads, mills, stores, and other apparatus of a market economy. The policies of the federal government changed, too. In the 1790s, President George Washington and Secretary of War Henry Knox advanced a policy of assimilation and perhaps even eventual political union. This policy was exchanged for Jackson's policy of Indian removal, defined in law by the Treaty of New Echota in 1835 and in fact by the deportation of the Cherokee in 1838–1839. The missionaries, too, presented a number of different and dynamic choices: first the Moravian missionaries, next the Congregationalist and Presbyterian ABCFM missionaries, and finally the Baptist and Methodist missionaries. The missionaries also presented different political options to the Cherokee. The first missionaries were funded in part by the War Department and considered themselves bound not to interfere with it. Later missionaries, like Samuel Worcester and Evan Jones, were willing to defy federal and state governments on behalf of the Cherokee and to hold forth a Christianity that made claims about justice in this life as well as salvation in the next. However, when removal seemed unavoidable, some missionaries counseled the Cherokee to give in to the removal party, and several converts to Christianity took a leading role in making the case for removal, sparking apostasy among other converts.[7]

The choices offered to potential converts were shaped by the Cherokee themselves. Among the first converts to Christianity were leaders like Charles Hicks, who favored assimilation. Cherokees also mounted religious opposition to the missionaries and to Christianity. Cherokee rituals, especially the Green Corn Dance and ball plays, were constant competitors with Christian rituals. The increasing importance of Cherokee visionaries and conjurers with the Ghost Dance movements starting in 1811 sharpened the distinction between Christianity and the Cherokee religion, which might otherwise have been considered nonexclusive systems. By the time of the Treaty of New Echota, both Cherokee *adonisgi* (medicine men/priests) and the Christian converts who signed the fraudulent treaty had made the choice stark, so that ambiguity of allegiance was no longer possible.

The majority of Cherokee who never opted for Christianity, or who were never even confronted by the choice, still had to choose their cosmology. William McLoughlin, a historian of Cherokees and their missionaries, explains how Cherokee cosmology took on a different meaning because its economic, political, and social frame changed: "The attachment to the old cosmology weakened slowly but surely between 1789 and 1839. . . . The young found it difficult to understand the symbols embedded in their sacred rites and myths; the symbols did not elicit a spontaneous emotional response. If they wanted to know, they had to ask. The Cherokee religion was no longer imbibed unconsciously from infancy."[8] For the Cherokee, as for all native inhabitants of the United States, traditional religions were never completely displaced, but they were also no longer simply traditional.

✠

When the missionaries arrived at the start of the nineteenth century, the Cherokee had a complex set of beliefs. In many respects, Cherokees and Christians held ideas that were at odds with one another. Even the way that Cherokees and Christians categorized their ideas was asymmetrical. Cherokee ideas that missionaries characterized as a religion might better be called a cosmology, because rituals like the Green Corn Dance and myths like the story of the origin of corn and game were not limited to a specific religious context but instead were part of an explanation of the whole world. Observance of rituals, for example, did not just determine one's favor with the gods, but also the success of the corn, one's position within the political system, and the health of one's body. To be sure, Christianity was a cosmology as much as it was a religion, but for white Christians there was a separation of categories between religion, economy, politics, and medicine. The conversion that missionaries were asking for was not just a request to exchange one religion for another, but a request to switch the way identity was categorized.

The notes of John Howard Payne, an actor and journalist (most famous for writing the song "Home, Sweet Home"), provide a glimpse of this cosmology. Payne made a number of travels through the Cherokee Nation, interviewing and taking notes on many aspects of Cherokee life, especially religion. He was aided by the missionary Daniel Butrick, who also gathered interviews from the Cherokee. Payne intended to publish his amateur ethnography and completed work on one volume out of a planned six, carefully documenting his claims with citations to specific Cherokee informants. His thesis—a common one in European and American studies of Indians—was that the original Cherokee were lost Israelites who practiced the religion of the Old Testament, from which their descendants had fallen away. This thesis doubtless clouds his ethnography, for example, when he referred to the Green Corn Dance as "maimed rites," "shorn equally of its pristine splendor and solemnity." The general tenor of the first volume is the similarity between Cherokee religion and the ancient Hebrew religion of the Hebrew Bible.[9]

The Cherokee told Payne a number of things about their cosmology, but they were careful to do so on their own terms. When Sickatower, one of Payne's interviewees, was repeating a Cherokee prayer, apparently in the presence of Payne and Principal Chief John Ross, Payne laughed and Ross smiled at something in the prayer. At that, Sickatower "declined proceeding." He said that was all there was to the prayer, though Payne had earlier heard seven verses for each of the clans. Sickatower "showed no ill temper, was extremely respectful, but firm. He thought his communications were not understood with the reverence he considered due to his cherished holy mysteries, and to all our persuasions uniformly answered that he had told all."[10]

Payne recorded a number of Cherokee stories about the creation of the world. According to the stories that "the older Cherokee" told Payne, the world was made by "the Creator . . . whose abode is in the centre of the sky." This Creator "in the beginning directed certain lines to points upon the earth," which were the four cardinal directions. He created four men: "In the North, was placed the Blue Man; in the west . . . the Black Man was placed . . . ; and to the south was sent the White Man, the man of purity and peace; but the first, and the original of all, was the red man, he was placed in the east (supposed to signify the sun)." These four beings now had power over the world "as Agents of the Great Being of all" and were worshipped, but "our final and the most fervent of our prayers" were due to the Creator.[11]

This creation myth was significant in the encounter between Cherokee and Christian cosmologies because it described humans as having multiple origins. These multiple origins implied essential differences between people groups. Each ethnic or racial group could have its own religion, customs, and laws. What was obligatory for the white man in the south was not necessarily obligatory for the red man in the east. These creation myths framed the stories of the origin of corn and game, as well as the particular instructions given to the Cherokee. These ways were good for the Cherokee and a part of their identity, but they were not obligatory for whites. In contrast, the prevalent Christian idea was of a single origin of humans in one creation act. The Christian creation story implied a unitary, universal religious principle for all ethnicities. From the Christian cosmology, missionaries could argue that all people needed to adopt faith in Jesus Christ; from the Cherokee cosmology, the Cherokee could argue that the religion of the whites was good for the whites, and the religion of the Cherokee was good for the Cherokee.[12]

The Cherokee creation myths were certainly in circulation before the encounter with Christian missionaries and likely before encounters with whites. As Christian missionaries insisted on the conversion of the Cherokee, the Cherokee found resources within their mythology to resist conversion. Catharine Brown, the most publicized of Cherokee converts, used these myths for exactly this purpose. Her biography was compiled by an administrator of the ABCFM, and everywhere it emphasized that Brown was a prodigy in the speed with which she learned English and adopted Christianity. Nevertheless, even this biography notes that Brown first "supposed, that the Cherokees were a different race from the whites, and therefore had no concern in the white people's religion; and it was some time before she could be convinced, that Jesus Christ came into the world to die for the Cherokees."[13] Indeed, Catharine Brown had to be persuaded to adopt the Christian idea of the unitary origins of humans. "Her apprehensions respecting the human race were so imperfect, that she supposed her own people a distinct order of beings. But soon she learned that God 'hath made of one blood all nations of men.'"[14]

In contrast to the amateur ethnology of Payne, missionaries to the Cherokee were interested in Cherokee cosmology as professionals formally trained in theology.[15] The missionaries cared about Cherokee cosmology because of their practical desire to win more converts. But they were also interested because of their ideas about natural theology. Christian theology of the early nineteenth century regarded God's revelation as coming in two ways. The first, available to all people, was God's revelation of himself in nature. From nature, it was supposed that anyone could discover certain essential facts about God: that He existed, that He was a creator, that there was a final judgment. Cherokees came to missionaries already holding these ideas, and missionaries took that belief as justifying their concept of natural theology. But there was a second kind of revelation, in which God spoke through Jesus Christ and later through the Bible. This special revelation was available only through the means of Christian Scriptures, and hence only to those who had those Scriptures. Furthermore, the content of this revelation, specifically knowledge of Jesus Christ, was necessary for salvation. It was not surprising to missionaries, then, to find that the Cherokee had no prior knowledge of Jesus. ABCFM missionaries saw the same kind of encounter between Christian revelation and indigenous cosmologies in their missions around the globe. In those encounters, natural theology took on increasing importance at the beginning of the nineteenth century, because the Enlightenment emphasized the universality of knowledge. Furthermore, American theology in the nineteenth century became primarily interested in apologetics, and natural theology had an outsized importance for defending and justifying the faith.[16]

The knowledge that the missionaries gathered of Cherokee cosmology had two effects. To be sure, missionaries did regard Cherokee cosmology as deficient and Christianity as necessary for salvation, as scholarly treatments of missions often point out. But the more significant fact for conversion was that missionaries saw in the Cherokee cosmology a preparation for Christianity. Missionaries did not find Cherokee beliefs to be all false, but saw them as containing important truths about the Christian God. John Howard Payne, for example, found what he thought were creation stories that paralleled the Genesis account with the creation of a red man from clay like Adam (Hebrew word meaning "red"), a god named Ye-ho-waah after Jehovah, a flood, a character named E-qa-ha-yi for Abraham, and a lawgiver named Wãsi for Moses. There was an exodus narrative, and a great king who probably stood for Solomon. There were parallels, too, between the opening word of a prayer, Ho-yannah ("hear me now"), and the word *hosanna* in the Psalms. Even Christian practices such as the Lot (a method of making decisions practiced by Moravians) had parallels in Cherokee practices of conjuring with crystals, roasted meat, and beads.[17]

Cherokee converts to Christianity adopted the same idea about religious parallels. Catharine Brown and Atsee, or John Arch, lamented their former ignorance of special revelation, but also believed that their Cherokee mythology had been a preparation for their conversion to Christianity.[18] For all their dissimilarities, Cherokee cosmology and Christian religion had enough points of congruity that the gulf between them, however large, could be bridged. Though the content and the categories of religious ideas were different, there were enough connections that conversion did not entail an entirely foreign view of the world. It is difficult to explain where these parallels may have come from. Some were, of course, purely coincidental. Other parallels may have come about because Cherokees had already learned about Christianity. This is entirely possible, since Payne prepared his work after widespread efforts at missionizing the Cherokee and even longer contact with whites. It is not surprising, however, that Cherokees had heard of Christian ideas before direct contact with the missionaries. Arch, who was a hunter who lived in a remote part of the Cherokee Nation and who "belonged to the most uncultivated portion of his tribe," nevertheless had heard of Christian ideas of a final judgment before he arrived at the Knoxville mission station.[19]

All the missionaries who recorded conversion narratives were interested in this similarity between Cherokee and Christian beliefs, because they tried to evaluate their potential converts' beliefs within the framework of Christian theology. Sometimes missionaries (with the notable exceptions of Daniel Butrick and Samuel Worcester) erroneously assumed that Cherokee ignorance of Christianity meant they had no religious ideas of their own. As Anderson noted of Catharine Brown, "When she entered the school, her knowledge on religious subjects was exceedingly vague and defective."[20] In general, missionaries concluded that Cherokee beliefs prefigured Christian doctrine. Catharine Brown's father, John Brown, was described as having an idea of a "Supreme Being" and of "rewards and punishments, after the present life," but his beliefs were not detailed. Catharine Brown's beliefs were similar. John Arch believed in a "Great Being above" but thought God did not take notice of humans. He believed that men ceased to exist after death, but he had heard that there were rewards and punishments and believed he was bad enough to deserve punishment if that were the case. Still, without the missionaries, the Cherokee did not have the revelation in the Scriptures "of the Saviour of the world."[21]

✠

The very first missionaries to arrive in the Cherokee Nation were the Unitas Fratrum, more commonly known as the Moravians. The Moravians were a Pietist group whose origins were in Central Europe but who had spread throughout Europe, North America, and the Caribbean because of their missionary zeal.[22] They brought with them uncommon practices, not least of which was making important decisions by casting a lot so that the decision was controlled by God. The Moravian missionaries had difficulty deciding where to settle their first mission station, so they left the decision to the Lot. The Lot chose Springplace, near the home of James Vann, a wealthy Cherokee planter and store owner. Whatever the role of chance or providence in the establishment of Springplace, its location near Vann's store revealed the position of the Cherokee and the missionaries within a market economy.[23]

The conversion of the Cherokee and the efforts of the Christian missionaries took place within a series of wrenching economic changes for the Cherokee. The broader context was the loss of Cherokee land to white settlers, which had the effect of reducing the supply of game and the fertility of land, while at the same time making the Cherokee Nation an island within the polity and economy of the United States. The Cherokee livelihood had been in transition since the arrival of Europeans. From the first, the transition included markets, as the Cherokee learned to hunt and trap for furs to satisfy nearby European traders, who in turn sold to distant European markets. For the Cherokee, unlike the Europeans, the market transition occurred before the agricultural transition. From earliest contact, the Cherokee were traders in a fur market. But by the beginning of the nineteenth century, overhunting had so depleted stocks of game that it became increasingly difficult for Cherokee men to make a living from hunting.

A more wrenching and total economic change was the transition in kinds of agriculture. For centuries, the Cherokee had been farmers. Cherokee women cultivated beans and corn using wooden implements that did not cut deeply into the soil, and their agricultural practices did not root the Cherokee to one place. The transition to a more European style of agriculture happened under two auspices. First, overhunting due to the market economy, combined with the loss of Cherokee land to whites, made the traditional Cherokee economy less feasible. Second, it was the policy of the U.S. government, beginning with George Washington, to "civilize" the Cherokee by making them farmers so that they could gradually be incorporated into the

Union. The Cherokee were encouraged to become a type of Jeffersonian farmer, though the more successful Cherokees became
plantation owners rather than yeoman farmers. Men (not women)
were to farm the land with the deep-furrowing plows of the whites
and were to raise subsistence crops and cash crops like cotton
and tobacco.

All of these economic transitions were fiercely debated within
the Cherokee Nation because they upended the Cherokee cosmology. Since politics, economy, and religion were all intertwined
in Cherokee cosmology, the transition to a rooted agricultural
economy became a wedge for Christianity. If the economy and religion were so closely linked for the Cherokee, then to change the
economy was to open Cherokee minds to religious changes as well.
Not all of the Cherokee who adopted white agriculture were converts, but many who became converts were adopters of American
agricultural ways.[24]

The location of the Moravian missionaries in Springplace, near
the store and the federal road, was useful because the missionaries
were near the Cherokee but not in the capital town of New Echota.
Being outside the Cherokee towns, the mission was not under the
cultural dominance of the Cherokee. Being near James Vann's store
put the Moravians near their benefactor, and also near the most visible connection of the Upper Towns to the market economy. The
federally funded road that came through the Cherokee Nation and
passed by James Vann's store connected the Moravians that much
more closely to the primary artery of commerce in the Cherokee Nation. Later missionaries, such as those from the ABCFM who settled the Brainerd station in Tennessee, followed similar strategies of
locating near roads, often building their own mills, and thus becoming a hub of the market economy near their location.

Though the Cherokees and missionaries lived within a market
economy, they also lived within a gift economy. This gift economy
was both a material reality and a spiritual ideal.[25] The missions did
not function as market economies because a market implies a surplus, and during many years at Springplace and Brainerd there was
never enough. In the early years of the Springplace mission, the missionaries barely operated at subsistence, while the Cherokee around

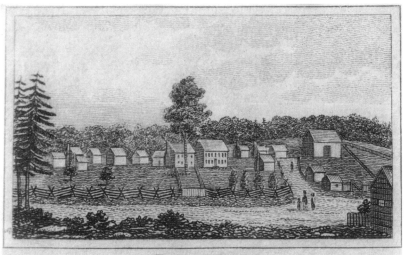

BRAINERD
a Missionary Station among the Cherokees.

FIGURE 2.1 A woodcut depicting the ABCFM Brainerd Mission Station, near what is today Chattanooga, Tennessee. It shows the school buildings, farm buildings, and living quarters, which made up the mixed economic, religious, and familial space of the mission. From Penelope Johnson Allen research notes, correspondence, and photographs, Special Collections, University of Tennessee at Chattanooga, MS-002-04-01-03-001, http://cdm16877.contentdm.oclc.org /cdm/ref/collection/p16877coll7/id/32.

them were often worse off. The Springplace mission was set up as a system of subsistence agriculture. At Brainerd, the mission settlement included a mill and other components of a market economy, but the number of missionaries and pupils resident at Brainerd made for a higher drain on resources, and the mission sometimes ran dangerously low on food and clothing (Figure 2.1). Though the missions had aspirations to self-sufficiency, Brainerd never turned a profit and depended on the donations of white Christian benevolent organizations. Both mission settlements felt obligated to provide what they could for poorer Cherokees in their vicinity. Even in prosperous times, the missionaries might have quoted Jesus's words, "The poor ye have always with you."

The missionaries and the Cherokees each had a hospitality culture that attempted to meet the needs of guests. So when Cherokee travelers came to the mission stations, they could usually expect a meal and lodging. The real proof that the missionaries were operating in a gift economy is the way that they viewed some economic transactions. When hard times were upon them, the missionaries were often asked to sell their food. This they were reluctant to do, needing the food for themselves and their pupils. But they almost always sold anyway, though the transaction was unfavorable to themselves. The items that changed hands were not part of mutually beneficial market transactions, but rather mutually obligated gifts.[26]

Just as important as material realities were the spiritual ideals that the missionaries saw themselves presenting. Whether food for the body or sacramental meals, the missionaries saw themselves as holding forth gifts, not goods. Many Cherokee saw the missionaries as a threatening imposition of the market. Others, such as Margaret Vann, saw the missionaries as offering a gift, and conversion as an invitation to mutual obligations in Christianity.

✠

It was in this context that the first Cherokees converted to Christianity. The Moravian missionaries called these early converts their "first fruits." The term had a theological as well as a metaphorical meaning. The Gambolds and Wohlfahrts at Springplace subscribed to a "first-fruits theology" common to Moravians in their missions around the world. They believed that the first converts would be elites, who would in turn influence others to convert. Though the Moravians were themselves humble people, they aimed to convert the powerful first without slighting the humble, including slaves. Their first and second converts, Charles Hicks and Margaret Vann, were indeed elites and were even related to one another, but they converted under very different circumstances.[27]

Margaret Vann's first substantive interactions with the Moravians were the result of her husband's beatings. The Moravian diary often recorded what they heard or saw of James Vann's drunken rages, including beating and even executing one of his slaves by burning him alive.[28] That Vann was a tyrant was well known. John Howard Payne recorded in his notes that Vann's "impetuosity and decision sometimes degenerated into cruelty."[29] That was to say the least. On June 18, 1805, Anna Rosina Gambold wrote, "We heard horrible things about what he had done again last night, especially that he mistreated his wife so badly that it cannot be repeated."[30] Whether Vann's abuse of his wife was a beating, or rape, or something else, Brother Jacob Wohlfahrt tried to rebuke James Vann for his behavior but found him away from home, while Sister Dorothea Byhan visited Peggy Vann.

The private visit of the two women together was the kind of interaction that seems to have been most significant in Peggy Vann's conversion. We have a record of the conversation only from Byhan's perspective, but she may have been the only one able to talk much. When Byhan asked Vann "whether she does not sometimes pray to the Savior when she is in distress," Vann answered that she did, "and then she could not speak any more for crying." Such visits were dangerous. When Vann returned the next day, he again "knocked his wife to the floor" and raged against Wohlfahrt for questioning his power within his household. Wohlfahrt tried to walk a delicate line between making peace within the Vann household, rebuking James Vann, arguing for the gospel, and preventing Vann from expelling the missionaries.[31]

Peacemaking and private conversations were the primary mode in which Moravians interacted with Cherokee and African slaves. For example, the missionaries "had a further heart-to-heart talk" with Vann's slave Demas "and asked him to be concerned with the eternal well-being of his soul." With the slave woman Jenny, "we took the opportunity to speak *especially* with her."[32] Acts of bargaining were common. For instance, Wohlfahrt, a carpenter, refused to make a coffin for an executed slave until he was permitted to preach to blacks at the funeral. He then based his sermon on the text, "We must all appear before the judgment seat of Christ."[33]

Peggy Vann interacted with the missionaries probably more than any other person in the vicinity of Springplace. In part this was because, as the wife of Vann, she had more leisure and freedom and lived closer to the missionaries—though she was by no means free of labor and by no means free of Vann's restrictions. But it was also because she sought out the comfort of the missionaries, especially of the women, and interacted with them in times of sorrow. One such instance occurred at the deathbed of the Christian slave, Caty. Her death, like many deathbed scenes common in evangelical (especially Methodist) literature, was a time of singing hymns, discussion of the gospel, and the joy of the dying believer mixed with sorrow on the part of those attending her death. Caty was a deathbed convert, for she said "she had never prayed when she was healthy." After she called out to God during her sickness, the Moravians concluded, "We have a faithful hope that the loyal Savior has taken her soul to Himself in grace."[34]

Having witnessed a conversion in the flesh, Peggy Vann was exposed the next day to conversions in print. Vann had been touched by Caty's conversion and had spent the night "thinking about . . . the heavenly blessings that she would one day enjoy with the Savior." Pressing home their opportunity, the two missionary women "read her several stories of remarkable conversions, and then a part from the devotional work, *Something for the Heart*."[35] These conversion narratives were undoubtedly narratives of Protestant converts, possibly Moravian converts, and common fare for religious publishers. By educating Peggy Vann about these Protestant patterns, Byhan and Wohlfahrt trained her to experience them herself. In Vann, the ideals of the genre would be turned into actual experience.[36]

For Vann, the crucial restraint was her husband, who had sometimes forbidden her to attend Moravian services. But when James Vann died in 1809, Peggy Vann was free to set her own course. Her sporadic attendance at the Moravian Sunday services became more regular. And it seems that she began to regard the Moravians more favorably than she did her family. Her mother-in-law, usually called Mother Vann, despised Peggy and the missionaries and did what she could to come between them. Peggy began spending entire days and nights at the mission house in order to attend services.[37]

It was at one of those services that Vann had the experience that set in motion her conversion. The Moravians practiced a liturgical Christianity and celebrated Christian holy days along with their own observances from Moravian history. In April 1810, the Moravians at Springplace were commemorating Holy Week. In a series of services, beginning on Palm Sunday and intensifying during the week until the sorrow of Good Friday and the joy of Easter Sunday, the small gathering of Moravians ritually reenacted the life, death, and resurrection of Jesus. On Maundy Thursday, the commemoration of the Last Supper, the entire community experienced an intimate presence of Christ:

> During the reading of the great and important story of this day, such a powerful feeling of the gracious presence of our dearest Lord, Who suffered and made retribution for us, prevailed that one could not describe it at all. There was such loud crying when Brother Gambold began to sing the hymn "Most awful Sight, my Heart doth break!" etc. that it was really just mumbled. In brief, it was as if the bloody Giver of Mercy, overburdened with our guilt and distress, passed before each soul personally!

The observance affected Vann, who "was so moved that she continued crying for a long time afterward and could not speak a word." On her way home in the evening, she would only say, "Oh, how I felt! I thought I would faint!"[38]

Those events finally gave Peggy Vann the desire to be baptized. In several private conversations between Vann and Anna Gambold, Vann declared, "My heart was completely with you!" Vann was also willing to declare that she believed in Jesus, a type of confession that missionaries often asked the converts to make. Given the amount of interaction that the women had, Peggy Vann must have known what her answer meant not just to herself but to the missionaries as well: "In answer to the question whether she was prepared to set aside all other considerations, to subscribe completely to Him who bought her with His precious blood, to be His eternal property, Who had pursued her from her youth with indescribable faithfulness and love, she repeatedly answered very joyfully, 'Yes!'" And so on June 16, 1810, when Vann declared her desire to be baptized, she was propounded as a baptismal candidate before the Moravian mission conference.[39]

Though the missionaries likely considered Vann to be a believer, she had to go through a formal process of conversion, which for the Moravians was synonymous with becoming a church member. First came catechesis, or formal instruction in the doctrine of the church, and also a waiting period to test sincerity. Brother Gambold instructed Vann and had her read *Idea Fidei Fratrum* (*An Exposition of Christian Doctrine, as Taught in the Protestant Church of the United Brethren*), a doctrinal text written by August Gottlieb Spangenberg in German and translated into English for the use of missionaries and converts.[40] Vann's catechesis lasted for nearly two months.

On August 13, the Moravian day commemorating the first love feast of the United Brethren, Vann was dressed in white and at her wish left alone in a room, "lying with her face down and her hands raised in a folded position." She was then brought into the service. The service was an emotional time. They sang "the spiritual song 'Come Holy Ghost, come Lord our God!'" invoking the presence of the Holy Spirit. The prayers and singing were punctuated by "a general crying" and the loud cries of Vann's sisters and slaves. Brother Gambold asked Vann a number of questions about her beliefs, which was a ritual performance of the knowledge and faith she had gained during catechesis. Finally she was baptized.

The conversion of Peggy Vann was typical of how women—held forth as a model of piety—were expected to convert. It is noteworthy that Mother Vann, or Worli, who expressed so much hostility to the missionaries, followed her daughter's example and was converted herself in May 1819; she was baptized as Mary Christiana. Peggy Vann's conversion emphasized emotion and the heart. Most of all, it was a conversion that came about because of the intimate personal interactions of women. Vann's conversion was not entirely at an end, for she still had to be admitted to the Lord's Supper. She was finally motivated to present herself for the Lord's Supper after a reading of missionary accounts, this time of Moravian missions to the Inuit.[41]

Present at Vann's baptism in August 1810 was her uncle, Charles Hicks. He told the missionaries that he, too, had an inexpressible experience at the baptism of Peggy Vann: "He could not describe the feeling that he had experienced during this baptismal service. He said again upon leaving that he hoped that the impression of what he had enjoyed here today would stay with him the rest of his life."[42] Hicks had long been a "friend" of the Moravians, stopping in at both the

Springplace mission and later the ABCFM mission at Brainerd. Hicks was a powerful friend for the missionaries to have. He was present at the meeting where the Cherokee granted permission to the Moravians to settle and build a school; his son Jesse Hicks became a pupil. Charles Hicks became second principal chief in 1817 and principal chief in 1827. As such, he was exactly the kind of person whom the Moravians tried to cultivate with their "first-fruits" theology.[43] Hicks was exposed to the Moravians' religion in a number of ways. He was witness to many of their services in his travels through the Cherokee Nation; the powerful service at the baptism of Margaret Vann was one. Hicks also read and discussed with the Moravians literature that they gave him. He read more Moravian books after Vann's baptism pricked his interest, including sermons and texts that detailed the conversion of two Muslims and "Greenlander," the latter likely a convert at another Moravian mission. Like Vann, he too was trained in the genre of conversion before experiencing it himself.[44]

Hicks's interest in Christianity was especially pricked after a special service where the missionaries unveiled an image of Jesus crucified. The painting was displayed on Good Friday in March 1812— two years after Vann had expressed her desire to be converted. The Moravians received a regular stream of publications and missionary journals for the use of the ministry, but the painting of the suffering Christ was an unusual item. The painting, which fit well with the Moravians' "blood and wounds" theology, was used to convey the emotional weight of sin and redemption to those viewing it. It was displayed in candlelight during the season of Holy Week, already a dramatic time when the death and resurrection of Jesus was ritually reenacted. The painting was accompanied by John Gambold's prayers for the conversion of "every heathen nation," and Peggy Vann explained the meaning of the painting to the other Cherokees gathered. Ritual, painting, prayer—all came to emphasize the wounds of Christ in an emotional, intimate bond. The experience prompted Hicks to ask for baptism.[45]

The spring of 1812 brought another event that needed interpretation: an earthquake. A series of earthquakes shook the Cherokee Nation, centered on New Madrid, Louisiana Territory (now Missouri).

The earthquakes, accompanied by food shortages, hailstorms, and drought, were universally believed to require a supernatural explanation.[46] Many Cherokee regarded these earthquakes and poor harvests as a sign that they had violated their responsibilities. This sense of failure had roots in the myths of the origin of the corn and game, in which two sons killed their mother, from whom came corn, and disobeyed their father, from whom came the game. The earthquake became the catalyst for a new Cherokee religious and nationalist movement, sometimes called the Ghost Dance movement, led by the prophet Charley. This renewal movement competed directly with Christianity and was often led by full-blood Cherokees and the traditional *adonisgi*, whom the missionaries called "conjurors." But some Cherokee turned the traditionalists' message on its head by finding in the earthquake a reason to convert. Charles Hicks began his conversion at this exact moment, finding in the earthquake not a reason to embrace the Cherokee cosmology more fully but to embrace the Christian religion instead. And the Ridge, an assimilationist Cherokee, came as close as he ever did to Christianity because of the earthquake, though he ultimately chose not to convert.[47]

Shortly after Holy Week, Hicks sent a letter to the Moravians at Springplace, asking to be baptized. It took exactly one liturgical year for Hicks to move from awakening to baptism. The delay was due in part to catechesis, perhaps because of the Lot, but primarily to the travels that Hicks had to make because of his leadership within the Cherokee Nation. The timing was set by Hicks himself, who asked to be baptized on Good Friday (April 16, 1813), a day now as significant in his personal calendar as in the Christian calendar. Hicks was approved for baptism on the basis of his knowledge of the faith—and perhaps also by consulting the Lot.[48]

On Good Friday, Hicks, the missionaries, and a gathering of Cherokees and slaves met in the Springplace barn for the baptism, witnessed as well by Hicks's son Jesse, who was a pupil at the Moravians' school, and his Cherokee wife. Hicks, like Vann, was asked a series of questions, to which he "publicly confessed that he no longer wants to live for and serve the evil spirit, but rather our Savior Jesus Christ," the traditional renunciation of the devil. Hicks was christened "Charles

Renatus"—Charles Born Again. Something happened during the baptism, perhaps a breeze blowing through the barn, which the Christians took as a sign of Christ's presence. Gambold wrote in the journal that there was "a breeze of the peace of our crucified Lord; this cannot be described." The breeze too was a matter for interpretation. When the missionaries asked Hicks's wife whether she had experienced "something special inside," she said yes. But when Charles Renatus later tried to evangelize his wife, he told the missionaries, "she could not yet grasp it at all, and her answer was only, 'The Indians do not believe that!'"[49]

✠

It would be impossible to describe individually the biographies of all the Cherokees who converted to Christianity. Hundreds converted, but few left behind narrative accounts. Those who did, like Catharine Brown and John Arch, left narratives compiled by missionary headquarters from the journals and letters of missionaries in the field. Nevertheless, it is possible to describe the experiences of Cherokee converts generally by paying attention to interactions between Cherokees and missionaries and to the explicit rituals of conversion, by which the professed inward change was subjected to the judgment of congregations.

The first significant, sustained interaction that a Cherokee, whether a child or adult, was likely to have with a missionary was at one of the mission station schools. The Moravian Springplace missionaries started their mission without a school, but they were pressured into founding one by the Cherokees and by the Presbyterian minister Gideon Blackburn, who opened a school in 1804. Thereafter, the mission and the schoolhouse were synonymous institutions. The Cherokees, who at the start of the century had far more ability to control their territory than they would in the 1830s, obliged missionaries to provide schools to teach English. Cherokee parents, especially parents who were themselves of mixed blood or had children of mixed blood, sent their children to the schools to learn English. Missionaries regarded schools as opportunities to teach Christianity along with civilization. Missionary groups were obligated to have schools lest the Cherokees find their competitors—Baptists, Methodists, the ABCFM, Moravians— more appealing.[50]

The schools were not themselves the most important contributions to the conversion of the Cherokee, though they did teach hundreds of Cherokee children English and Christianity. Rather, they were important as sites of interactions between the Cherokee and the missionaries. Cherokee parents chose to send their children to the schools, and Cherokee leaders considered English education a matter of national concern, so they chose to accept and interact with the missionaries as educators. This brought the pupils and their parents into close contact with Christianity.[51]

The schools exposed children and parents to the liturgical practices of Christianity. Students learned the rhythms of daily prayer and of the church calendar. With the Presbyterians at Brainerd, they used a simplified church calendar that revolved primarily around partaking of the Lord's Supper observances, the observance of the Christian Sabbath, and days of preparation for communion. With the Moravians at Springplace, they learned a fuller church calendar, which included appropriate days of observances for every age, including young boys and young girls. They also learned Christian doctrine well enough that the missionaries thought the children could explain it to adults.

The schools were a place where students were evaluated by, and perhaps internalized, evangelical Protestant piety and morality. The missionaries observed what they called the "character" of their students. The evaluations that the Brainerd missionaries made of their pupils were compiled on several lists that contained such information as their name in English and Cherokee, the dates of their arrival and departure, and their original residence. The lists also kept track of how much students had learned. Allen Radcliff could "spell in 2 syllables"; Robin Burns could "read in easy lesson & write"; Henry Buckingham could "read & write"; and Edward Hicks had knowledge of "grammar, common arithmetic, Burrels Astronomy." The missionaries also evaluated moral character. Dealing with 218 students on one list and 79 on another did not permit fine gradations. Instead, students had to be quickly summarized or fit into a category.

So Robin Burns had learned basic reading although he "was not at school steady, Rather wild," and Henry Buckingham had learned his lessons despite being "rather dull." But the judgments most often fell into one of two types. Some students were judged by the criteria of civility: some were "respectable" or a "respectable young lady," others were "industrious," and still others "mediocrity." Yatsoo was judged "a wild creature just from the woods."

Often the terms missionaries used were the typical steps of conversion. So pupils who demonstrated the beginning signs of conversion were classified into an ascending series of stages. Their character was first "promising," then "hopefully pious," and finally "pious." The category "pious" implied that missionaries believed the person to be inwardly converted, even if baptism had not yet followed. David Brown and John Arch had already been inwardly converted when they were listed as pious.[52]

The schools also created a family atmosphere. The schools necessarily boarded their pupils, which meant that the children spent as much or more time with the missionaries as they did with their families. The gendered division of labor at the missions made them function like white families, as opposed to Cherokee families. Men (usually ordained ministers) functioned as the spiritual leaders, and the women oversaw the daily care of the children. The daily life, and especially worship, of the missions functioned like a family more than like a church. Samuel Worcester, the corresponding secretary of the ABCFM, visited the Brainerd mission and remarked about the evening devotions more than the church service: "At evening prayers, I was forcibly struck with the stillness, order, and decorum of the children, and with the solemnity of the family worship. A portion of the Scripture was read, with Scott's practical observations; a hymn was sung, in which a large portion of the children united; and Mr. [Ard] Hoyt led the devotions of the numerous family." The practice at the mission house was much like that recommended to Protestant families in the tracts published by the American Tract Society. The father (that is, the missionary) led the family in evening devotions, which included prayer, singing, and reading from the Scripture— in this case from a version of the Bible that contained devotional commentary.[53]

The missionaries assumed the right of a family to name its children. This practice must be considered distinct from the Christian practice of giving baptismal names, for the missionaries often renamed Cherokee children before they were baptized. Children were often named after notable evangelical Protestants, including ABCFM missionaries. The list of their names reads like a who's who of early nineteenth-century evangelicals: David Brainerd, John Newton, Jeremiah Evarts, Lyman Beecher, Cyrus Kingsbury, Jedidiah Morse, Benjamin Tappan, Samuel Newell, and two Samuel Worcesters.[54] Some children were named after lesser lights who were notable chiefly for publishing conversion narratives. The name Caroline Smelt was given to a seven-year-old Cherokee girl. Harriet Newell, who died at age nineteen on the way to India as a missionary had a ten-year-old Cherokee namesake in Tennessee.[55] Occasionally the names bestowed connected Cherokee children to the network of benefactors that supported the missions. Ann Porter received her name "in compliance with the request of a Society of Ladies in Wilmington, Delaware." Vinson Gould and Mindwell Woodbridge Gould were named after the pastor and his wife of "a society of young gentlemen in Southampton," Massachusetts, who funded their education. And then there was the improbably named Boston Recorder, named after a religious newspaper—a sign of the power of print to shape converts in more ways than one.[56] Not all of the children on the list had white names; about a quarter of them used only their Cherokee name. Some were named after Cherokee notables, such as John Osage Ross, the "little Osage captive" who was named after the principal chief of the Cherokee Nation and who later became a convert. Occasionally, a white infant was named after a Cherokee convert, as in the case of Catharine Brown Chamberlin, the daughter of a missionary.[57]

When one member of a Cherokee family became knit to the missionary family, it was not uncommon for the entire family to convert. Almost all of Catharine Brown's nuclear family converted after she did. Her father, John Brown or Yau-nu-gung-yah-ski, had three wives, giving Catharine Brown six half siblings and two full siblings. Of that family, there were several converts: John, a full sibling, "who died in the Christian faith," and his wife Susannah, "who is a professor of religion"; David, a full sibling "of whose piety hopes have been entertained for almost five years"; Polly and Susan, half siblings who were "esteemed pious." They converted because David Brown, Catharine's brother, instituted family devotional practices with his father's permission, after only he and Catharine had converted. David led the family in devotional practice in the morning and evening after the pattern he had learned at Brainerd, praying before and after meals and reading and interpreting the Bible to his family. Rufus Anderson, the secretary of the ABCFM, wrote, "It appears, therefore, that of Mr. Brown's family no less than nine have become hopefully pious."[58]

Converts came to regard the missionaries as family, without necessarily giving up their birth families. Peggy Vann thought of the Moravian missionaries as her family because of her abusive husband. John Arch and Catharine Brown described an implicit competition between Christian and natural families. In both their narratives, the convert's father came to the mission station to reclaim his child. Both Brown and Arch desired to remain with the Christians but found themselves bound to honor their parents. In both cases, the converts managed to remain with the church. These events undoubtedly occurred because there are dozens of examples in the missionary journals of parents' reclaiming their children. Recounting these events also served a narrative purpose: it allowed missionaries to demonstrate that they had accepted converts into their families.[59]

✠

Moral and religious education was preparation for conversion, but not conversion itself. The experience of God converting the heart had a common pattern among Protestants, but there were distinctive variations among the different denominations. The ABCFM missionaries, who were mostly New England Congregationalists under the local authority of southern presbyteries, tended to promote more formal if no less emotional conversions.[60] The Moravians were distinctive in blending missionary effort and liturgical piety, along with their other pietistic practices. The Baptists and Methodists—upstarts from the perspective of the other denominations—were more exuberant, outwardly displaying the work of the Holy Spirit. Even as these different missionary organizations attempted to convert the same Native American nations, they each had a very different base of support, and thus a radically different way of conceiving how Cherokee converts would brought into the new American nation. The ABCFM had its constituents among wealthy New Englanders who favored a "national evangelism" that would put Christianity at the center of the nation via home missions, missions to the Indians, and an expansionary print culture that reached many individuals in the new nation. The upstart Baptists and Methodists had their supporters among the poorer whites who migrated west, and they were in the early republican period far less nationalist than the ABCFM. The Moravians were even more divorced from the project of expanding and Christianizing the nation, owing their allegiance to the international Unitas Fratrum, not the United States. Missions to the Cherokee were thus one skirmish in an ongoing contest between different kinds of Christianity over the center and periphery of the nation. The missionaries were offering the Cherokee rather different forms of Christianity with rather different implications for their potential converts.[61]

Officially, the missionaries of the various denominations agreed to curb outright competition for Cherokee souls. While the denominations were not above competing for the souls of their own countrymen, they felt that missions were too important for competition to hinder the work. The Moravian Abraham Steiner proposed to the Brainerd missionaries "that no sectarian differences may be known among the heathen." Steiner also asked that members of one church be accepted for communion at another—the most important kind of cooperation for two groups that valued the sacrament so highly.[62] Tensions were higher between the ABCFM and the Methodist and Baptist missionaries. So when Daniel Butrick wrote to Jeremiah Evarts reporting that several ABCFM converts had become Methodists, he stated what might not be obvious to the mission board: "Here I feel compelled to state that our Methodist brethren have hitherto conducted [themselves] with great propriety, and I think have manifested a Christian spirit in this place. They know us to be Presbyterians, and we suppose them to be Methodists, yet I do hope we love each other."[63] There were occasionally interdenominational meetings where souls were won on a nonsectarian basis.[64]

Reception more than supply, however, determined how the Cherokees received Christianity. Cooperation did not mean that the missionaries gave up on their own patterns of conversion, and so the Cherokee chose between the different ways to convert. By and large, they opted for the style of the Baptists and Methodists.

The Methodist type of conversion was likely to happen much more quickly, with all the emotion of the conversion released at once. And it was also more likely to happen in the group setting of a revival meeting and in the Cherokee language. Elizur Butler described a Methodist revival meeting held in 1830. The meeting began with a white Methodist preacher describing a council held in hell by state legislators and the president of the United States for the purpose of stealing the Cherokees' land. Then six clergymen, including Cherokee preachers and interpreters, had their turn. They all exhorted at once, and "after some persuasion by Cherokee preachers, interpreters, and singers, a number came up to the alter [*sic*] to be exhorted, prayed for, and converted. The congregation rushed forward each seeking the nearest place to the alter." The entire congregation prayed at once, in Cherokee and English. There were exuberant displays of the Spirit: "At the same time, also singing, shouting, spatting of hands, and screaming. In the alter some were prostrate on the ground, some lying on benches, some apparently fainting, some crying &c &c."[65] This type of conversion, influenced by the new measures and their accompanying changes, had none of the slow catechesis of the ABCFM or the Moravian conversions. While it focused on character, it was character that could be transformed in an instant. The Methodists cared about character no less than the ABCFM, but they expected it to be imparted by the Holy Spirit in conversion and then after conversion to be developed with the methods of piety. And so, "disgusted," Butler wrote, "I came home with my faiths for the Cherokees very much diminished—It seems as if such a religion could never benefit them—a religion calculated to draw the vilest characters into the church. Today a man may be considered a horsethief, an adulterer, a drunkerd, and tomorrow be considered by the methodists a good christian."[66]

The ABCFM churches, on the other hand, drew on New England's long tradition of detailed examinations before converts could be admitted to full church membership and the consequent right to take the Lord's Supper. David Brown, for example, "gave a relation of his religious experience & answered such questions as were put to him relative to his supposed gracious change. His relation & answer were satisfactory, & he was admitted by unanimous vote, a candidate for baptism." The gracious change of conversion was ultimately for God to judge, and it was hoped that conversion in this theological sense would take place prior to baptism. But before conversion could be made outward and visible, congregations felt themselves responsible to evaluate the conversion and to be cautious of those who covenanted with them.[67]

If the bar of entry was high at ABCFM churches, it was unpredictable at Moravian churches due to their practice of the Lot. The Moravians wished to do only the things that pleased the Lord, whom they saw as actively superintending every detail of their conduct. When faced with difficult decisions, they would cast a lot to determine whether someone should be accepted for baptism or for the Lord's Supper. These decisions by the Lot had the effect of delaying or blocking some Cherokee conversions to the Moravian faith and discouraging some believers.[68]

Many Cherokee converts sought out the Baptists and Methodists if they were turned away by the ABCFM. William Chamberlin, an ABCFM missionary, thought that the Cherokee rejected the need for building moral character in favor of the immediate moral transformation of the Methodists: "If you say anything to them about a new heart, they will appear surprised and . . . answer, 'Why, I joined the Methodists.'" Daniel Butrick noted that "several who have been suspended from this church united with the Methodist Society" and had gone on to be, "to say the least, apparently moral, and attentive to religious instruction."[69]

It was not church discipline itself that the Cherokee converts rejected, but church discipline decided only by white believers. Joining churches, whether founded by the ABCFM and the Moravians or the Baptists and the Methodists, was an important step for the Cherokee in defining their own conversion, because by being admitted to the membership of the church they gained the right and duty of judging other converts' conversions. When Cherokee names showed up on the lists of membership next to the names of missionaries, the Cherokee had taken an important step toward making Christianity their own.[70]

☩

Making conversion their own was closely linked to the question of language, in ways mundane and cosmological. Missionaries understood that they would need to learn the Cherokee language in order to gain many converts. The Moravian and ABCFM missionaries were able to speak with Cherokees, mostly of mixed race, who spoke English. For the Moravians, the language barrier was doubly difficult since their native language was German. It was the desire to learn English that prompted the Cherokee to permit missionaries in the first place, with the stipulation that they provide schools. The Moravians were reluctant to take on the task of teaching English; the ABCFM was eager to do so but always found itself turning away students for lack of space. Cherokee parents wished for their children (and often for themselves) to learn English, and hundreds did. The earliest converts were the ones with the greatest facility of languages. Their conversion narratives depicted them as linguistically gifted. The narrative of Arch's life described him as having no education except in the letters of the alphabet, which later gave him an urge to seek out missionaries for education. Brown's narrative emphasized the speed with which she learned English and to read and write. For both, to be a linguistic prodigy was to have the ability to be a spiritual prodigy. But converts also had to learn to speak the language of Christianity. Peggy Vann, for instance, in preparing a birthday celebration for her second husband, Joseph Crutchfield, wrote a prayer: "My dear Joseph! The God of all Grace, who hath called us unto eternal Glory by Christ Jesus, after that You have suffered a While, make you perfect, establish, strengthen, settle You." She had learned not only English but the pietistic, biblical argot of evangelicalism.[71]

The Cherokee proved to be better linguists than the missionaries because few of the missionaries learned to speak Cherokee with any fluency. They never learned in part because they never found teachers. When asked, Cherokees often refused to teach the missionaries. Early in the Springplace mission, Anna Gambold told two Cherokee "that she would really like to learn their language." In reply, "they shook their heads, pointed close to the earth, and said, 'Yes, if you were still a small child, then it would happen. Now, it is too late.'" Charles Hicks had also told the missionaries that they would likely never learn the language unless they had started as children.[72]

The missionaries were also skeptical that the Cherokee language had the resources to convey the theological ideas necessary for conversion. Missionaries eagerly learned phrases they thought would be useful, such as a name for God learned from Nancy Falling, which they guessed meant "our Daddy above." Just as the missionaries thought that the Cherokee had the rudiments of natural theology but not enough knowledge for salvation, so they worried that the Cherokee language could express only rudimentary ideas about God. The missionaries had it on good authority that the language could not express the necessary ideas, such as the idea of a transcendent, self-existent God as opposed to a supernatural being. When they met Thomas Wilson, a Cherokee who had been educated by Quakers in Pennsylvania for five years, they "asked him to tell us a word for God, or the highest being, the Great Spirit, or the Creator of all things. He admitted that he could not give any sufficient expression for these. The only expression one could force by putting together several words from the Cherokee language was 'He who made me.'" Even that phrase they could not record for future use, because "neither he nor we were able to write it down phonetically because we did not have letters for it."[73]

The missionaries had to face the problem of how to spread Christianity when they could not speak the language of their converts. The visiting Lutheran minister Dr. Gotthilf Mühlenberg, an expert on botany (though not Cherokee), advised them that it was "completely impossible to impart to them the right ideas about God or spiritual things" in the Cherokee language, and so the only way to reach most Cherokee was to educate their children, who could then be Christians and native speakers. The Springplace Moravians demurred, thinking it was possible for a truly converted Cherokee to express the doctrines of Christianity effectively in the native language.[74] The ABCFM, too, tried both techniques, training children to speak English and to be Christians, as well trying to train adult speakers of Cherokee. The only truly effective speakers of Cherokee among the missionaries were ABCFM missionaries Daniel Butrick, Evan Jones, and Samuel Worcester.[75]

The missionaries were never content, however, to think that English (or German) was the only language in which Christianity could be expressed. When Chiconehla, mother of a convert who had died, came to the Springplace missionaries asking to learn English— whether for mundane or spiritual reasons is difficult to tell—they assured her, "God understands all languages." The pupils at their school added, "And even if you speak very softly . . . He understands you."[76] The father of Jeremiah Evarts (the Cherokee pupil, not his missionary namesake) told the Brainerd missionaries that his neighbors "laugh at him, & tell him he cannot know anything about religion, because he cannot understand English." His thoughts, unprompted by the missionaries, were different: "He knows God can understand him in his own language."[77]

In fact, Cherokee was a far more powerful and conceptually rich language than the missionaries knew. At the end of the nineteenth century, the ethnologist James Mooney, working for the federal Bureau of Ethnology, reported the distinction between the Lower, Middle, and Western dialects, as well as the difficult (for Euro-American ears) tonal quality of the language.[78] In one sense, it is surprising that the missionaries thought Cherokee such a poor language, given the opposite stereotype that Native Americans were natural orators. It was only in retrospect that the missionaries came to the conclusion of Rufus Anderson, that Cherokee was "a language, that is said to be more precise and powerful, than any into which learning has poured richness of thought, or genius breathed the enchantments of fancy and eloquence."[79] Once the language had the syllabary (characters representing syllables rather than phonemes), invented by Sequoyah, and a print publication, the *Cherokee Phoenix*, the missionaries who actually understood the language knew that it was far easier for a Cherokee speaker to learn to read Cherokee than for an English speaker to learn to read English. Given the important role that print and literacy played in missions and evangelism, this was no small praise.[80]

It was the Cherokee themselves who did the work of crafting the linguistic apparatus necessary for conversion. This was a fact that the missionaries acknowledged daily as they depended on their Cherokee pupils or adult converts to do the work of translating, whether for business or evangelism. Even more important, it was the Cherokee Sequoyah, sometimes called George Gist or George Guess, who invented the Cherokee syllabary, starting in 1809 with an ideographic system, and completing the syllabary in the early 1820s, well before most of the missions were well established. Sequoyah had seen printed texts, including a copy of the Bible, but he was a speaker of Cherokee only and had not been educated by missionaries. His syllabary was an ingenious script that represented the sounds of individual syllables in the Cherokee language, some eighty-six in all. Students reportedly could learn the characters in several days of study, and because the characters corresponded directly and regularly to the sounds, they were able to learn to read much more quickly in Cherokee than in English. The missionaries' impressions were confirmed by an 1835 census from the War Department, which reported about 50 percent of Cherokee households had at least one literate person. Sequoyah himself did not intend the syllabary for the use of the missionaries, though he taught it at the Dwight mission, but missionaries quickly recognized how powerful the syllabary was. With the help of Samuel Worcester, the ABCFM chairman Jeremiah Evarts, and the Cherokee leaders John Ross and George Lowry, Sequoyah's syllabary was cast into type, and a printing press was set up in 1827 at New Echota, funded by the ABCFM.[81]

Cherokee converts mined the richness of their language to transfer the texts and ideas of Christianity into their native language. Two Cherokee in particular were influential in translating the New Testament into Cherokee: John Arch and David Brown, the brother of Catharine. John Arch began his ministry by preaching sermons in Cherokee after a missionary preached them in English, and "after sermon, [he] read a chapter to the people, translating it into the Cherokee language as he went along, and making remarks upon it." About 1821, he translated the third chapter of the Gospel of John into Cherokee, which was circulated in manuscript copy among the Cherokee. The missionaries wanted to send Arch to their missionary school in Connecticut, but he refused, feeling an urgency to remain with the Cherokee. He died of dropsy in 1825 before accomplishing much by way of translation.[82]

What John Arch began, David Brown continued. Brown was one of ten Cherokee converts from Brainerd who went to the ABCFM's mission school in Cornwall, Connecticut.[83] He had earlier helped John Pickering develop an alphabet for translation into Cherokee. The ABCFM's official history recorded that the Cherokee demanded that the Bible be translated into the syllabary rather than into the alphabet: "The Cherokees would hear of nothing but their own alphabet for their own language. David Brown, their best scholar, must translate the New Testament; and as, owing to his long residence at the north, his knowledge of the Cherokee was imperfect, several of their most skillful orators must assist him." Furthermore, Charles Hicks urged Brown to translate from the Greek, rather than English. Brown was aided in his translation by George Lowry, a convert who would eventually become both the assistant principal chief and a deacon and ruling elder of a church. By September 7, 1825, Brown's translation was complete. The ABCFM history celebrated this Cherokee accomplishment: "The translation of the New Testament, from the original Greek, into the Cherokee language, in an alphabet invented by another Cherokee, was completed."[84]

Brown's initial version, imperfect by any standard including his own, circulated in manuscript. It was not the only version of the New Testament available, since both the ABCFM missionary Samuel Worcester and the Baptist missionary Evan Jones, along with his son John B. Jones, produced their own versions. All three were published serially in the *Cherokee Phoenix*, the first Cherokee-language newspaper, whose editor was the convert Elias Boudinot. The newspaper eventually published articles in both English and Cherokee, including both religious and political news, though Boudinot was decidedly of the assimilationist party and eventually of the party for removal. The *Phoenix* was thus the Cherokee's own platform for publication. Boudinot also assisted Worcester in publishing the Bible and other religious literature. Worcester had to rely on Boudinot for the translation, and Evan Jones relied on Jesse Bushyhead. Cherokee converts determined which of the printed versions, Worcester's or Jones's, they would receive. The whites debated fiercely about which version was superior. At stake was the translation of the word rendered in English as *baptize*. But also at stake was Jones's competence as a scholar of biblical languages, which Worcester fiercely attacked. Even the Baptist mission board sided with Worcester and the ABCFM and for a time ordered Jones to use Worcester's version of the Scriptures instead. Yet the Cherokee much preferred the text of the Jones translation, which the bilingual convert John Foster described as "the most correct, that is better Cherokee, more easily understood and more gladly received by full Cherokees." As the historian William McLoughlin concluded, "In the end, the Cherokees made the choice," for they both preferred the Baptists' translation and, by and large, chose the Baptist denomination as their own.[85]

The translation and printing of Christian texts embedded the Cherokee into the vast evangelical publication network, as they had already been embedded into the evangelical missionary network. Some historians have seen the project of missions to the Cherokee as complicit in the project of colonialism.[86] But it was missionaries like Worcester and Jones who fought attempts by Georgia and other states to control the Cherokee and remove them across the Mississippi. The ABCFM, Baptist, and Moravian missionaries formed a united front to oppose the removal of the Cherokees, with which the Methodists agreed in a separate statement. They termed the removal "an event to be most earnestly deprecated" as an injustice that would "arrest their progress in religion [and] civilization."[87] Samuel Worcester of the ABCFM lent his name to the U.S. Supreme Court case *Worcester v. Georgia*, in which the court defended (to no avail) the Cherokee's right to territorial integrity; Worcester had to spend eighteen months at hard labor in a Georgia prison to bring the case before the court. Jones too was an advocate for the Cherokee, coming as near as any white man to becoming a Cherokee, for he was formally adopted by the nation and traveled with them on the Trail of Tears as part of the obligation imposed by kinship and gift.[88]

Historians have also seen a colonial project in the missionary use of language. One scholar writes that "missionary power, like that of English colonizers," relied on "an assumption about the universalism of truly religious language."[89] If translation did indeed imply these epistemological problems, it also answered them. For Cherokee Christianity was not couched in some universal language, but in Cherokee. Cherokee converts translated the texts of Christianity, printed and distributed them, and wrote and sang their own hymns in their own language. They chose denominations (mostly the Baptists) whose rituals most closely accorded with their own. When the ABCFM refused to ordain ministers, the Cherokee turned to denominations that would or to those who valued ordination less. Though many white missionaries considered Cherokee medicine to be a part of Cherokee conjuring and urged converts to forsake it, some converts continued to practice traditional medicine while practicing Christianity. When the Cherokee were forcibly removed to Oklahoma, they persisted in their Christianity despite distrust of most missionaries—and after a period of declining numbers and apostasy, the numbers of Cherokee Christians grew following removal.

Translation can thus stand for something bigger: the process by which the Cherokee received Christianity. When Cherokee converted to Christianity, they also translated Christianity. Christianity was not a universal but a particular religion. And it became a religion as traditional—that is, as handed down—as the traditional Cherokee cosmology. Missionaries on the ground and especially Cherokee converts understood that it was the Cherokee themselves who were making over Christianity.

✠

The process of creating a Cherokee Christianity from translation was well under way when the Cherokee were forcibly removed from their lands beginning in 1838. Daniel Butrick and Evan Jones traveled with the Cherokee on the Trail of Tears. Their records show how Cherokee Christians became less dependent on the missionaries at the same time that they lost control over their territory.

When Daniel Butrick went to the prison camps at New Echota, Butrick was upset to find Cherokee, even Christians, playing cards and profaning the Sabbath. Butrick warned them that he would not return on the Sabbath unless they stopped these activities. And in response to the argument that they were doing so because the whites were maltreating them, he could not escape providential thinking: "True, they might say their enemies were cruel, but suppose they were, how did they get this power over them unless the Lord was angry with them, why should He thus give them up."[90] Butrick actually agreed with the reasoning of the card-playing Cherokee prisoners. He blamed the card playing and blaspheming of God's name not on the Cherokee, but on the whites and in particular on the federal and state governments. By making it a criminal offense for the Cherokee to govern their rightful territory, the federal and state governments had subjected the Cherokee to anarchy and to the depredations of white traders. Thus "the country was soon filled with liquor to over-flowing; and stores of liquor & cards were set up to induce gambling, while white gamblers were strolling through the country, seeking whom they could destroy." Butrick was thus keenly aware that the moral problems of the Cherokee, as he saw them, were structural and not individual. He also saw the essential competition, in this instance, as not being that between Cherokee traditionalists and missionaries but that between missionaries and Cherokee converts against the ungodly whites of Georgia—"that evil, that unfeeling, unmerciful, conscience seared, heart hardened state."[91]

Butrick thought that the structural problems of the Cherokee Nation were not those of an unconverted, "heathen" nation but the problems rather brought by a white, converted but apostate, nation. Butrick regretted the influence of white civilization, because it taught the Cherokee to treat "all the duties and ordinances of religion, not as unenlightened heathen, but with all that contempt and acrimony peculiar to the Voltaires of the present age." And so Butrick regretted "that any Cherokee had the least knowledge of the English language" because white so-called "professors of religion" had taken advantage of them. "Because they understand English, the dark rhetoric of hell has an immediate and distinct effect on their minds, and they are pressed into the service of darkness."

The converts had not learned to pray in Cherokee but to blaspheme in English.[92]

Butrick, like Rufus Anderson, came to the conclusion that the mission to the Cherokee did not involve civilization toward white ideals before conversion. Rather it involved individual, spiritual conversion bearing moral fruit, which would then permit the Cherokee to create a more virtuous civilization than those of white governments and society. Ironically, though whites took away the Cherokees' land, their forcible removal created an indigenous Christianity. Cherokee converts, for the most part assimilationists, had accepted the Christianity offered to them by missionaries from several traditions. While the Cherokee converts remained in their ancestral homeland, they had already begun the work of translating Christianity into their own idiom. Removal dislocated the Cherokee from the roots of their traditional cosmology, even as it forced Cherokee Christians to practice their faith independently of the missionaries that had brought it to them. The set of religious options available to the Cherokee were thus transformed.[93]

By the time of removal, the Cherokee Christians formed a small but significant portion of the population. In 1839, according to the judgment of one historian, "perhaps 8 per cent of the total Cherokee population, 1,250 out of 16,000, were officially listed as 'members.'"[94] In their forcible statement opposing removal, the united missionaries undertook the fullest accounting of the number of Cherokee converts who were full members of their congregations. They estimated that there were 167 Cherokee Presbyterians out of 219 total Presbyterians; about 45 Cherokee Moravians; about 90 Cherokee Baptists; and about 850 Methodists of whom most were Cherokee ("including those denominated seekers").[95] These numbers were considered to be extremely low by the mission boards. Indeed, they were lower than they might have been, had the Moravian and ABCFM missionaries been quicker to ordain Cherokee ministers, and had the Cherokee *adonisgi* not had justice on their side when they associated Christianity with the political oppression of the United States. But in another sense, the numbers were extraordinarily high given that there had been only two generations of converts. The growth in Christianity after removal and the decline of missionary influence was proof that Cherokee Christianity had become an indigenous religion. McLoughlin estimates that in 1860 "no more than 12 to 15 percent of the Cherokees were formally members of the Christian churches."[96] Yet Cherokee Christianity continued because it was a living tradition that Cherokee converts had received not simply as the missionaries transmitted it but in an idiom that they shaped for themselves, not as a commodity but as a gift.[97]

3

Hope

AFRICAN AMERICAN CONVERTS
AND THE JUBILEE

IN 1871, THE beleaguered Fisk University sent a group of students on a musical tour. Fisk had been founded five years earlier in Nashville by the American Missionary Association as a school for recently emancipated African Americans. With the school's funds nearly exhausted, eight singers and a pianist traveled throughout the Northeast to raise money. Midway through their first tour, the choir took a new name for itself: the Fisk Jubilee Singers. The word *jubilee* was pregnant with meaning, for it evoked the biblical command to "hallow the fiftieth year, and proclaim liberty throughout all the land unto all the inhabitants thereof" by declaring freedom for all slaves.[1] Fisk students had recently experienced their own jubilee, and that word ran through the songs that they sang.[2] The Fisk Jubilee Singers were one of the first groups to popularize spirituals—the Christian songs of slaves—and because of their tours and those of similar musical groups, spirituals were collected into songbooks during the 1870s. If the Jubilee Singers performed anything like the repertoire contained in those books, their concerts were a manual of the new birth, a guide to Christian conversion in song.[3]

The spirituals covered every aspect of conversion, beginning with a call to the sinner to pray for salvation before the coming judgment of Christ: "O sinner, you'd better get ready, / For the time is a-coming that sinner must die. / O sinner man, you had better pray, / Time is a coming that sinner must die."[4] They laid out a progression from "sinners" to "seekers" to "Christians" in martial language reminiscent of both the recent civil war and the eschatological language about warfare in the Bible.[5] Sinners were invited to move toward conversion through prayer—"I think I hear the sinner say,/Come, let's go in the valley to pray"—with the promise that the reward of the conversion would be the crown promised in the Book of Revelation: "You shall wear the starry crown,/Good Lord, show me the way."[6] This prayer for salvation would be difficult but would ultimately bring forgiveness of sins: "That's why this sinner has to pray so hard,/To have his sins forgiven."[7] After someone converted, the spiritual "Chilly Water" might accompany a public baptism (Figure 3.1),[8] but for conversions forbidden by masters, there was "Peter, Go Ring Them Bells," "a secret prayer-meeting song" sung "when any one confessed religion."[9] The spirituals took into account the sharp differences between Arminian Methodists and Calvinist Baptists, the two groups that won the most converts among African Americans, yet these differences were combined into two verses of the same song: "I'll be baptized on the Methodist side,/And a Methodist will I die"; "Oh Hardshell Baptist is my name,/Hardshell till I die;/I've been baptized in the Baptist faith./Going to die on the Hardshell side."[10] Ultimately, salvation would come through the true master: "Oh, reign salvation in my poor soul,/Reign master Jesus, reign!"[11] Salvation was expressed in terms of freedom, both in this world and the next:

> This is the year of jubilee
> You shall gain the victory;
> The Lord has set His people free,
> You shall gain the day.[12]

The spirituals were not the only Christian songs emphasizing conversion; that theme ran through the hymns and songs of Protestants generally. What distinguished the spirituals was their reliance on the prophetic, eschatological portions of the Bible: they were full of visions and prophecies and hope in the last days. In one of the Fisk songbooks, a note before the spiritual "In That Great Getting Up Morning" pointed out that "this song is a remarkable paraphrase of a portion of the Book of Revelation, and one of the finest specimens

FIGURE 3.1 A baptism in a river near New Bern, North Carolina, in 1907. After Emancipation, Baptists were the largest group among African American Christians. "New Bern, N.C.," Durwood Barbour Collection of North Carolina Postcards (P077), North Carolina Collection Photographic Archives, Wilson Library, UNC-Chapel Hill, http://dc.lib.unc.edu/cdm/ref/collection/nc_post /id/697.

of negro spirituals."[13] Though historians have properly argued that Exodus and Moses metaphors were central motifs of African American Christianity, eschatological imagery and theology were just as central in spirituals and African American conversion narratives.[14] One of the first and still most persuasive interpreters of the meaning of spirituals was W. E. B. Du Bois, who himself attended Fisk University in the 1880s, where he became an agnostic.[15] Du Bois dismissed these eschatological references as only a "comforting dream" and a "deep religious fatalism" that cemented the slave's "place at the bottom of a new economic system" since they were only "the doctrines of passive submission embodied in the newly learned Christianity." He was more positive in a passage connecting the Civil War and the eschatological:

When emancipation finally came, it seemed to the freedman a literal Coming of the Lord. His fervid imagination was stirred as never before, by the tramp of armies, the blood and dust of battle, and the wail and whirl of social upheaval. He stood dumb and motionless before the whirlwind: what had he to do with it? Was it not the Lord's doing, and marvelous in his eyes?[16]

Du Bois was correct to emphasize a connection between eschatology and the freedom brought by the Civil War, which was the central idea of African American conversions. But he was wrong to believe that for slaves and freedpeople, Christianity was merely passive. Rather this eschatological hope—in which the Day of the Lord might break in on slaves and freedpeople every day but especially in the moment of emancipation—was the defining element of a cosmos that African Americans deliberately crafted in order to differentiate their own Christianity from the Christianity or irreligion of their masters.

There was a strong connection between the eschatological meanings of the genre of African American conversions and conversions around the time of the emancipation jubilee. It is seen in the African-American conversion narrative created during slavery, in particular the eschatological themes that were prominent in many of the narratives. Of the Christian virtues of faith, hope, and love, African American conversion narratives had a distinct theme of hope, including visions drawn from the apocalyptic parts of the Bible. This connects African American conversions to the larger history of the Christianization of the United States during the nineteenth century.[17] Historians have recently shown that Islam persisted among slaves long into the antebellum period, and they have long known that conjure, African animism, and other such practices existed alongside, mixed with, and competed against Christianity.[18] The Civil War was a decisive eschatological moment that provoked many enslaved holdouts from Christianity to become Christians once they were free. While the Civil War was a crisis for white Protestant Christianity's biblical interpretation and moral order, it became a theological fulfillment for black Christians and potential converts among the freedpeople.[19] African American slaves created a new tradition within Christianity premised on conversions defined by experiences that brought home the prophetic passages of the Bible. When the Day of the Lord appeared during the Civil War, just as the eschatological predictions of slave Christianity had said it would, more and more freedpeople adopted that form of Christianity. Emancipation not only allowed newly freed black Christians to come forth and build their churches, it also encouraged freedpeople to convert to a Christianity whose eschatological claims validated the gospel message.[20]

African American conversions were both similar to, and different from, Protestant conversions generally, just as black Christianity was both a part of Protestant Christianity and a tradition unto itself.[21] Investigators into African American conversions have differed on this point. It was the opinion of Paul Radin, who gathered a number of conversion narratives and published them in *God Struck Me Dead*, that "the Negro conversion experiences . . . conform to the normal pattern for all such experiences," in other words, that black conversion narratives were the same as white conversion narratives. Radin's collaborator Clifton Johnson, on the other hand, thought slave Christianity was different because he did not believe that Christianity itself "made any appeal to them"; he made the strong claim that "the antebellum Negro was not converted to God. He converted God to himself."[22] Far more persuasive is the account of Albert Raboteau, for whom the Christianity of the enslaved was unquestionably Christianity, but a version that was fundamentally and deliberately different from the Christianity of masters. As Raboteau puts it, "The slave knew that no matter how sincerely religious a slaveowner might be, his Christianity was compatible with slavery and theirs was not."[23] Although it grew out of older Protestant traditions, African American religion became a category unto itself because, as Eddie Glaude puts it, "African American religion emerges in the encounter between faith . . . and white supremacy."[24] The question is why Christianity would be a live, appealing option to any slave or freedperson.

African American Christianity was different because it was oriented toward hope. Hope was based in the prophetic scriptures, and the prophetic scriptures were calls for justice.[25] The black Christianity that Du Bois regarded as an opiate in fact produced far more powerful visions. The self was buffered from neither the blows of the master nor from visions of Christ and of heaven and hell; secular time was enforced by the master's clock that drove production in the field, but true time was measured by election before the creation of the world and the coming Day of the Lord.

Time was the element that tied together many of the African American conversion experiences. A conversion that is eschatological has a distinct relationship to time. The prophetic portions of Scripture on which individuals modeled their conversions described events that could only be future in terms of secular clock-and-calendar time. Eschatological time, however, stood over and above secular time. When eschatological time broke in upon converts, they were closer to the eschatological events than they were to the day-to-day events happening in secular time. The vision of hell and judgment, heaven and reward, brought one closer to those ostensibly future events than to the day of labor regulated by the master's clock.

Another way to bend time was with typology. The slave who was whipped was more like Christ, who had undergone the same beating, than she was like the master who did the whipping. When Nat Turner, the slave rebel who was about to be hanged, skinned, and beheaded, was asked whether he repented of leading an uprising of slaves, he responded, "Was not Christ crucified[?]"[26] Where eschatology brought one close to the future, typology brought one close to the past because the antitype (fulfillment) stood in for the type (figure). In other words, eschatological and typological African American conversions made the Day of Judgment and liberation and justice immediate, present, now. Such experiences are not supposed to be a part of modernity, certainly not the modernity of a person deeply embedded in the secular time of slave capitalism.[27]

A fundamental difficulty in approaching African American conversions is noting how they change over time, rather than viewing them statically. Thanks to early twentieth-century interviews conducted on a small scale specifically about religion by researchers at Fisk University and on a much larger scale by interviewers for the Works Progress Administration during the Great Depression, we have a far richer set of sources for the history of slaves and freedpeople than we would otherwise.[28] Because these interviews date from a narrow band of time, and because there are few chronological markers in the interviews, it is difficult to avoid reading them synchronically, even though the conversions themselves happened over a wide range of time. The narratives were also often intended to obfuscate human time in favor of eschatological time. A few narratives detail ordinary life, yet those human details are usually set in an eschatological frame that broke in on the converts in radical moments.[29] Thereafter, the world would be different: the convert had seen the true nature of things. The conversion narratives deliberately conflate these two times. Given the similarity of their biblical imagery, it is difficult to make claims about how the conversion narratives changed over time.

Both the social question about when African-Americans were Christianized and the cultural and religious question of the meaning slaves and freedpeople made out of their conversions are fundamentally concerned with timing. Both are connected to the period around the Civil War, a moment that had eschatological implications. The eschatological content of the conversion narratives points to a different dynamic of conversion for African Americans. African American conversion narratives were characterized by a rejection of the "buffered self" and of the pervasiveness of secular time. Converts were not impervious to the external influences of spirits or angels. Nor were they buffered from the blows of the master. However hard the master's clock drove slaves working in the field, true time was measured by election before the creation of the world and the coming Day of the Lord. African American converts were part of a spread of Protestantism in the United States. Black Christians after emancipation had one of the highest rates of Christian affiliation of any racial or ethnic group. Yet their conversions, shaped during slavery then experienced in ever increasing numbers after emancipation, deliberately took on a eschatological pattern.[30]

✠

Christianity among enslaved Africans and their descendants in British North America, and later the southern United States, was born in the midst of a fundamental contradiction. The spread of Christianity was one of the justifications for enslaving Africans in the colonial period and, eventually, one of the prevalent arguments for the legitimacy of paternalist slaveholding. Yet in the colonial period, many masters prohibited slaves from converting from fear that Christian baptism might free the slaves, since the original theoretical basis of slavery was the non-Christian status of the enslaved. Protestant missionaries, such as the Anglican Francis Le Jau, who was sent by the Society for the Propagation of the Gospel, complained that masters had no interest in converting slaves.[31] Though white missionaries and a few masters tried to evangelize slaves, many masters resisted or permitted evangelism only if missionaries emphasized the Christian duty of obedience so that slaves would not believe the their conversions were an occasion to claim rights of freedom or equality with their masters. Slaves recognized that this preaching was at best a bowdlerized form of Christianity. Though Christians had long believed that anyone could and should become a Christian, slaveholders in Virginia actively cultivated the idea that Africans were "hereditary heathens," incapable of being truly converted and so legitimately enslaved. By the end of the seventeenth century, Virginia had legally established race, rather than religion, as the basis of enslavement. Yet Christian slaveholders continued to use their religion to justify slave owning. For instance, slaveholders applied the so-called biblical "curse of Ham" to Africans and identified it with dark skin.[32]

By the Civil War, a Christian defense of slavery was fully developed and sufficiently secure that the notion of "hereditary heathens" had been replaced with the paternalist argument that bondage was good for slaves because slavery resulted in their conversion, or at least their subjugation to Christian masters. The Presbyterian minister Robert Dabney argued that slavery was ordained in both the Old and the New Testaments, that slavery had elevated Africans from "the degrading effects of paganism," and that slavery made possible "more than half a million adult communicants in Christian churches."[33] Racism based on science, particularly biological evolution, did not fully develop until the second half of the nineteenth century. The Christianity of masters was thus productive of the concept of race; slavery in the United States was in part constituted by religion. To be sure, though racism was defined scientifically, instantiated legally, protected constitutionally, enforced violently, and motivated economically, a religious justification did crucial work in legitimating its power.

In the first half of the nineteenth century, any number of barriers lay between slaves and Christianity, though slaves and free African Americans had participated in the eighteenth-century awakenings.[34] The first limitation was the potential for thinking of slave owners as God. The word *master* was a significant term within the Bible, being used as a term of address for Jesus in the Gospels, and that term is given theological weight in the New Testament epistles. Yet the New Testament epistles also enjoined slaves to "obey in all things your masters according to the flesh."[35] Catechisms for slaves often referred to slave masters without making the distinction that Paul did between the earthly and heavenly masters.[36]

A striking example of the confusion this could cause came from the narrative of Henry "Box" Brown, who escaped to freedom in 1849 by mailing himself from Virginia to Philadelphia in a box. When Brown was a child, he "really believed my old master was Almighty God, and that his son, my young master, was Jesus Christ," in part because he believed his master controlled the weather, but also in part because of his "exclusive control over all the actions of his unfortunate victims." The adult Brown said that the sort of obedience that slaves were expected to render to their masters was idolatry; he thought that the master "probably . . . did not dislike our reverential feelings towards him." Brown had to be catechized out of his reverence by his mother, who taught him that when the slaves spoke of their master, they meant "our Saviour in heaven." The decisive religious event of his life was not just his conversion, but the moment he was taken out of the box in Philadelphia. Brown identified with Christ's resurrection; his box was a "sojourn in his temporary tomb," and after rising he recited a messianic psalm: "I waited patiently, I waited patiently for the Lord, / And he inclined unto me, and heard my calling."[37] The typology of the box and the tomb, like eschatology, bent time so that in that moment Brown was closer to the day of Jesus's resurrection than he was to the secular time around him. The theme of emancipation from the master accompanied by conversion to God was common in the slave narratives. In Leonard Black's narrative, for instance, his salvation by the Holy Spirit was immediately followed by his escape from his master.[38]

When masters were not usurping the position of God, they often beat and imprisoned slaves to keep them from religion. Thomas

Anderson in Guyandotte, Virginia, converted to Christianity and became a Baptist in 1804. His master "was an unbeliever, or tried hard to be." When his owner learned that Anderson had become a Christian, he "supposed my religion was all a fancy, and said he could and would whip it out of me. He took me up and tie me, and scourged me until feeling of flesh was almost gone." During the beating, Anderson called out to God, and the owner "cursed me, and said: 'Will you preach to me?'" Anderson defied his master: "You can take a gun and shoot me or kill me, as you please, and all for nothing; and that is all you can do: for I know I have a life you cannot touch, and the fear of you will not keep me from doing anything my new Master tells me to do. And if He let you take this poor bruised body of flesh, I feel it ain't worth much." In the eyes of the law, though, Anderson's "body of flesh" belonged to his master, and the law imposed all kinds of restrictions on Anderson's Christian practice. Not least were restrictions on movement, controlled by an extensive system of patrols and passes, and restrictions on association, which attempted to keep slaves from meeting for political and religious purposes.[39] Anderson had to delay joining the white Baptist church because "that I could not do without my master's consent, (as it is against the laws of Virginia for slaves to join without consent of their masters.)" Anderson was able to join the church only because his earlier defiance led his owner to think that if the church "thought best to receive him he had no objections; and for his part, he thought if there was a Christian in the world, Tom was one." Reflecting back on the torture he had received for becoming a Christian, Anderson wrote, "I now feel glad that I could suffer patiently for my new Master."[40] Anderson appended to his narrative a request for aid to build a church, but he added, "I am sorry to say it, but it is no less true, that the greatest opposition I meet with is the opposing spirit of those who profess the Christian religion."[41]

Virginian Anthony Burns decided to become a Baptist under the dual excitement of a camp meeting and the spread of the Millerites, followers of William Miller who announced that Jesus would return in 1843. To join the church he had to ask "for leave to be baptized; no slave being suffered to comply with that command of the Saviour or admitted to the church without a written permission from his owner." His owner, Charles F. Suttle, at first refused, and only eventually relented. Burns became a pastor to the nearby Baptist slaves, and in 1854 he escaped slavery to Boston, only to be extradited by federal forces under the Fugitive Slave Law despite mass demonstrations. When his freedom was eventually purchased by abolitionists, Burns briefly became a pastor in Indiana before harassment led him to move to Ontario, where he continued in the ministry.[42]

When Bethany Veney was going through "precious seasons" of awakening on her way to conversion, her owner decided "he was not going to have me running to meeting all the time any longer," and so he sent her to another plantation, "there to stay until I should get over my 'religious fever.'" Only after she prayed for God to change his mind did he say, "as if 'rent by the Spirit,'" "Well, I'll go to the devil if you ain't my match! Yes: go to meeting, and stay there."[43]

Elizabeth was raised in Maryland by Methodist parents. In 1777, when she was eleven, she was sent to work at a different farm. A beating with a rope by the overseer brought to mind her mother's words and set in motion her conversion: "After this time, finding as my mother said, I had none in the world to look to but God, I betook myself to prayer." It took six months, but Elizabeth converted through a sinner's prayer: "I fell on my knees and prayed the best I could the Lord's prayer. Knowing no more to say, I halted, but continued on my knees. My spirit was then taught to pray, 'Lord, have mercy on me—Christ save me.'" Alone with no family and only the hell of her overseer's beatings, the religious alternative to her master's world came through a vision drawn from the eschatological books of the New Testament. Her sinner's prayer was accompanied by a vision of a "director" who led her to hell, succeeded by a vision of Christ in heaven: "Then I thought I was permitted to look straight forward, and saw the Saviour standing with His hand stretched out to receive me. An indescribably glorious light was in Him, and He said, 'peace, peace, come unto me.' At this moment I felt that my sins were forgiven me, and the time of my deliverance was at hand." In accordance with her eschatological vision, Elizabeth became a preacher of the gospel when she was forty-two.[44]

Thomas Jones became a Methodist despite the efforts of his master, who had no religion. The day after the eighteen-year-old Jones went

to a Methodist prayer meeting, his master whipped him with a cow-
hide. One white Christian who was present tried to protect him; another slave owner argued that a "slave was worth more money after
he became pious than he was before." But Jones's master replied that
"religion was all a damned mockery, and he was not going to have
any of his slaves praying and whining round about their souls." Jones
kept praying during the whipping, though his owner threatened to
kill him if he would not stop. The slave owner prevented Jones from
going to the Methodist love feast the next Sunday. Jones did go to
the Friday prayer meeting, hoping "to forgive master for his cruelty
to me," for which he was whipped again. Jones joined the Methodist
church in the next six months.[45]

In 1840, James Watkins attended a Methodist camp meeting in
Maryland although his master had denied him permission. At the
camp meeting, which was segregated with whites in the front of the
audience and blacks in the back, Watkins longed to "find this
Jesus. . . . I thought if I could but find out this great man I should
be free from slavery as well as from sin." Watkins was converted by
going apart from the meeting, where "I poured out my soul to the
Almighty, in my weak and ignorant way, beseeching Him earnestly
to pardon my sins." After "three or four hours . . . my prayers were
answered in a very unmistakable manner. My heart was so filled with
the love of God that the fear of the whip, or even of death, was entirely taken away from me." When he returned to the slave quarters,
having been long absent, his master with his sons forced Watkins to
strip at the whipping post and tied his hands to a beam above his head
in preparation for a beating. Watkins "reminded him that every
stripe he laid on my back would be registered in heaven, and rise up
against him at the day of judgment." The slave owner and his sons
tried to whip him, but Watkins recorded that "the Lord stood by me
on this occasion and paralysed the arm of my master, for he seemed
utterly unable to lift the lash or give me a single blow." Watkins was
no idealist—he continued to call Maryland "the Land of Stripes"—but
he believed that "Christianity is life, and light, and freedom."[46]

The beatings that Anderson, Elizabeth, Jones, and Watkins experienced happened in Virginia and Maryland, where slavery's defenders believed it to be a benevolent and paternal institution. As the

population of African Americans grew in the Chesapeake area, slave owners sold their slaves to the rapidly expanding Deep South plantations in a crescent of lands through Georgia, Alabama, and Mississippi, and most of all along the Mississippi River itself. The scale of the forced migration was huge. Steven Deyle estimates that between 1820 and 1860, "at least 875,000 American slaves were forcibly removed from the Upper South to the Lower South." In the Lower South, especially along the cotton and sugar plantations of the Mississippi River, the conditions of exploitation were unspeakably brutal.[47] The possibilities of conversion were limited by the location where slaves found themselves, and their location depended on where they had been sold.

On the Mississippi plantation where Henry Cheatam worked, there were no baptisms, because the overseer did not want the slaves to be religious. The pace of forced labor left no time for religion anyway. In the Upper South, slaves were more often given task work and had at least some time to direct as they chose. In the Deep South, slaves worked in gangs driven by overseers with whips and clocks, without a moment in the day to call their own. After becoming free, Cheatam became a member of Corinthian Baptist Church in Alabama.[48]

Charlotte Rogers was sold from Virginia to a Louisiana sugar plantation sometime around 1844. Her owner sometimes locked her up on Sundays in the plantation jail to keep slaves from socializing, a ban that extended to holding church meetings and praying. When Rogers met Aunt Jane, another woman who had been sold from Virginia to a nearby plantation in Louisiana, she told Jane that "I had not been in a church since I came here." She found Louisiana foreign, especially because her owners were Catholics, as were most of the religious people she knew. Rogers converted to Protestantism because of Jane, who "was the cause of so many on our plantation getting religion. We did not have any church to go to, but she would talk to us about old Virginia, how people done there." Jane insisted that the "beads and crosses we saw every body have was nothing. She said people must give their hearts to God, to love him and keep his commandments; and we believed what she said." If Aunt Jane had not imported evangelical Christianity to Louisiana, Rogers could not have converted.[49]

Slaves' experience of religion was often shaped in reaction to the Christianity of their masters.[50] This was articulated at length by Frederick Douglass, for which his opponents tried to "brand me with being an infidel."[51] When Douglass's owner, Thomas Auld, "attended a Methodist camp-meeting . . . and there experienced religion" in August 1832, Douglass "indulged a faint hope that his conversion would lead him to emancipate his slaves, and that, if he did not do this, it would, at any rate, make him more kind and humane." On this score he was disappointed, for "it neither made him to be humane to his slaves, nor to emancipate them. If it had any effect on his character, it made him more cruel and hateful in all his ways; for I believe him to have been a much worse man after his conversion than before." Auld's commitment to Methodism was not a sham, for he "prayed three times a day and became an exhorter and leader of a Methodist class, and further proved himself an instrument in the hands of the church in converting many souls." But Auld only felt obliged to evangelize his slaves when certain Methodist ministers were present; otherwise he made no effort to bring them Christianity. Christianity made Auld a worse master because it justified his slaveholding and his treatment of slaves.[52] Douglass relates one chilling incident:

> I have said my master found religious sanction for his cruelty. As an example, I will state one of many facts going to prove the charge. I have seen him tie up a lame young woman, and whip her with a heavy cowskin upon her naked shoulders, causing the warm red blood to drip; and, in justification of the bloody deed, he would quote this passage of Scripture—"He that knoweth his master's will, and doeth it not, shall be beaten with many stripes."[53]

Douglass regarded this pattern as common among slaveholders. Edward Covey, to whom Douglass was hired out for a year, "was a professor of religion—a pious soul—a member and a class-leader in the Methodist church," but he also had "a very high reputation for breaking young slaves."[54] Douglass could not resist by slowing down his work, because his master worked with his hired slaves and, when returning to them in the fields, would surprise them like the biblical "thief in a night." Douglass's way of confounding his master was by sometimes refusing to play his assigned role during morning prayers. Because Covey was a "poor singer," Douglass had "the duty of raising the hymn." Sometimes when Covey nodded at Douglass to begin the hymn, Douglass would refuse, reporting that "my noncompliance would almost always produce much confusion. To show himself independent of me, he would start and stagger through with his hymn in the most discordant manner." In this rare moment of humor within Douglass's *Narrative*, we see how Douglass exposed the deception of the master. Covey "prayed with more than ordinary spirit" and "seemed to think himself equal to deceiving the Almighty."[55] To Covey's example Douglass added the Reverend Rigby Hopkins, any slave's last choice for a master, for "I should regard being the slave of a religious master the greatest calamity that could befall me."[56]

Responding to accusations that he was irreligious, Douglass made it clear that he was arguing against "the *slaveholding religion* of this land, and with no possible reference to Christianity proper; for, between the Christianity of this land, and the Christianity of Christ, I recognize the widest, possible difference."[57] In his 1829–1830 *Appeal . . . to the Coloured Citizens of the World*, David Walker repeatedly argued that the "white Christians of America, who hold us in slavery, (or, more properly speaking, pretenders to Christianity,) treat us more cruel and barbarous than any Heathen nation." He blamed white Christianity for hindering African Americans from becoming Christians because slaveholders' patrols broke up church meetings and would "absolutely beat a coloured person nearly to death, if they catch him on his knees, supplicating the throne of grace."[58] Henry Box Brown put the matter yet more bluntly:

> Let me tell you my opinion of the slaveholding religion of this land. I believe in a hell, where the wicked will forever dwell, and knowing the character of slaveholders and slavery, it is my settled belief, as it was while I was a slave, even though I was treated kindly, that every slaveholder will infallibly go to that hell, unless he repents. I do not believe in the religion of the Southern

churches, nor do I perceive any great difference between them, and those at the North, which uphold them.[59]

Frederick Douglass maintained his connection to Christianity. He had been converted when he was a teenager, and he was licensed as a lay preacher by the African Methodist Episcopal Church in New Bedford, Massachusetts. Later in life, he attended the Metropolitan African Methodist Episcopal Zion Church in Washington, DC, even as he seems to have adopted the liberal or naturalistic view of Jesus as in no sense divine espoused by the European scholars David Friedrich Strauss and Ludwig Feuerbach.[60] Douglass himself interpreted the Civil War in eschatological terms, though he laid the stress on man's work rather than God's, to the dismay of some black clergy. On the day on which the Emancipation Proclamation took effect in 1863, Douglass was waiting with a crowd in Tremont Temple in Boston for "the trump of jubileee, which everybody wanted to hear . . . a bolt from the sky which should rend the fetters of four millions of slaves."[61]

Slave Christianity often had to be created in close proximity to the master's Christianity. At Camp Hill, Alabama, Sara Colquitt converted in the white church near the plantation: "Us used de white folks' church in de morning. I j'ined de church den, 'cause I always tried to live right and wid de Lord."[62] At Carrollton, Alabama, slaves on the Bonner plantation who converted joined the white Baptist church. Siney Bonner recalled that some of the slaves wanted to have their own meetings, but the master prevented their ecstatic worship.[63] Amy Chapman was converted and baptized by a white minister into the Baptist church near the plantation in Livingston, Alabama, because there was no black church—perhaps because her master prohibited one. Nevertheless, she interpreted her own sufferings and the sufferings of her fellow slaves as like Christ's. She told how the overseer "tuk my ol'est brother an' had him stretched out jus' lak you see Christ on de cross; had him chained, an' I sot down on de groun' by him an' cried all night lack Mary an' dem done." She was herself whipped with the "cat er nine tails when I was stark naked"—the unusual name for the whip recalling how Jesus had been stripped and tortured. These descriptions were all the more poignant since one of her favorite songs began, "I saw him hangin' on a tree/In agony an' blood/He fixed his languid eyes on me/As near his cross I stood." It was Christ's suffering that she had herself experienced that led to conversion: "He seemed to change me wid his death."[64]

Josiah Henson was able to convert only because of a white baker named John McKenny whose "character was that of an upright, benevolent Christian. He was noted especially for his detestation of slavery, and his resolute avoidance of the employment of slave labor in his business." Henson was reluctant to become a Christian because of the barriers his master erected, but his mother told "me that I could never become a Christian if I minded beatings—that I must take up my cross and bear it." Henson saw God's love in contrast to the master's scorn and felt the power of love to change his master.

> In sharp contrast with the experience of the contempt and brutality of my earthly master, I basked in the sunshine of the benignity of this divine being. "He'll be my dear refuge–he'll wipe away all tears from my eyes." "Now I can bear all things; nothing will seem hard after this." I felt sorry that "Massa Riley" didn't know him, sorry he should live such a coarse, wicked, cruel life.

Henson become a Methodist minister only because of the slightly greater degree of freedom afforded him as superintendent of slaves on a Kentucky farm; much of his narrative was taken up in figuring out ways to travel and preach despite whites taking away the pass that allowed him to travel under the watchful eye of the slave patrols.[65]

✛

In the accounts of their conversions, African Americans crafted their own alternative form of Christianity. The central institution that could set expectations for conversion was the church, which judged the testimony of its potential members, though it might be many years before someone felt able to join. Their narratives sometimes testified to the means by which the community made experiences, especially eschatological visions, a prerequisite for having "got religion." One woman, Molly, was converted in Columbia, Tennessee, sometime between 1873 and 1875. When she was interviewed, she said, "I have been a member of the church for fifty-four years. I came through when you had to be a thoroughbred, and I mean I am a thoroughbred," referring to someone who had experienced an authentic conversion. She pointed to her generation as one that had known religion as evidenced by the prevalence of visions and dreams and ecstatic experiences.[66] Charity Anderson, who complained about many things in the younger generation, thought that the "world is gettin' wicked'er and wicked'er, sin grows bolder and bolder, and 'ligion colder and colder." Her own generation of converts around the time of the Civil War had been able to demonstrate their conversion experiences.[67] Another woman insisted on the necessity of experience: "We must see, feel, and hear something, for our God talks to his children." She "joined the church after nearly ten years of experience."[68] God told another convert in a vision, "Nobody can talk about the religion of God unless they've had a religious experience in it."[69] Experience in some cases could be so powerful that it validated a person who took on an important role, as in the case of the convert who joined the church immediately after his experience and preached the next Sunday.

Dissenters from the norm of an ecstatic conversion offered the most powerful testimony to the power of the church in shaping conversion experiences. One anonymous convert at the end of the nineteenth or beginning of the twentieth century said, "My religion means as much to me as anyone else, but I have not had all of the varied experiences that most of the older people say they have had. I have not had a chance to see any kind of funny forms or anything like that to make me afraid." Instead, this convert trusted in "the greatest book in the world, the holy Bible" and justified his or her lack of ecstatic experience with a quotation: "Repent, believe, and be baptized, and you shall be saved." This repentance—along with the feeling of "the spirit in my soul"—was more akin to the white Protestant definition of justification by faith rather than conversion by eschatological hope.[70] This late conversion without an eschatological experience demonstrates the significance of the post–Civil War period as one where such experiences were less prevalent; African Americans who had not gone through slavery and emancipation did not experience the eschatological meaning of the faith in quite the same way.

✠

African American conversions showed a progression from more typical evangelical models at the beginning of the nineteenth century to increasingly ecstatic, eschatological models by the middle of the century. White evangelical conversion narratives of the eighteenth and early nineteenth centuries could be quite ecstatic, even if the eschatological component taken from scriptures like the Book of Revelation was not very common. Among many groups, the visionary aspect of some conversion narratives became less prominent on account of the codification of the white Protestant conversion process around the sinner's prayer. At the same time, African American conversion narratives became increasingly eschatological around the period of the Civil War. The African American conversion thus exhibited some of the characteristics of the instantaneous, codified conversion narrative shared with white evangelical narratives, but translated those moments into eschatological terms.

The early nineteenth-century narrative of Noah Davis, who later became a minister, has many of the same characteristics as white evangelical conversion narratives. As in those narratives, he had been raised in the faith as a child but regarded such catechesis as insufficient, and he sought the moment of conversion in a prayer: "Having always, from parental training, purposed in my mind to become religious before I died, I thought that now was the time to begin to pray." His conversion was accompanied by the unsettling thought that God knew everything about him, including his sins, and that he had no ground for considering himself saved. Conversion was necessary because he could not inherit religion. Crucially, he rejected inherited religion from his mother and the religion of his master: "The reflection occurred to me, 'Your mother is a christian; it may be she can save you.' But this suggestion appeared to be offensive to God. Then came another thought,—'As my master was a rich man, could he not do something to help me?' But I found no relief in either." After five weeks of hard praying, Davis felt no closer to conversion. Then conversion came in a moment as he prayed.

> While I sat thus, hoping and praying, light broke into my mind—all my trouble left me in an instant.
> I felt such a love and peace flowing in my soul, that I could not sit longer; I sprang to my feet, and cried out, "Glory to God!" It seemed to me, that God, whom I had beheld, a few seconds previously, angry with me, was now well-pleased. I could not tell why this great change had taken place in me; and my shopmates were surprised at my conduct, saying, that I must be getting crazy. But, just at this moment, the thought came into my mind, that I was converted.

Davis's conversion was accompanied by a vision of Christ: "I felt joyful in my heart; and while trying to pray, I thought the Saviour appeared to me. I thought I saw God smiling upon me, through Christ, His Son. My soul was filled with love to God and Jesus Christ."[71]

Jarena Lee had a powerful and fairly typical conversion in 1804.[72] She, like many people in the eighteenth-century conversion narratives, felt herself "driven of Satan . . . and tempted to destroy myself" by drowning. Though she lived for a time with Roman Catholics and heard Episcopalians, Methodists, and Presbyterians preach, her conversion came under Richard Allen, bishop of the African Methodist Episcopal Church, who had catechized Lee.[73] For Lee, the definitive mark, coming just moments after the reading of the text of a sermon, was that "for a few moments I had power to exhort sinners, and to tell of the wonders and of the goodness of Him who had clothed me with *His* salvation." It was not uncommon in conversion narratives for the person to feel an urgent need to share the gospel with others (which was, after all, one of the polemical points of the conversion narratives). But Lee's case was unusual in that she was immediately impelled to publicly proclaim the gospel and to do so as an exhorter, a formal role within the church to which she had not been appointed.[74] While she was exhorting, "the minister was silent, until my soul felt its duty had been performed, when he declared another witness of the power of Christ to forgive sins on earth, was manifest in my conversion." Here was a curious juxtaposition of ministerial silence, signifying the importance of Jarena Lee's speaking for herself, and ministerial authority to explain the meaning of Lee's exhortation as a sign of her conversion.

Jarena Lee also had an experience of entire sanctification. To the standard evangelical pattern of conviction of sins, repentance, and faith leading to justification, Methodists added a second experience of "entire sanctification"—the knowledge that one was not just justified from sins but freed entirely from even the tendency to sin and made completely holy. Where Lee's conversion came from the word of preaching, her entire sanctification came from a word of prayer. After her conversion and before her entire sanctification, she prayed at four o'clock every day for three months. One day after praying, she realized—by hearing a voice speaking to her saying, "Ask for sanctification"—that she "had not even thought of it [sanctification] in my whole prayer," a forgetfulness she attributed to Satan. So she prayed to God, "Lord *sanctify* my soul for Christ's sake." The response was instantaneous: "That very instant, as if lightning had darted through me, I sprang to my feet and cried, 'The Lord has sanctified my soul!'" For the Methodists, the moment of entire sanctification often took the form of a second conversion experience. In Jarena Lee's case, both were instantaneous experiences, though the preparation was long. And in both cases, the conversion came in response to a prayer.[75]

But the thread of visions began early. Quamino Buccau became a Christian in New Jersey in 1780 or 1781, when he was eighteen. After seeing a vision that he could not interpret and hearing "a noise like half-a-dozen horses, coming after me," Buccau "went to the barn, where, after earnest exercise in prayer, he slept upon the straw." In the field the next day, the moment of conversion came: "Being in much distress, the gracious words of the Saviour were distinctly revived to him, 'Let not your heart be troubled. Ye believe in God, believe also in me.'" Buccau knew at that moment he had received the "unspeakable gift."[76]

Direct experiences of God in voices and visions became increasingly widespread in African American conversion accounts. Visions often happened while alone: alone plowing the fields, alone in the woods, alone in the cotton patch. The visions cannot be explained away by any simple "medical materialism," as William James would have put it. But they did often happen in the heat of work, or while hungry, after a whipping or after being sold, or during other events that left the body weakened and the soul ready to receive an ecstatic experience. One man, for example, was consumed by a desire to be reunited with his mother after the Civil War and by the thought, "Remember the promise you made to your mother to meet her in glory." He vowed "not to eat anymore until I had found God." After several days of fasting, he collapsed while chopping cotton in the field, "sprawling out with my face to the ground . . . [and] immediately lost sight on the world."[77] One convert detailed the process by which she came to her vision:

> It took me about three weeks to "come through" with my religion. . . . I prayed every day all day long, in a big, open field that was just being opened up as new ground, for three weeks. When I was out there neither did I eat a thing nor drink more than a little water. This seems strange to you, but for three weeks I ate only four pones of bread about the size of your hand. I was full up to my throat, and I did not want anything to eat.[78]

One fifteen-year-old was converted when she saw a vision after going "about five days without eating."[79] The anonymous dissenter from the need for seeing visions for conversion refused to participate in the practices that led to visions: "I think if I would have had to spend time in a cemetery or some secluded place for two or three days I would have never been converted."[80]

What these clues suggest is that African Americans had an established practice—not unlike the meditative or ascetic practices of many other mystics—that prepared the body through exhaustion for spiritual experiences. These practices did not necessarily have anything to do with hoodoo. The convert quoted about fasting for three weeks did not believe in conjurers (though she did use root doctors) because God told her, "There ain't no such thing as conjurers."[81] These practices were similar to the custom of black preachers who began sermons by complaining of a bodily ailment or poor health as a sign that the power of the sermon came not from the minister's talent or preparation but from the Holy Spirit.[82]

Other conversions happened in company. One fifteen-year-old convert was put under intense pressure by her father, "a fiery preacher," and her mother, "a very devout Christian": "After I was fifteen they told me that I should get religion." She tried for over a year, including during a revival. When she had her vision, "I told my mother what had happened. She kissed me many times and told me that I had been converted, and I went my way rejoicing." In this case her parents' pressure—and presumably, the pressure of the congregation—impelled her to conversion; it was her mother's approval that persuaded her that she was converted.[83] The influence of families, and in particular of mothers, was a common theme. One man told how the slaves would sing after work was done: "Soon everybody would be gathered together, and such singing! It would be long before some of the slaves got happy and started to shouting. Many of them got converted at just such meetings. There was so much fire among them when they started to praying and shouting, clapping and shaking hands and shedding briny tears, something had to move."[84]

The conversion experience for African Americans was often described as being killed or struck dead. That language came from eschatological passages in the Bible about heaven and reward, or hell and judgment. The biblical language of being born again or of resurrection, common as a theological and moral idea among white Protestants, was lived as an experiential and visionary idea for black Protestants. One convert said, "I am not hell-scared or devil-dodging, for I know that I have died and don't have to die anymore." Another said, "I was fifty-two years old when the Lord freed my soul. About three years before I was killed dead and made alive again. . . . I truly died and saw my body. I had a temporal and a spiritual body. My spiritual body had six wings on it, and when I was barked at by the hellhounds of the devil I arose and flew away."[85]

The African-American conversion narratives contain striking examples of concern about damnation. One account used the same language as Jonathan Edwards's "Sinners in the Hands of an Angry

God," describing a vision of "my old body suspended over a burning pit by a small web like a spider web."[86] Salvation from damnation came by faith. One narrator was told by a voice in a vision, "I have saved you through grace by faith, not of yourself but as a gift of God."[87] Another said, "I saw him [the Lord] through the eye of faith and heard his voice through the spiritual ear until the heart understood.[88] Accounts often included visions of hell as a "sea of glass, and it was mingled with fire." The lake of fire was taken directly out of the Book of Revelation.[89] Often the narratives included warnings of death or hell. One girl saw an ice pick and heard a voice say, "You got to die and can't live again." Very often the narratives included a vision of someone—sometimes God, sometimes an angel or a man or woman—who promised that the convert would not be harmed. The visionaries often saw Jesus as a man and sometimes God the Father as a man. One woman said, "A man once told me that he saw God as a natural man with a hickory shirt on and lying in a high feather bed."[90] One cannot escape the sense that the African American converts lived in a world of danger—from their masters, from employers, from soldiers, from everyone. As one convert put it, "Through the spirit I have come to see the meaning of the thicket briars, the snakes, the dogs, and the cows. They were my enemies."[91]

The salvation from these many enemies came in the form of eschatological hope. The ecstatic, otherworldly conversion experience by which one became marked as a saint was a dress rehearsal for the eventual glorification of the saints at the last day. This eschatological metaphor was captured clearly in a sermon taken down by a Fisk University researcher: "Oh, brothers! Ain't you glad that you have already been in the dressing room, had your everlasting garments fitted on, and sandals on your feet? We born of God, aha! are shod for traveling."[92] Conversion was the dressing room for eventual eschatological salvation.

✠

When the Civil War and emancipation came, African Americans associated their conversions with those events. One man who was "about twelve or fourteen years old" was sold during the war to a slave trader taking slaves to Louisiana. The mistress, "a Christian woman," was persuaded to sell because she "thought the war would come and all the slaves get freed."[93] The sale later came to be a parallel to a conversion experience, which included a vision of the Lake of Fire. "The darkest hours of my life as a slave came just before freedom, and in the same way, in my trials with sin, when everything seemed lost I was delivered."[94] A child of a former slave, who was born in June 1861, often heard her mother say, " 'I am so glad I am free.' I did not know then what she was talking about. I thought she meant freedom from slavery."[95] The antebellum United States was a hothouse of millennial fervor, and when the war came, it took on an eschatological meaning for many Americans. The rest of the country appropriated what enslaved preachers had been saying: that salvation would come when God showed his hand of deliverance and freed the captive from bonds physical and spiritual.[96]

Many former slaves who converted did so after emancipation.[97] By one estimate, at the start of the Civil War, "between 15 and 25 percent of adult slaves were aligned with Christian denominations."[98] Emancipation also brought Christian missionaries from the North to the South to evangelize as well as to educate freedmen and freedwomen. Edward Blum has estimated that "between 1861 and 1889 northerners contributed an estimated $20 million in cash to the relief associations" and that "more than eight thousand northerners" came to the South. Freedpeople and missionaries—at least, those missionaries who stayed more than a few months, and especially women—lived together closely and broke down racial barriers, not least in Christian worship. The most significant of the missionary groups was the American Missionary Association (AMA), which established schools for freedpeople throughout the South. Ostensibly nondenominational but mostly Congregationalist, the AMA had only marginal success in establishing churches. It was very successful with its schools, which also educated blacks in the particular form of Christianity practiced by the Northern missionaries.[99] During Reconstruction, African Americans by and large left interracial churches to form their own churches and denominations, in their own buildings, and under their own leadership.[100]

Emancipation provided an eschatological impetus to salvation. Anthony Abercrombie of Alabama attended religious meetings in a brush arbor, since the slaves had no meetinghouse. But he did not

convert until two years after the "surrender," when he "took consideration and j'ined up wid de Lawd." Abercrombie claimed to be one
hundred years old when interviewed, and he attributed his long life
to a promise from the Lord that he would live 120 years if he converted and stayed on the straight and narrow.[101] Oliver Bell recalled
that "Ol' Mistus read the Bible to us an' got us baptized in de river
at Horn's bridge, but dat was atter de surrender," though they had
secret prayer meetings before emancipation.[102]

The end of the war was also an opportunity for freedpeople to reject the Christianity of their masters. Jennie Bowen recalled that on
the Fisher plantation in Alabama, slaves were required to attend the
Presbyterian church on the plantation. But after she left the plantation in Camden, Alabama, and moved to Mobile, she became a Baptist.[103] When Emma Crockett was a slave, she didn't go to church, but
later she became a member of the "New Prophet Church" (perhaps a
Pentecostal church).[104]

One Tennessee narrator named Charlie was converted after the
war. He was born sometime between 1843 and 1845 and so was about
twenty during the war. His brother Jeff had run away probably in
1863; he came back for Charlie in 1864, and they both escaped to the
contraband camps during the Battle of Nashville in December 1864.
Charlie and Jeff experienced harrowing escapes during the battles,
once being asked to escape in an ironclad on the Cumberland
River. Charlie succinctly described the situation: "Times were so
desperate along these days. All I did was to call on the Lord. 'Lord,
save me; save me, Lord!' He saved me, and that is why I trust in him
today." Charlie "never did hear from my brother, or about the boat
in which all those people had hidden. I don't know whether the boat
got sunk and all got drowned or not, but thanked God for my spared
life."[105] Charlie was later converted because of an experience of God
in the woods, combined with an invitation to a revival meeting.
This conversion enabled Charlie to rebuke one white man for whom
he worked after the war because "you call yourselves Christians and
pray for the widows and orphans, but you don't do anything for them,"
and it also enabled him to forgive his former "Mars' Bill" when he
encountered him thirty years after the war. He forgave his former
owner because "I love you as though you never hit me a lick, for the

God I serve is a God of love, and I can't go to his kingdom with hate in my heart."[106]

One woman was converted in 1876. She believed that "I have always been a sheep. I was never a goat."[107] Another woman heard a voice while chopping in the field: "My little one, I am God Almighty. I have loved you from the foundation of the world, even with an everlasting love. I have freed your soul from hell, and you are free indeed."[108] Yet another convert was "a new creature in Jesus, the workmanship of his hand saved from the foundation of the world. I was a chosen vessel before the wind ever blew or before the sun ever shined."[109] That language was eschatological, deriving from passages in the Gospels where Jesus foretold a future judgment where he would separate the sheep from the goats, and it was also about election. This salvation, predestined from the beginning of time and to be consummated at the eschaton, had to intersect a particular moment of time. She "was in my house alone, and I declare unto you, when his power struck me I died." The vision of God in the Trinity and the devil was confirmed by the sign that when she was baptized, the rain lifted for the occasion.[110]

Another man had a vision of coming "to a snow-white wall with large gates. . . . When the gates flew apart I saw a beautiful city, the length and breadth of which I couldn't tell. There was no sun, but it was as bright as day when the sun is in midheaven." Another convert "saw the city. It was the prettiest place that I ever saw."[111] The imagery of a beautiful city lit by God himself was taken from the book of Revelation. Also from Revelation was a vision where the man "showed me a large book and my name written in it."[112] This book of life was seen by other African American converts. It was an eschatological record, as opposed to a congregational record, of conversion. Likewise this convert was baptized in a vision by Jesus himself, and only later was he baptized by a minister.

✠

Because of their experience of slavery, conversion for African Americans came to be highly charged with eschatological significance. While African Americans converted like other Protestants and were indebted to the forms of Protestantism, by rejecting their masters' Christianity but not Christianity itself, they created their own highly distinct form of Protestantism. This form of Christianity took root during the times of slavery, and then its eschatological predictions were proved correct by emancipation, which was in no small part made possible by the efforts of African American soldiers and escapees.[113] African American Christianity, freed from the shackles of slavery, went on to create its own kind of religious tradition in the spread of African American churches with their own distinctive types of conversion.

The African American Christian tradition, then, represents a distinct case in the spread of religious choice in the nineteenth-century United States. Prior to emancipation, African American Christians endured the most widespread instance of religious persecution in U.S. history. A massive exertion of state power as well as private violence—manifested in slave codes, slave patrols, and the domestic slave trade, which brought enslaved African Americans to the even more brutal regime of the Deep South—severely limited the ability of slaves to convert to Christianity and to practice their religion once they had converted. Though the Christianity of slaves was vibrant, its practice in black churches and denominations, in white-controlled churches, or in the brush arbors of secret congregations was constrained. That same exercise of power also had the ability to tamp down, though not completely eliminate, the remains of animist or Islamic religious practices carried over from Africa, thus clearing the way for Christianity.

After emancipation, African Americans carved out a freedom to convert to Christianity. A best estimate of the percentage of enslaved adults who were formally aligned with a Christian denomination is 15 to 25 percent.[114] By the time the U.S. Census Bureau began collecting data on church membership at the end of the century, the rate at which African Americans affiliated with black churches had grown rapidly. By 1890, some 59 percent of adult African Americans were adherents of some Christian church, whether it was a black denomination or a predominantly white denomination. By 1906, some 61 percent of adult blacks were church adherents of those denominations; by 1916, 68 percent; by 1926, 66 percent. In other words, over the course of the five decades since emancipation, African Americans had more than doubled their rate of affiliation. African Americans easily exceeded the rate of Christian affiliation among whites, which was perhaps 45 percent in 1890 and 56 percent in 1926.[115] Furthermore, black Christians mostly chose to affiliate with black denominations, coming out of the white led denominations in the years following the Civil War and gaining new converts for those denominations. By 1926, over half of black Christians were in black Baptist denominations, with another quarter in black Methodist denominations.[116] Black converts thus created a distinct religious tradition focused on an eschatological experience of conversion, and after emancipation they exercised their freedom of religious choice to choose that tradition over others.

4

Kingdom

MORMON CONVERTS AND THE
PRIMITIVE GOSPEL

In 1843, two ministers squared off against each other in a public debate in Lexington, Kentucky, that lasted eighteen days. Such debates were common, though this one—eventually reported in a volume of 912 large, closely printed pages—was unusual in its length. People flocked to theological debates because they were entertaining, but also because they touched on key issues of public and personal interest. The primary subjects of the debate were "Christian baptism" and "spiritual influence in conversion and sanctification." The two sides in the debate shared a belief that conversion was crucial, even as they disagreed about its nature.[1]

One of the debaters was Nathan L. Rice, a Presbyterian minister trained in a tradition that valued the Westminster Confession and catechisms as the authoritative interpretation of the Bible.[2] His opponent was Alexander Campbell, who had left the Presbyterianism of his youth to become a Baptist when he emigrated to the United States from Scotland in 1809. In his reading the Bible did not permit the baptism of infants. But in continuing to study the Scripture, he concluded that baptism was necessary for the "remission of sins," a doctrine that Baptists rejected. By 1830, Campbell had started his own movement, called the Disciples of Christ, or simply the Christians, which aimed for the "restoration of the ancient order of things" by adhering strictly to what could be found in a plain reading of the Bible.[3]

Those two forms of Protestantism had very different ideas about what made Christianity authoritative. The Old School Presbyterians insisted on evaluating biblical interpretations by testing them against creeds and doctrinal statements. Restorationist Christians trusted only the plain words of the Bible, understood apart from any creed. They therefore differed on crucial questions such as the meaning of baptism and conversion.

Both debaters often insinuated that their opponent's views of authority had led to the proliferation of competing denominations. Campbell claimed that the writing of creeds divided Christians but a plain interpretation of the Bible would unite them. Rice countered that the private interpretation of Scripture unguided by creeds was bound to lead to error. "It is impossible to know what men believe by the mere fact that they profess to receive the Bible as their rule of faith," he claimed, because "all classes of errorists, Arians, Socinians, Universalists, and even Shakers and Mormons, profess great regard for the Bible."[4]

Rice sought to score a point against Campbell by associating him with the Mormons, who came on the scene a little more than a decade before the debate and were just beginning to gain ground in Kentucky. The Mormons claimed to have a new revelation, the Book of Mormon, which would restore Christianity to its ancient purity. In fact, some people who had sought a restored gospel with Campbell ended up finding it with the Mormons instead. Rice pointed out, for example, that Sidney Rigdon had been one of Campbell's "most popular preachers" but had since "sworn allegiance to Joe Smith." And Rice tried to make his audience worry about Mormon growth. Campbell had claimed that "error . . . often gains converts more rapidly than truth." Rice pointed out that Campbell "boasts of his rapid increase of numbers, as evidence conclusive that his principles are correct! His argument would prove the Mormons right."[5]

Campbell had in fact been one of the earliest and strongest critics of the Mormons. In 1831 he penned a lengthy review mocking the Book of Mormon. He claimed that the stories in Joseph Smith's new revelation were occasioned by "every error and almost every truth discussed in N. York for the last ten years." Campbell thought that God had perfectly revealed his will for the church about those questions, and that the job of Christians was to search the Scripture to find out God's will. In Campbell's view, Smith had given up on the Bible's authority and ginned up a new revelation to resolve the pressing debates in American Christianity. As Campbell put it, the Book of Mormon claimed to decide "all the great controversies—infant baptism, ordination, the trinity, regeneration, repentance, justification, the fall of man, the atonement, transubstantiation, fasting, penance, church government, religious experience, the call to the ministry, the general resurrection, eternal punishment, who may baptize, and even the question of freemasonry, republican government, and the rights of man."[6]

In his debate with Rice, Campbell sought to distance himself from Mormonism, and he disclaimed his former associate Rigdon. Campbell was right that he had sought "the ancient order of things" in the Bible alone, whereas Joseph Smith had received new revelation. But Rice had a point in linking Campbell with the Mormons: what Campbell sought and what Joseph Smith sought had an essential similarity. Both wanted a resolution to vexed questions about salvation, baptism, and church authority, and both thought that the generally sinful state of the church required restoration by returning to its ancient purity. The desire for a pure and primitive church was shared by large numbers of American Christians, even if they never became disciples of Alexander Campbell or Joseph Smith.[7]

The issues at stake in the debate between Rice and Campbell—and for that matter between Campbell and Smith—had enormous implications for how individuals would navigate the complexities of the American sect system. Should potential converts depend on interpretations of the Bible that they had received, or must they search through the Bible themselves unaided? Or did salvation depend on a new revelation that would return the church to the way it had once been? In Kentucky, as in most other places in the United States, groups that claimed to have a restored Christianity were proliferating. In time the most significant of these would be the Mormons, who attracted attention for their size and rapid success, though they were only one restorationist group among many.

Restorationists occupied a space between belonging and not belonging to the nineteenth-century Protestant mainstream. Their new revelations and innovative interpretations of the Scriptures earned them no favor from other Christians, who often treated them—especially Mormons and the utopian sects—as belonging to a new, anti-Christian religion. But converts to these movements saw the matter differently. They thought of their new faiths not as innovating but as restoring an ancient faith. Converts to these groups saw themselves as returning to the epitome of the religion to which they already belonged—a familiar rather than a foreign faith. What Campbell and Rice were debating, and what the people in the audience were attempting to decipher, was how to understand the religious groups that were sweeping through the United States, claiming to be simultaneously old and new.

⳨

Until the 1830s, anything that could be called Mormonism was literally un-thought of. Joseph Smith—a failure early in his life, who was derided for publishing a "golden Bible," and who married dozens of women—did not seem to be a likely candidate to lead a successful church. But by the time of his death in 1844, there were perhaps 26,000 Mormons. It was not simply the rate of growth that distinguished Mormonism as a new group on the scene of American religious life, however. The Methodists were also a new movement, and they reported only 3,233 adherents in 1773 at their first annual conference in British North America. By 1817, thanks largely to conversion, they had grown to 225,000: a growth rate that far exceeded that of Mormonism.[8]

Mormons, however, resembled other religious offshoots of mainstream Christianity in the nineteenth century. These groups shared a few distinguishing traits: they had a distinct origin within relatively recent times; they were marginal to more commonly accepted religions; and they were characterized by new revelations or at least innovative biblical interpretations.[9]

One example was the "kingdom of Matthias," founded in 1830s New York by Robert Matthews. Matthews claimed to be both the transmigrated soul of the biblical apostle Matthias and his genetic descendant. Claiming the gift of prophecy, he founded a group that lived in a home in New York and preached judgment on New York and the reordering of marriage relationships. (Matthews once met Joseph Smith, presenting himself to Smith as "Joshua the Jewish minister.")[10]

In the 1830s, the seminary student John Humphrey Noyes concluded that he had been perfected from all sin. He founded a community eventually located in Oneida, New York, and preached the perfectibility of human beings in this life. The commune featured "complex marriage" (though with the aim of "male continence"), where all members could have sex with anyone else who consented and where children were raised in common. Though the commune survived only till 1881, never growing beyond a few hundred members, their work ethic continued into the Oneida silver company.[11]

Another new community was the United Society of Believers in Christ's Second Appearing, known more popularly as the Shakers. In the 1740s, the Shakers ("shaking Quakers") broke off from the Quakers in England. Their most important leader was Mother Ann Lee, who preached and received revelations requiring celibacy and the abandonment of marriage. She considered herself the second, female manifestation of Christ, while Jesus had been the first, male manifestation. Not merely a prophet, she was thus the second coming of Christ. In 1774, the Shakers arrived in New York and grew rapidly, establishing colonies throughout New England, New York, New Jersey, Pennsylvania, Kentucky, Ohio, and as far west as Indiana. As they grew during the 1820s through 1860s, they received spiritual messages and visions, and communicated these manifestations of the spirit in dances, gift drawings, and speaking in tongues. Shakers practiced the equality of the sexes in the belief that God was both male and female, lived communally, and practiced celibacy. Celibacy ensured that most Shakers were converts, though the Shakers also indentured children and took in orphans. Perhaps 20,000 people joined the Shakers during this period.[12]

As a final example, the late nineteenth century saw the rise of many black Israelite groups. Distinct from African Americans who became Jews by converting into a Reformed or Orthodox Jewish congregation, these groups formed around leaders such as the prophet William Saunders Crowdy, who founded the Church of God and

Saints in Christ, or Rabbi Wentworth A. Matthew, a Christian
minister who founded the Commandment Keepers Church of the
Living God, the Pillar and Ground of the Truth. Whether these
groups featured a charismatic prophet like Crowdy or focused
more on the Old Testament, they gradually replaced Christian
practices with those derived from Judaism and "cabalistic science,"
motivated by a desire to return to the origins of Christianity in
Judaism.[13]

Though wildly diverse, most of these groups shared a key characteristic. They believed that one could cut through the confusion of
so many different religious groups by choosing a plainer interpretation of the Bible or, better yet, by receiving a new revelation that
clarified the Bible's message. Restorationists were characterized by
their look back to a pure era of the primitive church, but looking back
to a golden age also meant that restorationists were looking forward
to the day when God would restore the church to its primitive purity and they would experience the perfection of God's promises.

Protestants generally, but especially the kinds of biblically centered
Protestants who were prominent in the United States, had long subscribed to Christian primitivism. The common narrative was that
God in Christ Jesus had revealed himself and founded the church in
the first century but that it quickly became corrupted by false doctrines and false practices unsanctioned or even condemned by the
church's sole authority, the Bible. The epitome of error was the Roman
Catholic Church, which (Protestants claimed) featured corruptions
of doctrine, such as the belief that salvation came by works rather
than faith; corruptions of practice, such as prayers to the Virgin
Mary; and corruptions of institutions, such as the papacy. Where
the Roman Catholic Church claimed to carry forward the tradition
of the apostles, primitivists urged a return to the founding principles of the church as authoritatively revealed in the Bible, which
contained everything necessary for faith and practice. God had revealed in the Bible how the church should function, even down to
the specifics of how it should be governed, and the job of faithful
Christians was to recover that model from the Scriptures and put it
into practice. Such claims were especially strong among Baptists, for
example, who rejected the nearly universal Christian practice of

infant baptism as an initiatory rite since they could not find it in the Bible.[14]

Often Christian primitivists coupled a return to the distant past with a view to the immediate future. Either Christ would soon return and reestablish the pure church, or the church would purify itself before Christ's return. Either way, return to the purity of the original church was, they believed, characteristic of the end times. The middle of the nineteenth century was rife with Christian millennialism, most notably the movement started by William Miller. Miller was a Baptist who claimed to have learned from a close reading of the Scriptures that Jesus would return sometime between March 21, 1843, and March 21, 1844. As that date passed, he set various other dates. The final predicted date, October 22, 1844, came to be known as the Great Disappointment. Yet Millerism, or Adventism, continued as a movement long past that date, with the largest number of converts becoming Seventh-Day, or Sabbatarian, Adventists. Led by Ellen Harmon White, this group coupled a belief in the soon return of Christ with the idea that the Christian day of worship was properly the Sabbath, that is Saturday rather than Sunday, and that the change to Sunday worship had been a corruption. Millerism was just a striking example of a broader obsession with the end times that permeated large parts of American Christianity. And many American Protestant groups associated the imminent return of Christ with widespread evangelism.[15]

To be a restorationist did not imply traditionalism or conservatism in religion—quite the opposite, for the times of the primitive gospel as described in the Scriptures were filled with prophecy, with the moving of the Spirit, with the hope of Christ's return. To be truly primitive meant that one would not just remember but actually relive prophecy and life in the Spirit. Often it meant the presence of a prophet, such as Mother Ann Lee, Robert Matthews, or Joseph Smith, or the addition of a new book of scriptures, such as the Book of Mormon. To become old, one had to become new.

This combination of primitivism and millennialism, expressed in so many different sects, was itself a reaction against the sect system. Restorationists argued that other denominations were corruptions of genuine Christianity. One Mormon evangelist, Parley Parker

Pratt, described the situation of American churches as analogous to the time before Christ when miraculous "gifts had ceased" and the Jews were divided into a "multitude of sects, none of which were right." According to Pratt, it was the miraculous gifts of Jesus and the apostles that succeeded in establishing Christianity, in the same way that the Mormon apostles like Pratt were restoring it.[16]

Yet ironically, at the same time that prophets or preachers called their followers to return to primitive Christianity and forsake many false choices, they made yet another religious option available. Mormonism called its followers to exercise a choice of belonging expressed repeatedly in ritual action. Joseph Smith viewed his followers as restoring corrupt Christianity, and he positioned the Book of Mormon as continuing the story of the Christian Bible. But unlike most Christian denominations (except Baptists and Campbellites), the Mormon "restored gospel" demanded that people be rebaptized at conversion.[17] Mormon conversion accounts are filled with mentions of the moment of baptism, which acknowledged that converts accepted the restored gospel and repudiated a claim to saving power in any previous baptism. Part of the genius of Mormonism was that it gave its adherents ways of expressing their affiliation in an ever-growing array of ritual practices. Temple sealing, patriarchal blessings, and polygamous marriage—not to mention removal to Nauvoo, Illinois, or to the Great Basin—required converts to continue to express their commitment.

Mormonism, then, was a paradoxical faith. Joseph Smith received revelations that created a new religious community, yet the basis of that community was the claim to have the restored gospel. Though Mormonism originated as a response to the proliferation of many religious groups, it became yet another choice among many. It was these paradoxes that Mormon converts had to deal with, beginning first of all with Joseph Smith himself.

⁺⁺

Joseph Smith Jr. was born in 1805 in Vermont to a family of poor farmers. When his parents lost their farm, the Smiths migrated to Palmyra, New York, and continued to struggle economically. The family's religious affiliation was as tenuous as their finances. Smith's mother, Lucy Mack Smith, had been raised a Congregationalist but had only the loosest affiliation to that denomination.[18] His father, Joseph Smith Sr., had religious feelings but was skeptical of religious organizations. Smith himself encountered a number of different Christian groups. Western New York was known as the "burned-over district" for the number of revivals and upstart sects in the region.[19]

Smith's closest encounter was with Methodism. His wife, Emma Hale Smith, was reared a Methodist, and Smith found himself "somewhat partial to the Methodist sect" and occasionally attended Methodist class meetings with his wife.[20] Smith also occasionally attended Presbyterian services in Palmyra. He reacted strongly against Presbyterian doctrines such as predestination, and his later revelations were consistently anti-Calvinist. He felt keenly the need to choose between the different churches, and he was dismayed over deciding which was correct.[21]

According to a history that Smith wrote in 1832 and then retold in an official church history that he began in 1838, the future Mormon prophet had his first visionary experience in 1820. While many of the details of the first vision, including the date, are uncertain, Smith's later recollections, written during a pivotal decade in the growth of Mormonism, show the meaning he expected conversion to have for his followers.[22] At the age of fourteen, Smith encountered a revival that began with the Methodists but then became "general among all the sects in that region of country." Despite the general awakening, Smith was alienated by the way that different faiths contended for converts: "Some were contending for the Methodist faith, some for the Presbyterian, and some for the Baptist." He later wrote that "when the Converts began to file off some to one party and some to another," he saw "priest contending against priest, and convert against convert so that all their good feelings one for another (if they ever had any) were entirely lost in a strife of words and a contest about opinions." Smith objected to the competition not least because he felt the pressures of choosing the right option to save his soul. "I often said to myself," he later recalled, "what is to be done? Who of all these parties are right? Or are they all wrong together? if any one of them be right which is it?"[23]

Agitated by these questions some time after the revival, Smith went out into the woods to ask God for help in deciding. It was the first time he had ever attempted "to pray vocally."[24] Smith's 1832 account of retiring to the woods to pray was modeled on many conversion accounts, which commonly described sinners who went into solitary places to attempt their first prayer and returned converted. Even Smith's sense that he was "filled with the spirit of god" and that "the Lord opened the heavens upon me" was not unusual for an evangelical conversion account of this period. As part of this account, Smith wrote that he "saw the Lord and he spake unto me saying Joseph my son thy sins are forgiven thee," and he received the promise that "all those who believe on my name may have Eternal life." His conversion account, like so many others, found its meaning in the forgiveness of sins.[25]

This 1832 account, which was an almost wholly conventional evangelical conversion narrative, had a hint of an additional meaning. Smith heard God say, "Behold the world lieth in sin at this time and none doeth good no not one they have turned aside from the gospel and keep not my commandments." That language was a pastiche of biblical quotations, and its condemnation of general wickedness was not very precise.[26] Smith would later make the meaning of that revelation far sharper.

Smith's 1838 account of his first vision had a different focus. Instead of going into the woods to pray for the forgiveness of sins, Smith wrote that he went to pray "to know which of all the sects was right, that I might know which to join." The two questions were of course related, since one had to join the right church to be forgiven, but the second account emphasized the general apostasy of the Christian churches instead of Smith's personal forgiveness for sin. The account also differed in that Smith saw a vision of "two personages," implied to be God and Jesus Christ. During the vision Smith asked his question about which church to join, and "the Personage" replied that he "must join none of them, for they were all wrong."[27]

In the 1838 account, Smith recalled that he told a Methodist minister about his vision and was surprised when the preacher said "it was all of the Devil" because revelation had ceased. Telling other people his story "excited a great deal of prejudice against me among

professors of religion." Such opposition is not surprising, for Smith
had begun to depart from the common form of conversion narrative to a different kind of religious experience that was sharply critical of all other Christian groups.[28]

The first vision was followed by another, which led to the Book of
Mormon. In 1823, Smith said, the angel Moroni led him to golden
plates containing texts which told the story of an ancient biblical
civilization. By 1827, Joseph Smith was engaged in translating the
golden plates into the Book of Mormon, a labor known only to members of his family and a few close associates: Oliver Cowdery, David
Whitmer, and Martin Harris. During this time Smith continued to
receive more revelations from Jesus Christ, John the Baptist, the
apostles Peter, James, and John, and other figures who appeared in
the golden plates. He finished his translations and published them
in 1830 as the Book of Mormon.

Yet even before the book was published, in May 1829, Smith and
Cowdery received a vision of John the Baptist, given by the authority
of the apostles Peter, James, and John. John the Baptist conferred on
Smith and Cowdery "the priesthood of Aaron, which holds the keys
of the ministring of angels and of the gospel of repentance, and of
baptism by immersion for the remission of sins." Smith first baptized
Cowdery in the Susquehanna River, then Cowdery baptized Smith.
As Cowdery was baptized, "the Holy Ghost fell upon him and he
stood up and prophecied many things which should shortly come
to pass," and once Smith was baptized he "also had the Spirit of
Prophecy."[29] Smith and Cowdery thus returned to the times of the
apostles, and Smith became the prophet Joseph. Their act of baptism
for the remission of sins accompanied by prophecy and the work of the
Spirit was soon replicated in the lives of many Mormon converts.

✠

By 1829, Joseph had received a new book of revelation in the soon-
to-be-published Book of Mormon, the priesthoods of Aaron and
Melchizedek, and the gift of prophecy through the Spirit. He also
knew the mode of receiving converts into his restored church: baptism by immersion for the remission of sins. Smith's view on bap-

tism was thus similar to that held by Alexander Campbell and other restorationists, who (unlike Catholics and Reformed Protestants) saw baptism as valid only for conscious believers, but whose reading of the Scriptures (unlike Baptists) made baptism instrumental in forgiving sins. Smith had received the answer to his dilemma about which sect he should follow. None of them was true, because they had all been corrupted, but Smith was to be the prophet of the restored gospel. Very rapidly, beginning with his own family, Smith attracted followers to his restored gospel.

Lucy Mack Smith, Joseph's mother, felt some of the same pressures in her adolescence that her son felt in his. She experienced an "anxiety of mind" because of her desire "to obtain that which I had heard spoken of so much from the pulpit—a change of heart." It is not surprising that Lucy Mack, in the midst of the Second Great Awakening in New England, frequently felt the pressure to be converted. Yet she did not manage to have a satisfactory change in heart because she could never demonstrate to everyone else that she had made the correct choice. She expressed the problem in these terms: "If I remain a member of no church, all religious people will say I am of the world; and, if I join some one of the different denominations, all the rest will say I am in error. No church will admit that I am right, except the one with which I am associated." The horns of her dilemma were worldliness (closely associated with irreligion) and a religious commitment that would always be questioned by other denominations. Furthermore, Mack had imbibed enough Puritan primitivism to think that none of the denominations available to her were good choices, since "seeing they are all unlike the Church of Christ, as it existed in former days!"[30] She remained unbaptized and unaffiliated into adulthood.

After marrying, Lucy Mack Smith found a minister who permitted her to be baptized, probably around 1820, without having to join any particular denomination. Joseph Smith Sr. was "much excited upon the subject of religion," according to his wife, "yet he would not subscribe to any particular system of faith, but contended for the ancient order." Both Lucy and her son experienced visions, including a vision where she cried out, "I beseech thee, in the name of Jesus Christ, to forgive my sins."[31] Joseph told his family (and others, who scoffed) about his visions and his translation of the Book of Mormon. He told his mother in no uncertain terms that the Presbyterian church she eventually joined was false. Finally, Lucy Mack Smith found in Joseph's revelations the primitive church she had not found in Congregationalism, Methodism, or Presbyterianism.

Lucy Mack Smith made that commitment decisively on April 6, 1830, after her son received a revelation from Jesus Christ that he was to reestablish "His Church once more here upon the earth" on that "precise day."[32] Smith wrote down instructions for how the church would be organized, in a revelation known as the Articles and Covenants. These instructions were later included in the Doctrine and Covenants, a canonical book for the Latter-day Saints first published in 1835.[33] Where other restorationists had to search through the examples given in the Bible to piece together how the church should operate, Smith's revelation provided an exact blueprint.

On April 6, thirty people assembled and voted to make Smith and Cowdery the leaders of the church. They were confirmed by Smith and took the Lord's Supper. Not everyone who was there had been baptized, and only Smith and Cowdery had been baptized in the new dispensation. During the meeting, several people "became convinced of the truth" and decided to join the newly formed church. Among those, Smith wrote, "my own father and mother were baptized, to my great joy and consolation."[34] Lucy Mack Smith's baptism, like many later baptisms into the Mormon church, was an implicit repudiation of the Christian baptism that she had already undergone. It was a step that many people would soon take to follow the restored gospel. Val Rust estimates that from 1829 to 1830 some 260 people were baptized as followers of Joseph Smith, with more than 1,400 baptized by the end of 1834.[35]

Two episodes in her later life illustrate how Lucy Mack Smith's conversion became typical of other Mormon conversions. In June 1844, a mob murdered her sons Joseph and Hyrum. In 1845, a general conference of the church was held to determine, among other things, whether the church would move to the west and who would succeed Smith. Lucy Smith was an important symbol on that day. According to the *History of the Church*, "Mother Lucy Smith," like a biblical matriarch, said "she was truly glad that the Lord had let her see so large a congregation." Lucy Mack Smith asked the congregation "whether they considered her a mother in Israel." Brigham Young asked the congregation to reply, on which "One universal 'yes' rang throughout."[36] The moment was clearly a power play on Young's part, to get Lucy's approval for Young's leadership and the move to Utah. Yet that play showed how Lucy received an honorific title of "mother in Israel," in that her spiritual struggles had begotten Joseph's, and Joseph's had begotten thousands of others.

When the Mormon apostle Orson Pratt published Lucy Mack Smith's memoirs in 1853, he emphasized not only the book as a history of the prophet Joseph but also that "the events which have occurred in connection with the history of this remarkable family, are . . . of infinite importance in their bearings on present and future generations."[37] Smith began by recounting the history of her father, Solomon Mack, and her brother, Jason Mack. Solomon was a convert during the First Great Awakening, and her brother while not yet sixteen "became what is termed a seeker" who "held that there was no church in existence which held to the pure principles of the Gospel." The rest of the document emphasized that her son Joseph had reinstituted the true principles of the gospel.[38] The apostle Pratt aimed to use the document to spread the Mormon faith.

✢

The followers of Joseph Smith soon numbered many people outside the Smith family. These early converts established the themes that would mark later generations of converts, who would find some of the same attractions in the restored gospel of Joseph Smith and who would emulate the example of these early Latter-day Saints.

The conversion of Parley Parker Pratt showed a longing for primitivism and a desire to escape the modern sect system through an ancient baptism. Pratt was born in 1807 and grew up in Burlington, New York. His family attended Presbyterian, Baptist, and Methodist churches, yet Pratt recalled that his father "belonged to no religious sect, and was careful to preserve his children free from all prejudice in favor of or against any particular denomination, in which the so-called Christian world was then unhappily divided."[39]

Pratt reported that when he was a young man, he questioned his father about the form of conversion that had developed in the Second Great Awakening. Though evangelicals claimed they practiced this form directly from the Bible, Pratt complained that there was "so manifest a difference between the ancient and modern disciples of Jesus Christ." He observed from the Scriptures that "if I had lived in the days of the Apostles, and believed in Jesus Christ, . . . Peter or his brethren would have said to me, '*Repent and be baptized in the name of Jesus Christ for REMISSION OF SINS, and you SHALL receive the gift of the Holy Ghost.*'" With so clear a message, Pratt said he would have "known definitely and precisely what to do to be saved." Pratt contrasted this apparently clear biblical command with the current practice: "*now* we go to the religious minister for instruction, and he tells us we must experience a mysterious, indefinite and undefinable something called religion before we can repent and be baptized acceptably." Though this reported conversation quite obviously draws on Pratt's later beliefs as a Mormon apostle, there is no reason to think that he misrepresented the disagreement he experienced as a young man with the evangelical pattern of conversion.[40]

In fact, Pratt tried to be baptized by the Baptists, though "I lacked that '*experience of religion*' which they always required." Pratt finally heard of primitive baptism from the preaching of Sidney Rigdon, at the time a preacher for the Disciples of Christ, founded by Alexander Campbell, but eventually a Mormon leader (and finally an apostate from Mormonism). Having discovered the restorationist movement, Pratt was primed when he encountered the Book of Mormon in a print edition from an "old Baptist deacon" in Newark. In New York, he "demanded baptism" from Hyrum Smith (Joseph Smith's brother) but was actually baptized by Oliver Cowdery in Seneca Lake, New York. For Pratt, the baptism gave him confidence that he "had authority in the ministry." The next Sunday he preached from both the Bible and the Book of Mormon, so that "four heads of families" were baptized.[41] Pratt went on to become one of early Mormonism's most energetic evangelists until killed by the former husband of one of his plural wives.

Pratt's search for a primitive baptism was akin to that of Mary Brown. She joined the Methodists when she was thirteen. She recalled that it was the "only church I knew much about," but that didn't mean she didn't have opinions from the Scriptures. When she was baptized, she asked the minister whether he believed "baptism to be a duty for us to obey," meaning a duty that brought about salvation, and he replied that "baptism was not a saving ordinance" but was only "to answer a good conscience." She disagreed from her reading of the New Testament. She also wished to be baptized by immersion, but he had her kneel in the water rather than join her in the river to immerse her. After being married, Mary Brown Pulsipher and her husband, Zerah, heard the gospel of the Latter-day Saints in New York. When the Mormon preacher taught that "baptism by immersion was the only right way" and that baptism was "for the remission of sins," she replied, "That looks right." They were baptized along with "about twenty" other people in 1832. At the same time, she was healed of her rheumatism. The preacher had promised her healing, and when she came out of the water, she said, she "left my cane, [and] went home rejoicing." The next day, the preacher confirmed Mary Pulsipher into the church and gave her the gift of the Spirit. The Pulsiphers later went to Kirtland, Ohio, and she remained a Mormon over fifty-two years until her death. Her narrative is structured around the contrast between her powerless and, to her mind, unbiblical baptism into the Methodist church, and her powerful baptism with healing, the presence of the Spirit, and the remission of sins.[42]

Newel Knight's conversion also came by baptism, but it demonstrates the connections between conversions to Mormonism and the pattern of prayer that Protestants had developed. Newel Knight was the son of a family that supported Joseph Smith while he translated the Book of Mormon. Because the Knight family were Universalists, they were interested in Joseph Smith's message. The young man Newel frequently spoke with Joseph about "the important subject of man's eternal salvation." Knight attended prayer meetings but could not bring himself to actually pray. Prayer in his narrative was a sign— as in Finney's preaching, the ATS tracts, or many Mormon accounts, including Joseph Smith's first vision—that someone was willing to be saved. Knight thus "deferred praying until next morning, when he retired into the woods." Even there he could not pray: "He made several attempts to pray, but could scarcely do so—feeling that he had not done his duty, but that he should have prayed in the presence of others." The emphasis that Knight placed on prayer shows that he saw it as the pivotal moment in salvation.[43]

In Knight's case, the reluctance to pray had serious consequences. When Joseph entered Knight's house, he found "his visage and limbs distorted and twisted in every shape and appearance possible to imagine," then some power tossed Knight around the room. Knight was possessed by a demon. After Smith cast it out, Knight was converted. The scene had echoes of the ending of the Gospel of Mark, where Jesus promised his disciples that a sign of their ministry would be casting out devils.[44] Though Knight's conversion account did not mention that biblical text, it scarcely needed to. Just as in the Acts of the Apostles, the "Spirit of the Lord descended upon" Knight. Unlike in Acts, he reportedly levitated so that "my shoulder and head were pressing against the beams" of his house.[45] Knight's conversion account had many of the features of the evangelical conversion narrative: the preaching of the Word of God and the attempt at a sinner's prayer. But Knight also had an ecstatic experience, demon possession, and the descent of the Holy Spirit as in the times of the apostles.

The conversion of William McLellin shows the pull of the Mormon community on new converts. William McLellin was a schoolteacher in Paris, Illinois, in 1831 when two Mormon missionaries came to town. Their preaching bore elements of millennialist and restorationist preaching, which McLellin might have heard elsewhere. But it also contained much that was new, including an explanation of why the Book of Mormon was divine revelation, preaching on the "signs of the times," and the testimony of David Whitmer about having seen an angel. What impressed McLellin most was that the missionaries "expounded the Gospel the plainest I thot that I ever heard in my life, which astonished me."[46]

Most of the people McLellin talked to were not persuaded by the "Mormonites. They though[t] they were generally a very honest people but very much deluded by Smith and others." McLellin, though, found the message persuasive enough to travel to Independence, Missouri, arriving by August 1831. It was the community there that really persuaded him to become a Mormon, because after he "talked much with those people" he "saw Love, Peace, Harmony and Humility abounding among them." He was also persuaded that the elders "had the power of deserning spirits," a gift of the Spirit listed in the New Testament. He had a chance to talk with Hyrum Smith for four hours about the origin of the Book of Mormon and to attend a prayer meeting.[47]

He continued, like many a Protestant, to pray the next morning, as he "rose early and betook myself to earnest prayr." His prayer convinced him to ask Hyrum Smith to baptize him, "because I wanted to live among a people who were based upon pure principles and actuated by the Spirit of the Living God." He was immersed, then confirmed on the banks of the river, and was overcome by a feeling of being "very happy, calm, and pleasant during the day until evening." Despair "respecting my own salvation" came over him in the evening, but the evening prayer and especially the ministry of Newel Knight overcame that. Knight (perhaps by experience with other converts) "was enabled to tell me the very secrets of my heart and in a degree to chase darkness from my mind." He was confirmed by another meeting in the morning, where "Peace, order, harmony and the spirit of God seemed to cheer every heart, warm every bosom, and animated every Tongue." Crucially, he "saw more beauty in Christianity now than I ever had seen before." Having been baptized and confirmed on his second day in Independence, he was told "it was my duty to become an Elder in the church and go and preach the Gospel" the next week.[48]

McLellin's conversion—which took only about a month from first proclamation to his commissioning as a missionary—thus brought together many of the themes of Mormon conversion. He was in motion as a convert: quite literally, from Illinois to Missouri, then back out on the road to convert others. He found conversion in the love and peace of a community, knit together by the Holy Spirit. His conversion found its definitive form in rituals of private prayer but also in rituals of baptism and confirmation. He joined a new church but thought of it as the fulfillment of Christianity.

For McLellin, it was a short-lived sense of community at best. By 1838, he had lost confidence in the leadership of the Latter-day

Saints and worked against the church. The church in turn excommunicated him on May 11, 1838. McLellin and Smith engaged in an ongoing verbal battle, which nearly turned to blows. In 1844–1845, McLellin followed Sidney Rigdon when he broke away from the main LDS body after Smith's death and Brigham Young's succession, and McLellin was made an apostle by the Rigdonites. By 1847, he backed David Whitmer, one of the first three witnesses to the Book of Mormon who had split from Smith in 1837 to form a different dissident group called the Whitmerites. Before his death, McLellin would be affiliated with at least two other groups that had split from the main body of Mormons. For McLellin, the search for the perfection of Mormon community and the endless choosing between one schismatic group or another went hand in hand.

✠

The conversions of these early Mormons had some distinctive elements that became characteristic of Mormon conversions generally. The pattern of Mormon conversions developed out of several sources. Not least was the general desire for primitivism by which so many potential converts judged the Mormon message and found it appealing. Then there was the interplay between the preaching of the many Mormon missionaries and their hearers' responses. There was also the strong influence that Joseph Smith's revelations and the Book of Mormon exerted on potential converts. Both the Book of Mormon and Smith's other revelations tended toward the same kind of pattern. They gave the expectation that large numbers of people would convert in response to a far-flung mission effort, despite fierce resistance to that message. Their theology made conversion a matter of explicit choice to accept or reject the Mormon message. And they emphasized baptism for the remission of sins as the decisive act of conversion.

Some of Joseph Smith's earliest revelations prepared him and his followers to receive many converts despite opposition. In a revelation of March 1829, Smith heard the voice of Jesus promising that "if this generation harden not their hearts, I will establish my Church among them." The vision told Smith that the "field is white already to harvest" and that "there is no gift greater than the gift of salvation." Yet the revelation also warned Smith that "Satan doth stir up the hearts of the people to contention, concerning the points of my doctrine," thus preparing him for opposition to the message. Even in this early revelation there was a strong implication that conversions were a matter of choice and that those who heard the message might "reject my words."[49]

The revelation on the organization of the church on April 6, 1830, spelled out many more details. Just as in Smith and Cowdery's baptism, the connection between salvation and baptism was made explicit: "As many as would believe and be baptized, in his holy name . . . should be saved"—language drawn from a literal reading of the New Testament. Even when many evangelical denominations took the New Testament plainly, they tended to make salvation more a matter of a convert's heart and less a matter of the actual administration of the sacrament, as did the Methodist minister in Mary Pulsipher's narrative. Baptism was only for believers who "have truly repented of all their sins and are willing to take upon them the name of Jesus Christ." There was to be no question of the mode of baptism, for which the Book of Mormon and Smith's revelations gave specific instructions. The person doing the baptizing was instructed to "go down into the water with the person who has presented himself or herself for baptism" and "immerse him or her in the water." And baptism, in the words of the New Testament, was for the remission of sins, meaning that it actually brought about salvation. A revelation of April 1830 clarified that everyone who joined the church must be baptized, even if they had previously been baptized into a different Christian group. This procedure obviously denied the validity of baptism by any other group, implying that only the Mormons had the power of salvation.[50]

Salvation was made even more explicitly a matter of choice. No one could become a member of the church "unless he has arrived unto the years of accountability before God, and is capable of repentance"—an age that Smith identified as eight years old. Not only must converts be old enough to make a choice for themselves, they also retained the ability to later reject the gospel. The question of whether someone could lose his or her salvation after an experience of faith was one that contemporary Protestants were wrestling with. Smith's revelation was clear that "there is a possibility that man may fall from grace" and so lose his salvation. That theology led to a practical provision in the revelation: a procedure for blotting out the names of those who had left the church. Not only must one make a choice to become a Mormon, one had to continually choose to remain a Mormon.[51]

The Book of Mormon likewise set up a typical pattern for conversions, through stories rather than through explicit rules. Many converts became Mormons more because of the existence of the sacred book than by reading it.[52] At least in the early days of Mormonism, preachers tended to emphasize the Bible in their preaching. The Bible as a text was more familiar to their audiences, and it brought with it an enormous authority. Mormon preaching of a restored gospel from the Scriptures could fall on ground that was already ready to hear that primitivist message.[53] Yet preachers pointed to the existence of the Book of Mormon as a powerful sign that God had sent his message through the prophet Joseph. The "Testimony of the Three Witnesses" and the "Testimony of the Eight Witnesses" at the back of the book authenticated the book as a new revelation. More important than those witnesses was the claim that the Book of Mormon was self-authenticating. In other words, by reading the book, converts came to immerse themselves in its world and to find that its claims were true. Very early in the book, readers would learn that "the most plain and precious parts of the gospel of the Lamb . . . have been kept back by that abominable church" but that the "plain and precious" gospel would be restored—a claim many of them were well prepared to receive.[54]

The claim that the Book of Mormon was influential in many individual conversions primarily for the fact of its existence is not to say, however, that the contents of the Book of Mormon did not affect conversions to Mormonism. Missionaries read the Book of Mormon and shaped their preaching to its plan of salvation. Converts often read it as well, or at least heard parts of it preached. In several places, the Book of Mormon created the controlling story of what a conversion looked like.

The Book of Mormon makes it explicit that religious faith is a matter of choice. The Book of Alma tells the story of a man named

Korihor, who is an "Anti-Christ" who "began to preach unto the people that there should be no Christ." It is not hard to see in Korihor a figure of nineteenth-century irreligion. Yet Korihor is not punished, the book explains, because one's religion could only be a matter of choice. Thus "if he believed in God it was his privilege to serve him; but if he did not believe in him there was no law to punish him." The book quotes the Old Testament call "Choose ye this day, whom ye will serve" as a proof text.[55] Another passage explains that "even if it were possible that little children could sin, they could not be saved," the implication being that they could be neither damned nor saved because they had not consciously made a choice.[56]

The Book of Mormon describes several individual conversions in detail, and these accounts are significant for the way in which they were replicated in the lives of Mormon converts. In one of the Book of Mormon narratives, Alma the Younger sets out on a journey to destroy the church and is miraculously knocked to the ground. Alma is unable to speak for three days, but at the end he "cried within my heart, 'O Jesus, thou Son of God, have mercy on me, who am in the gall of bitterness, and am encircled about by the everlasting chains of death.'" After that conversion moment, Alma recalls "what joy, and what marvelous light I did behold," and he has "memory of my sins no more." This narrative, clearly derived from the miraculous conversion of the apostle Paul in the Book of Acts, is similar to the sinner's prayer of evangelical conversions. Alma's conversion prepared Mormons to expect sudden, decisive conversions.[57]

In another part of the Book of Mormon, the book of Enos describes a conversion that centered on a prayer of repentance. Enos was converted, if not in an instant, then after a day of praying. As in so many conversion narratives from the early nineteenth century, including Joseph Smith's first vision, Enos went into the forest where he "kneeled down before my Maker, and I cried unto him in mighty prayer and supplication for mine own soul." After his prayer, "there came a voice unto me, saying, 'Enos, thy sins are forgiven thee, and thou shalt be blessed.'"[58] Descriptions of conversion in the Book of Mormon were clearly grounded in the evangelical milieu in which Joseph Smith developed early Mormonism.

Conversion in the Book of Mormon also required a belief in prophecy. For instance, Alma the Younger says that when his father converted, "there was a mighty change wrought in his heart," and "he preached the word unto your fathers, and a mighty change was also wrought in their hearts."[59] The Book of Helaman described a pattern of conversion that included repentance and faith, specifically in "the holy scriptures, yea, the prophecies of the holy prophets." Everywhere in the Book of Mormon, the question of whether or not one believed prophecy was front and center. Nephi, who experiences the first conversion in the Book of Mormon, comes to believe as the result of a vision and of prophecy.[60] Readers of the Book of Mormon, a new work of revelation, were thus constantly encountering stories of people choosing to believe or disbelieve in new revelation.

Unlike typical evangelical conversion narratives, the Book of Mormon describes conversions of large numbers of people. After Alma the Younger converts, he challenges the atheist Korihor and strikes him speechless. He then sends out a general call for all infidels who heard Korihor's message to believe, and "they were all converted again unto the Lord."[61] He later encountered another group of people, the Zoramites, who believed in and worshiped God yet did not believe that there would be a Christ.[62] Alma encouraged the Zoramites to try to grow faith like "a good seed," implying that they could actively work to develop their faith, while another prophet, Amulek, urges the Zoramites not to "procrastinate the day of your repentance until the end."[63]

The universal mark of conversions in the Book of Mormon, especially the Book of Alma, is baptism. Every time the prophet Alma preaches to a new group of people, he baptizes many of them. In one typical account the people of the land of Zarahemla "were baptized in the waters of Sidon and were joined to the church of God; yea, they were baptized by the hand of Alma." A later adaptation of the Book of Mormon into more dramatic prose included an image of Alma baptizing in the river, just as Joseph Smith's revelations required (Figure 4.1). It was a scene that many converts to Mormonism reenacted.[64]

Early Mormon conversions followed a distinct pattern, the roots of which can be found in the revelations of Joseph Smith and the Book of Mormon, and in the experiences of the first Mormon converts. The conversions of the Smith family were, of course, influenced by their

FIGURE 4.1 A baptism from the Book of Mormon, as illustrated in *Cities of the Sun*, a novelistic expansion of stories from the Book of Mormon. In this illustration, the prophet Alma baptizes one of the many groups of people that he converted. This scene of a river baptism by immersion would be replicated in the lives of many converts to Mormonism. Elizabeth Rachel Cannon, *Cities of the Sun* (Salt Lake City, UT: Deseret News, 1910), 21.

relationship to their remarkable family member. Many conversions of people close to Smith were not so very different, though. They might not have been related to Smith by blood, but they had actually met the prophet, saw him working at translating the Book of Mormon or receiving revelations—sometimes directly addressed to them. There can be no mistaking the fact that the charismatic prophet was the locus of early Mormonism until his death in June 1844.

But in the fourteen-year period between the publication of the Book of Mormon and Joseph Smith's death, the Latter-day Saints grew so impressively that it would be a mistake to attribute that growth to Joseph Smith alone. The new believers were simply too numerous, coming from too many scattered places and converting under the influence of too many different Mormon evangelists. Even in his lifetime, most of these new converts, including those who converted outside the United States in places like England, entered the church long before they could ever have met Joseph Smith. Even in the heady early days of the Mormon movement, there was a reliable pattern for winning and naturalizing converts to the faith, which relied on the influence but not the presence of the prophet.

✝

Our best way of understanding how people came to be Mormons comes from manuscript records that Mormon missionaries sent back to their leaders in Kirtland, Nauvoo, or the Great Basin. Either on the road or after returning home, these missionaries described the people they evangelized, the number of baptisms and ordinations they performed, the resistance they encountered, and the content of the message they preached. These manuscript accounts, which bear a remarkable similarity regardless of place and personality, describe how Mormons presented the opportunity to convert. Many Mormon converts (at least the men) became missionaries, so there was little distinction between the proselyte and the proselytizer. One person's experience of conversion was replicated in his converts until it became a pattern. Doubtless many Mormons' conversion narratives shaped their memories to conform to their fuller understandings of the faith.[65] Regardless of what one thinks about the reliability of this or that narrative, the narratives as a whole amounted to a pattern that trained missionaries in how to produce conversions and potential converts in how to experience them. Reading these accounts synoptically, we can also see the outlines of how converts might typically have first encountered Mormonism.

An inhabitant of a settlement who had never encountered the Mormon message was likely to first hear Mormon preaching through a session scheduled by a pair of missionaries (Figure 4.2). When missionaries came to town, they "gave out appointments" at various places. These appointments would specify the place and time of meeting, though they did not always clearly specify the content of the meeting. The pair of missionaries might remain in the same location for a day, for several days, or for as long as a couple of weeks. They held their meetings in whatever venue they could obtain permission to use. Occasionally, churches would grant permission to use their buildings, at least before Mormonism became better known and stirred

FIGURE 4.2 Mormon missionaries and church members in Sanderson, Florida, in 1897. Throughout the century, Mormon missionaries traveled all around the United States, preaching at whatever buildings or locations were made available to them and gathering converts into congregations. Southern States Mission photograph collection, PH 3793, box 3, folder 17, item 3, Church History Library, Church of Jesus Christ of Latter-day Saints, Salt Lake City, Utah, https://dcms.lds.org/delivery/DeliveryManagerServlet?dps_pid=IE7714432.

up more opposition. Just as often, the meetings were held in a public place, such as a school, or in a private home. Occasionally, Mormons would go door-to-door to invite people, as Horace Cowan did in Villanova, Pennsylvania. Nothing about this procedure would have seemed unusual to the inhabitants of the town or village. Itinerant ministers of various denominations, especially Methodists, also gave out appointments. The appointment for public preaching was perfectly familiar and would offer little clue as to the distinctive content of the Mormon message.[66]

Other times, though, the first encounter with the Mormon missionaries might be at the religious meetings of one's own denomination. Mormon missionaries often attended services of Baptists or Methodists and requested permission to speak. How long they could speak depended on whether the people listening regarded the preaching as being distinct and heretical or whether it seemed familiar and faithful to Christianity. Joseph Coe, for instance, asked to speak to a meeting of Baptists and Presbyterians but "was stopped in a very few minutes."[67] Occasionally, the missionaries gained a longer hearing, and sometimes they even won over the clergy. Mormon missionaries presented themselves not as a new movement with distinct beliefs but as a restoration movement within the Christian tradition, and converts often regarded them this way. Missionaries saw themselves as being like the apostle Paul visiting the synagogues, as when William McLellin received a revelation from the prophet Joseph telling him to go to the East and preach in the "sinagogues."[68] The missionaries were universally disdainful of the clergy whom they encountered, almost always calling them "priests" (it was not a compliment) even though denominations such as Baptists, Disciples, or even Methodists would never use that term themselves. The term drew on popular anticlericalism to imply that "priests" used "priestcraft" to keep their subjects from hearing the restored gospel out of selfish, financial concern.[69] Other times those ministers were more directly called "hireling priests" who preached for "filthy lucre." The missionaries pointed out to listeners that they, like Jesus's disciples, traveled without "Purs or scrip."[70] This proclamation had a stern edge of potential judgment and condemnation of the existing congregations that non-Mormons were a part of: Hazen Aldrich saw himself as "lifting a warning voice in the congregations of the wicked."[71] The missionaries therefore saw it as a duty to preach their message in the churches.

The preaching that a potential convert heard was certainly distinctive, but it also related to what people might have heard from other sources. The preaching of early Mormon missionaries had both restorationist and millennialist elements. The restorationist strain emphasized that the Mormon gospel wished to return to primitive Christianity; the millennialist strain emphasized that their message was being preached in the last days, with judgment near at hand. William McLellin, for instance, spoke "on the covenants and the promises, the glories of the Millenniel day" while he also "exhorted them to embrace the truth and flee from the wrath to come." He "spoke about an hour on the manifest difference between the church of God and the world in all ages that the Bible gives account of," thereby establishing the Mormon claim to be the only truly biblical church. The links between primitivism and the millennialism were "prophecy after prophecy and scripture after scripture, which had reference to the book [of Mormon] and to these days."[72] A listener in the audience would not have thought restorationism or primitivism to be in conflict with millennialism. The content of both of these messages demonstrated the time in which one was living—and thus the decisions that one made—were happening in sacred time. The sacred time of Mormon preaching implied immediacy and urgency. Horace Cowan proclaimed that "the morning of the resurrection and the redemption of the saints draweth nigh and the hour of his coming is nigh."[73]

More often than not, sermon texts were taken from the Bible rather than the Book of Mormon. The Bible was familiar and resonated with potential converts, and (as many other preachers were doing) it was more than possible to get primitivist and millennialist teachings from the Bible itself. The missionaries, like Joseph Coe, sold or distributed the Book of Mormon whenever they had copies, not unlike the American Bible Society colporteurs. But the Book of Mormon was simply too scarce to be made available to everyone. When William McLellin was converting, he bought a Book of Mormon from the missionaries and soon gave it away to another person. When he met more Mormon missionaries, they had run out of Books of Mormon to sell or give him.[74]

When the early Mormon missionaries preached, they more often testified about the Book of Mormon than preached from it. Harvey Whitlock treated the book as divine revelation but mostly described it, giving "some particulars respecting the book and some reasons why he believed it to be a divine revelation."[75] Sometimes William McLellin did not even have a Book of Mormon available for himself.[76] His partner therefore gave a "brief history of the book of Mormon, of its coming forth." But for most of the sermon, he "reasoned upon and expounded prophecy after prophecy and scripture after scripture, which had reference to the book and to these days." In another place, he spoke "on the subject of the coming forth of the book of Mormon about 1 ½ hours."[77] Converts certainly came to regard the Book of Mormon as important, and they often made every effort to read it. But the simple fact that the Book of Mormon had been translated and printed authenticated Mormon preaching to people who already found plausible the idea that the gospel had to be restored.

In their preaching, the Mormon missionaries set forth a clear summary of the Mormon beliefs and practices that were necessary for salvation. They called these a "plan of salvation," implying both a salvation history of how God was saving people, and a set of steps or experiences through which the convert should go.[78] After explaining the Mormon belief in the Bible and Book of Mormon, McLellin preached that "we believe, that faith in God, Repentance and Baptism (by immersion) in the name of the Lord Jesus, for the remission of sins and Laying on of the hands of the Elders for the reception of the holy Spirit, is the plan by which sinners may become reconciled to God or become christians."[79] Parley Parker Pratt, describing his mission efforts around 1835, gave a similar summary description of the steps involved in a Mormon conversion. In Pratt's description, missionaries "preached the Word, and baptized such as desired to be obedient to the faith; confirming them by the laying on of hands and prayer in the name of Jesus Christ; thus the Holy Ghost and the gifts thereof were shed forth among the people, and they had great joy." He emphasized that "many great and marvellous things were prophesied" and that "many persons were carried away in the visions of the Spirit."[80]

The common elements that Mormon missionaries expected of conversions, then, were preaching, faith, baptism, confirmation (and, for men, usually also ordination), and the manifestation of the works of the Spirit. Most of those steps had their roots in the evangelical Protestant pattern of conversion, yet each was made distinctly different. Evangelicals regarded the preaching of the Word as a divinely blessed action that produced faith; Mormons shared that belief but preached a restored gospel. All Christian denominations practiced baptism; Mormons insisted on baptism as a matter of adult choice, thought of it as an efficacious sacrament, required the mode to be immersion, and demanded that all converts undergo rebaptism. Confirmation was a rite practiced by the more liturgical Christian denominations, such as the Catholics and Episcopalians, who also baptized infants, yet Mormons adopted it as a sign of belonging to the church and practiced it immediately after baptism. Only the more ecstatic of Christian groups saw manifestations of the work of the Spirit, but Mormons expected them as a matter of course during conversions.

A potential convert who heard the preaching, and perhaps thought that it was authenticated by the Book of Mormon, would be called by the missionaries to the decisive act of baptism. Baptism was an action that was recognizable and meaningful within the wider systems of belief from which converts came. Baptism was performed whether or not the convert had previously been baptized: it thus functioned as a renunciation of one's previous religion as much as an appropriation of one's new faith. The missionaries described baptism as an act of obedience. Nathan West preached for two weeks in Winchester, Indiana, where "many believed but only two obeighed, to wit Austin Hammer and Hannah York, whom I Baptized."[81]

Converts in the earliest decades were making a significant step by being baptized. This can be seen by how few baptisms there were, relative to the effort that the missionaries made. Most missionaries held many more meetings than they held baptisms. Benjamin Clapp traveled 4,444 miles through Alabama and Mississippi in 1845 and held 176 missions but baptized only 118 people.[82] In his 1835 travels for several months through Missouri, Illinois, and Indiana, Edward Partridge baptized no one.[83] Horace Cowan held 153 meetings in New York and baptized 70.[84] In the aggregate, there were a great number of baptisms.

But converts felt the weight of the meaning of baptism place by place, not in the aggregate. Occasionally, there were baptisms of a dozen people or more, but far more often the number of people baptized in any one place was two or three. To be baptized in such small groups was to make a deliberate stand against the Christian churches in one's community. When people were baptized in groups of two or three, they were often related to one another, like two sisters who were baptized and confirmed together, or Charles Dalton's mother, brother, and sister, who were baptized together in Wisconsin.

A convert who went forward for baptism, and perhaps even a potential convert who merely heard the missionaries preach, would know that he or she was transgressing the norms of the community in a way that they would not by, say, listening to a preacher of a different denomination or by switching Protestant denominations. The most common strategy to avoid Mormon preaching was to refuse to let them hold meetings, as did one "pious" Baptist deacon. In another town, Methodists deliberately held a class meeting at the same time as a Mormon appointment, to keep their members from attending.[85] At other times, there were debates—often about prophecy or the authenticity of the Book of Mormon. Sometimes the resistance took the form of violence. In his travels through the South, Elam Luddington reported that there were "eggs throwed" and windows broken in to disrupt meetings.[86] Especially in the South, missionaries could face physical violence and even extrajudicial killings.[87]

Even if there was no violence, converts could expect resistance from families and neighbors. At a meeting held by Samuel Smith, "the daughter of Mr Barna would have been baptized but her farther would not let her."[88] Other people "gladly recd the word, but would not submit to the book of mormon," perhaps implying resistance to the specific claims of Mormonism.[89] Truman Waiter had to dispute with two "Pharisaical Presbyterians" who, he reported, invited him to explain his message but really debated and "abused" him so that he was obliged to leave.[90] A convert who chose to be baptized was making a serious, hotly contested choice.

After the converts came up out of the waters of baptism, the missionaries laid hands on them and confirmed them. This often happened immediately after baptism, or in some cases a day later. Confirmation was supposed to convey the Holy Spirit, and converts frequently felt manifestations of the Spirit. After baptism by Samuel Smith, converts "were filled with the Holy Ghost and glorified God."[91] When Joseph Coe laid hands on children and converts, the result was "the effusion of the Holy Ghost and ministering angels."[92] At one of William McLellin's baptisms, eight people received the gift of tongues.[93]

Baptism and confirmation were often accompanied by healings. Healings and manifestations of the Spirit demonstrated that potential converts were living both in primitive Christianity and in the last days, and thereby authenticated the missionaries' message.

Horace Cowan recorded that one convert was baptized but slipped and sprained her ankle in the water. He immediately healed the swollen ankle, confirming the power of his message.[94] Daniel Stephens claimed a blanket power to heal and "laid hands on many that were sick which were healed of diverse diseases."[95] Charles Dalton made the message of healing explicit when he healed a man in Wisconsin named Lorenzo Dowd, who "had been confined to his bed for two years." After preaching at the man's home, Dalton asked the crowd if they believed the Bible, and they responded, "If Lorenzo is healed we will beleive Mormonism." He healed the man, who was able to change his clothes and dine with them at the table. Skeptics doubted the miracle, though, saying, "He could have done it before if he had of tried."[96] William McLellin healed a leg "struck with the num[b] palsey"—an ailment that resonated with biblical healings of the lame.[97] Parley Parker Pratt healed a blind woman in Toronto.[98] It is at least possible that some Mormon missionaries claimed to be able to raise the dead, and potential converts at times wanted missionaries to raise the dead as proof of the validity of their message.[99] One missionary said that when converts "receive his Holy Spirit, they may Prophesy, See Visions, Discern Spirits, Do Miracles, Cast out Devils, Heal the sick, &c. and even . . . [like Paul and John] by faith to be enwrapped in the spirit and caught up to behold the wonders and glories of God's Throne and the order of the eternal world."[100]

After converts became Mormons by baptism and by signs and wonders, the question was what would happen to them next. The missionaries would soon move on, and converts needed some kind of structure to continue in their faith. Usually, the missionaries ordained one of the men to be an elder. Almost all Mormon male converts were ordained to be priests—another distinctive feature of Mormonism. The elders would be leaders of the churches that were formed from the new converts. These churches or meetings were often very small. Edward Partridge made a trip in 1835 to visit congregations: he visited twenty-five congregations attended by about seven hundred people, or between twenty-five and thirty people on average at each congregation. He "found the churches doing as well as could reasonably be expected."[101] These churches seem to have

been rather larger than many of the congregations that the missionaries went to, such as the eight member congregation that Lewis
Robbins visited,[102] or the two churches in "Letter B" and one church in
New Hampshire that Horace Cowan founded.[103] On the whole, these
churches were scattered, small, and isolated. This was especially
the case in the South, which saw comparatively few converts.

Yet those small churches were linked by missionary routes that
overlapped with one another. Often, more than one pair of missionaries would visit a settlement. There were multiple opportunities to
attend an appointment when the first missionaries came to town,
then there might be more opportunities when other missionaries arrived. Missionaries joined up and separated every few months, so
the teams of missionaries were different. In the 1840s, at least, missionaries tended to leave in August and come back in June. The missionaries' travels linked the new converts together, connecting
them to a larger Mormon world.

But converts were also invited to join "places of gathering of the
land of zion and the land of jerusalem."[104] In the early days of Mormonism, that meant gathering in Kirtland, Ohio, in Jackson County,
Missouri, or later in Nauvoo, Illinois, as nearly all the missionaries
had done themselves. To gather in was an opportunity to be close to
the prophet Joseph, and some of the missionaries could testify that
they had been baptized, confirmed, or ordained by the prophet himself. Yet gathering in also changed the way that converts experienced
their new faith.

✠

Early Mormonism appealed to converts because they saw it as the
restoration of the primitive gospel. That primitive gospel featured a
renewed emphasis on choice, as defined in the Book of Mormon and
practiced in the ritual of baptism for the remission of sins. Yet that
choice presented itself as a return to an earlier version of Christianity.
Mormon missionaries in the 1830s and early 1840s spread that choice
by traveling and proclaiming their message wherever they went, deliberately trying to visit as many places as possible. The edges of that
choice were sharpened, however, by two aspects of Mormonism.

First, for the duration of the nineteenth century, Mormons practiced a deliberate policy of "gathering in" converts to a central location. Second, as the Mormon message spread, so too did anti-Mormonism. These two factors constituted Mormonism as a distinct kingdom.

Joseph Smith received his revelations in western New York, and he organized the church in Palmyra in 1830. The movement grew significantly and attracted scores of converts who became missionaries. Yet by 1831, the church had moved west to Kirtland, Ohio. The Mormons constructed their first temple in Kirtland, and Smith received continuing revelations that developed the movement further. Mormons also formed their own bank called the Kirtland Safety Society—the beginnings of a long-standing Mormon preference for establishing their own economic institutions.[105] Converts were usually asked to, and often did, gather at Kirtland, which became the center of Mormonism. At the same time, Smith dictated a revelation identifying Independence, in Jackson County, Missouri, as "Zion." The Saints were to gather there to prepare for the second coming of Christ. Yet in 1833, anti-Mormon settlers managed to force the Mormons out of Jackson County; and in 1836, the Missouri legislature created Caldwell County for the Mormons. In 1838 Smith and the other main leaders settled in the town of Far West, Missouri, leaving Kirtland behind.

The policy of gathering in continued in Missouri for several years, until Missouri and Mormon militia came into conflict. The Mormons were forced to leave Missouri and settled in Nauvoo, Illinois, in 1849. The Mormons built a second temple in Nauvoo. The Mormons' political and commercial autonomy grew during their time in Nauvoo, where they ran the city government and even had their own "Nauvoo Legion." Converts poured into the city from around the United States and, indeed, from European countries as well. Smith introduced new practices, including baptism for the dead and the practice of polygamy. Though Smith always publicly denied practicing polygamy, these practices radically distinguished Mormonism from Protestant Christianity and stoked anti-Mormon fires. In 1844, Smith, who was the mayor of Nauvoo, ordered a newspaper called the *Nauvoo Expositor* destroyed when its first issue published salacious critiques of Smith and the Mormon church leadership. When non-Mormons called for his arrest, Smith was imprisoned in Carthage, Illinois, without protection and was killed along with his brother Hyrum by an anti-Mormon mob.

After some wrangling to determine who would succeed Joseph Smith as leader of the Mormons, Brigham Young gained the support of most of the Mormons. Relations between the Mormons and non-Mormons grew worse, and Young eventually led the Latter-day Saints west to settle near the Great Salt Lake in 1847. Over the next several years, the "Mormon Exodus" moved a majority of the adherents of the faith to Utah.[106] Migration to Utah became the norm for many Mormon converts in the United States and abroad. Brigham Young said that emigration "upon the first feasible opportunity, directly follows obedience to the first principles of the gospel we have embraced."[107] Migrants to Utah received support from the Perpetual Emigration Fund, which was founded in 1849 and lasted until the federal government dissolved the corporations owned by the church in 1887. The fund supported converts who were unable to pay their costs to gather in to Utah; they were then expected to repay the costs so that the fund could in turn support other migrants. Perhaps some 30,000 Mormon converts migrated through the aid of the Perpetual Emigration Fund alone, and many more came on their own or with support outside the fund.

Mormon converts migrated for a variety of reasons that pulled them to the Mormon kingdom and that pushed them from their homes. Mormon migration to the United States was certainly encouraged by the more general trend toward increased immigration to the United States. Especially in the late 1840s and 1850s, emigration from Ireland, Great Britain, Germany, France, and the rest of Northern Europe to the United States was encouraged by poor economic prospects, a surplus of labor, and failed revolutions in those countries.

One such migrant was William Adams, who was born in Ireland to Protestant parents. He was religiously trained and remembered defending the "doctrine of everlasting punishment where sinners would be burning in hell for everlasting without end, which was the belief of the Sectarian religious denominations." In 1840, he heard the preaching of two Mormon missionaries, Theodore Curtis and William Black, who "proclaimed that the gospel of Jesus Christ had been restored to earth by a holy angel from heaven to Joseph Smith, a prophet of God in these last days." He studied the Scriptures and rejoiced that the priesthood was restored and that "the gifts of the spirit were enjoyed, the speaking in tongues, the interpretation of tongues, prophesying, etc." He was baptized on March 26, 1842, and confirmed the following Sunday. He originally founded a church in Ireland "which numbered about twenty members," but after the Methodists resisted the group, he left Ireland on the last day of 1843 and traveled to Nauvoo. He arrived in Nauvoo on April 10, 1844, just a couple of months before Joseph Smith was murdered. He then gathered with the Saints in Utah, making the journey to the Great Basin in 1849.[108]

Richard Ballantyne made the journey from Scotland to Utah. He attributed his turn to Mormonism to the Christianity his father had handed down to him. He described his father as a pious man who memorized large portions of the Scripture and who "would not take a drink of cold water till he had first given thanks to his Maker." Though he "died before hearing the fullness of the Gospel" as proclaimed by Joseph Smith, yet Ballantyne thought "he no doubt would have received it had he lived." Ballantyne, a "ruling elder" in a Presbyterian church, had "an open vision of the Son of Man" while he was walking one morning. His own visions seem to have predisposed him to believe the accounts of Joseph Smith's visions. He was first introduced to Mormonism in a letter from his sister, who had met Orson Pratt in Scotland. It took a year of his "investigating the work that I might know whether it was of God and true, or of man" before he was converted to Mormonism in 1842, along with his mother and sister. Ballantyne became a Mormon because he had "obtained a witness of the Holy Ghost that Joseph Smith was a true prophet, and the Book of Mormon a divine Record." He was baptized "for the remission of sins" despite the "risk of losing all my friends, my business, and good name, by being baptized." He did in fact alienate the pastor of his Presbyterian church by giving him a Book of Mormon, though he was "too timid to step forward as a public preacher."[109]

Within a year, he had saved enough money to migrate to Nauvoo with "a large company of Saints," arriving in November 1843. He expressed his "joy, thanksgiving and praise to our God for thus safely landing us among His own Covenant people," declaring that "henceforth this people are my people and their God my God." Ballantyne went on to own a "provision store" on the counsel of one of the elders, which was a part of "God's government in Zion." He was married and sealed, ordained a priest and then a high priest, and served a mission to India.[110]

Ballantyne's niece, Hannah Thompson, was converted in Scotland about the same time. She recalled that her uncle Henry (brother to Richard) was the first to hear Mormon preaching from Orson Pratt and George D. Watt and to "yield to baptism for the remission of sins, and the laying on of hands for the gift of the Holy Ghost." Conversion spread through the family. Her mother was the next to convert, and she had her children, including Margaret and Hannah, baptized "when we reached the age of accountability." The age of accountability was when someone had a sufficiently free will to be aware of his or her sins and choose to convert. Her father, on the other hand, was "too high minded to embrace the Gospel of Jesus Christ, as had been revealed to Joseph Smith the Prophet." But he did not stand in the way when her uncle Richard sent for her and her two sisters to come to Utah as some of the first funded by the Perpetual Emigration Fund. Her father remained in Scotland. But when Richard Ballantyne went through Scotland in returning from his mission to India, he converted his brother-in-law and brought him to Utah. When she was nineteen, Hannah Thompson became the second plural wife of an English convert.[111]

The other factor that sharpened the choice to convert to Mormonism was persistent anti-Mormonism. Anti-Mormonism took many forms. The earliest forms of anti-Mormonism were resistance from the Christian denominations who viewed Mormonism as a heretical and delusive sect. Early Mormonism began with a new revelation, and as it developed new theologies, temple rituals, and practices like baptism for the dead, its difference from Christianity only became more apparent. Once Joseph Smith privately announced the doctrine of plural marriage and the practice became widely known, no other part of Mormonism stirred up more antagonism. Just as in the debate between Campbell and Rice, many Christians actively opposed Mormonism, writing innumerable tracts and books that purported to expose the deceptions of Joseph Smith and his new religion.[112]

Mormons were not reluctant to flex political muscle in places like Kirtland and Nauvoo. Their distinctiveness in religion was coupled to a tendency to run their own affairs and to trade with one another. Mormons also feared violence against their homes, persons, and meeting places. The westward movement of Mormons occurred largely because of the continued resistance that they felt, sometimes coupled with violence. In 1838, for instance, a Missouri mob killed seventeen Mormons and injured others in Caldwell County.

The most powerful form of anti-Mormonism came from the coercive power of the state. In Ohio, Missouri, and Illinois, the Mormons faced resistance from state governments, including their militias. Mormons and non-Mormons more than once fought each other in armed battles. Once most Mormons moved to Utah, they enjoyed considerable independence, especially since the federal government was otherwise occupied with the crisis over slavery and the Civil War, though President James Buchanan did send an army expedition to Utah in 1857–1858 that skirmished with Mormon militia. Mormons even proposed their own state, called Deseret. But after the Civil War, the federal government turned to squash polygamy and the separate political kingdom of the Mormons. The fight against polygamy was linked to the fight against slavery, "the twin relics of barbarism." The Mormons lost a test case, *Reynolds v. United States* (1878), to see whether there was a constitutional exception to laws against polygamy for religious conscience. The Edmunds Anti-Polygamy Act (1882) made it easier to enforce the laws against polygamy, and most of the leadership of the LDS church was driven underground. Then the Edmunds-Tucker Act (1890) unincorporated the LDS church and seized most of its property. It was not until well after Mormons officially abandoned the practice of polygamy in the 1890s that the Mormon church experienced anything approaching freedom of religion.[113] While Mormons continued to make converts, Mormonism's notoriety made clear that a decision to convert was neither simple nor free from consequences.

A large part of the anti-Mormon effort came from those who had converted to Mormonism and then left the faith. While every

religious group had apostates, Mormon apostates were especially
numerous, with even high-placed leaders of the founding generation defecting. And Mormon apostates were especially virulent in
their critiques of the group they had temporarily joined.[114]

One such exposé was published by Frank Johnson, a "disillusioned
convert" to Mormonism. Johnson recognized the origins of Mormonism in Joseph Smith's original vision, while adding a sneer:
"[W]hen Joseph Smith . . . was a boy of 14 he became very anxious
as to which of the three churches where he lived he should join.
(There is no evidence that he was fit to join any; but plenty to the
contrary.)" Johnson had been a Disciple of Christ who heard Mormon
preaching in 1899, then converted and traveled to Utah. He accused
the Mormons of being interested only in "money, money, money, all
the time; no Gospel at all." He claimed that the missionaries told him
polygamy had been abandoned, only to find that Mormons continued
to practice it secretly when he arrived in Utah. He called on Christians to continue to resist Mormonism and portrayed the issue as one
of religious competition between true Christianity and falsehood.
Christians should "help others to know the facts as to the real character of the Mormon system, that they may not fall into its snare and
may both hinder the efforts of its emissaries to make fresh victims
and help the Western work for its deluded people." And the best way
to do that was "by loving, Christian gospel work," that would help
Mormons to an "experience of personal salvation in Christ."[115]

David Claiborne wrote a tract about, as the subtitle put it, "how
he was lured into Mormonism, and how he found the light again."
Claiborne's narrative illustrates how Mormon converts, especially
outside of Utah, faced immense pressure about the choice they had
made. Claiborne was born into a Baptist family in South Carolina
in 1868. He was "inclined to be of a religious disposition" as a child
and experienced his "first conversion to Christianity" in 1887. He
converted because of the preaching of the Salvation Army, then
joined Mount Morris Baptist Church. About the same time that he
grew estranged from the church and the pastor, he received tracts
from Mormon missionaries. He converted to Mormonism after "six
months of reading Mormon books, and tracts, and numerous talks
in private and in public." He found the Mormon practice of baptism

by immersion familiar and their unity appealing. He was baptized on June 22, 1901, in Jersey City in New York Bay and ordained to the Mormon priesthood. Yet soon he went to a YMCA lecture against Mormonism and was visited by Protestant missionaries who sought to dissuade him. "After reading this lot of literature," likely including exposés by other ex-Mormons, he was in an "awful state of mind, and could not rest night or day." After repenting of his Mormon conversion, he was again received by the Baptist church.[116]

Apostates from the Mormon church, whether they were Sidney Rigdon early in the century or Claiborne at the end of the century, did much to define the boundaries of Mormonism. They showed that converts who had chosen to join the church might just as well choose to leave it.

✠

Yet most Mormon converts chose to remain. Mormonism grew rapidly, taking in members from across the United States and from Europe and sending missionaries around the world. From its humble beginnings with six members in 1830, it had nearly 284,000 members on the books by 1900.[117] While Mormons remained small compared to Baptists, Methodists, and Presbyterians, they had an impact out of proportion to their size. The animosity that Mormons generated and the capillary reach of their pairs of missionaries meant that Mormonism presented itself to many more Americans than actually joined the church or migrated to Utah. Mormons may have been pushed to the margins of American geography, but they remained central to the concerns of American religious life.

In one crucial way, Mormonism was the epitome of religion in the nineteenth-century United States. The spread of the evangelical call for conversion in missions, evangelism, and the distribution of conversionary literature in the Second Great Awakening were matched by the proliferation of religious groups that one could join. Denominational competition, like the debates between Rice and Campbell, or the preaching of Mormon evangelists and the resistance of Christian ministers, pushed more and more people into deciding which religious group they would join. Many restorationist groups, from the Millerites to the Shakers to the Disciples of Christ, tried to establish the certainty of their faith by resorting to a primitive reading of the Scriptures or new revelation. Mormons, with the prophecies of Joseph Smith and the Book of Mormon, were the most successful of the restorationist groups, and they spread their message far and wide. Confronting many people with the restored gospel, they obligated them to choose for or against Mormonism. Thus Mormonism represented a protest against the sect system, even as it became yet another option within that system, further entrenching religion in the United States as a system of choice.

5

Sincerity

JEWISH CONVERTS
AND RESISTANCE TO MISSIONS

SARAH JANE PICKEN COHEN spent half her life as a Jew, and half as a Christian. Her name tells the story of her two conversions. Jane Picken was born in New York to a Scottish Presbyterian and an English Anglican. Orphaned as a child, Jane spent her youth under the tutelage of a "confirmed Deist," who parodied Methodist hymns and "utterly rejected revealed religion." As a result, Picken grew up knowing little of her parents' Christianity. In 1806, she met Abraham Cohen at a party in Philadelphia. Cohen was the son of the *hazzan* (cantor) of Congregation Mikveh Israel, a prominent Philadelphia synagogue. Within three weeks, they were engaged.[1] A quick courtship did not ensure a quick intermarriage. Abraham's father, Jacob Cohen, backed by the synagogue leadership, would permit Abraham to marry only a Jew. Abraham Cohen was called before the leaders of the synagogue and questioned by his father, who wanted "his only son to represent him when he was no more." Abraham was obligated to swear an oath "to marry none but a Jewess."[2]

Cohen hesitated before trying to persuade Picken to convert, yet he found a willing proselyte. Cohen "portrayed in glowing colors the beauties of the Jewish religion, as handed down in the laws of Moses" and argued for "its divine origin, being the first and only true religion." Picken was persuaded on intellectual and aesthetic grounds, agreeing "to adopt the faith of the Jewish church" because "there was great sublimity in the representation he had given me." Though Cohen explained Judaism as a system of theological truth, Picken was stirred more by the aesthetic aspects of Jewish rituals and holidays, especially the lighting of Sabbath candles and the Sabbath meal.[3] Having agreed to become a Jew, Picken lived for thirty days with the Lurias of Philadelphia, relatives of her soon-to-be mother-in-law. Among the Lurias, she was "instructed in the rites and ceremonies of the Jewish household duties, with dietetical prohibitions and usual modes of living."[4]

Once her training as a Jewish wife was complete, Jane Picken was ritually converted, a process that she described in greater detail than any other nineteenth-century American woman who converted to Judaism. The leaders took Picken to the river several miles outside Philadelphia, where "a nice little bath-room had been built over this beautiful stream, with a flight of steps to descend."[5] The bathhouse, which covered the synagogue's *mikveh* (ritual bath), completely hid the convert and her female attendant from outside eyes for modesty's sake. Wearing a veil and white robe, Picken walked down the steps into the water with her attendant, whose job was to make sure she was completely immersed. She was "pressed under the water, and allowed to rise" three times. She stepped out of the water and was robed as the elders sang a hymn.

During the ceremony, she received a new name as a proselyte. A common choice for female converts was Ruth, after the biblical Moabite who became a Hebrew, but Jane became Sarah, after the wife of the biblical patriarch Abraham. Though an orphan, she was reborn as a proselyte with a new genealogy: "bat Avraham Avinu," "the daughter of Abraham our Father." A week later, she married her own Abraham and took his surname Cohen, the ancient Hebrew word for "priest." For the rest of her life, she would sign her name "Mrs. S. J. Cohen."[6]

Though the change of name symbolized a total transformation, Cohen worried that her conversion had been merely nominal, as she came to question the sincerity of her conversion to Judaism. Looking back on her life as an elderly widow who had returned to Christianity, Cohen saw sincerity as the central concern in both her "ceremonial" conversion to Judaism and her "heart" conversion to Christianity. One way of judging sincerity was by the standards of the *halakhah* (Jewish law), which required an examination of a proselyte's reasons for converting. Her nephew Raphael Moses believed that "she went through the usual probation of converts so as to ascertain whether she was influenced by any other motive than a conviction of the truth of Judaism."[7] Certainly, the *halakhah* required, and American synagogues usually followed, the practice of questioning converts about whether they believed in the unity of God and were sincere in their conversion, even though in Cohen's case there could be no doubt that her motives were mixed. It is difficult to know whether Cohen accurately remembered the questions put to her fifty years earlier, but she later maintained that "I had only to express my wish to become a proselyte—no inquiry was made as to my motive or former belief in joining the Jewish church."[8]

Though the ceremony of conversion had remade her into a new person, Cohen tried to think of her new religion in terms of the old. Before converting, she had seen in the "Jewish rites . . . nothing but what the most devout Christian might conform to." She kept a strictly observant Jewish home for several decades during her marriage, while her husband served as *hazzan* in Philadelphia and then Richmond. "I remember visiting her at her house in New York, in my boyhood," wrote Raphael Moses, "when she was scrupulously particular in adhering to all Jewish forms, dieting and others."[9] But she persisted for several years in thinking of the Sabbath meal "like the Christian communion."[10] When her first son was born, she found the circumcision so trying that she prayed she would have no more sons. From that date, she began "close self-examination," which led to the feeling that she had "erred, grievously erred, in forsaking my people."

In 1814, after her first son died at the age of four, Cohen fell desperately ill.[11] On what she thought was her deathbed, her doctor and a friend, both Christians, urged her to turn to Jesus. Cohen had a vision of Satan, arrayed like "one of the gay throng I had mingled with in former days," then a vision of Jesus, bleeding, who promised, "Though thy sins be as scarlet, they shall be white as wool."[12] In the morning, Cohen felt that "my load of sin was gone, gone" and that "my soul [was] redeemed from death." In contrast to her life as a Jewish convert, Cohen thought, "*This* was conversion—deep and heartfelt conversion."[13]

The Cohens' marriage was shaken—but not broken—by her conversion. Abraham was furious at the change in his wife, but after the initial shock, he was willing to permit his wife her Christianity, provided she kept it a secret. Sarah too wished to do everything possible to keep the marriage together, but she warned that she could bear to "be called an apostate, but never a hypocrite."[14] The marriage survived because it had already been strong: Sarah Cohen always insisted that her husband was a good and gracious man. The Cohens lived together for a decade more. There were struggles over raising the children: Sarah taught her second son, Henry, the Lord's Prayer, and Abraham forbade him to recite it. It was Henry's precocious conversion to Christianity and his death from scarlet fever that forced the couple's final separation. They separated in 1831 after twenty-five years of marriage. Of their daughters who survived to adulthood, one chose to live with her father as a Jew, and two with their mother as Christians.[15]

The Cohens were able to work out a temporary *modus vivendi* because of a shared vernacular idea about conversion. They both believed that their births and education shaped their natural religions, which conversion could not change. Thus Abraham reconciled himself to his wife's reconversion on the grounds that she had "descended from Christian parents, who in early life instructed you in the Christian religion." But he could not become a Christian himself because his Judaism was "that blessed religion to which by birth I am entitled, and grafted more firmly by the force of education." In explaining her husband's anger to her readers, Sarah asked that they "readily make allowance for one who was a Jew by birth and principle, descending in a direct line from the priesthood."[16] This idea was a frequent resort of husbands and wives trying to work out the difficulties of intermarriage.[17]

Though Cohen's return to Christianity was seen to confirm this theory, by the end of the century conversions across religious lines had shaken, though not totally defeated, the idea of a natural religion. Jews by and large did not convert to Christianity, despite a widespread missions movement, in large part because they crafted an alternative narrative of conversions that called the sincerity of converts into question.

✠

Converts both to and from Judaism were consumed with questions of sincerity. Jews who became Christians had to conform to the requirements of heart religion, as in Cohen's "heartfelt" return to Christianity, while Christians who became Jews had to meet the test of their motives required by the *halakhah*, as in Cohen's conversion to Judaism. The heart versus ritual, grace versus the law—however reductive those concepts were, and however little Jews and Christians understood one another's faith, the dichotomies between those terms shaped the boundaries between the religions. As in so many other questions, the two religions had very different and incompatible conceptions of what constituted sincerity, and they therefore mischaracterized and mistrusted each other. Converts between Judaism and Christianity had their sincerity tested not just by the religion that received them, but by the religion they had left. At issue was whether converts could actually make a sincere choice of a different religion. In the middle of the century, Sarah and Abraham Cohen concluded that choosing a different religion could not erase the imprint that birth and education made on a person's religious identity. By the end of the century, culture gave wider latitude for individual self-fashioning in general, but in this specific case Jews and Christians came to think of sincerity in terms of economic metaphors. In the unending polemical debates between Jews and Christians, carried on in newspapers, books, and pamphlets, on street corners and in homes, synagogues, and churches, converts had their sincerity tested in the assayer's fire.

The public test of sincerity contributed in no small part to limiting the numbers of conversions of Jews to Christianity. While it would be a half century more until the United States could be called the land of "Protestant-Catholic-Jew," the crucial point settled by the end of the nineteenth century was that Jews would not have to convert before fully taking their place as citizens. The history of conversions between Judaism and Christianity is as much a history of Jews who did not convert as those who did. The result was that conversions between Judaism and Christianity took on a peculiar cast, and its possibility received greater scrutiny and doubt than other types of conversions. Yet Jews, who were constantly mission-ized, had to continually justify their refusal to convert.[18]

Not only did Jews manage to hold their own; in the United States, Jews even made proselytes out of Christians. To be sure, Christians had converted to Judaism in early modern Europe, but often secretly and at risk of life and property, because Jews were usually forbidden by law to proselytize. In America, Christians were free to convert to Judaism. Polemicists such as Isaac Mayer Wise trumpeted them in Jewish papers, religious enthusiasts like Warder Cresson published their narratives to encourage others to convert, and journalists re-ported on conversions to Judaism as a matter of public interest but not concern. For Protestants, converts to Judaism were a reminder of the limits of their religion. These proselytes also raised a number of practical religious and legal questions for Jews. Sometimes the question was whether conversions were valid according to the *halakhah;* other times, the question was whether Judaism's central mission was to convert the Gentiles to pure monotheism.

Christians actively missionized Jews, but Jews were far more re-luctant to proselytize Christians, both because they had a different conception of salvation and from a long-standing caution about making proselytes. Because of their numbers and status as the ma-jority religion, Protestant Christians had the political power to shape laws toward Christian ends. Then, too, during the nine-teenth century the proportion of Jews in the general population never rose above 1.4 percent.[19] Christians could convert to Ju-daism only at places where there were Jews, but everywhere Jews went, there were Christians.

✠

The competition between Judaism and Christianity carried over from the Old World, but in America, the competition proceeded under New World rules.[20] Sephardi Jews had memories of Catholic persecution under the Spanish and Italian Inquisitions in the not-so-distant past; Ashkenazi Jews recalled ongoing oppression under the Russian empire. After immigrating to the United States, Rabbi Max Lilienthal wrote an exposé of forced conversions in Russia. As a young German rabbi educated in both traditional Jewish learning and *Wissenschaft des Judentums*, Lilienthal had been hired by the czarist regime to modernize the education of Jews. After a few years, Lilienthal grew disillusioned with his job, accusing Czar Nicholas I and earlier czars of supporting liberal education for Jews as a cloak to convert Jews to the "Greek religion," that is, Orthodox Christianity. Writing in the *Asmonean*, Lilienthal explained how Russian Jews were pressured by the state to convert. Liberal education—otherwise a positive good—was intended to strip Jews of their identities. The czar required reports about how many Jews were being converted, a none-too-subtle hint to underlings that the numbers were too low. The state also made a point of impressing Jews into the army, where advancement required conversion to Orthodox Christianity. Jewish soldiers were taught Christian catechisms. One general drove all his Jewish soldiers at bayonet point into a church and had them forcibly baptized.[21]

Conversions of Jews by state-sponsored force were not limited to Russia. The most famous nineteenth-century case was that of Edgardo Mortara, a Jew born in Bologna, Italy, in 1851. When Mortara fell sick as an infant, a Catholic servant girl performed the rite of emergency baptism. Mortara was thus, in the eyes of the Roman Catholic Church, a Christian; because Bologna was at the time part of the Papal States, the church was also the civil authority. In 1858, five years after the baptism, Mortara was taken from his family by force since the law forbade Jews to raise Christian children. After a trial, Mortara was permanently removed from his family and adopted by Pope Pius IX. Mortara himself took the name Pius and became an Augustinian friar and preacher. The Mortara affair caused an international uproar. The British Jewish leader Sir Moses Montefiore tried to have Mortara returned to his parents, and the American press inveighed against Catholic tyranny.[22]

Other cases of forcible baptism and kidnapping were less well known. Augusta Ellis Johnson and Abraham Johnson married at Congregation Shearith Israel in New York in 1847, then lived in Lima, Peru, where Abraham was a merchant. In 1868, the widowed Augusta Johnson wrote a series of petitions to Alvin P. Horey, the U.S. minister to Peru, begging for his intervention in the case of her son, Joseph, who had run away from home. Joseph had been detained in the Convent of the Descalzos with the support of Peruvian authorities. On exactly what basis the Spanish friars took Joseph is unclear, but Horey saw what purported to be a letter from Joseph to Bishop Thespia that stated, "He believes the Catholic religion to be the true one, and is fully determined to embrace it; but that for this desire you opposed him and threatened him with personal violence should he carry his wishes into effect." Joseph was baptized on October 2, 1868. Augusta Johnson disputed that her son was able to make his own choice of religion: "You certainly cannot pretend that a boy of 14 years old, raised according to the Jewish faith be a competent judge as to what is or what is not the true religion." It is unknown whether Joseph was restored to Johnson, though it is unlikely, despite her plea that "American citizens whatever be their faith or religious creed must and will be protected, by our government."[23]

In the United States, however, Jews felt that they lived under a fairer set of ground rules. As Gershom Mendes Seixas, the *hazzan* of Shearith Israel in New York, wrote to Hannah Adams in 1810, "the United States of America is perhaps the only place where the Jews have not suffered persecution, but rather the reverse."[24] Though the federal Constitution's protection of religious freedom was terse, not to say cryptic, most states had fuller guarantees of religious freedom, especially protecting freedom of conscience.[25] In particular, the Constitution's provision that no test oaths would be required for holding an office was a gain for Jews, who had been excluded from office by such oaths. American Jews had substantial reason to think that the state would not coerce them into conversion and might even protect them against the religious majority.

Jews saw these constitutional provisions not just as laying down legal boundaries, but as setting the tone for religious freedom in society. Historian Sarah Barringer Gordon has called this tendency "popular constitutionality," meaning that religious actors often regard "the spirit of the law" as being normative, though legal authorities treat the law as being considerably more constrained.[26] It was just this phenomenon that gave Jews the powerful argument that their religion was as legitimately American as Protestant Christianity. Isaac Leeser, a prominent Jewish leader in Philadelphia and editor of *The Occident*, linked the question of sincerity of converts and liberty of conscience. A reader wrote to Leeser, complaining of "the habit which Jewish editors have got, of treating all professed converts from their ranks as sheer impostors." Leeser thought the more important question was what proselytizing did to a society where religions had unequal numbers of adherents. While he admitted that "a Christian individual" might have "the moral right to persuade an individual Jew to embrace his belief," he argued that *"combinations* of many to act upon the few are an anomaly in a free country, where the few have an equal right to pursue their religion as the mass, or rather the greater masses around them."[27]

Still, none of this precluded interreligious wrangling over the use of state power to encourage conversions and over whether to be American meant to be a Christian. It did mean that religion was fought over at a lower level of law. The conflict came at the level of the law of incorporation and the building of institutions; it came over people who tried to persuade neighbors to convert. So while religious conflict between Judaism and Christianity was everywhere present—as indeed it was between most other religious groups in America—it was a conflict that took place primarily in social and cultural terms, and at most in the level of everyday law, and not at the highest reaches of society's power to define and exclude.[28]

✠

The conversion of the Jews had long been a concern of Christians in North America, extending back to the earliest days of Massachusetts Bay before there may even have been any Jews in the colony. John Eliot, the missionary to the Indian nations of New England, believed that the Indians were Jews and that their conversion would bring about the end times.[29] The earliest known conversion of a Jew in North America was the 1722 conversion of Judah Monis, who took an instructorship in Hebrew at Harvard College, despite the New England clergy's apparent doubts about the sincerity of his conversion.[30]

The first group of Christians established to evangelize the Jews was organized in Boston. The founder was Hannah Adams, whom we have already met as a writer of history and religion. Correspondence with the French abbé Henri-Baptiste Gregoire convinced her to begin a *History of the Jews*. She was rescued from a writer's penury by an annuity paid by a number of "benevolent gentlemen" who had also founded the Boston Athenaeum, including Josiah Quincy, Stephen Higginson, William Shaw, and Joseph Buckminster. Because of her limited sources, the *History* mostly concerned itself with how Christians had treated Jews since the destruction of Jerusalem. Adams paid attention to places where Jews received guarantees that they would not be forcibly converted or where they were threatened with forcible conversion. Adams objected to "the mistaken zeal of those who sought to convert them by force." She also took special note of conversions to Christianity, from ancient times, through Europe in the Middle Ages, to Judah Monis in colonial Massachusetts.[31]

From studying Jewish history, Adams was moved to attempt to convert Jews. A friend recalled that people thought of Adams as a walking version of her books, but "many said, 'if you want to know Miss Adams, you must talk to her about the Jews.' And this last was, indeed, a subject that always called forth the energy of her mind."[32] Close to home, she corresponded with Ezra Stiles, a Congregationalist minister and president of Yale College who was insatiably curious about other religions. Stiles had corresponded with Gershom Seixas and repeatedly attended the synagogue at Newport when rabbis visited from Europe or the Caribbean. Adams's research also connected her to a broader transatlantic network involved in the conversion of the Jews. She read the conversion narrative of Joseph S. C. F. Frey, a Jewish convert to Christianity who was serving as a missionary with the London Society for Promoting Christianity among the Jews.[33] Adams opened a correspondence with that society and formed her own.[34]

The Female Society of Boston and the Vicinity for Promoting Christianity amongst the Jews was founded in 1816. It had among its members elite women of Boston, but at a subscription rate of only 52 cents per year ($10 for a lifetime membership) even people of lesser means, like Hannah Adams herself, could join. The leaders of this movement were not evangelical Christians, but mostly Boston Unitarians.[35] A handful of auxiliary societies formed mostly in Massachusetts to funnel donations to the Boston society. The society accomplished little. It passed along most of its donations to the London society to translate the New Testament into Hebrew and to educate Jewish children in Bombay. Other than $30 spent on "the assistance of a destitute Jew," the society's reach was limited to hopes of acquiring "a couple of male orphans . . . whom they may take under their protection, and educate in the principles of Christianity," following the model of the London society.[36] The lifetime membership proved not to be a bargain when the society folded after a few years.

Local attempts to evangelize the Jews moved to the national stage when the American Society to Colonize and Evangelize the Jews was founded in New York in 1820.[37] With its purpose clearly stated in its title, the group ran into difficulty when it sought incorporation. In New York, as in all the other states, corporate charters were seen more as instruments of governance than of business. For example, in Massachusetts after the Revolution, some two-thirds of corporations were "bodies politic," such as towns, and the rest were mostly benevolent or religious institutions. Legislatures granted corporate status only to institutions that advanced the public good.[38] The New York legislature balked at incorporating an organization to convert Jews, and it required the group to change its name (and nominal purpose) to the American Society for Meliorating the Condition of the Jews (ASMCJ). Mordecai M. Noah, the editor of the Democratic Party paper *The National Advocate* and an up-and-coming politician, thought he had instigated the legislature to force the change "from delicacy towards me." "While the party had a Jew for their political editor," Noah reported, "it would be rather ungracious, under his very nose, to pass an act converting him to Christianity." Noah objected to the organization's vague name, however, and preferred an "honest and candid avowal of the real object" of evangelism.[39] The stronger objection may have been constitutional. New York's constitution guaranteed liberty of conscience, and the grant of quasi-governmental powers to a corporation to evangelize Jews was judged to violate the religious liberties of that group.[40]

The charter permitted the ASMCJ to establish "a colony" in New York for Jews who had already converted to Christianity in Europe.

The colony was to be a "refuge for those who embrace the Christian faith—cast out and deprived of the means of obtaining subsistence." The society had heard of converts who had "been obliged to return to Judaism to keep themselves from starving" and feared that destitution might keep other Jews from accepting Christianity. The ASMCJ purchased a farm in Westchester County, New York, where Jews would learn agriculture and trades. Mordecai Noah saw the farm in a different light: the ASMCJ "endeavoured to obtain converts by appealing to their cupidity—by bringing them on a farm—by providing for their indolent wants—by making religion comfortable, luxurious, and desirable." Noah denied that charity could lead to honest conversion: "A bad Jew, thus purchased, can never make a good Christian."[41]

Over the next three decades, the ASMCJ was a moderate success as an institution. Its board boasted prominent men, most notably Secretary of State John Quincy Adams as an honorary vice president. The organization did face ongoing difficulties in unifying the various Protestant denominations represented in its constituency. But by its fifth year, the ASMCJ had 322 auxiliary societies, mostly in New York, New Jersey, and New England, and these societies raised an impressive amount of money. The ASMCJ was among the earliest organizations of the benevolence and reform movement that swept the nation following the War of 1812. The ASMCJ also reached across the Atlantic. Besides its connection to the London Society, the ASMCJ had an agreement with the German count Adelbert von der Recke, who presided over an institution for Jewish proselytes called Düsselthal Abbey in the west of Germany, on which the ASMCJ modeled its farm. Von der Recke sent some of his most promising converts to the ASMCJ to serve as missionaries. For thirteen years, the ASMCJ published a newspaper, *Israel's Advocate*. It sent missionaries traveling throughout the country, preaching and raising money.[42]

The ASMCJ was able to gain such a widespread network because of the symbolic importance of converting the Jews. The "stiffneck" of Jews refusing to convert to Christianity was a common theme in the Christian New Testament. Nineteenth-century Christians also added a highly specific concern for the end times. At least since the sixteenth century, Jews were vaguely associated in Protestant eschatology with the coming of the end times. The leaders of the ASMCJ made their interpretations of prophecy much more specific. The conversion of the Jews would lead to the end of the world, since the book of Revelation prophesied that 144,000 converted Jews would evangelize the world. These prophetic ideas were repeated with only small variation and little originality in every sermon delivered at the annual gatherings of the ASMCJ and its affiliate societies. Historians have usually attributed the rise of dispensational Protestantism to John Darby, C. I. Scofield, and other writers at the end of the nineteenth and the beginning of the twentieth centuries. But dispensationalists were able to find receptive ground for their innovations because American Protestants had long been prepared to regard the conversion of the Jews as the harbinger and consummation of the age. The theological concerns were the same: the prophecies of Revelation and Romans 9–11 about God's program for the Jews were interpreted not through supersessionism (the doctrine that the church had entirely replaced the people of Israel in redemption history) but through the idea that God worked in different ways at different periods of time and would return to the redemption of Israel. The key term of the sermons to the ASMCJ was *dispensation*, used in the same technical sense as the later *dispensationalism*.[43]

The only thing the ASMCJ was not good at was converting Jews. Its annual reports struck an endlessly hopeful note, but reported conversions were few and mostly unsubstantiated. Only a handful of Jews ever lived on the Westchester farm, and few of them went on to be missionaries. The ineffectiveness of the ASMCJ demonstrated the limits of voluntary organizations to coerce. Unlike other moral reform movements, such as abolition and temperance, the evangelism of Jews in America could never use the coercive power of the state to accomplish its aims.[44]

The legacy of the ASMCJ was the Jewish converts who immigrated to the United States to become missionaries for the organization. These included the Polish convert Bernard Jadownicky, the German converts Erasmus H. Simon and his wife, Frederick Gustavus Primker, John Edward Zadig, John David Marc, and J. S. C. F. Frey.[45] These converts had a disproportionate effect in promoting

efforts to evangelize Jews in America. Marc's letters and Frey's narratives, along with Frey's presence in New York, had spurred American Christians to organize the Female Society of Boston and the
ASMCJ in the first place. At annual meetings, convert missionaries
gave advice about how to convert Jews.[46] These missionaries, by their
actions and the reactions they spurred in the Jewish press, set the
prototype for missionaries to the Jews for the rest of the century. The
most famous of these, and the most hated, was Joseph Samuel Christian Frederick Frey.

✛

Frey was born Joseph Samuel Levy in Franconia, Germany, in 1771,
the son of a Hebrew tutor who also served a minor role in the synagogue in Maynstockheim. Frey received a Jewish education typical
of preemancipation Germany. Contrary to later stories that circulated about him, Frey was neither ignorant of Judaism nor ordained
as a rabbi. As in many narratives of converts from Judaism, he described his Jewish education at length, in particular complaining that
the Hebrew Bible was mostly passed over in favor of the Talmud.
Frey later recalled being inoculated against Christianity through the
reading of the *Toledot Yeshu* (a parody of the Christian Gospels),
though of all the details of his education, this is perhaps the one most
likely to have been embellished for Christian readers. He later became a *shohet* (ritual slaughterer) and claimed to have been a *hazzan*
in a German synagogue. Education was a favorite theme of both conversion narratives and missionary pamphlets, the idea being that
education shaped one's future religious experience and that small details of one's education, such as an encounter with the Bible, could
be the seeds of a future conversion. Frey regarded his Jewish education as a proto-Christian past, in much the same way that a Christian
interpretation of the Hebrew Bible understands it as a proto-
Christian Old Testament.[47] Furthermore, explaining Jewish customs
aroused Christian readers' reliable fascination with Jews.[48]

 After finishing his education around age twenty-two, Frey "resolved to travel," seeking a position as *melammed* (tutor), *hazzan*, or
shohet. If Frey told the truth in his memoirs, he lost several possible

jobs because of his strict observance; his critics claimed he was simply incompetent. Desperate and impoverished, Frey went to Schwerin to take a (nonexistent) position as a tutor. He traveled with a Christian merchant's clerk and with a nonobservant Jew. The Christian tried to persuade both Jews to convert, and a line that the clerk spoke to the non-observant Jew lodged in Frey's memory: "You . . . are neither a Jew nor a Christian, neither cold nor hot. If you think yourself freed from the Jewish ceremonies you should become a Christian."[49]

Frey was forced out of Schwerin by a law that forbade Jews from staying overnight in the city, and he took lodging in Gistrow at the same inn as his "Christian friend." Frey attended synagogue services on Friday night. At the synagogue, "the most honorable Jew in the place," who knew his father, invited him to dinner the next night. The impoverished young man decided to play both angles. On Saturday morning, after a troubled night, Frey wrote a letter to the clerk to "inquire into the truth of Christianity," quite probably as a ruse to seek a job, then returned to the synagogue for services.

Frey was stricken when he returned home from the synagogue. Never mind the act of inquiring after Christianity; the physical act of writing was a violation of the Sabbath. The argument his Christian friend had made to the nonobservant Jew hit Frey with a new force: "My conscience was now awakened, and it loudly told me that I was no longer a Jew, for that I had broken the Sabbath." Whether Frey's inquiry after the truth of Christianity was genuine, or whether it was simply a ploy for a job from the friendly Christian tobacco merchant, or both, cannot be determined from Frey's account. But by writing on the Sabbath, Frey at once inquired after the truth of Christianity and inadvertently destroyed his sense of identity as a strictly observant Jew.[50]

For three years, Frey was instructed twice a week by a Lutheran pastor. The catechesis emphasized intellect, not piety, and it soon produced an intellectual conversion: "My judgment was soon convinced that Jesus of Nazareth was the Messiah, and that his doctrine brings much greater glory to God, and peace and good will towards men, than that of Moses." On May 8, 1798, Frey was baptized by sprinkling by a Lutheran minister. At the baptism, Joseph Samuel

Levy became Joseph Samuel Christian Frederick Frey. His priestly surname Levy was replaced by three names indicating his conversion: Christian, a tribute to his new religion; Frederick, meaning "gift of peace"; and Frey, from the German *frei*, meaning "free."[51] Frey then underwent a lengthy series of other conversions. He attended the meeting of a group of Pietist Christians, with whom he experienced a heart conversion: "From that moment, I was led to rejoice in the salvation of God my Savior, and felt the love of God shed abroad in my heart." Frey moved to London to train to be a foreign missionary but was instead kept on by the London Society as a missionary to the Jews. After immigrating to the United States, Frey became a Presbyterian and, later, a Baptist, which entailed being baptized a second time by immersion.

Frey's life became the best-known story of a Jewish convert in the antebellum United States. Frey's credibility was tested the moment he disembarked in New York. An anonymous pamphlet, *Tobit's Letters to Levi; or, A Reply to the Narrative of Joseph Samuel C. F. Frey*, set out to discredit Frey. The most serious allegation was that Frey had committed adultery while in the employ of the London Society. Frey's departure from England to the United States lent credence to this claim among Jews. The charge probably did little harm to Frey among Christians, who hired him for the ASMCJ anyway. The other main allegation was that Frey was worthless as a missionary. Hannah Adams read in the *Christian Magazine* before Frey's arrival that he had converted thirty-one Jews.[52] Tobit, who likely had information from London, asserted that Frey had converted only the poor or shiftless among London's Jews, who were interested only in handouts from the missionaries rather than Christianity. Tobit's refrain was that the missionaries got what they paid for—not very much. Jews in New York reprinted a lengthy and witty London tract against Frey by Jakob Nikelsburger, who had challenged Frey to a debate that Frey apparently never accepted.[53] Some early Jewish periodicals in America got their start in part from opposing Frey and the ASMCJ. Several years later, Isaac Leeser published articles against Frey in the first two issues of *The Occident*.[54]

Allegations against Frey appeared more credible once Christians developed their own suspicions about his finances. Frey spent several decades as an agent of the ASMCJ, preaching mostly to Christians and raising funds. In 1821, for example, Frey was paid $893.03 in salary and expenses, a respectable if not a lavish amount, while he helped raise $5,841.29. But by 1840, Frey cost the society more than he brought in, and British and American Jews alleged that Frey had his hand in the till. In a special report delivered to the ASMCJ and printed at his own expense, Frey tried to clear his name. Though publishing his conversion narrative had brought him fame, it was publishing his narratives and other books at his own expense that gave him financial trouble.[55] Frey had to write books because he "had but little opportunity of preaching to my Jewish brethren. . . . As I could not preach to my brethren, I resolved to write to them." When Frey was sent to London in 1838 to raise money for the ASMCJ and sell books to pay his debts, the ASMCJ either did not trust him or could not afford him, so he went on the three years' journey accepting only an expense account without a salary. Even his expenses were disputed. Frey, unable to raise money in Britain or to sell his books, was turned down for the money he requested. The ASMCJ resolved that though "this Board are pained to learn that the pecuniary circumstances of Mr. Frey are in such an embarrassed condition as he describes . . . this Board is not bound to grant him any aid, nor has he any claim whatever upon this Society." Frey was left only the humiliation of stating his case in a pamphlet and requesting that donations be sent to his house.[56]

In part, Frey was discredited because his self-created persona was a lightning rod for opposition. His shifts in religious opinion also drew scrutiny. Further, he largely failed at the financial tasks with which he was entrusted. Because of his fame, Frey became the prototypical convert to Christianity from Judaism, and suspicions about his probity help explain why there were so few others.

✠

Over the coming decades, whenever Jews became Christians, they were accused of converting because they were paid to do so or were too shiftless to get a job. Such converts were frequently mentioned in print, often by name, by Jews seeking to shame the convert. For example, a young man named David converted to Christianity in Philadelphia in 1848. A Jewish printer appended a description of David's conversion to a reprint of a tract written by an English Jew against the British efforts at Jewish evangelism. The printer claimed that David was "well known to be a lazy, indolent individual" who was "not capable of earning his living by physical means." One Mr. Bokum, a missionary, deceived by David's "shrewdness," paid for David's lodging at a hotel, "clothed him in a decent suit of apparel, and gave him twenty-five dollars in cash" before the baptism. Whether or not Bokum intended the gift as a bribe or as charity, the printer claimed that David would take advantage of Christians by an "appeal to the purses of a duped community whenever he wished for money." The printer added that the expenditure of $160,000 by the ASMCJ had netted only the "wonderful conversion of TWO individuals." He warned Christians that "Christian priestcraft . . . forces the mite from the widow's purse" to pay for ill-conceived missions to the Jews, and so he appealed to the "servant girl [to] keep her coppers, and the rich, humbugged enthusiast his gold and silver."[57]

Isaac Mayer Wise, a prominent rabbi and leader of the American Reform movement, made the same appeal to Christians to keep their money: if Christians knew that "not five Jews a year are converted in this country; and secondly, among the five converts there are generally three rascals and two vagabonds, they would not throw away their money."[58] "Those who call themselves converted Jews are certainly impostors, that really believe nothing," Wise wrote, "but profess to believe anything for the sake of money and honours."[59] He claimed that Jews who converted did so only to get jobs offered by organizations like the ASMCJ, to become missionaries and live on Christian funding, or even to accept an out-and-out bribe from missionaries—a kind of conversion signing bonus. It was common in Jewish publications for Wise or other writers to offer details of a conversion that disproved its authenticity. Missionaries were scorned as hirelings.[60]

Wise also argued that attempts to convert Jews were un-American. He accused the ASMCJ of being "not an American but an English institution," unsuited for a democracy. He saw no problem with Christian missionaries evangelizing non-Jews, and wrote, "Our

American missionaries and missionary societies never show any disrespect to Judaism." Attempting to stake out a place for Judaism
within the U.S. denominational system, Wise argued that the good-
hearted Christian "considers the Synagogue the same as the Methodist, Baptist, Lutheran or other churches." Citizens were bound to
respect Judaism and Jews' right not to convert or be proselytized,
because to disrespect the adherents of a sect other than the one to
which one belonged was to "see himself in the unpleasant condition
of disrespecting the majority of his fellow citizens." Only "well paid
hirelings" spurred on by "superstition which are thrown on our shores
from all parts of Europe" attempted to convert Jews in a democracy.[61]
Wise was less sanguine about Christian-Jewish relations three decades later when he published his *Defense of Judaism versus Proselytizing
Christianity.* Nevertheless, he argued in that text that "all morality
and morals depends upon the intelligence" and upon "conscience"
rather than upon religion. Wise thought that even differences in religion were negligible for the purpose of citizenship because so long as
a religion promoted morality it made good citizens.[62]

Economic and political arguments were the most powerful anti-
dotes to the choice posed by missionaries, because they addressed the
questions of the sincerity of converts and their place in the political
and social order of the United States. These arguments, though,
floated on a sea of apologetics about the interpretation of the Bible
(and, more rarely, the Talmud), the identification of Jesus as the Messiah, and the fulfillment of prophecy. These apologetics, which
were as ancient as the split between Judaism and Christianity, were
endlessly repeated on the one side in sermons and books calling
Christians to greater missionary efforts and reassuring them of the
truth of their religion, and on the other side in Jewish defenses of
their faith and refutations of Christian polemic. Christians read, for
example, chapter 53 of Isaiah as a prophecy of Jesus, whereas Jews
interpreted the passage as referring to the suffering of the nation of
Israel. On the strength of several passages in the Gospels, Christians
took Isaiah chapter 7 to refer to a prophecy of the virgin birth of
Jesus, while Jews took the prophecy as being fulfilled in the birth
of Isaiah's child in Isaiah chapter 8. Any nineteenth-century argument between Jews and Christians rehashed these points. Warder

Cresson, for one, minced no words, giving nine "reasons why no honest Jew can convert to Christianity"—all of which had to do with the interpretation of the Scriptures. The primary power of these polemics was not in providing reasons for people to convert, since few seem to have been persuaded, but in building up reasons for Jews and Christians to remain in their religions. For those who came in contact with missionaries, the need for such apologetics began to shift the basis of remaining from habit to choice.

⚜

These choices were pressed upon Jews and Christians as they more frequently encountered one another over the course of the nineteenth century. At the start of the Revolution, there were somewhere between 1,000 and 2,500 Jews in the thirteen colonies, comprising at most 0.1 percent of the population. In 1800, because of the migrations forced by the Revolution, there were the same number of Jews, but they now comprised only 0.04 percent of the growing population. Christians and Jews encountered one another mostly in Newport, Rhode Island; Charleston, South Carolina; and other urban seaports. By the 1830s, the Jewish population began to grow faster than the general population, thanks in large part to immigration from Europe. By 1900, there were about a million Jews in the United States, comprising at least 1.25 percent of the population.[63] Jews still lived in cities on the Atlantic Seaboard, most notably New York and Philadelphia, but there were also large Jewish populations in Cincinnati, Memphis, Nashville, Galveston, and San Francisco, as well as other cities and towns.

The growth in the Jewish population was not just a quantitative change but a qualitative shift from the "mythical Jew" to the "Jew next door."[64] For Christians, Jews were often present in the imagination: Jews were (usually stereotyped) characters in novels, subjects of histories, the topics of sermons, and, of course, the people of the Bible. Converts like Samuel Freuder sometimes made a living demonstrating Jewish prayers and other rituals to curious Christian audiences. Every Jewish conversion narrative described the Jewish home and education, especially rituals, for the benefit of an inquiring

Christian readership.[65] The result was that Christians assumed they knew Jews' thoughts intimately—better than Jews did themselves, in fact, because Christians knew from the Bible why Jews were "blinded" from the truth of the gospel. But as more and more Jews became Americans, everyday interactions of Christians with actual Jews led to a new kind of experience. When Christians got to know Jews, Christian assumptions were challenged, in a few cases at least, to the point of converting to Judaism. Jews, on the other hand, usually lived in a society where Christians were more common than Jews.

Jews and Christians often met each other in the religious services of the other faith.[66] It was not uncommon for Jews in a community without a synagogue to attend a Christian church for religious worship. Isaac Leeser, after noticing the increase in the number of Jews and synagogues in the United States, nevertheless observed that "in no other [country], except in Australia, are they living in many instances so isolated and removed from Jewish influence." The result was that Jews attended Christian congregations and, Leeser complained, "we have heard of instances where such persons had seats in churches, and were regular attendants, and contributed the same as the Christians to the expense of the establishment."[67] Because many Christian groups in the nineteenth century emphasized morality over doctrine, Jews could, for the most part, make common cause on moral questions. But Leeser warned that Jews "may think nothing of their visits; but the eyes of others are upon them, and it is not unlikely that a mere presence from curiosity may be trumped before the world as an evidence of a desire to be converted"—let alone the very real danger that they might actually become converts.[68]

Jews did not typically attend Baptist or Methodist congregations, which were known for evangelism, nor Catholic services, which Jews associated with medieval persecution. The ideal congregation for Jews was Episcopalian, whose dignified liturgical worship seemed uplifting, or best of all Unitarian, where the denial of "Christology" meant that they could worship without mention of Trinitarian dogma.[69] Nineteenth-century Reform Judaism felt a certain kinship with Unitarians in their shared pursuit of a rational religion that recognized the unity of God. Nineteenth-century Reform rabbis even had good words to say for Jesus as a moral teacher once he was stripped of divinity.[70] For example, Aaron Lazarus and his family attended services at an Episcopal church in Wilmington, North Carolina, and were friends with the priest, Adam Empie. This strategy backfired, however, when Lazarus's son, Gershon, converted to Christianity and was baptized. The priest appears to have converted him under the misapprehension that his father had given permission. Remarkably, the father was willing, if reluctant, to grant permission for the conversion once the son reached his majority. This compromise was a heartfelt wish that the son would not convert, coupled with a grudging acknowledgment that the son's religion would be his own choice. Within six months, the boy had renounced his baptism after weeks of study with an Episcopal bishop and with his grandfather, Jacob Mordecai, who had become an expert in Jewish apologetics.[71] Toward the end of the nineteenth century, missionaries also tried to reach Jews with street corner preaching and in missionary halls, but few Jews could be reached through these efforts. Though missionaries' reports do mention Jews attending services, these attendees were as often as not there to police and report on the missionaries or to speak to Jews who might defect. Occasionally, these encounters ended in brawls.[72]

Some Christians frequented Jewish synagogues, especially Sunday lectures delivered by well-known rabbis. Lectures were popular entertainment throughout the nineteenth century, whether on the Chatauqua circuit or in theological debates between denominations. Reform rabbis often offered lectures about religion, politics, or history on Sundays, not just because Sunday was the state- and society-sanctioned day of rest, but to keep Jews from Christian services. Rabbis who gave these lectures were conscious that they had non-Jews in their audiences, and sometimes they tailored their lectures to them. Rabbi Joseph Krauskopf of Philadelphia gave a series of lectures on conversions, refuting Christian ideas of conversions but arguing for the ability of Jews and Christians to live together without proselytizing each other. (Krauskopf called Jews who left Judaism "perverts." In the nineteenth century, the term *pervert* was occasionally used for someone who had left a faith, the opposite of a "convert" who had joined a faith, even as the term was taking on its pejorative sexual connotation toward the end of the century.)[73] The most daring form of rabbinical lecture, which formed a genre of its own, was the public statement of what Jews thought of Jesus: a worthwhile moral teacher, but not the Messiah, and certainly not God. There were also reports of Christians attending Jewish services as paid musicians, sometimes provoking complaints that there were more Christians than Jews in attendance.[74]

Entering the door of a church or synagogue might be the first step to conversion. Max Rossvally's conversion was set in motion when he attended a church service in Washington, DC, on a whim. David Stern converted a man who became convinced of the truth of Judaism after attending his lectures.[75] This evidence points to a frequent, often voluntary mixing of Jews and Christians even in one another's religious institutions, thereby presenting choices to both groups about whether to be Christians or Jews.

✠

The encounter that led to the most conversions was marriage. In the nineteenth century, as today, most conversions occurred when people married across religious lines.[76] Such conversions were private family affairs, and people who converted for marriage did not add their voice to the public polemics between religions. Yet because they were private, intermarriages led to questions about sincerity, not unlike public conversions. The claim, whether made on the basis of *halakhah* or theology, was that a person who converted for marriage was doing so for love or family, not God, and that therefore his or her conversion was unreliable.

Intermarriage between Jews and Christians could be a wrenching experience for parents and couples, and Jews thought they got the worst of the bargain. Most ethnic groups in America practiced endogamy; but as a smaller population, Jews had a harder time finding suitable matches, and intermarriage was more often a possibility. Jews who married Christians were likely to convert to Christianity. Malcolm Stern estimates that before 1840, only twelve Christian spouses out of 150 mixed marriages converted to Judaism; in most of the other marriages, the Jewish spouse became Christian. Any intermarriage raised the question of what religion the children would be. This question was complicated by the *halakhah*, which regarded someone as a

Jew by birth if he or she had a Jewish mother. It was possible, therefore, for children to be Jewish in the eyes of the *halakhah* but to be
raised in Christian homes; it was also possible for people to be raised
as Jews who were not halakhically Jewish. Jonathan Sarna argues that
Jews were able to practice endogamy primarily because most other
Americans practiced endogamy, whether that meant that Protestants
married Protestants while Catholics married Catholics, or that Italians married Italians while Germans married Germans and the Irish
married the Irish. Just as the perpetuation of the Jewish identity in
the family was the primary concern in resisting missionaries, so a
strong family and avoiding intermarriage were the best defenses
against conversion.[77]

Jews regarded conversion because of intermarriage with suspicion.
The *halakhah* considered their motives to be mixed and therefore invalid.[78] But the stipulation against conversion for mixed motives was
mostly honored in the breach. Custom was willing to bend that requirement on the theory that if people were going to marry anyway,
it was better that they should marry as Jews than as Christians. These
concerns about intermarriage played out in the life of many Jews and
Christians married to one another. David B. Nones, the scion of a
wealthy Jewish mercantile family in Philadelphia, married a Christian while in Cádiz on a voyage. Nones wrote an anguished series of
letters to his parents asking their forgiveness and blessing, though
"your feelings will be wounded." Nones "sacredly promise[d] . . . in
the presence of my Creator" that his wife would convert to Judaism,
but "with her will & not forced." He made preparations to travel to
England, where there was a significant Jewish community that was
freer than the Jews of Spain. In England, the conversion would be
performed with "all the requisite forms & informations useful," that
is, with the proper rituals and instructions in Judaism. And in case
there was any doubt on the matter, Nones assured his parents that
"my principles are & will be through life the same" and that he
would not become an apostate.[79] Intermarried spouses usually
promised that the non-Jewish spouse would convert, and that he or
she (most often she) would do so of her own free will.

The potential proselyte and the Jewish spouse usually had to persuade congregations and rabbis to accept them. Orthodox rabbis
tended to balk at converting intermarried spouses. When in 1892

Rabbi Isaac Pereira Mendes of Savannah converted Mrs. F. A. Ehrlich, he did so only because he was persuaded that she was acting "of her own free will and accord, no mercenary motives, but simply a pure desire and love for our holy religion," and even then he disclaimed conversions in general and left the final responsibility for authorizing the conversion with the board of his synagogue.[80] Besides encouraging suspicion of converts, the *halakhah* considered children Jewish if they were born to a Jewish woman, whether or not she was a convert. But if a woman were a convert, she could not marry a *kohen* (priest). Though in some cases, as in Sarah J. P. Cohen's, the question seems not even to have been raised; in other cases, it provoked letters to English halakhic authorities to ascertain the best course of action. Nathan Marcus Adler, the state-sponsored chief rabbi of Great Britain, received a number of such queries whether a convert or the child of a converted woman could be allowed to marry a *kohen*. In his *responsa* (written rabbinical decisions), he always answered no.[81]

In 1775, Benjamin Jacobs petitioned Shearith Israel on behalf of the woman whom he was about to marry civilly: "The Lady, whom he is about to espouse, Being desirous to live as a Jewess; Joins with him in this petition, and Begs that she may be married according to the manners and customs of the Jews, as it is her desire, to live in the strict observance of all our Laws and customs." In his case, there was an appeal to a London *beth din* (Jewish rabbinical court), as in many cases of question about the *halakhah* of conversion.[82] But even more interesting were couples who petitioned for conversion and religious marriage after they had been civilly married. In 1793, Moses Nathans, a member of the board of the Philadelphia synagogue, tried to have his wife converted. Nathans had lived with his wife in a civil marriage for eight years, and they had three children. The *parnas* (president) of the synagogue, Benjamin Nones, sent letters to London synagogues to see whether this was permissible. They had a Jewish marriage in 1794.[83] Anna Barnett petitioned Mikveh Israel to be converted. She acknowledged that she "has not the happiness to be born a Jewess and favoured immediately from the God of Israll" but that she wanted to join the congregation and "become a Jewiss." She claimed this, "not as a favour, but as a right" since she felt obligated of "living up to the divine precepts of the Bible." Accordingly, she agreed to "submit to such ceremonies as are necessary."[84] The significance of these conversions was that these women and families desired to become Jews after living with a Jew for some time but not converting. Won over by family pressure or by the love of Judaism, converts successfully pressured congregations to take them in the interest of preserving the family line.[85]

Suspicion of intermarried converts never died out, but Isaac Mayer Wise nevertheless delighted in publicizing them in the *American Israelite*. At one Memphis synagogue, two conversions occurred in as many weeks. Mrs. A. Paterson, a Catholic, received the given name Leah, then married David Lowenstein; Lucy Franklin, an Episcopalian, received the name Rachel and married J. Danheiser. Congregations witnessed both women as they "publicly renounced Christianity and embraced Judaism." Wise wished that "as they advance in years they may also advance in knowledge and love of their new faith."[86] In another synagogue, a mother was converted and her daughter was married on the same day, a "spicy item of news" for the newspapers, according to Wise. The mother had long had a civil marriage to a Jewish man, and her daughter, Miss Raunch, possibly considered herself a Jew. But when the daughter married Mr. Cohen, "the bride's mother, a born Christian, was received into the covenant of Judaism by Dr. Wise, and remarried her husband."[87]

Regardless of suspicions for practical or halakhic reasons, the rituals of conversion and the certificate that they had been performed declared the converts to have been genuine and remade them into children of Abraham. It was rare that conversion certificates mentioned ulterior motives, even marriage. One exception was Marie Berthelot, a Catholic converted by Max Lilienthal in 1852, whose certificate noted her civil marriage to a Jew. Children of proper converts were considered Jews even if the convert later reneged. Life could be messier than law, but the trend was toward the acceptance of converts even if they converted for marriage.[88]

✢

The requirements of the *halakhah* meant that a number of people who considered themselves Jewish but did not meet the legal requirements underwent conversion rituals. Abraham Kirkas first attended Congregation Shearith Israel in New York in 1848, and in March of that year he came before the *beth din* to become a Jew in accordance with the law. He told quite a story. His grandmother and unmarried mother, who were probably Jews, traveled from Thessaloniki in Asia Minor to Jerusalem by boat, but were beset by pirates who enslaved them and sold them to a "rich Gentile" in Beirut. The Gentile, Kirkas, who was probably a Christian but perhaps a Muslim, married Simcha, the younger woman, to whom Abraham was born. His name probably signified his mother's wish that her son be a Jew. After Abraham's father died, his mother made her wish plain on her own deathbed, when she enjoined her son, "See that thou makest of thyself a Jew."

When Kirkas tried to fulfill his mother's dying wish, he found he was unable to do so in Syria. He asked to be converted by the Jews of Beirut, but they "did not wish to make a proselyte of me for fears of the laws of the country." Syria, which controlled Beirut, was then under Ottoman control and had laws against converting Jews. His grandmother suggested traveling to the west to become a proselyte. In a touching speech that inverted the pledge of Ruth, the biblical archetype of the convert to Judaism, to her mother-in-law Naomi, the older woman promised to "journey with thee from the east to the west, until I shall see thee in the Jewish religion, living according to the words of the law." Traveling by way of France and England, Kirkas and his grandmother eventually immigrated to New York, in "this free country America." Though Kirkas's story might have aroused suspicion, he produced letters from Syrian, French, and English rabbis vouching for its truthfulness.[89]

Kirkas went through the process of conversion detailed in the *halakhah*. The *beth din* before which he appeared on March 26, 1848, had three members led by Samuel M. Isaacs, the second rabbi to immigrate to America. Isaacs was joined on the court by the *parnas* of Congregation Shaaray Tefillah and by the *shohet* of Congregation Shaaray Zedek. Both were laymen who undertook the role because of the scarcity of rabbis. The court questioned Kirkas about his motives, whether he was converting "perhaps for love of money, or for love of the daughters of Israel." Kirkas knew to emphasize that his conversion was undertaken only for the sake of God and that his promise to his mother was "of my own free will." Satisfied with Kirkas's sincerity, they instructed him in the basics of Jewish theology, such as "the Divine Unity, and the prohibition of idolatry." After his conversion, Kirkas was expected to keep the law, so the court instructed him about "the major and minor commands," in part to test the sincerity of the proselyte. Kirkas was circumcised by "a specially qualified and skilled Mohel [ritual circumciser]," probably because of medical concerns about an adult circumcision. He also received a new name. Many adult male converts to Judaism received the name "Abraham, son of Abraham our father," but Kirkas's given name was already Abraham. He was thus given the new ceremonial name, "Isaac son of Abraham our Father" for use in the synagogue. The conversion was not complete until he returned, after healing from the circumcision, to be immersed in the *mikveh*.[90]

The *halakhah* of conversion contained in the Talmud set forth a specific set of commands about how to make proselytes. The commands were intended to make the convert completely Jewish, but the laws first tested his or her sincerity. The proselyte was supposed to appear before a rabbinic court, which would ask, "What did you see that prompted you to convert?" and to remind the proselyte that "the people of Israel were afflicted." This was a test of the convert's sincerity, for if he was discouraged easily, he was to be let go. Many nineteenth-century rabbis took this command seriously, as in the case of David Stern, who several times rebuffed a potential proselyte. According to the Talmud, the potential convert was also informed of the major and minor commandments of the law. If a man accepted the yoke of the law, he was immediately circumcised by a *mohel*. After he healed in about a week's time, he was immersed in a *mikveh* and again pledged to obey the laws without mental reservation. A woman who accepted the law was only immersed in the *mikveh*. Though not mentioned in the Talmud, there was a practice of giving the convert a conversion certificate, a number of which survive from the nineteenth century (Figure 5.1).[91]

The purpose of this ceremony was to make the convert into a complete Jew. As the convert rose from the waters of the *mikveh*, he would be "treated like a Jew in every respect." Another practice ce-

FIGURE 5.1 A detail from the conversion certificate of Jacob Bar Abraham Abinu, dated November 22, 1819. This certificate explains that the convert was circumcised by a *mohel*, renamed, and immersed in the *mikveh* at K. K. Shearith Israel in New York, "he being fully sensible of the truth of the Jewish faith and the Unity of the Divine Being." Conversion certificate of Jacob Bar Abraham Abinu, copy made January 3, 1820, Jacques Judah Lyons P-15, American Jewish Historical Society, Boston and New York, http://search.cjh.org:1701/beta:CJH _SCOPE:cjh_digitool1112696.

mented this new identity. In the words of the Talmud, "A person who converts is like a newborn child."[92] This meant that the convert's sins were forgiven, and it also meant that the convert had no family. The person who converted received a new Jewish name and a new lineage: "son of Abraham, our Father" or "daughter of Sarah, our Mother." Some converts adopted this name for their everyday life, as did Warder Cresson; others used it only in the synagogue; others combined the two names, such as Sarah Jane Picken Cohen. This genealogy moved the convert from being a Gentile to being someone who had a genealogy in Israel. This new status could not be lost. Even if someone renounced his or her conversion, that person was legally regarded as an apostate Jew, not a Gentile.

The sociological reality, however, was often more complicated, and there was a recurring idea that people were religious by nature rather than by choice. The renunciation of conversion, which in retrospect often appeared inevitable, was attributed to the religious nature of the individual. The question was how to treat the convert, and on this matter the Talmud was of two minds. Converts "delay the arrival of the Messiah" and were as "the scab of the skin"—probably because they did not keep the commandments and made Jewish families genealogically impure.[93] But to counter the tendency of the convert to apostatize, and on the basis of the many biblical commandments, the Talmud warned against oppressing the convert. Indeed, in bad times converts were presumed to be sincere, and in good times they were more suspect. Good motives meant being persuaded of the truth of Judaism out of love of Torah, while motivations of money, prestige, or coercion were suspect. Though in America, where there were few rabbis and where the "synagogue community" had become a "community of synagogues," it could be difficult at the beginning part of the century to follow these stipulations, Jews tried to make halakhically valid conversions.[94]

Kirkas's conversion shows how differently conversion functioned for Judaism than for Protestant Christianity. Kirkas's conversion was predominantly legal, not emotional or experiential. To be sure, the *beth din* had an exacting procedure to test his sincerity and goodwill, not to mention free will. And he did have to give his assent to matters of both creed and practice. But whereas a Christian conversion happened because of an inward change, with baptism or access to the Lord's Supper as confirmatory rites, Kirkas was not a Jew until after the completion of the rituals of circumcision and immersion. The ritual aspect also demonstrated the importance of the judgment of a congregation or community. Kirkas required the approval of the New York *beth din* to convert, which was administered by lay and rabbinical members of three synagogues representing the "community of synagogues." To be sure, Kirkas required such approval because he went the route of an orthodox conversion. Eventually Judaism, like Christianity, became increas-

ingly fractured, giving converts the option of choosing which congregation's approval to seek.

✝

In an age when conversions were often public and polemical, Warder
Cresson sparked the major cause célèbre of conversions to Judaism
in the antebellum United States. Cresson's religious inclinations were
a minor matter of state policy, but his conversion became a major test
case for the religious freedom of Jews.[95]

Cresson was born into a Pennsylvania Quaker household in 1798.
The records of the Gwynedd Society of Friends show that Cresson
attended the meetings in his early adulthood and marriage, but fell
off in attendance in his late twenties. When Cresson joined the
Shakers in 1829, the Friends removed him from their membership.[96]
Cresson was deeply interested in the Bible as a work of prophecy,
noting details of passages from prophets such as Isaiah and Daniel.
In his tract *Babylon the Great Is Falling*, he mustered these prophecies
as arguments against Orthodox and Hicksite Quakers alike, as well
as against the economic system of Pennsylvania.[97] These prophetic
themes recurred throughout his life, as Cresson tried to see the signs
of the times in light of the Bible, especially the Old Testament. Once
he encountered Isaac Leeser, Cresson began to turn his withering
critique from Quakers to Christianity in general.

In Cresson's prophetic system, Jews played the leading role, as they
did for most millenarians. (After all, their source materials were the
Jewish scriptures.) Even before he met Leeser, Cresson anticipated
the restoration of Jews to the promised land, a common theme in
Christians' understanding of prophecy. Leeser, too, believed in the
eventual, though not imminent, return of Jews to Palestine.[98] Cresson
seems to have heard of Leeser, a prominent leader in nearby Philadelphia, through his published sermons and new periodical, *The Occident*, first published in 1843. Cresson also sought out Mordecai
Noah. In 1844, Cresson applied to the State Department to serve
without pay as U.S. consul in Jerusalem, and in May he received his
commission from Secretary of State John C. Calhoun. After receiving a strongly worded critique from a former treasury secretary

who described Cresson as a religious enthusiast bent on converting Jews and Muslims in Palestine, Calhoun rescinded the commission within a week. But it was too late. Cresson was already at sea. He arrived in Palestine believing himself to be a consul and exercised the powers of the office for several years.[99]

Jerusalem had only four years earlier been restored to Ottoman rule with the help of European powers, after being annexed by Egypt. Jerusalem's political fate remained tenuous, but North African Jews increasingly swelled the tiny population (which was only 15,000 or 20,000) and rebuilt synagogues with the permission of their Muslim rulers.[100] Many Christian missionaries also came to Jerusalem, drawn by the irresistible combination of a Jewish population, a prophetically significant location, and state support for their efforts. In 1840, the British, with German support, established an Anglican diocese. Catholic and Orthodox churches maintained a larger presence in Jerusalem, as European powers reestablished diplomatic missions in the city.[101] Travelers to the east often recounted their tales of Jerusalem, and the English novelist William Makepeace Thackeray encountered Cresson, reporting that "he expects to see the millennium in three years, and has accepted the office of consul at Jerusalem, so as to be on the spot in readiness." Thackeray also reported his doubts that the Anglican mission had converted even a dozen Jews.[102]

In several works that he published in Jerusalem, Cresson critiqued the missionaries as ineffective and claimed to have lived in quarters vacated by failed American missionaries. Though Cresson participated in Christian worship services, his distaste for missionaries grew into a rejection of Christianity. Cresson was learning exegetical details from Jews in Jerusalem that encouraged his study of prophecy. At the same time, he doubted that Christianity was the fulfillment of the prophecies of the Hebrew Bible. The main claim of Christians was that the Hebrew prophecies were fulfilled spiritually in the church, but Cresson thought that was no fulfillment at all. A true fulfillment must be first literal and then spiritual, and so he judged Christianity lacking.[103] He put this critique pungently in one pamphlet, calling what the missionaries offered "sawdust" in exchange for the "good old cheese" of Judaism. By 1848, Cresson acted on his conviction that "salvation was of the Jews." "I remained in Jerusalem in my former faith until the 28th day of March, 1848, when I became fully satisfied that I could never obtain Strength and Rest, but by doing as Ruth did, and saying to her Mother-in-Law, or Naomi (the Jewish Church), 'Entreat me not to leave thee . . . for whither thou goest I will go.' . . . In short, upon the 28th day of March, 1848, I was circumcised, entered the Holy Covenant and became a Jew."[104] Cresson took the name Michael C. Boaz Israel, son of Abraham.

Within two months, Boaz Israel had departed Jerusalem to return to Pennsylvania, intending to set his affairs in order, sell his property, and return permanently to Jerusalem. By his appearance alone, his family could tell that he had changed: he wore a full beard, rather common for nineteenth-century men, but also sidelocks tucked behind his ears, and a large velvet *kippah* that covered his entire skull, both signs of observance of the Torah. His diet and observance of other Jewish laws marked his conversion. He attended worship at the synagogue Mikveh Israel, and he stumped on the street advancing his arguments for Judaism over Christianity. He asked that his wife (she said, demanded) become a Jew. After four years of absence (his family said, abandonment) the family was unwilling to be reunited in Boaz Israel's new religion. His wife, Elizabeth Townsend, had made her own religious choices, having converted from the Quaker meeting to the Episcopal Church.[105] She and some of Cresson's children tried to retain the family property by having a court declare him insane.

Boaz Israel fought to retain his property and his dignity. He saw the case in prophetic terms: he was a symbol of Judaism, his wife a symbol of Christianity.[106] His Jewish co-religionists saw the accusation as a battle "waged against my Right of Religious Liberty, for becoming a Jew," because the court recognized conversion to Judaism as evidence of insanity.[107] They feared that civil disabilities might be attached to Judaism at the level of local jurisdictions through property laws. Seventy-one witnesses spoke in Cresson's defense at the trial, including prominent citizens such as Mordecai M. Noah. There were some bizarre witnesses, such as a doctor who claimed to be able to tell from hair roots whether someone was insane. (Cresson passed his test.) The general line of defense was religious liberty. Cresson won his case because he and his defenders changed the focus from questions about abandoning his family and about his ability to administer an estate to the question of religious freedom, which the republican traditions of the country and Pennsylvania valued.

Cresson's defense attorney, Horatio Hubbell, summed up his position in a ringing concluding argument. Hubbell appealed to Jefferson's dictum that one could believe in "twenty gods or no god" without harming society. Cresson could not treat polytheism as flippantly, having stated that "my persecutors tried hard to condemn me upon the ground of mono-mania, let me inform them, there is no mania or madness as bad as Poly-mania, or Poly-theism, for that is rank idolatry and Insanity."[108] Like Jefferson, Hubbell argued that finding truth depended on free inquiry, even to the point of conversion: "God help the honest and conscientious inquirer, if, after he finds that one creed is not true, he should not be at liberty to adopt another, without incurring the danger of being branded a madman."[109] The strongest argument that Hubbell presented was that conversion was common: Cresson's wife and many of the witnesses and officials at the trial had also converted. Even the doctor who examined Cresson had converted from Judaism to Christianity.[110]

Cresson won his case when the judge instructed the jury that Cresson's Judaism could not be used as evidence of insanity, thereby clinching the legal principle in favor of minority religions. Newspaper accounts generally favored Cresson, though they also mentioned people who opposed the outcome of the trial. Though the federal Constitution said nothing about a right to convert, most newspapers appealed to the Constitution, appealing to the spirit rather than the letter of the law. The press defended the right to convert to either Christianity or Judaism. And like Hubbell, they cited converts such as Orestes A. Brownson, "who changes his religion every year," to demonstrate that conversion was acceptable, even normal, for Americans.[111] In summing up the trial, Isaac Leeser identified the criterion for judging conversions that mattered most: "Whatever may have been the eccentricities of Mr. Cresson, and we are willing to admit them, he was a sincere convert to our religion."[112]

Having won his case, proved the legal point, and publicized his arguments in *The Key of David*, Michael C. Boaz Israel departed Pennsylvania for Jerusalem. He married Rachel Moleano and fathered a son and daughter. Isaac Leeser reported that Cresson had established a farm outside Jerusalem. In a reversal of the ASMCJ's plan, Boaz Israel established poor-relief farms for Jews, and like a good Jeffersonian, he feared manufacturing and advocated for internal improvements related to agriculture.[113] He also hosted as a guest a second novelist, the American Herman Melville.

✝

Melville visited Jerusalem in 1856 on his own spiritual quest, but where Cresson had found the Promised Land, Melville found only spiritual desert. Melville drew on that trip and his interview with Cresson when writing the semiautobiographical poem, *Clarel: A Poem and Pilgrimage in the Holy Land*, published in 1876. In more than 18,000 lines, Melville described the doubts that Clarel, an American seminary student, and his companions felt about their Christianity, spurred in part by the encounter with varieties of religions. In Melville's poem, readers encountered fictional Christians who had converted to Judaism, and fictional Jews who had converted to Christianity.[114]

For all the real conversions between Christianity and Judaism in the nineteenth century, readers probably encountered more fictional than factual conversions. Conversions to Judaism were uncommon, and when they occurred, they were probably publicized in newspapers for just that reason. But stories of conversions of Jews to Christianity were ever-present in the nineteenth century. So common were these stories, which were mass-produced on stereotype presses with their stereotypical plots, that the credulous nineteenth-century reader might have been forgiven for wondering how a Jew could enter a church or read a Bible or tract without instantly becoming a Christian. A story was even published about a Jew who converted upon being sent to prison.[115] Indeed, that was the question that animated these narratives: Why would Jews not accept the Christian Gospel so plainly and frequently proffered to them? The millennial expectation of mass conversions that had animated the ASMCJ never died out, and at the beginning of the twentieth century would once again burst out in full flame.

These conversion relations were significant not just as texts, but as commodities. They often bore pledges of what the profits of their sale would do. For example, the 1859 London edition of *Thirza* promised the profits from the sale to a "Jewish Converts' Institution." An Episcopal congregation in Mississippi published the novel *Zerah* to raise money for their church building. Reports of the conversions of Jews flooded the market, traveling back and forth on a network where Boston, New York, London, and Berlin were the main publishing nodes.

The narratives were often set in biblical times. The most famous was *Ben-Hur: A Tale of the Christ*, written by former Union General Lew Wallace. That book outsold Harriet Beecher Stowe's more famous novel, *Uncle Tom's Cabin*. In the novel, the story of the Jewish main character, Judah Ben-Hur, is interwoven with an account of the life of Jesus of Nazareth. Ben-Hur becomes a Christian after witnessing Jesus's execution.[116] Wallace's historical novel was preceded by the much less well known novel *Zerah, the Believing Jew*. Like *Ben-Hur*, *Zerah* described the life of a first-century Jew who encountered Jesus and early Christians and converted to Christianity. The novel owed a great deal of its structure and plot devices to the familiar Protestant conversion narrative. *Zerah* wove a fictional narrative around lengthy italicized quotations from the Gospels. The distinguishing of source materials points to a text organized not as fiction and fact, but as Word of God and human production.[117] Another of these novels was *Thirza; or, The Attractive Power of the Cross*, a German novel translated into English and published in London and in Boston by the Massachusetts Sabbath School Union. The character Thirza, daughter of a rich Jewish merchant, had read the New Testament as a child before her father had stopped her, and this reading encouraged her desire to know more about Jesus. When she entered a church and heard a sermon explaining that Jews were under the curse of God for crucifying Jesus, she fainted, then after reviving had a conversion experience under the ministrations of the preacher and his wife.[118] The willingness of Christian writers and publishers to blur the line between the actual conversion narrative and the novel called into question the reliability of other narratives of Jews converting to Christianity.

✠

A notable characteristic of public conversions from Judaism to Christianity is that many converts became Christian ministers.[119] In 1902,

A. E. Thompson estimated that "125 American pulpits are occupied by Hebrew-Christians."[120] Among these Jewish-Christian ministers was the medical doctor Max Louis Rossvally, who converted from Judaism to Christianity after the Civil War.[121] After hearing the urban revivalist Dwight Lyman Moody preach many times in New York, in 1876 Rossvally started a mission to the Jews in New York called the Hebrew Christian Association.[122] Rossvally thought that Christians had shamefully neglected their duties to the Jews: "Conversions among the Jews occur so seldom, simply because so very little is done for their spiritual welfare." Besides the opportunity to convert Jews, New York presented an opportunity to gather Jews who had already converted into a congregation, since the *New York Daily Witness* reported that "there are upwards of 200 converted Jews in New York City."[123] The first meeting was attended by sixty people, their ranks swelled by non-Jewish Christians. A "converted Jewess" named Esther King gave testimony about believing in Christ and being cast out by her family after converting.

The Hebrew Christian Association had a long but tenuous existence. The organization moved from location to location, sometimes meeting in churches, but preferring lecture halls or the Young Men's Christian Association as places more likely to attract a Jewish audience. The gathering of Jews who had converted to Christianity as a separate church was a new kind of Christianity that developed in the late nineteenth century because of missionaries to the Jews. In December 1898, the convert Maurice Ruben began a mission to the Jews in Pittsburgh supported by a network of churches and prayer meetings called the Friends of Israel Union of Pittsburgh. The mission, called House of the New Covenant and later Friends of Israel Mission to the Jews, met for worship separately from other Christians. The mission supported itself, at least in part, by the publication of the magazine *The Glory of Israel*. Christians purchased the magazine for themselves and "for their Jewish and Christian friends." Its pages were full of polemics, including invited disputes with Jews, along with the occasional conversion narrative.

Sometimes Jewish religious leaders also tried to become Christian ministers, as in the tragic case of David Stern.[124] Stern emigrated from England bearing the titles doctor and rabbi. He made connections among the more radical of the Reform rabbis in America: Kaufmann Kohler, Emil G. Hirsch, and Bernhard Felsenthal. For a time, he lectured in various congregations and aided other rabbis, and then he managed to obtain a pulpit position in Wilkes-Barre, Pennsylvania, for a few years. But Stern was too radical even for the radicals. He held that the obligations of Judaism extended only to religion and that Judaism had no ethnic or racial component at all. "Every adherent of Judaism" but not "every Jew" was "duty bound to carry out its doctrines."[125] In other words, Judaism was a belief system that one could opt into, but one's birth as a Jew carried with it no obligation to be a Jew in religion. Stern's ideas manifested themselves in a willingness to convert at least one Gentile, as well as to marry a Jewish man to a non-Jewish woman without requiring her conversion.[126] The rabbis who were Stern's benefactors had followed their principles fairly far down the road of Reform. Hirsch's own progressive Chicago congregation met on Sundays, rather than Saturdays, and Felsenthal was vice president of the Free Religious Association in 1879 when Felix Adler was president. But Hirsch publicly criticized Stern for his views, Kohler refused to support Stern, and Felsenthal kept up a correspondence with him but did not recommend him for rabbinical posts.[127]

With Hirsch's criticism, Stern's career took a turn for the worse. He lost his temporary position in Wilkes-Barre and sent anguished letter after anguished letter to prominent rabbis, asking for recommendations to pulpits, then turned accusatory when he was passed over. He tried his hand at a Sunday lecture series but was unable to gain a sufficient audience to support himself. In desperation, he made an attempt to convert to the Episcopal Church and become a minister. Probably there was no Unitarian church in the vicinity to turn to. Exactly what Stern intended is unclear in retrospect, even to him. He seems to have thought that he could continue to preach a unitarian idea of God and to hold the same ethical ideas, regardless of whether he called himself Jew or Christian. In this he resembled Felix Adler, the son of a Reform rabbi, who had started the New York Society for Ethical Culture in 1876 to encourage a religion of ethical deeds rather than creeds. Stern pronounced himself unafraid of "dogmatism," by which he meant that he was not afraid of his more traditional critics, nor did he regard doctrinal labels as significant.

But Stern was a party of one. The Episcopal Church rebuffed his attempt at conversion.

When Bernhard Felsenthal opened his mail on April 27, 1885, he found a note from Stern, announcing that he had committed suicide. A. B. Weil, a prominent citizen and merchant, described Stern's death to the rabbi, which was also reported in the *New York Times*.[128] No generalization should be drawn from Stern's suicide: his death was too personal, too individual. Yet other attempted converts found, like him, that there was a boundary between religions where they thought there should be none. A few years after Stern's unfortunate tale, another, better-known rabbi tried to convert to Unitarianism. Solomon H. Sonneschein was the rabbi of a congregation in St. Louis who was in danger of losing his position. He traveled to Boston to inquire whether Unitarians would take him as a member. For Sonneschein, as for other rabbis, the attempt at conversion was not a simple attempt at a livelihood, but also an ideological statement about the lack of boundaries between religions as institutions, provided that they espoused a spiritual, unitary idea of God that was to be worked out in moral action. The Unitarians were reportedly receptive to the idea and even seemed to be willing to forgo the rite of baptism if Sonneschein would convert. But to actually treat religious boundaries as porous was a step too far even for the most radical Jews and Christians. Sonneschein was put on trial in the religious press and in rabbinic correspondence, and even the popular press took notice of the controversy. In the end, Sonneschein was forced from his pulpit and discredited as someone who had tried to cross a forbidden line.[129]

Sonneschein and especially Stern were marginal cases among nineteenth-century converts, but their experiences demonstrate that though boundaries between religions could in theory be porous, they were not in fact. The idea of religious pluralism—that each religion had some truth to it—would be espoused at the World's Parliament of Religion in Chicago just a few years after the Sonneschein episode. Yet few people in the nineteenth century were willing to consider conversion to be an insignificant passage—and those few who thought so received intense scrutiny from progressives as well as conservatives.

The boundaries of conversion between Christianity and Judaism were especially complicated because they were not just religious but racialized. Stern's theory of Judaism as a voluntary religion was opposed to "Renan's theory of a racial monotheistic instinct."[130] Ernest Renan, a French philosopher and Orientalist who had drifted away from the Catholicism of his youth, achieved his greatest fame with the 1863 publication of his *La Vie de Jésus*. That book, which was banned by the Roman Catholic Church, was immediately translated into English and became a best seller. Renan depicted Jesus as a Romantic individualist who necessarily owed nothing to Judaism: "Far from Jesus having continued Judaism he represents the rupture with the Jewish spirit." That Jewish spirit was more often termed a "Jewish race." Though Renan professed that "no one is more disposed than myself to place high this unique people," the word he most frequently associated with the Jewish race was "defect." Renan's racial thought was not the fully developed antisemitism of the late nineteenth century, but it suggested that races had distinctive characteristics, or spirits. The Jewish "particular gift," according to Renan, "was to contain in its midst the extremes of good and evil."[131] Renan's basic premises, that races had particular characteristics and that Jews were a race with unfavorable characteristics, were widely accepted on both sides of the Atlantic.

In the United States, race as a category was particularly fraught, because race was thought of as a dichotomy between black and white. Stern's solution was to decouple the religion from the racial concept, but most Jews sought to positively associate their identity with whiteness.[132] In one sense, religious conversion challenged race as an identity, because it was an identity chosen rather than ascribed. Over several generations, converts to Judaism or Christianity could lose their racial markers. For the most part, though, race constrained religion when it came to Christianity and Judaism. Converts from Judaism to Christianity such as Freuder or Rossvally may have chosen their religion, but they never lost their racial or ethnic markers as Jews.

✠

By the end of the nineteenth century, Reform Judaism expected large numbers of converts to "pure monotheism," not unlike the anticipation of Christians that Jews would all convert to Christianity in the end times. For both religions, the idea was that one religion would subsume the other: Jews would recognize Christianity as the fulfillment of Old Testament prophecy; Christians would reject their religion's admixtures of paganism to return to Judaism's monotheism. Neither side achieved these predictions, of course, but American Reform Jews made enough converts to hold their own against Christian missionaries.[133]

Conversion to Judaism from Christianity was more difficult religiously than other types of conversions. Conversion to Judaism, in particular, required an entirely new religious vocabulary, a new way of practicing religion that emphasized ritual explicitly, as opposed to Protestants' explicit spontaneity and implicit ritual. Christian converts to Judaism could never expect to gain knowledge of rabbinic sources or the familiarity with Jewish customs required of a rabbi. When W. E. Todd tried to convert to Reform Judaism and study for the rabbinate, he was turned down by rabbis Emil G. Hirsch and Edward Nathan Calisch.[134] These religious barriers to conversion were somewhat lessened over the course of the century, as Reform Judaism and liberal Christianity developed in more compatible ways.

In rabbinic correspondence and even in newspaper accounts, there are instances where Gentiles discreetly, rather than publicly and polemically, converted to Judaism. As David Stern put it in a query about a potential convert, "in a small community like ours, the probable effect of such a step upon public feeling must be taken into consideration." The fear of inciting Christian animosity by making converts openly was one that rabbis had to consider, even if they were free to make the converts. These converts typically had some previous interaction with Jews, such as attending synagogues to hear lectures or visiting preachers. For example, David Stern reported that a Catholic priest attended his lectures in Wilkes-Barre and said that Catholicism was "for the masses" and Judaism "for thinkers."

Stern made a convert of "a certain Mr. Macintosh, a Scotchman by birth and a florist by trade." Macintosh had apparently heard Stern's lectures and possibly had been attending the synagogue in Wilkes-Barre. He approached Stern and asked to become a Jew. When Stern queried Felsenthal about the case, he wrote, "He presents to have been 'converted' by my Sunday Lectures of last season."[135] The quotation marks around the word *converted* spoke to the difference between Jewish and Protestant ideas of conversion. Macintosh found himself persuaded of the truth of Judaism as Stern preached it, and considered himself converted, whereas for Stern conversion was a ritual and a status.

But for a reformer like Stern, such a ritual was not obviously desirable. For one, there was no obligation for Macintosh to become a Jew to be saved. Nor was there any reason for Macintosh, whom Stern found to be "a pure Theist," to become a Jew to advance the work of monotheism. Besides his worries that making a convert might arouse ire, Stern thought he could "do more towards undermining superstition and spreading truth whilst remaining a nominal Christian than he can possibly do by publicly professing Judaism"— demonstrating an essential similarity between Unitarian Christianity and Judaism unique to Stern's radical wing of Reform. Accordingly, Stern tried to dissuade Macintosh from converting. If not exactly following the Talmud's guidelines, he followed its spirit by investigating Macintosh's motives. Stern found that "there is no woman in the case" and considered him a sincere believer in the truths of Judaism. As custom required, Stern attempted to dissuade him by first accusing "the man of ulterior motives." The sticking point was whether to circumcise Macintosh or not. Though Stern used the threat of circumcision as a way to dissuade Macintosh from potentially converting, he claimed never to have had the intention of actually performing the operation. When a doctor informed them that the procedure was unsafe, and when Felsenthal's letter confirmed that he thought circumcision inadvisable, Stern withheld the circumcision.[136]

Male converts to Judaism often claimed a medical reason why they should not be circumcised. Henry Berkowitz, rabbi of Congregation B'nai Jehudah in Kansas City, sent a circular letter to over a dozen rabbis in a similar case, to decide whether to admit a convert without circumcision. The majority, including such well-known rabbis as Hirsch, Felsenthal, and Krauskopf, agreed to forgo the circumcision.[137] The question of whether to require circumcision was a vexed one that occupied many sessions about proselytes in the founding years of the Central Conference of American Rabbis.[138] It is not too surprising that potential converts wished to avoid an operation whose debilitating pain they might have read about in the biblical account of Shechem.[139] But the concerns were not merely personal. People occasionally died from the operation, which was a serious one for an adult. There were rabbinic precedents in cases where more than one son had died after being circumcised of not requiring circumcision, since the overriding concern of the *halakhah* was to preserve human life. Though in the last quarter of the century, circumcision for male infants became more widely practiced for hygienic reasons, there remained enough medical concerns about the practice for adult males that Reform rabbis had reason to cite medical practice as a reason not to circumcise.[140] Bernhard Felsenthal published a book in German about proselytes that opposed the practice of circumcision altogether.[141]

⁜

Samuel Freuder's life was the mirror image of Sarah Jane Picken Cohen's. He was born a Jew, lived seventeen years as a Christian, then returned to Judaism. But where Cohen had reconciled her return to Christianity with the notion of an inborn religion, Freuder justified his return to Judaism by calling into question whether it was possible for a Jew to make a sincere choice to become a Christian.

Freuder was born in Hungary, the son and grandson of the *hazzan* of an Orthodox synagogue. He pursued rabbinical studies in Berlin, where he studied *Wissenschaft des Judentums*, the historical scholarship of Jewish religion. There he became acquainted with the emerging German Jewish Reform movement, which appealed to him once he got over his initial shock. He immigrated to the United States in 1883, studying at Hebrew Union College in 1884.[142] Entering the college brought him within the ambit of Isaac Mayer Wise, leader of American Reform Judaism. He remained enrolled at Hebrew Union College for three more years while filling a pulpit in a Georgia synagogue, preaching in English. It is unclear whether Freuder received a rabbinical diploma in 1886 from the college, but he took several positions as pulpit rabbi, receiving Wise's endorsement each time.[143] After a short, unsuccessful spell with a congregation in San Diego, Freuder had an equally disastrous tenure as a rabbi for Congregation B'nai Israel in Davenport, Iowa. Wise attributed Freuder's lack of success to his failure to listen to the wishes of his congregation. In Iowa, Freuder pursued a more radical Reform agenda than his congregation, which only a decade earlier had considered itself Orthodox, could tolerate. In 1891, before the congregation could dismiss him, Rabbi Freuder announced his conversion to Christianity.[144]

Freuder converted, he later claimed, because he hoped to find in Christianity the solution to the dilemmas of Reform Judaism. Where Freuder had struggled to find the dividing line between commandments in the Hebrew Bible that were essential and those that were not, Christianity had at least solved that problem. Furthermore, Freuder found Jesus of Nazareth appealing as a teacher of morality and true religion. An appreciation of Jesus' moral teachings was not uncommon among late nineteenth-century Reform Jews, whose public lectures often praised Jesus while rejecting "Christology" as a Pauline accretion.[145] Freuder claimed that he converted because he thought "Judaism could no longer resist the buffets of the winds and waves of the modern spirit," but Christianity, having already abandoned the law, could inaugurate the "brotherhood of man."[146] These explanations reflect Freuder's religious trajectory and the sometimes blurred lines between radical Reform Judaism and liberal Christianity in the late nineteenth century.

Freuder's baptism was the scene of just one of the many shouting matches (and occasional fisticuffs) that took place between Jews and Christians in Christian mission halls and on Jewish street corners in nineteenth-century cities. Freuder was baptized at the Chicago Hebrew Mission by a professor at the Chicago Divinity School. As the waters of baptism trickled from the hand of the minister down Freuder's head, a cadre of Jews who had assembled to watch Freuder's apostasy headed for the exit. While the congregation sang a hymn, "a few [of the Jews], on reaching the door, turned around and shouted to me, 'How much did you get for this?' "[147]

For the next seventeen years, Freuder lived as a Christian. For a time, he demonstrated Jewish rituals and customs to Christian audiences. During most of his time as a Christian, he was a missionary to the Jews. Then in 1908, at a gathering of Christian evangelists to the Jews at Park Street Church in Boston, Freuder denounced missions to the Jews and renounced Christianity. He eventually published an anticonversion narrative, *A Missionary's Return to Judaism*, in which he sought to demonstrate his sincerity as a Jew and the insincerity of Jewish converts to Christianity.[148]

Freuder carefully constructed a conversion narrative that was the inverse of the typical conversion to Christianity, which described the soul before conversion as incomplete, sinful, distant from God, and under judgment. In Freuder's narrative, his soul was sick and his self divided *after* conversion. The ever-present theme of Freuder's story, which he tried to convey in his last speech as a Christian to assembled missionaries to the Jews, was this: "You don't know what it means and costs for a Jew to be baptized—the rended soul, the disrupted family, the desertion of friends, the loss of respect."[149] Freuder turned the question of sincerity on its head. Conversions, he claimed, moved Jews from sincerity to insincerity. Freuder could not so neatly flip the standard calculus of sincerity because all the evidence he lined up to disprove the sincerity of converts from Judaism necessarily called into question his own sincerity.

Freuder's other challenge to the standard conversion narrative was the charge that conversions were not a matter of the heart, but of the pocketbook. Freuder accused converts (and especially converts who became missionaries) of becoming Christians in pursuit of money. Freuder had a host of stories about the greed of converts that played off stereotypes of the money-hungry, dishonest Jew: the convert who asked for travel fare and other small expenses at every turn, the potential convert who received a dime for attending a mission hall meeting, or the actual convert who received money from the missionary for testifying to his conversion—money drawn from the missionary's own take from the offering or from wealthy Christian donors. Another story told of a group of unscrupulous but entrepreneurial Jews who learned the stock phrases of conversion narratives and testified at meetings for laughs and for money to buy their meals. Freuder added that "it was not impossible, though highly improbable," that the impostor "acted his part so well that even the missionary was deceived." In telling that story, Freuder was implying that because false converts were skillful at manipulating conversion stories, genuine conversion narratives could not be discerned from lies.[150]

The anecdotes added up to a system: Jews were converting not because they received the gift of the gospel, but because they had been purchased in market transactions. Freuder described how this market functioned. Wealthy Christian donors gave funds to missionaries and mission houses. These missionaries in turn passed on gifts (read: bribes) small and large to entice Jews to feign conversion. The potentially convertible Jew came to the mission hall for a dime or a meal, might be baptized for the sum of $20, and sometimes stayed on for a career as a missionary, taking a salary to convert others. The missionaries' reports of these conversions to donors were like so many balance sheets, intended to keep the money flowing. In the missionary system, Jews—like financial instruments—were convertible to cash. Despite labeling himself as an exception, the pattern he described could be demonstrated by the life of Freuder himself: a jobless rabbi turned seminary student, then missionary, then colporteur or Bible salesman, then lecturer demonstrating the "morning prayers of a Jew" before paying Christian audiences, then finally a missionary again, who turned into an anti-missionary Jewish publisher. The bottom line of Freuder's accounting was that "professional converts" were running a "business of turning Jews into Christians."

✠

At the end of the nineteenth century, Christian missionaries looked over their ledgers to estimate the numbers of Jews converted to Christianity. Given how few American Jews converted to Christianity, American missionaries turned to estimates of world Jewish conversions. The most frequently cited number—attributed to a missionary to the Jews of Breslau, J. F. de Le Roi—estimated the total number of Jewish conversions worldwide during the nineteenth century to be 204,540. This absurdly precise number was repeated uncritically in many sources.[151] The most thorough American writer about American Jewish missions, A. E. Thompson, threw up his hands at trying to estimate the number of converts: "It is foolish to attempt to number Israel, . . . nor can the number of conversions be tabulated except in the Lamb's Book of Life." The additional difficulty for Thompson was distinguishing "the number of *professed* conversions" from genuine conversions, and so he did not simply repeat de Le Roi's numbers, but divided them between Protestant, Roman Catholic, and Greek Orthodox churches. (Thompson was disinclined to count non-Protestant conversions as genuine.)[152]

The number of Jewish converts was especially small when set against the large numbers of Jews who entered the United States in the 1880s and 1890s. This mass immigration sparked xenophobia and antisemitism, to which missionary publications were not immune, so that some missionary reports were at once alarmist and optimistic. One publication warned that recent Jewish immigrants were especially hard to convert because they came from Eastern European countries "where Talmudism still has a strong hold upon the people," that young Jews were abandoning their religion for crime, and that "Jewish leaders deny the fundamental truth that ours is a Christian country and that our institutions are Christian." Yet they estimated that "5,208 Jews were baptized in the United States and Canada between 1870 and 1900, while from 1895 to 1901 the number of Jewish baptisms in the same countries was 1,072. As far as ascertainable, 323 Jews were baptized in 1905, and 376 in 1906 in America."[153]

Both Jews and Christians recognized that an additional question was relevant: how much were Christians paying to convert Jews? Thompson wrote that "in this commercial age the first question usually asked of the missionary is, 'Does your work pay?'" In compiling his detailed statistics about missionary societies in America, Thompson was able to include a column about "Annual Income," but no figures at all about conversions. Jewish leaders scoffed at these figures and calculated alternative statistics that donors had paid thousands of dollars for each Jewish convert. Samuel Freuder quoted missionary estimates that 13,400 U.S. Jews were baptized in the nineteenth century, then observed, "How many of this number were baptized more than once and how many failed to stay 'baptized' the reports do not say."[154]

Thompson, writing for Maurice Ruben's periodical, countered with alternative statistics. Thompson insisted that the denominator of the fraction should not be the number of Jews converted, but the number of Jews yet to be converted. There were only sixty full-time

American missionaries in the United States with a total amount expended of $45,000. "In other words," Thompson wrote, "we value the soul of an American Jew at three and three-quarter cents. The entire Christian world sets a slightly higher value on a Jewish soul, and expends five and one-half cents a year per capita in Jewish evangelization."[155] Max Rossvally held that conversions of Jews were priceless: "If for a world a soul be lost,/What can the loss supply?/More than a thousand worlds it cost,/A single soul to buy."[156]

These accountings were wholly incompatible, as Jews and Christians saw the same phenomenon from opposite sides. Likewise, Jews and Christians never could agree whether missions to Jews were an insult to Judaism or an act of love for Jews. Conversions between Judaism and Christianity happened within a matrix of institutions—families, congregations, society, race, politics, and the law—that shaped the way people converted and which paths they could take. The most important of these controlling influences was the persistent market metaphor, which brought into question the motives of converts. The effect was to dampen the number of conversions and to convince both Jews and Christians that conversions between their religions took place as a market transaction rather than a sincere choice, freely made.

6

Repose

CATHOLIC CONVERTS AND THE
SECT SYSTEM

THE PUBLIC PAPERS have already announced the Conversion of a Protestant Minister wrought at Rome, at the time of the miracles of the Venerable Labre. I am that Protestant converted to the faith."[1] With these words, John Thayer began his narrative of conversion to Catholicism, already a matter of some notoriety in his hometown of Boston. In the 1780s, Boston was the city least likely to produce a Catholic convert, though by the end of the nineteenth century, three out of four of its churchgoers belonged to that faith.[2] In fact, Catholics were legally barred from practicing their religion until the Revolutionary constitution of 1780. As a Congregationalist minister in his twenties, Thayer doubtless heard many sermons decrying "popery," but he may never have known an actual Roman Catholic until the French fleet sailed into Boston Harbor in July 1778. Thayer, who was probably of Huguenot ancestry and able to speak French, gained his first impression of Catholicism from the French chaplains. One of them, the priest Claudius de la Poterie, returned to Boston in 1788 to establish Boston's first Catholic church.[3]

In 1781, Thayer left his congregation and traveled to France and Italy to study republican politics, aiming "to acquire, by this political knowledge, a greater consequence in my own country." Denying any personal interest, he also took the opportunity to study Catholicism with a Jesuit priest and an Augustinian friar. Thayer finally gave up on Congregationalism because its leaders could not settle on doctrine: "There were not two among them who agreed in the most essential articles: what is more, there was not one who had not varied in his doctrine." From the Augustinian friar Thayer learned that Catholics distinguished between "articles of faith," for which belief was obligatory, and "simple opinions" on theological matters, on which there could be a wide latitude for variance. Catholics thus had a "perfect unity of faith" while maintaining "different opinions on many undecided points." Thayer's new idea about unity and liberty of faith stood in stark contrast to the common Protestant accusation that Catholics were told what to believe without reason and that their spiritual oppression unsuited them for political liberty.

Despite his "prejudice against Catholicks" and his "formal disbelief of the miraculous facts which are said to have happened among them," Thayer was in Rome while the city was awash in news of miracles surrounding the death of the mendicant pilgrim Benedict Joseph Labre. Labre was a French Franciscan who traveled from shrine to shrine in Europe practicing utter poverty. By 1783, he had mostly settled in Rome, living in the ruins of the Colosseum, begging his bread, and spending his days in Eucharistic adoration. When Labre died in April, dozens of sick people—some 136 by his confessor's count—attributed miraculous cures to his intercession in heaven. Thayer scoffed at the reported miracles, but when he set out to disprove them by interviewing Labre's confessor and four people who had been cured, he was "convinced by [his] own eyes." Thus shaken, he began reading an Italian account of a gentleman who converted to Catholicism, and before finishing the book he "exclaimed, 'My God! I promise to become a Catholick.'" On May 15, 1783, he was received into the church by abjuring the heresy of Protestantism.[4]

After his conversion, Thayer gave up his ambitions for political fame and studied for the priesthood at the seminary of the Sulpicians in France, an order that was sending many new priests to the United States. While the federal convention sweated out a draft of the Constitution in Philadelphia in the summer of 1787, Thayer wrote of his plans to return home to convert his countrymen to the Catholic faith, thinking that perhaps God "has only permitted and brought to an end, the surprising Revolution of which we have been witnesses, in order to accomplish some great design, and much more happy Revolution in the order of grace."[5]

✠

At the end of the nineteenth century, American Catholics counted up the converts they had gained as part of that religious revolution. Thayer stood at the head of most lists, along with several converts he had made in Boston.[6] The most prolific list maker was D. J. Scannell-O'Neill, whose series of articles eventually culminated in a book-length work, *Distinguished Converts to Rome in America*. The 3,000 names on the list were not exhaustive, for the rhetorical emphasis was as much on the dignity as on the quantity of converts: 8 converts who became bishops or archbishops (actually, there were 11); 202 converts who became priests; 115 medical doctors; 126 lawyers; 45 members of Congress; 372 ex-Protestant clergymen and 3 ex-rabbis; and the wives of many of the above, plus 260 women who became nuns (Figure 6.1). Richard H. Clarke had earlier published a list of about 700 names dating back to Thayer, and the Paulist missionary Alfred Young appended yet another list to his book, *Catholic and Protestant Countries Compared*. Though the zeal of the compilers sometimes exceeded the facts, these lists documented how Catholics made converts from the elites of American society.[7]

Another kind of list told a bigger but more subtle story. From 1852 to 1907, the Missionary Society of St. Paul the Apostle kept careful records of the converts they had won while fulfilling their vocation to evangelize Protestants. In six large manuscript volumes these Paulist Fathers—most of whom were converts themselves—chronicled how they had multiplied their efforts across time and space to win Protestants. At the middle of the century, the order comprised four priests based in a parish in midtown Manhattan; sixty-five years later, the Paulists had four mission bands scattered around the country. The Paulists alone heard the confessions of some 80,000 to 110,000 Catholics each year. An unknowable number of these were loosely affiliated Catholics whose "conversion" from sin at a Paulist mission marked the start of a real affiliation with the church, analogous to the conversions experienced at a Protestant revival. But they also made hundreds of converts from Protestants or the irreligious each year, nearly 6,000 over the course of the half century. Some of these converts were wealthy New Yorkers taking the waters at Saratoga Springs, the

STATISTICS OF THE LIST.

Converts	3000
Anglican Bishops	1
Protestant Clergymen	372
Jewish Rabbis	3
Clergymen to become Archbishops amd Bishops	4
Clergymen " " Monsignori	3
Clergymen " " Priests	135
Founders of Anglican Religious Orders	1
Members of Anglican Religious Orders	25
Converts who became Archbishops	4
Converts who became Bishops	4
Converts who became Abbots and Priors	5
Converts who became Monsignori	3
Converts who became Priests	202
Anglican Nuns	12
Convert Nuns to establish Religious Orders	6
Nuns	260
Medical Profession	115
Legal Profession	126
United States Senators and Congressmen	45
Governors of States	12
Mayors of Cities	8
Diplomatic Service	21
Educators	28
U. S. Army Officers	125
C. S. A. Army Officers	32
U. S. Navy Officers	23
Authors, Journalists, Musicians, Painters	206

FIGURE 6.1 Catholic missionaries and polemicists published many lists of converts to their church. The book-length *Distinguished Converts to Rome* listed 3,000 of the most prominent converts, and tabulated their claims to distinction, noting either their occupation before conversion or their influence within the Catholic church after conversion. D. J. Scannell-O'Neill, *Distinguished Converts to Rome in America* (St. Louis: B. Herder, 1907).

type who made it into *Distinguished Converts*, but more were the black and Irish servants of the wealthy. The Paulist records included converts from every class. Unlike the list compilers, who gathered their data from letters and their connections within the church, the Paulists counted only those people over whose heads they had personally poured the waters of baptism, on whose lips they had placed the sacred host, or over whom they had pronounced absolution.[8]

Extrapolating the total number of converts to Catholicism from these varied sources is impossible. As E. Rameur, a nineteenth-century French observer of Catholicism, put it, "a false delicacy prevents the Americans from including the statistics of religious belief in their census-tables. Estimates are very variable."[9] Scholars have most frequently cited an "estimated 700,000 conversions to the church from 1813 to 1893." That number is certainly wrong: based on his list of 700 converts, Richard H. Clarke guessed that converts and their descendants must have numbered 700,000, and twentieth-century scholars compounded that unfounded guess by assuming the number meant only converts themselves.[10] It is possible, however, to state the importance of conversion to the nineteenth-century Catholic Church. Rameur concluded that "the influence of immigration is not enough to account for the rapid progress of the faith."[11] The proportion of converts was sufficiently large that church officials could speak of the "convert element." When bishops confirmed new additions to the church, often a handful or more of adult converts were among the scores of children.[12] The label of "missionary church" imposed by the Vatican until the early twentieth century as an administrative distinction actually reflected that the Catholic Church was breaking new ground in the United States. Because the church was growing, converts rose to prominence in every aspect of church life: the journalist Orestes A. Brownson became a noted apologist and intellectual; the priest Isaac Hecker led the church's missionary movement; James Roosevelt Bayley even became the head of the American hierarchy as archbishop of Baltimore. Patrick Allitt has argued that converts were the primary intellectual drivers of the Roman Catholic Church on both sides of the Atlantic.[13] In short, converts made up much of the life of the American Catholic Church in the nineteenth century.

Conversions to Roman Catholicism fell into three distinct periods. Beginning with John Thayer's conversion in 1783 and continuing through the 1830s, conversions were scattered, and converts usually came from Reformed Protestant groups. The critical period for Catholic conversion was the 1840s through the 1860s. During this period, a wave of converts entered the church from American Episcopalianism, which was riven by the Oxford Movement, and from Transcendentalist and liberal Christian reformers dissatisfied with the theological underpinnings of reform. These Catholic converts became the agents behind a new movement to convert Protestants. From 1870 through the beginning of the twentieth century, missionary priests pressed the possibility of conversion on many Americans and won thousands of converts.

Though the converts' reasons were as varied as the individuals themselves, new Catholics showed a great deal of unity in the main reason they gave for converting. In theological terms, converts to the church yearned for "catholicity."[14] Many American Protestants, troubled by the multiplicity of sects in the American free market of religion, sought unity in a visible, orthodox church. The idea that the true church would be catholic—that is, universal across time and space—was an ancient doctrine with renewed appeal in the mid-nineteenth century. Because the Roman Catholic Church recognized Protestant baptisms as valid, many converts came to think of themselves as having always belonged to the Catholic Church.[15]

The Catholic Church in the nineteenth century labored mightily to overcome anti-Catholic prejudice and secure its rights within the American denominational system.[16] But in their search for catholicity, converts to Catholicism rejected the American denominational system even as Catholicism was winning its place within it. Therein lies the significance of conversions to Catholicism for understanding nineteenth-century U.S. religion. Converts who rejected the burden of choosing from among sects by picking Catholicism clearly demonstrated the inescapable obligation of religious choice.

✠

By and large, nineteenth-century converts to Catholicism in the United States joined the church because they were turning away from the proliferation of Protestant sects. After the Revolution, Baptists and Methodists grew rapidly, while fragmenting into dozens of independent groups. New movements such as the Disciples of Christ, the Shakers, the black denominations, and the Mormons formed on the basis of new theologies, new social pressures, and new revelations. Each sect claimed to know the way of salvation more perfectly than any other, if indeed any other could be said to have the truth at all. This menu of choices appealed to many Americans as they joined churches in ever-increasing numbers.

But tens of thousands became convinced that if so many sects could claim truth, then none of them actually had it. Stephen Blythe was a Bostonian who heard Father Thayer preach and eventually converted to Catholicism after experimenting with the Episcopal, Moravian, Universalist, and Swedenborgian churches and investigating Deism and Islam. He concluded, "In this chaos of creeds—amid this anarchy of sects and opinions, it is true with mathematical certainty that all cannot have truth on their side."[17] The most famous convert to Catholicism, Orestes Brownson, tried on almost as many religions as one could manage: Congregationalism, Presbyterianism, Universalism, Unitarianism, and Transcendentalism. When he was convinced that salvation came only through the church, he wrote that "we take it for granted that no serious Protestant can be satisfied with the present state of our Protestant world. The foundation of all moral and social well-being is in religion; and religion cannot coexist . . . with our sectarian divisions, dissensions, and animosities. Union is loudly demanded. We hear the cry for it from all quarters." Brownson thought that "the great evil under which we suffer is not so much *wrong* churchism, as it is *no*-churchism," his term for the inevitable consequence of Protestant fragmentation. He became convinced that one must "either accept No-churchism and say no more about it," or "if we must have a Church, and cannot have one without returning to the Roman communion, then, let us go to Rome."[18] While religion in the United States was becoming a voluntary system where one had to choose a denomination, some people tried to opt out of the system altogether by converting to the religion with the best claim to "catholicity."

"Catholicity" was an idea about Christianity, but it was also a common name for the Roman Catholic Church, a shorthand reference to the church by its most persuasive idea. Thus the Jesuit missionary priest Francis Xavier Weninger appealed to Protestants in his book *Catholicity, Protestantism and Infidelity*, and the former Episcopalian Fanny Maria Pittar described herself as *A Protestant Converted to Catholicity by Her Bible and Prayer-Book*.[19] In a series of lectures titled *Evidences of Catholicity*, Archbishop Martin John Spalding used the recently developed mode of evidentiary, rationalist apologetics to define an ancient idea about the church. He argued that four creedal descriptions of the true church—"one, holy, catholic, apostolic"—along with miracles, infallibility, and the primacy of the see of St. Peter, made up the definite marks of "catholicity," and that those marks were possessed only by the Roman Catholic Church. Catholicity was thus an idea that the true church was unified in doctrine and practice across space and time.[20]

The catholicity of the Roman Catholic Church was institutional as well as theological. By the middle of the century, Catholics were the largest minority faith in the United States.[21] Considered together, Protestants were far and away a majority, but Catholics argued that Protestant numbers should not be aggregated because they were fragmented into mutually incompatible groups. Catholics pointed out that even the pan-Protestantism of the American Bible Society and the American Tract Society did not imply unity in worship, polity, or doctrine. The convert from Episcopalianism Pierce Connelly bitterly denounced such interdenominational cooperation as mere shams of the Catholic church.[22] Institutional catholicity let Catholics argue—persuasively, to many converts—that they had primacy, tradition, the interpretation of the Scriptures, and history all on their side. Just as important, Catholics had a form of ritual and religious practice that, though foreign and even idolatrous to Protestants, nevertheless appealed to some people more than Protestant devotional practices stripped bare of ritual. Richard Clarke observed that each Protestant denomination had emphasized some truth that provided its adherents a road to Catholicism. In Catholicism, Episcopalians found their "love of religious antiquity and episcopacy"; Presbyterians, "the principle of ecclesiastical authority"; Methodists, the "intense culture of the personality of God and of the Saviour"; Puritans, "their hatred of Erastianism"; evangelicals, their "zeal . . . against mere formal religion."[23] Thus Isaac Hecker sought a "polemical theology" for the Paulists that would "develop the intrinsic notes of the Church."[24] Devotional and mystical practices, the saints, connections to the Blessed Virgin Mary, ecclesiastical authority, tradition, and antiquity—all these went by the name Catholic. Catholicity had all the variety of Protestant sectarianism, plus a visible unity.

The idea of catholicity had enormous intellectual appeal during the nineteenth century. Most famously, a party within the Church of England known as the Oxford Movement claimed that their church was a branch of the catholic church rather than a Protestant denomination. In a series of *Tracts for the Times*, Edward Pusey, John Keble, and John Henry Newman reinterpreted the liturgy and doctrine of the Church of England as compatible with Catholicism.[25] When the Oxford Movement came to the United States, it met firm resistance from bishops and congregations that emphasized the reformed, Protestant, and evangelical character of the Anglican tradition over its catholic heritage. As a consequence, many of the adherents of the Oxford Movement, like their intellectual leader John Henry Newman, found themselves pushed as much as pulled toward the Roman Catholic Church. Yet within a few decades, the Oxford Movement had taken root, and many members of the Protestant Episcopal Church considered themselves Anglo-Catholics. There was even a movement to rename the denomination the "American Catholic Church."[26] While some Episcopalians went on to become Roman Catholics, the Episcopal Church also won its own converts on the strength of its catholicity. After her father's death, Harriet Beecher Stowe, the famed author of *Uncle Tom's Cabin* and daughter of the Calvinist minister Lyman Beecher, left the Congregationalism of her youth for the Episcopal Church. Though Stowe had experienced a new birth as a Congregationalist when she was thirteen, as an adult she was drawn to the liturgy and sacraments of the Episcopal Church and came to reconceive of salvation in sacramental terms.[27]

Even the more resolutely Protestant found the idea of catholicity desirable. At a seminary in Mercersburg, Pennsylvania, church historian Philip Schaff and theologian John Williamson Nevin constructed a theology of "evangelical (*evangelische*) catholicism." For Schaff and Nevin, as for Newman, development was the key to locating catholicity in their modern age. Where most Protestants regarded the Reformation as a sharp break from the corruptions of Romanism and a return to the purity of the primitive church, Schaff and Nevin admitted a historical continuity between the medieval Catholic Church and the Reformers in order to preserve the catholicity of the Protestant churches. They envisaged a Hegelian dialectic between Protestantism and the Catholic Church. In Nevin's typology, the thesis of Petrine Catholicism and the antithesis of Pauline Protestantism were creating a new Johannine Christianity that would reunite Christendom.[28]

Both men stood by their "evangelical catholicism" despite severe difficulties. Schaff faced heresy trials twice for "Romanizing," though he was acquitted both times. For a period of five years beginning around 1850, Nevin privately considered converting to Roman Catholicism. He wrote publicly that "'the whole present state of sect Christianity is full of difficulty and discouragement,' since the sect system 'has no tendency whatever to surmount its own contradiction, but carries in itself the principle only of endless disintegration.'"[29] Nevin wrestled with the question, "How shall the demands of the old Catholic faith be satisfied in true union with Protestant freedom?" Doubting his dialectic, he wondered whether only conversion could resolve the difficulty. He corresponded with converts Orestes Brownson and James McMaster about being received into the church. McMaster indiscreetly wrote in the *Freeman's Journal* that "the day is not distant when another triumph will be added to the faith in the conversion of this profound and learned scholar" and asked readers to pray to that end. Nevin did not convert, mostly because Brownson's static idea of the church's magisterium contradicted his idea of catholicity as development.[30] But others in their staunchly anti-Catholic German Reformed Church did convert. Around 1871, two ministers, J. S. Ermentrout and G. D. Wolff, went over to Catholicism and were censured for denying that the Reformation was the "Roman Church . . . separating itself from all communion and fellowship with the Reformed Church."[31]

This idea of catholicity appealed not only to Episcopalian seminarians who read the church fathers and to émigré theologians who read the German Romantics, but also to intellectuals, authors and artists, the genteel, and intermarried Protestants and Catholics.[32] These varied conversions, however, were but part of a much broader movement of converts into the church, many of whom shared the same yearnings for catholicity as theological elites. One such convert was a Lutheran coachman in the employ of George Hecker, a wealthy flour magnate. George Hecker was a convert to Catholicism and the benefactor of his brother Isaac. When the Paulists preached a mission in New York City, this unnamed Lutheran was received into the Catholic Church. He had been reading Isaac Hecker's book, *Questions of the Soul*, in which Hecker laid out his diagnosis of American religion in its opening lines: "The age is out of joint. Men run to and fro to find the truth." Hecker offered a remedy that was no respecter of persons. Only the "Church of Christ" could answer "to the wants of the soul," whether the person "be king or slave, rich or poor, artist or laborer, in a word every individual of the race whether white or black, young or old, man or woman." The coachman found that these were "the very same questions his own soul used to ask, and that the Catholic Church alone could answer them."[33]

Conversions of both the working class and wealthy merchants demonstrate the peculiar position that nineteenth-century Catholicism occupied in the hierarchy of social and economic class. On the one hand, Catholicism was decidedly a religious tradition on the margins of social acceptability, given the pervasiveness of anti-Catholic prejudice among American Protestants. Because Catholicism was predominantly the religion of immigrants, Catholics were for the most part poorer than Protestants. Many converts gave up social status to become Catholics. Married Protestant clergymen such as Levi Silliman Ives gave up their livelihood because they could not become priests. Ives was left impoverished, and Archbishop Francis Kenrick established a convert relief fund and sought a position for Ives with great difficulty.[34] But on the other hand, by the end of the century, conversion to Catholicism gained new popularity among the upper classes caught up in the fashion for the Romantic, the medieval, and the Gothic. Those upper classes could afford to pay the social cost of converting in their pursuit of the antimodern.[35]

The conversions of the Hecker brothers illustrate how very differently Catholic converts could see their new faith when it came to economic relations. George and John Hecker both became wealthy from the family flour business and supported their brother Isaac. John converted to Episcopalianism, finding it sufficiently catholic for his taste, while George became a Roman Catholic and funded both his brother Isaac's sojourn as a mystic among the Transcendentalists and later his preaching tours across the country. George Hecker was not alone in his generosity to the church. Thomas Fortune Ryan, a wealthy New York magnate, and George Bliss, a noted attorney for railroads, insurance companies, and the federal government, both converted to Catholicism during the second half of the century. Ryan used his money to endow many churches; Bliss used his pull with President Chester Arthur to save the American College in Rome.[36]

Isaac Hecker, however, took a vow of poverty as a Redemptorist priest and lived ascetically for much of his life.[37] He saw his Catholicism as an alternative to the way that souls were shaped by capitalism. When Hecker addressed potential converts in *Questions of the Soul*, he told them that in the United States there was "a class of souls that cannot satisfy their natures with the common modes of life," who doubted that "he who amasses wealth" could be a follower of Jesus. "Christ was not only poor, he had also a great affection for poverty," and "as he approached death he became more and more enamored of poverty. His garments were stripped from his body and naked he was nailed to the cross." Where Protestants held that imitating Christ in his poverty was "not required of men, . . . [and] that no one can practise voluntary poverty," Hecker's gospel was that "voluntary poverty must be most precious in the sight of God if one is able by it to purchase the riches of heaven."[38] For Hecker, conversion was a mystical experience in the economy of grace—a gift, rather than a market transaction. The gift of grace obligated him to a vow of poverty and a life dedicated to converting others.[39]

Converts to Catholicism, unlike converts to Protestantism, at least sometimes saw their new faith as a rejection not only of the American sect system but also of capitalism. Protestants, in the judgment of Mark Noll, accepted capitalism without reservation while providing moral instruction in how wealth should be used; Catholics, on the other hand, sometimes challenged the structures of capitalism itself.[40]

This is not to say that conversions to Catholicism were driven primarily by political or economic concerns; they were not. But relations between Protestantism and Catholicism were fraught with politics. Protestants argued that republicanism and freedom were incompatible with Catholicism. Lyman Beecher wrote in his *Plea for the West* that it was "by the march of revolution and civil liberties" that the "triumphs of universal Christianity," in this instance meaning Protestantism, would be ushered in.[41] Catholic apologists—chief among them Orestes A. Brownson—argued that Catholicism was necessary for political liberty. Brownson has often been treated as the archetype of conversion to Catholicism. But Brownson was unusual rather than typical. Most converts were less concerned about politics in their conversion narratives than was Brownson.[42]

Many Catholic converts found the central characteristic of American religion—its multiplicity, its pluralism—incompatible with the expression of their faith. American Catholics valued religious liberty, even though Leo XIII rebuked American Catholics for accepting the separation of church and state.[43] But they deplored religious license and "indifferentism." Converts who grew weary of the continual variation and disputation of competing sects often found themselves embracing the church with the best claim to unity and catholicity. They converted because they formed bonds with the saints in communion, and because they experienced the power of the sacraments. What was American about American religion was not only the multiplicity of sects, but the yearning for catholicity that the multiplicity provoked.

✠

If catholicity was the mark of the true church, then an important question was what Protestants and Catholics thought of each other's eternal salvation. Almost all Protestants, especially evangelicals, regarded Catholics as unconverted and thus unsaved. Catholics relied on works rather than grace and faith, said Protestants, and thus had not experienced heart conversion. Evangelical minister and historian Robert Baird classified Roman Catholicism among the "unevangelical denominations in America," because even though Catholics "hold those doctrines on which true believers of all ages have placed their hopes for eternal life, yet those have been so buried amid the rubbish of multiplied human traditions and inventions, as to remain hid from the great mass of the people."[44] Catholics gave as good as they got. They proclaimed Protestants to be outside the true church and thus cut off from the sacraments, true faith in Christ Jesus, and the hope of eternal life. By rebelling against the faith of the church, embracing false doctrines, cutting themselves off from the Eucharist, and refusing to receive the forgiveness of the church in the sacraments of penance and last rites, Protestants were likely to die outside the church and without salvation.

But Catholics made a distinction based on baptism that most Protestants did not. They regarded Protestants as heretics but not as pagans. A pagan was someone with no connection to Christianity at all, someone who had never been initiated into the church. Though Protestants were heretics because they were in schism with the Roman Catholic Church, they had been initiated into the church through baptism. Catholics denied the validity of most of the Catholic sacraments mimicked by Protestants: Protestants were not validly ordained, the Protestant Lord's Supper did not perform the miracle of transubstantiation as priests did in the Eucharist, Protestants could not absolve penitents of sins, and even Protestant marriages, though valid, did not have a sacramental character. Nevertheless, Catholic theology defined Protestant baptisms as valid. Not all Protestants reciprocated. In 1845, the Presbyterian Church (Old School) declared Catholic baptisms invalid, even over the objection of their best-known theologian, Charles Hodge, who understood better than the General Assembly the consequences that decision had for the theology of Christian unity.[45] For Baptists, the question was never even raised; they regarded all infant baptisms as invalid because they were not performed after the heart conversion of a believer.

Catholics extended recognition to Protestant baptisms not entirely out of an ecumenical spirit but because they repudiated the practice of rebaptism performed by some Protestants. The sixteenth-century Council of Trent was the first to define Protestant baptisms as valid, even if performed outside the church. Catholic theologians always had a horror of rebaptism, which denied the essential nature of a sacrament as a work of Christ (*ex opere operato*) rather than of a minister. To repudiate rebaptizers, the Tridentine Catechism defined the essential form of the sacrament of baptism: it had to be performed with real water, though it was a matter indifferent whether the mode was sprinkling, infusion, or immersion, performed once or three times; and the baptism had to be performed with the Trinitarian formula, "in the name of the Father, and of the Son, and of the Holy Ghost." Though baptism was normally performed by a bishop or priest, it could be performed by anyone in an emergency. The laity and even non-Catholics could perform the rite, including "Jews, infidels and heretics, provided, however, they intend to do what the Catholic Church does in that act of her ministry." Many American converts knew this doctrine because the *Catechism of the Council of Trent* was the standard Catholic educational text until the publication of the 1885 *Baltimore Catechism*.[46]

This theology of baptism changed the mode and meaning of conversion for everyone who joined the Catholic Church from Protestantism. In cases when there was some doubt about whether baptism had been properly administered, such converts received baptism *sub conditione* (conditionally). In conditional baptism, the priest inaudibly added the words "if you are not yet baptized" to the baptismal formula—a literally tacit acknowledgment that a prior baptism might have elevated the person being received into the church from nature to grace and made him or her a part of the Catholic Church. Though different bishops had practices that varied in the details, conditional baptisms were usually performed privately (because the original baptism was perhaps valid) but with the full ceremonies of the church. Bishop Francis Patrick Kenrick, for instance, made "no distinction as regards the ceremonies between conditional and unconditional baptism of adults" but performed the ceremonies when the person "received baptism without ceremonies, as is always the case among the Sects."[47] But in cases where there was no doubt, converts were not baptized and the only ritual performed was the "abjuration of heresy" through the recitation of the Creed of Pope Pius IV. That Reformation-era creed prefixed the Nicene Creed with the declaration, "I, *N.*, with a firm faith believe and profess each and everything which is contained in the Creed which the Holy Roman Church maketh use of," and added to the creed a statement of belief in the seven sacraments, transubstantiation, and "the Holy Catholic Apostolic

Roman Church as the mother and teacher of all churches"—all of which the converted acknowledged to be the "true Catholic faith, outside of which no one can be saved."[48] This theology of baptism changed the imaginative possibilities for converts and the people who received them into the church. Priests who were inclined to evangelize Protestants could think of them as already a part of the church, only fallen away. Based on the theology of Thomas Aquinas, Protestants who had not purposely rejected the Catholic church, but sincerely desired salvation, might not actually be heretics but instead belong to the "Soul" of the church. According to Thomas's *Summa Theologiae*, an error was only heresy "when it is error *pertinaciously* maintained and *manifestly* against the faith." Therefore anyone, Clarke observed, "whether pagans or Protestants, who are in good faith and sincerely desirous of knowing the truth, are claimed as belonging to the soul of the Church."[49]

Many Catholic converts entered the church because they had come to regard themselves as already a part of it through baptism. Protestant clergymen were especially likely to come to this realization because of their theological training, but other Protestants learned of it from their reading. Levi Silliman Ives, the Episcopal bishop of North Carolina, ascertained the doctrine from the German theologian Johann Adam Moehler's *Symbolism*. Ives became "convinced, therefore, that I was originally placed by baptism within the pale and under the authority of 'the One Catholic and Apostolic Church'" and that to continue separated from it was "an act of deadly schism." Ives concluded that submitting to the Roman Catholic Church (which he did by handing over his episcopal ring to Pope Pius IX at Rome on Christmas Day, 1852) was not a betrayal of the Protestant Episcopal Church. That church could neither validly ordain him nor forgive his sins after baptism, but it could baptize him into the Catholic Church.[50] H. H. Wyman, who traveled from Congregationalism to Catholicism, felt by the time of his conversion that "not to have become a Catholic when I did would have been apostasy from my vows of baptism as a Congregationalist."[51] Isaac Hecker's biographer, Walter Elliott, wondered whether Hecker's spirituality before his conversion was attributable to nature or to the grace of his baptism as a child.[52]

As a young man, Nathaniel Augustus Hewit learned from his evangelical Congregationalist father, Nathaniel Hewit, that "a baptized person might claim all the privileges of a child of God which are signified by baptism, if he were willing to acknowledge and ratify his own part" in the baptismal vows. His father was referring to the Reformed theology of baptism as a sign of the covenant. Hewit "began at once to fulfill my part of the baptismal compact" by experiencing an evangelical conversion in which he "immediately prayed most earnestly for forgiveness." Before his conversion, he had "learned to despise and hate God and religion, and to disbelieve the Bible"; his evangelical conversion was his first attempt to grapple with the problem of infidelity.[53]

After his conversion, the earnest young man attended Amherst College, and then, beginning in 1840, he studied for the Congregationalist ministry at the theological seminary in East Windsor, Connecticut. The liberal tendency in Congregationalism bothered him greatly: he wrote to his parents repeatedly that Andover Theological Seminary was sliding toward Unitarianism and disputing the doctrine of "Plenary Inspiration." Hewit found it hard to "keep up friendship" with people who were denying Christ, especially one of his classmates who "thought the Atheistic hypothesis possible." Hewit admitted to questioning his own faith and wrote that "the unbelief with which I have to struggle is deeper" than Unitarianism.[54] Hewit found the New Haven theology of Nathaniel William Taylor taught at the seminary inadequate, and he criticized conversions under Asahel Nettleton's preaching since the "minds of his converts seem to have been very little directed to the contemplation of the sufferings and death and resurrection of the Saviour."[55]

Hewit preferred to read the fathers of the Christian church, John Henry Newman's *Lectures on the Doctrine of Justification*, Catholic theology, and *Brownson's Quarterly Review*. When he graduated from seminary, he became an Episcopalian and was ordained deacon, reserving the right to interpret the Thirty-Nine Articles in the sense of Newman's *Tract 90*. When Newman converted, Hewit followed him into the Catholic church. When he entered the church on March 25, 1846, he took the confirmation name Augustine Francis Hewit. The conversion to Episcopalianism, and even more the conversion to

Catholicism, caused a "sad and painful separation" with his father.[56] Hewit's conversion to Catholicism was both a turning away from "these days of scepticism and unbelief" to a turning to "recover at that time the grace which I had received in baptism." Hewit came to realize that he had been "united to the soul of the Catholic Church" in baptism though not yet a Catholic outwardly.[57]

The Paulist Fathers and other mission preachers confronted many Protestants with the doctrine that they were already a part of the Catholic Church. It was no coincidence that both Wyman's and Hewit's stories appeared in *From the Highways of Life*, a publication of the Paulist Fathers. In their hundreds of missions across the United States, the Paulists emphasized baptism as the moment of salvation.[58] The climax of a Paulist mission was the renewal of baptismal vows, which came with indulgences granted for the mission. Protestant observers often remarked about the power of this closing service. A "Protestant lawyer" thought the renewal of baptismal vows was a "most sublime scene," and he "lay awake the whole night."[59] In Cleveland, "a young girl, baptized a Cath[olic] but brought up a Prot[estant] went home after the sermon on judgment and cried all night. She could not be pacified or got to bed. The next morning she applied to be instructed and reconciled to the church."[60] In Plattsburg, New York, a workingman who had been baptized by one of his fellows in a slaughterhouse came to a mission expressing a desire to become a Catholic; when the priest asked about the form of his baptism, the priest was persuaded that it was valid and permitted him to take Holy Communion.[61] At North Bridgewater, Connecticut, an Episcopalian was received into the church because of the baptism of his infant. The Paulists recorded that "among the reasons he gave for becoming a Catholic," he said, "I had a dear little child who was baptized in the church, and I know she is gone to heaven, and I'm afraid I would never see her, if I did not become one too."[62] In New York City in 1858, the Paulists received many Protestants "besides others also who [though] baptized in the church had never professed themselves Catholics."[63]

☩

The Catholic doctrine of baptism created another asymmetry between Protestant and Catholic conversions. Though Catholic revivalism borrowed many elements from Protestant revivals, the pattern of conversions was different. Evangelical Protestants regarded conversion as the moment that interrupted and transformed one's life from sinfulness to salvation, while Catholics regarded it as one moment among many that repaired one's spiritual life.[64] The Catholic pattern of life brought a person genuinely and irreversibly into the church from infancy, while the Protestant pattern made the choice to become a Christian obligatory for each person.

The normative Catholic life was one regulated by and infused with the seven sacraments. It began with the sacrament of baptism performed soon after a child's birth, which brought the infant into the Catholic Church, invested him or her with the privileges of being a Christian, and washed away original sin and the eternal punishment for sins. When a child reached the age of reason around twelve years old, the child would be confirmed in the church by a bishop and receive for the first time the sacrament of the Eucharist, which he or she would then take at least yearly. Later in life, the person would most likely marry, and provided the spouse was a Catholic, the church would perform the sacrament of matrimony. If one instead became a priest or a nun, there would be a kind of marriage to Christ for a nun, or the sacrament of holy orders for a priest. Throughout life one would confess mortal and venial sins to a priest and receive absolution and penance in the sacrament of confession. And when one's life came to a close, a priest would anoint the dying person with oil in the sacrament of last rites, or *viaticum*. The normative life, however, was not typical, and much of the work of priests in their parishes, bishops in their dioceses, and the regular clergy on their missions was to "repair" breaches from these norms.

Conversion was the term for one of those repairs, and it was a term with a double meaning in Catholic theology. In its biblical and strict theological sense, conversion meant a turning from sin. Thus the Paulists could record that "a dramseller underwent a notable conversion" not because he was a Protestant who became a Catholic but because he was a Catholic who repented of his sins. In another instance, a Catholic who read anti-Catholic literature and threatened to join the Presbyterian church made the pastor of his parish "most anxious for his conversion during this mission." The term also had a broader theological meaning. Protestants used the word *conversion* as an umbrella term for both repentance (conversion) and faith. Catholic missionaries used the term this way as well. In Lexington, Kentucky, in 1855, for example, the Redemptorists made one convert "from atheism."[65] An adult convert from heathenism who was received into the church simply began the Catholic life from the start. He or she would be baptized, confirmed, undertake a general confession, and receive first communion.

When converts entered the Roman Catholic Church, they always did so through a ritual performed by a clergyman. One could not join the true church by fiat or choice alone. Protestants joined their congregations, but converts to Catholicism were "received." To be received, rather than to join, was to emphasize the stability of the church and the timelessness of the Catholic faith, which one might accept for oneself but on which one did not pass judgment. Paul Curtis, who resigned his Episcopal parish in Baltimore and traveled to England in 1872 to be converted by John Henry Newman, gave a detailed account of the rituals used in his conditional baptism, general confession, and confirmation. In a letter to a former parishioner, he explained that one of the "chief benefits of becoming a Catholic is just the fact that you find so much you don't understand, and that makes you feel as if you had gone back a long way, and turned baby again. And it's very nice to be a baby when you have such a grand thing as the Church to take you in its arms and carry you along." The rituals of conversion created this sense of trust for Curtis because he could submit to an authoritative mother church rather than having to search for the basics of Christian doctrine and then be perpetually uncertain of them: "It is so very nice to leave off pretending to know and to judge, and to be quite certain that you are where the judging will be done for you. I just believe whatever I am told, and I have been told nothing that I find any difficulty in receiving."[66]

✠

If theologies and practices of baptism and catholicity were the primary way that converts came into the Roman Catholic Church in the nineteenth century, their experiences varied widely over the course of the century. In the early republic, the natural rivals of Catholics in the United States were the Reformed Protestant churches, both the still-established Congregationalist churches in New England and also the Baptists who were growing both north and south. Their animosity was as old as the Reformation, but both Catholic and Protestant had to reckon with the new possibility of Enlightenment infidelity. Catholics and Protestants had long accused one another of being a halfway house on the road to atheism. Protestants argued that the excesses of Catholic "superstition" provoked people into rejecting faith altogether, while Catholics argued that the Protestant tendency to pare away the faith would leave nothing remaining. These arguments had a frightening immediacy in the age of the French Revolution, when Deists and rationalists published books like Tom Paine's *The Age of Reason* and Ethan Allen's *Reason the Only Oracle of Man*. Though the United States was not France, rationalism had a strong presence from the 1790s through the early decades of the nineteenth century.[67]

The basis of the debate between Protestants, Catholics, and unbelievers was mostly about how to acquire certain knowledge of religious truth. The debates thus set the parameters by which potential converts could seek out which religion to join. Those parameters were outlined in a dispute between John Carroll, the first Catholic bishop appointed in the United States, and a former Jesuit priest turned Congregationalist, Charles Henry Wharton. During the War for Independence, Wharton served a parish in Worcester, England, and then resigned his parish and returned to Maryland in 1783. He published a letter to the Catholics of his former parish explaining why he had rejected Catholicism. Carroll first replied anonymously as a "Catholic clergyman," and when his identity was found out he wrote publicly as head of the American church. As in every exchange between Catholics and Protestants, Wharton and Carroll debated the full range of issues since the Reformation: tradition, Scripture and the canon, transubstantiation, miracles, the use of images, and the veneration of Mary and the saints. But Wharton's complaint depended primarily on two linked arguments. Wharton argued that the Catholic doctrine *extra ecclesiam nulla salus* ("outside the church there is no salvation") falsely excluded other Christian denominations; furthermore, he argued that Catholics were kept from investigating the truth for themselves by papal claims about the infallibility of the church and papal bans on reading the books of other religions. Wharton here struck at both Catholic epistemology and piety, the way Catholics knew truth and the way they set out to learn it. He thought that a Catholic could not use reason "because . . . he cannot set out with that indifference to the truth or falsity of a tenet, which forms the leading feature of rational investigation."[68]

Carroll responded to Wharton on the issues of knowledge, authority, and piety. He offered a fundamentally different idea of what constituted appropriate inquiry into other religions. Carroll denied that the inquirer should take a Cartesian risk and abandon all presuppositions, citing on this point the English Catholic writer John Leland's *View of the Principal Deistical Writers*. Carroll argued that if one attempted to be "indifferent" to "doctrines or facts," or worse, if one "should actually disbelieve them," then one "must necessarily commence atheist, before he can fairly examine into the proofs of the existence of God." Carroll thought that one was more likely to find truth if one should "apply himself to it with a mind open to conviction, and a disposition to embrace truth." In other words, one was more likely to find the truth if one started out predisposed to the church. Carroll balanced his insistence that truth was best found within the Catholic Church with an argument that salvation could also be found outside of it. He distinguished between "*the communion of the church*" who participated in the sacraments and government of the Roman Catholic Church, and "*members of the catholic church*." These members were all "who with a sincere heart seek true religion, and are in an unfeigned disposition to embrace the truth, whenever they find it." Because the Council of Trent declared that people could be saved without "actual baptism" if they would desire baptism were it available, Carroll taught that "out of our communion salvation may be obtained."[69] Carroll thus articulated two seemingly paradoxical doctrines: that one could best find salvation within the authority of the church, but that baptism was truly catholic, encompassing those actually baptized in any sect as well as those who desired baptism. Converts to Catholicism would find that they could come to salvation only by putting themselves under the authority of the church, but they also were often taught that the church of Rome had already defined them as part of the Catholic Church.

Converts who came into the church during the early republic were pulled between infidelity, catholicity, and Protestantism. Stephen Blythe faced the dilemma that "out of the Catholic Church, there is no rational resource but Deism." He found that "many an example has there been of a Catholic, after rejecting the authority of his native church, becoming an Atheist." Blythe had seriously considered infidelity and turned to Catholicism to get as far from it as possible. A Protestant critic of Blythe's narrative agreed that "there is less distance than is thought between Skepticism and Popery; and that a mind wearied by perpetual doubt willingly seeks repose in the bosom of a Church which pretends to infallibility."[70] In 1835, Pierce Connelly came to regard Protestantism generally as suffering "deistical mutilation of her ritual." The "confusion" of Protestantism had left him afraid of infidelity, almost "utterly overthrown in faith and hope."[71]

This triangular nexus was at play in a set of conversions from infidelity and Protestantism in Vermont and New Hampshire. The first of these conversions was by Fanny Allen, daughter of the famed Revolutionary war leader Ethan Allen. Ethan Allen had stirred the opposition of Christians with his Deist publications in the aftermath of the Revolution. Though Fanny Allen was raised by her mother and stepfather, she was raised without any religion. Her parents had her baptized in her late teens by the local Episcopal priest, Virgil Barber, solely as an antidote against Catholicism before sending her to a convent in Montreal to learn French. At the convent, Allen was a skeptic and refused the nuns' entreaty to be pious. The turning point came when one of the sisters asked her to put flowers near the tabernacle and adore the reserved sacrament. Allen ridiculed the notion, but when she tried to enter the sanctuary with the flowers, she felt herself bodily barred at the doorway three times. She returned home to Vermont resolving to convert. Her parents and most of the people in the town were furious when they found a rosary wrapped in her handkerchief. Though her family did not care for religion, they tried to persuade her that the Protestant Episcopal Church was a better choice than the Roman Catholic Church. Allen was as independent-minded then as she had been when a skeptic, and she soon returned to Montreal and became a Catholic. She lived as a nun at the Hotel-Dieu convent, dying within a few years because of the severity of her devotions and the frailness of her health.[72]

Before Allen's death, she was visited by the Episcopal priest Daniel Barber, father to the priest who had baptized her into that church. Barber came to investigate her conversion as part of his own journey into the Roman Catholic Church. Barber was born a Congregationalist and had served in the Continental Army. In 1783 or 1784, he joined the Episcopal Church because he heard an Episcopalian call into question whether Congregationalists were a true church. Barber was persuaded that Congregationalist ministers lacked a line of succession back to the apostles since their ministers were not properly ordained by bishops. He was ordained an Episcopal priest three years later and served as pastor in Claremont, New Hampshire, for thirty years. During that time his son, Virgil Barber, also became an Episcopal priest and schoolteacher.[73]

Around 1818, however, the Episcopal foundations of three generations of the Barber family began to crumble. Daniel Barber again had his views on the apostolic succession shaken when he read a book challenging the ordination of the sixteenth-century archbishop of Canterbury, Matthew Parker. When Parker was consecrated archbishop during the reign of Edward VI, the Reformers had taken care that his ordination continued the succession back to the Roman Catholic Church. The question was much disputed, and Catholics never conceded the point, especially once the Tractarians elevated the importance of the idea of apostolic succession. Barber thus doubted whether he had ever validly received the sacrament of ordination, and he traveled to Boston to talk with the Roman Catholic bishop Jean-Louis Lefebvre de Cheverus, who was especially adept at dealing with converts. Cheverus gave him an armload of books to take back to his family, including saints' lives and John Milner's *The End of Controversy*.[74]

Virgil Barber and his wife, Jerusha, read Milner for themselves, as well as a booklet with a novena (a set of devotional prayers repeated over nine days) that he had borrowed from an Irish servant. Virgil made his own visit to New York to speak with the Jesuit priest (later bishop) Benedict Joseph Fenwick. In 1816, Virgil and Jerusha, along with their five children, were the first Barbers to enter the church, being persuaded by Milner's arguments about catholicity. Virgil then brought to New Hampshire the Dominican priest, Charles Ffrench, who preached a mission at Daniel Barber's home. Though she is little mentioned in the records, the linchpin of the family seems to have been Daniel's wife, Chloe Barber. She had also been reading Catholic books, and when she determined to convert under Ffrench, her other children as well as her sister, niece, and eventually nephew (a future bishop) converted. Daniel Barber was the first to investigate Catholicism but the last of his family to enter the church, after more than a dozen of his relatives.[75]

Milner's polemical work—read by nearly all converts who mentioned the books that influenced them—had brought the Barber family into the church. As Daniel Barber put it while justifying his choice in his memoirs, "I am a Catholic, because I have examined: do you the same, and you will be one too." Barber added that his newfound Catholicism and the unity of his family produced relief from the religious confusion of the United States. For proof of the difficulties that the Protestant denominational system had caused, he asked his readers to look into "our own country, into our neighborhood, into our own family. How rent and torn asunder, by dividing into sects and parties, even to the destruction of that love, peace and harmony."[76]

Though the Barber family found unity in Catholicism, their new faith divided their own family. Virgil and Jerusha Barber elected to live their lives like saints. Within a year, they had received a dispensation to annul their marriage. Virgil Barber entered the Jesuits; Jerusha became a Visitandine postulant. Their son was cared for by the Jesuits and eventually became one himself; each of their daughters was cared for by nuns, and they all took the veil themselves. The family was reunited one last time in 1820 at a chapel in Georgetown, where Virgil and Jerusha took their vows of religion while their children looked on. The father and son traveled to Europe for priestly training, and the mother and daughters went to separate convents. Virgil returned as a priest to Claremont, New Hampshire, where he managed to convert many in his former Episcopal parish to Roman Catholicism. When Bishop Fenwick visited the parish, he remarked that most of the Catholics there had converted within the last five years.[77]

Daniel Barber penned his memoirs from Saint Inigoes, Maryland. He moved there in his old age to follow his son and daughter-in-law, but also because he could live as a better Catholic in Maryland than he could in New Hampshire. There he found "not a family but such as are constant in reading, prayer, and works of faith."[78] Other converts besides Barber migrated to Catholic centers after their conversion. Stephen Blythe moved to the outskirts of Montreal, where he was confirmed in the church. Catholicism was difficult to experience in its fullness in places that conceived of themselves as Protestant. Lay Catholics throughout the colonial era, who were almost all born into their religion, had made do with a nearly priestless church.[79] Converts who joined Catholicism because it was a visible and not an invisible church wanted no such accommodation. The visible church offered sacraments, and in the case of confirmation required of converts, these rituals could only be performed by a bishop. Daily attendance at Mass or even Communion, not obligatory but nevertheless an ideal, was possible only at established places. The glories of the Catholic liturgy in the solemn masses could only be experienced in urban locations. Though converts made the hard choice to separate themselves from their family, in many cases they found that they wished to live where everyone was by default what they had become by choice. A number of the distinctive features of Catholicism promoted this kind of gathering. Nuns like Fanny Allen or priests like the Paulists lived together in community. Rome appealed to travelers like Isaac Hecker, Jane Sedgwick, and George and Anaïs Bliss. Montreal and Quebec City to the north, and Washington and Baltimore in the Southeast, appealed to converts as long as Catholics remained a minority group.

The critical period for conversions to Catholicism was the 1840s to the end of the Civil War. What made the period critical was not simply that people joined the church in greater numbers, but that the pathways into the church changed to encourage further conversion. This deep change came about in part because the Oxford Movement and Transcendentalism elevated the idea of catholicity among certain segments of Protestants, and in part because among some Protestants dissatisfaction with the chaos of American religion grew after forty years of a voluntary system. But it was converts to the Catholic Church during this period, especially priests like the Paulists or apologists like Brownson, who drove the growth in conversions by setting out to make Catholics of other Americans after the Civil War.

Beginning in the 1840s, converts came into the church in much greater numbers and for reasons that were more than individual. Jon Gjerde estimates that 60,000 people became Roman Catholics between 1831 and 1860.[80] Catholicity appealed primarily to two groups: those closest to Roman Catholicism and those furthest away. Catholics made converts from the Episcopal Church, a denomination that had preserved some Catholic practices and doctrines, and from Unitarianism or other liberal Christian denominations, which had rejected those doctrines entirely. Catholics less often made converts of evangelical or Reformed Protestants. Catholic missionary priests remarked on this trend themselves. Augustine F. Hewit wrote that most Catholic authors aimed to win converts either from the "extreme left" of Protestantism, meaning Unitarians and Transcendentalists, or from the most conservative Protestants, such as high church Episcopalians. On the basis of several decades of mission work, Hewit noted that "the greater number of converts in our own day have been either from the one or the other of these two classes." Isaac Hecker concurred in that assessment of the paths that converts took.[81] Hecker and Hewit themselves were both exceptions to and proofs of this rule. Hecker had been influenced by his mother's evangelical Methodism, and Hewit had been raised as a Congregationalist, but Hecker first associated with Transcendentalists and Hewit first became an Episcopalian before each became a Catholic.[82] E. Rameur also found that Protestant sects furnished converts in unequal numbers. Though it was "difficult to apply a statistical table to the study of the question of conversions," he noted that "the two sects which furnish the most [converts] are the Episcopalians, who, in their forms and traditions, approach nearest to the Catholic Church, and the Unitarians, who go to the very opposite extreme, and appear to push their philosophical and rationalistic principles almost beyond the pale of Christianity."[83] These two streams of converts became the dominant flows into the Roman Catholic Church, and anyone who became a

Catholic from reformed or evangelical Protestantism usually became an Episcopalian or a Unitarian first.

The American Catholic Church in the 1840s was very different from what it had been in the 1790s. After the Revolution, the church was still getting on its feet and had few priests and only one bishop. By 1840, there were many more priests, and the country's single diocese had been split into eighteen. Thus potential converts had more opportunities to interact with the church.[84] During this period, the church also held two of the three Plenary Councils of Baltimore, the American church's primary means of setting national policy during the nineteenth century. In 1852 and again in 1865, the assembled bishops passed legislation that regulated the way converts came into the church and established guidelines for cases of intermarriage. The second council laid plans for the evangelization of the United States.[85]

A crucial change came from converts themselves. A small but fervent group of converts headed by Isaac Hecker first joined together as Redemptorist priests, then founded a new religious order, the Paulist Fathers. This group had as its apostolate the conversion of Protestants to the Catholic Church. At the same time, Orestes Brownson established *Brownson's Quarterly Review;* James McMaster, an Episcopal convert who had traveled to Belgium with Hecker to study for the priesthood, published the *New-York Freeman's Journal and Catholic Register;* and Hecker and the Paulists founded the *Catholic World* to appeal to non-Catholics. Converts provided much of the material to the new Catholic Publication Society, which published dozens of conversion accounts, some as histories of early American converts like Demetrius Gallitzin and others by or about contemporaries like Joshua Huntington, James Kent Stone, and Francis Baker.[86] By the end of the 1860s, converted Catholics were primed to spread Catholicism throughout the United States.

The greatest flow of converts to the Catholic Church in the 1840s and 1850s came from Episcopalians who regarded themselves as catholic. At the General Theological Seminary in New York City, a group of students—among them Clarence Walworth, James McMaster, Arthur Carey, and Edgar Wadhams—trod very close to the boundary between Canterbury and Rome, and sometimes crossed it. These students saw themselves as the disciples of John Henry Newman, E. B. Pusey, and other leaders of the English Oxford Movement. Unlike the Tractarians, however, these youths were unordained (or sometimes in deacon's orders) and held no positions of note within the church. Though Newman argued for the compatibility of the Anglican church's doctrinal statements with Catholic doctrine in his famous *Tract 90*, the American students delighted in provoking the Protestant sensibilities of their co-religionists. Nearly all of them—including Walworth, McMaster, and Wadhams—had rejected the Reformed Presbyterianism or Congregationalism of their parents to join the Episcopal Church as young adults. They reveled in the jargon and paraphernalia of Catholicism. In Greek class, they translated a phrase from the New Testament as "do penance" rather than the Protestant rendering "confess," they bought rosaries, and they decorated the chapel for Christmas with garlands and a cross until forced to take them down.[87]

With youthful recklessness these students found the fissure in the Protestant Episcopal Church and drove a wedge into it. The Episcopal Church in the United States was emerging from the hard times it had suffered after the Revolution because of its connection to England and the loss of its privileges in disestablishment. By the 1840s, the church had produced its own prayer book, set up its own bishops and new parishes, established the General Theological Seminary to educate new clergy, and started to reverse its decline in membership. In addition, the Episcopal Church occupied a position of social prestige. The growth of the Episcopal Church put it in close proximity to the U.S. Catholic Church. The geographical centers of the Episcopal Church were New York, Charleston, and Baltimore— precisely the centers of growth for the Catholic Church.[88] Converts from the Episcopal Church to the Catholic Church most often converted at or at least spent substantial time interacting with Catholics at one of those locations.

But the Episcopal Church was divided into two parties. The "low church" or evangelical, party regarded the church as Protestant because of its roots in the Reformation, and it emphasized heart religion, interior conversion, and the doctrine of justification by faith alone. The "high church," or "catholic," party regarded the church as truly catholic because it continued the apostolic succession from the pre-Reformation Catholic Church in England and because it emphasized the sacraments. The Episcopal Church was sharply divided in its opinion of the Tractarians, but a sizable majority regarded supporters of the Oxford Movement as heretics and Romanists.

The students at the General Theological Seminary who called themselves catholics soon ran afoul of the Protestant wing. The most prominent test case involved Arthur Carey. When Carey presented himself for ordination in 1843, the pastor under whom he had served, Hugh Smith, and other clergymen questioned whether he held to the Thirty-Nine Articles (the doctrinal statement of the Episcopal Church) or whether his expressed views were too close to the Roman Catholic Church. Thanks to Carey's careful answers, the ambiguity of the Thirty-Nine Articles, and the support of Benjamin T. Onderdonk, bishop of New York and director of the seminary, Carey was ordained deacon. Whether Carey was indeed on the road to Rome or would have stayed in the Episcopal Church was never determined because he died eight months after being ordained at the age of twenty-one.[89]

The lengths to which the Tractarian-leaning wing of the Episcopal Church would go is illustrated by the peculiar baptism of Clarence Walworth. In June 1843, Walworth waded into the salty waters of the bay around New York City to be baptized for the second time. The Episcopalian minister who baptized him immersed Walworth three times while pronouncing the baptismal formula "in the Name of the FATHER and of the SON and of the HOLY GHOST." Afterward, the minister signed a certificate of baptism prepared in Walworth's hand, "heavily done in imitation of Old English lettering, ornamentally shaded with red." The Episcopal Church had not enjoined Walworth to be rebaptized, nor did it prescribe the "mode of 'trine immersion'" in its prayer book. This bizarre ritual, which borrowed elements from every branch of Christianity (and thus conformed to none of them) was Walworth's attempt to ensure he had a valid, catholic baptism.[90]

When he was a child, Walworth was baptized as a Presbyterian, in the faith of his family. He began attending an Episcopal church while practicing law, because his "fellow lodger" was the church organist. Bishop Onderdonk confirmed Walworth in the Episcopal Church in 1839, but Walworth later claimed that "no questions had been put to me as to what I believed or did not believe." His theological opinions were unschooled but broadly Protestant, save for a distaste for the doctrine of justification by faith alone. "With these convictions," Walworth thought, "I could without scruple have become a Presbyterian or Methodist as readily as an Episcopalian."[91]

His theology became better defined when he gave up his law practice in 1842 to become a student at the General Theological Seminary. The first shock came from James McMaster, an intelligent but impetuous student, who introduced Walworth to the doctrine of baptismal regeneration, though McMaster never managed to locate his proof text from the New Testament. The kindly Arthur Carey later identified the text in Acts and explained that baptism washed away sins and regenerated the soul. Walworth was persuaded very slowly, for he thought that "the idea of grace conveyed to the soul by means of a sacramental ceremony is something utterly inconsistent with the ordinary training of a Protestant mind." But once he was persuaded, this new doctrine was "the entering wedge of a new faith, far broader and deeper than any I then conceived of as possible."[92]

While Walworth was in seminary, baptism was a perpetual topic when catholicity was discussed. Some doubted that dissenting clergymen were truly ordained. At stake was the claim of Episcopalians and Anglicans that their church had maintained apostolic succession and thus was part of the "one true catholic apostolic church." Some of the seminarians maintained that dissenting clergymen were actually laymen, and because they held that baptism by laymen was invalid (a doctrine peculiar to high church Episcopalians), they concluded that Protestants were not in fact members of the church. Walworth was dismayed and could only exclaim that he "was the child of Presbyterian parents," as were some of his classmates, and that the "opinions expressed there so strongly and freely would sound very strangely at the firesides from which they had come." Carey, presiding over the meeting, defined those Protestants as "Christians" but not part of the "Church."[93]

In time, Walworth was persuaded that his previous baptism was invalid, and he asked Rector Caleb Clapp to rectify the deficiency with the waters of the Hudson River and Atlantic Ocean. The twenty-three-year-old confused catholicity with a kind of Christian pluralism, which he thought his baptismal rite and certificate guaranteed. Faced with many options, he tried to choose them all. The rite was designed to appeal to every possible Christian opinion of baptism. Catholics could not gainsay the baptism "on the ground of a want of intention on the part of the minister, since Mr. Clapp was a firm believer in the necessity of baptism, and would not administer it thoughtlessly." Episcopalians could not object to Clapp's credentials, since he was in holy orders from the Episcopal Church and not a layman. Baptists could not object that Walworth was "an infant and so incapable" of receiving baptism. Both Baptists and the Greek Orthodox Church had to admit that the mode of baptism was valid, "since the method of trine immersion was carefully used."[94]

Walworth aimed to make his second baptism incontrovertible. Yet no coherent theology motivated the idiosyncratic rite. In seeking to demonstrate his catholicity, Walworth thought he needed a ritual that would satisfy his Presbyterian parents, his Protestant aunt who brought him on trips to the American Bible Society, his skeptical and scoffing uncle, his Tractarian-leaning fellow seminarians, the judicious divines of his Episcopal church, the charge of excommunication from the papacy, and even the rites of the "schismatic Greeks" whom he knew only from his books. As he moved from Protestant indifferentism to the hothouse of the General Theological Seminary and eventually to Rome, Walworth was an example of a broader trend of people caught up in growing religious pluralism: they felt the need to change their religion but also the need to justify their religion to themselves, their family, and the world.

Such idiosyncratic attempts at catholicity within the Episcopal Church failed, in part because of the opposition of the Protestant wing, in part because of their own theological incoherence. Within two years of Carey's trial, nearly all of his fellow students with Romanizing tendencies had converted to Roman Catholicism. Wadhams and Walworth tried to found a two-person monastery in western New York but soon gave up the project and joined the Catholic Church. Charles West Thomson, a convert from Quakerism to Episcopalianism and a student at an Episcopal seminary in Philadelphia, also nearly converted in 1844–1845.[95] Levi Silliman Ives took a few more years to enter the Catholic Church—after coming under heavy fire in his diocese for trying to institute "papist" rituals and to establish a monastery and in the broader church for his defense of slaveholders.[96] Over the coming years, a number of Episcopal priests, among them Francis A. Baker (another future Paulist) and Alfred Curtis, left their parishes and converted to the Catholic Church as well.

✠

The future leader of this band of Episcopalian converts took an altogether different route to the church. Isaac Hecker, a working-class German American from New York, came to the church through evangelicalism and Transcendentalism. Hecker's mother was a Methodist, and at times Hecker attended Methodist revivals on his own. Though he never thought of himself as a Methodist, that evangelistic tradition influenced Hecker. Methodism was hardly the only tradition that Hecker knew, however. As a young man, he encountered Unitarianism in New York, he met the Mormon apostle Parley Parker Pratt in 1837, and he sometimes visited Shaker settlements in New York and Massachusetts. Working out of his family's bakery, Hecker participated in democratic and Fourierist reform movements and corresponded with Orestes Augustus Brownson, one of the reform leaders.[97]

Hecker's connections to radical political reformers, especially Brownson, led him to fall in with a number of Unitarians and Transcendentalists. Beginning in 1843, he spent months at the utopian communities at Brook Farm and Fruitlands in the company of Transcendentalists such as Bronson Alcott, Charles Dana, Charles Lane, Sophia Ripley, and William Henry Channing. For all its individualism, anti-Trinitarianism, and denial of dogma, the environment at Brook Farm was actually a greenhouse for converts to Catholicism, because its emphasis on spirituality led into Catholic devotional practice and its emphasis on the universal brotherhood of man led into the dogma of catholicity. Besides Hecker, Sophia Ripley also converted to Catholicism. Nathaniel Hawthorne traveled to Rome after living at Brook Farm and seriously considered Catholicism, while his daughter Rose became a Catholic nun named Mother Alphonsa. It is likely that William Henry Channing and his wife, Julia, would also have converted were it not for worries about their public reputation.[98] Charles Dana wrote to Hecker about his vision "of a society which shall be a church & a church which shall be a society" and which he called "that Holy Catholic Church which both you and I have at heart." He thought that "we shall best discharge our unspeakable debt to her [the Roman Catholic Church] by passing into the new Church." And James Kay Jr. argued with Hecker that "all the action of Christendom has been retrograde since Apostolic times" so "we arrive at Association as the true Church." These Transcendentalists thought that they had catholicity, even with their individualism, and for a few of them their catholicity led them to the Catholic Church.[99]

With their labor at the bakery and their investments in flour and shipping, Hecker's brothers, John and George, willingly afforded Isaac the leisure to develop his spirituality. Unlike his mercantile brothers, Hecker wrote that "my work must be devotional. It must be music, love, prayer." Hecker had a number of visions at this time, including one that prefigured his commitment to virginity. Hecker had begun to be acquainted with the Catholic mystical tradition, having read the life of the saint and founder of the Redemptorists, Alphonsus Maria de Liguori, and he later interpreted his visions as falling within that tradition. Hecker also lived so severe an ascetic life that he may have damaged his health. He baked bread for the community but ate none of it for himself, living mostly on raw vegetables and fruits. The hallmark of Hecker's spirituality was his belief that the Holy Spirit was guiding him into the church.[100]

Hecker was dissatisfied with Transcendentalism because it was too diffuse and individualist and could not meet his longing for catholicity. He worked out the problem in a long series of letters with Orestes Brownson, to whom Hecker signed his letters "deinen Sohn." (Within a few years, Brownson would be addressing him as "Father Hecker.")[101] He and Brownson determined to convert to the catholic church at roughly the same time. This left Hecker and Brownson with the problem of determining which church was truly catholic. The choices were between the Episcopal Church, which they considered to be a branch of the true church, and the Roman Catholic Church. Hecker wrote to Brownson that "at present I am not a member of any branch of the Catholic Church, but whatever branch I may be led to unite myself to, it would be as a Catholic to labor for the reunion and catholicity of the Church, as the prerequisite to all other movements which have for their object the advancement of Humanity."[102] Hecker first questioned Samuel Seabury, rector of the Episcopal Church of the Annunciation in New York City, about the catholicity of his church. Seabury made a strong argument that the Episcopal Church was catholic and the Roman Church was not. Hecker wondered whether some of the practices of Rome, especially the "assumptions of power assumed by the Pope of Rome," made the Roman Catholic Church "cling to exclusiveness and her practices which are not Catholic." Nevertheless, Hecker wrote to his brothers that the Anglican church could not really claim catholicity either because of its separation from Rome.[103] Hecker was so concerned with catholicity that when he visited a group of Shakers at the village of Harvard, Massachusetts, he asked them how "they justify their departure from the Catholic Church." "Their replies were very dubious and unsatisfactory," Hecker recorded, doubtless because they could scarcely conceive of the question that was agitating him.[104]

Brownson and Hecker both settled on the Roman Catholic Church as fulfilling their desires for catholicity. Brownson was the first to decide: "I do not as yet belong to the family of Christ. I feel it. I can be an alien no longer, and without the Church I know by my own past [e]xperience that I cannot attain to purity and sanctity of life. I need the counsels, the aids, the chastisements and the consolations of the Church. It is the appointed medium of salvation, and how can we hope for any good [e]xcept through it?" Hecker soon replied, "The life that leads me to the Church is deeper than all thought and expression and if I attempt to give a reason or to explain why I am led to the Church afterwards I always feel that it never reaches the reason and I feel its inadequacy. Let men say as they may it is only by grace that we come to the knowledge of the truth as it [is] in Jesus."[105]

As he made plans to enter the Roman Catholic Church in 1844, Hecker also made plans for a pilgrimage of voluntary poverty. For a period of weeks, perhaps months, Hecker fell into a spiritual malaise while waiting for conditional baptism because "it is a rule of the Church to defer the baptism of adults for a short time." In a letter written to Brownson on August 2, the very morning that he was to be baptized, Hecker described a plan to revive the ardor of a conversion not yet consummated. He planned to take "a penetential journey to Europe, even as far as Rome. To work my passage over the sea and to work walk and beg whatever distances I may go. A better penance I cannot think of." Hecker hoped to take along an unusual traveling companion, the "one person who can live on bread and water and sleep upon the earth, who can walk his share; if he should consent to go I might go. It is Henry Thoreau I mean."[106]

Henry David Thoreau might seem like an odd companion for a pilgrimage, but Hecker, himself a former Transcendentalist, was looking for someone to share the simple life and the rejection of the capitalist market.[107] Quoting the Gospels in his proposal to Thoreau, Hecker wanted to go "without purse or staff, depending upon the all-embracing love of God," for traveling in Europe and kneeling before shrines would "prove the dollar is not almighty." In his reply, Thoreau wrote that his soul leaped at the idea, because such wanderings rekindled "fresh faith in a kind of Brahminical, Artesian, Inner Temple life." But Thoreau could not comprehend Hecker's conversion to Catholicism: "The other day, for a moment, I think I understood your relation to that body; but the thought was gone again in a twinkling."[108]

Hecker had to break off his letter to Brownson to receive the waters of baptism, but he resumed the correspondence a few weeks later: "My project of going to Europe has so far failed. Henry Thoreau is not disposed to go and under the present circumstances I am not inclined to go on such a tour alone. This has thrown me back on the languages which may be of much more permanent good to me than the monk tour." Hecker did not bring up the question of whether Brownson might join the pilgrimage, but of course Brownson could not: he had a large family and burdensome financial obligations, which kept him from Hecker's kind of piety. Only someone as detached from family and the economy as Hecker or Thoreau could contemplate such a pilgrimage.[109]

Hecker's renunciation of the world came through the more conventional means of joining the regular clergy living under vows of poverty, chastity, and obedience. In 1849, Hecker, Walworth, Hewit, and several other converts joined the Redemptorists, an order of priests who gave missions throughout the country. After joining the church, Hecker had written the Redemptorist superior, "I believe that Providence calls me . . . to America to convert a certain class of persons amongst whom I found myself before my conversion."[110] The Redemptorists provided the best opportunity for Hecker and the others to fulfill that call. For a period of a week or two, the priests preached several times a day and heard thousands of confessions. Hecker so delighted in teaching the rosary that he became known as "Father Mary." The aim of such missions was to revive Catholicism among the many Irish and German immigrants, many of whom had only the most tenuous connection to the faith of their youth. The Redemptorists brought Catholics back into the fold, often hearing adults' first confessions and giving them their first communion.[111]

During the five years that Hecker and the convert priests were Redemptorists, they made scores of converts at their missions. Hecker would sometimes end his missions with "an extremely eloquent and popular lecture on Popular Objections to Catholicity."[112] But Hecker always thought that the Redemptorists made an inadequate effort to convert Protestants, who flocked to the missions unbidden. In 1855 Hecker published *Questions of the Soul,* and in 1857 he published *Aspirations of Nature,* arguing that the longings of individual souls and the collective good in the United States could only be found in conversion to the Catholic Church.[113] The Redemptorist provincial, as well as the bishops who granted permission for the missions, favored evangelism but could ill afford to pay attention to Protestants when there were so many unchurched Catholics.

Hecker traveled to Rome to present his proposal. But when he arrived in Rome, the rector major of the Redemptorists, who thought Hecker had made the journey without permission from his American superiors, disgraced him and expelled him from the order for breaking his vows of obedience and poverty. Hecker persisted in his plea, spending months in Rome working through Cardinal Alessandro Barnabò and the Congregation de Propaganda Fide (the Vatican institution that oversaw the United States) to bring his case before the pope. Hecker could not gain an audience until he met

George Loring Brown. Brown was one of many artists in the American colony at Rome, and after a few months in Hecker's company, he converted to Catholicism. Hecker wrote to his Redemptorist brothers that the conversion "has operated greatly in our favor, for it has gone through all the papers in Europe, & you should know that here in Rome a conversion excites among the Italians a great interest." The conversion caught the attention of Pope Pius IX, who granted Hecker permission to establish a new order, with a rule to be approved later.[114]

Hecker arrived back in New York in March 1858. The former Redemptorists bound themselves voluntarily, without vows, into a new community that they called the Missionary Priests of St. Paul the Apostle, taking as their apostolate the conversion of Protestants. By the middle of April, they had gone on their first mission, making five converts in Watertown, New York, and then fifteen at St. Bridget's Church in New York City. By the end of the Civil War, the Paulists had held 167 missions, at which they had received 422 converts. From the parish in New York, the Paulists traveled up and down the Eastern Seaboard and into the Midwest and South. While most of their missions were in places like Boston and New York where there were many Catholics—but also many non-Catholics—they also went to newly established dioceses and small hamlets and made converts from the prevailingly Protestant population (Figure 6.2).[115]

The Paulists' success won the approval of the wing of the American hierarchy that desired to Americanize the church by accepting the separation of church and state and by making more room for individual initiative.[116] The bishops invited Hecker to preach at the Second Plenary Council of Baltimore, where they assembled to legislate for the unity and discipline of the national church, recently in effect divided by the Civil War. The church also faced the task of evangelization, especially of freedpeople. The Paulists thought that "a great apostolate awaits among the colored people of the southern states" and noted that it was "lamentable to see how little has been done in the past for the conversion of the Colored people." But the Paulists seldom traveled in the South after the war, and they made few black converts.[117] At the council, Isaac Hecker preached on "The Future Triumph of the Church," predicting that Catholicism

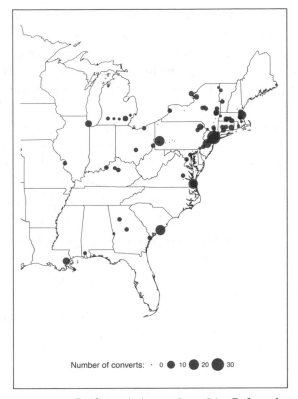

Number of converts: · 0 ● 10 ● 20 ● 30

FIGURE 6.2 Paulist missions, 1851–1865. Before the
Civil War, the Paulists tended to travel up and down
the East Coast by railroad or ship. Data: *Chronicle of
the Missions Given by the Congregation of Missionary
Priests of St. Paul the Apostle*, six manuscript volumes,
Paulist Fathers Archives, New York, 1:163–66; 2: flyleaf; 5:318–20.

would spread across the country through the working of the Spirit
because only the church satisfied the desire for catholicity that was
the spirit of the age.[118]

In 1868, Hecker's call for evangelism was echoed in a papal invitation to Protestants around the world to return to the "One Fold of
Christ." Pope Pius IX wrote a letter addressed to "all those who,
whilst they acknowledge the same Jesus Christ as the Redeemer, and
glory in the name of Christian, yet do not profess the true faith of
Christ, nor hold to and follow the Communion of the Catholic

Church. And We do this to warn, and conjure, and beseech them with all the warmth of Our zeal, and in all charity, to consider and seriously examine whether they follow the path marked out for them by Jesus Christ our Lord, and which leads to Eternal Salvation."[119] James Kent Stone, the Episcopalian president of Hobart College in New York, read the appeal at first with "rather contemptuous pity for the august Writer," since Stone thought he had solved the "Roman problem" and regarded himself "as a genuine Catholic—an Israelite indeed." But when he was a boy, Stone had seen Pope Pius IX in Rome, and he imagined the pope personally reading the letter to him. After reading Moehler's *Symbolism*, he came to the conclusion that "surely, if there be a Kingdom of Heaven upon earth, it must be known by marks which cannot be mistaken. Yes! I knew it when I had found it. And I found it as in the parable, like a treasure hidden in a field—the self-same field up and down which I had wandered for years, and where I had often trampled it under my feet." Stone resigned his college presidency and renounced his Episcopal ordination, converted to Catholicism in December 1869, and—after the death of his wife—became a Paulist priest in 1872.[120]

As an order, the Paulists fell on hard times after the Civil War. Because of illnesses and fewer priests, they had to restrict their efforts to their New York parish and discontinue missions from 1866 to 1871. But new converts like Stone swelled their ranks by the 1870s, so that the Paulists became known as an order that took in converts who became priests and put them to work making more converts. When those new Paulists went on to other orders, just as James Kent Stone went on to join the Passionists, they brought with them a concern to make converts.[121] By 1870, the convert movement had gone through its critical period and was ready to spread across the United States with renewed Paulist missions.

✠

During the Gilded Age, Catholicism became attractive to the upper classes, especially in New York. Wealthy elites had the financial and social capital to afford private chapels, the importation of European sacramentals, and the personal indiscretion of converting to a religion out of the mainstream. Until they converted to Catholicism, these converts were often Unitarians or Episcopalians, less out of reforming zeal than as a class marker.

Among these converts were the family of George Bliss. Bliss was a Massachusetts Yankee descended from the Dwights of "the bluest orthodoxy." Bliss himself had no particular interest in religion, and even at Unitarian Harvard, he was censured for sitting during prayers. In 1846, Bliss traveled to Rome and met Pope Pius IX.[122] Bliss became a lawyer to capitalists, serving as the federal district attorney for New York and a lawyer for Mutual Life Insurance and other large corporations. He married his second cousin, whom he admired in part for "her independence . . . in becoming an Episcopalian when all the influences about her were Unitarian." In their household, Catherine Bliss was the religious leader, not least because her first conversion from Unitarianism to Episcopalianism showed her to be the only person with an interest in religion. Though they had agreed to split time between churches, George went most often to Catherine's Episcopalian church. In 1884, in the midst of a prolonged illness, she suddenly converted to Catholicism. Bliss was "very angry and threatened separation &c., and even threatened to kill myself, though I never meant that." Catherine converted George only with the greatest difficulty. She left Catholic books lying around the house for George to read. Anaïs Casey, a female client of her husband's who was also a convert, prompted Catherine to invite Monsignor Thomas Capel to speak with George. While the Paulists took their name from the "Apostle to the Gentiles," Capel was known as the "Apostle to the Genteel," spending his time making converts among the American upper classes. In 1884, George became a Catholic in a semisecret conversion in the Blisses' private chapel. The secret lasted only to the next morning. Bliss traveled that evening to Washington, DC, and in the morning at the White House President Chester Arthur congratulated him on his conversion, the news having been published in one of the New York papers.[123]

When Catherine died, George Bliss married Anaïs Casey, and the newlyweds spent their honeymoon on a European tour, including several months in Rome. The Blisses went to a Mass celebrated by Pope Leo XIII, who blessed them. Unlike Hecker's proposed "monk tour," the Blisses traveled with considerably more than purse and staff and certainly more than two tunics. Their travelogues recalled meals taken, art purchased, and powerful people visited. Nevertheless, this extravagant trip both encouraged and expressed George Bliss's emerging piety; unlike Hecker's, it was underwritten by wealth inherited and earned on the capitalist market rather than by begging. Bliss later used his connections with President Arthur to save the American College in Rome when it was in danger of being shut down by the pope's many European enemies, for which Pope Leo made him a Commendatore of the Order of St. Gregory.[124]

Another upper-class convert was Jane Minot Sedgwick II, who offers a window onto the reading and devotional practices of converts. Sedgwick was born into a wealthy and accomplished family in Connecticut. Influenced by her friends Mary Langtree and Mary O'Sullivan, she converted from Unitarianism to Catholicism in 1853 and spent several years in Rome; but she also lived in Stockbridge, Massachusetts, where she endowed a church.[125] Before her conversion, Sedgwick spent a great deal of time in catechesis, keeping a series of notebooks in which she recorded her thoughts and readings. Her conversion was intensely laborious and made possible only by the leisure that her family afforded her. Judging by her notes to herself, Sedgwick was an extraordinarily diligent catechumen but one who must have put her priests through a workout. She asked standard questions about doctrines, such as whether Christ's words "this is my body" were meant to be taken literally or symbolically, but also such technical questions as whether the Benedictine editions of the church fathers added spurious passages to support Catholic doctrines. Sedgwick's journals contain many quotations from the church fathers, and since she was fluent in several languages, it is even possible she read them in the original. But most of her reading came from Catholic sources, such as Cardinal Nicholas Wiseman's *Lectures on the Real Presence of the Body and Blood of Our Lord Jesus Christ* and Milner's *End of Controversy*, as well as catechisms in French and Italian. She read works by American converts, such as Peter Burnett's *A Protestant Lawyer Converted to Catholicity* and Isaac Hecker's *Questions of the Soul*. Like Hecker, Bliss, and the artist George Loring Brown, she traveled around Rome and its environs visiting shrines

and viewing Catholic art. She kept a catalog of the shrines and cata-
combs she visited and the religious experiences she had there. And
she recorded the meaning of all the religious symbols in the artwork
she had seen, including the bark of St. Peter, the boat that symbolized the Catholic Church.[126]

Her journey was connected to the pattern of piety and mortifica-
tion that Sedgwick was taught by her confessor, a Redemptorist. She
sent to New York for books, including such a weighty tome as the
Canons and Decrees of the Council of Trent but also *The Life and Death
of the Child of Mary*, "a lovely book for those who are devoted to the
Virgin." Her reading was supplemented by prayer, for she ordered a
rosary from New York as well. Her confessor directed her to the lives
of the saints. She read the life of St. Philip Neri, a saint known for
prayer and joy. Neri was commonly mentioned by converts like
Hecker but was also noted in Ralph Waldo Emerson's "Essay on
Conduct." Sedgwick took these books to heart, trying to foster a devotional practice that continually recognized "how to practice the
Presence of God." She resolved to make the Act of Faith (a Catholic
prayer) before each action and to recognize "that God is the witness
of every thing I do."[127]

Sedgwick's conversion to Catholicism at Baltimore from her
family's Unitarianism was hard on her family, but her friends, some of
whom were also converts to Catholicism, welcomed the news. When
Mary O'Sullivan learned that she had converted, she wrote, "Your
note gave me great happiness, and from my inmost soul I rejoice at
your being as you say one with me in the Catholic Faith."[128]

✠

When the Paulist Fathers resumed their missions in the 1870s, they
did so on an increased scale. Before the Civil War, they averaged about
30 converts per year. From the 1870s to the 1890s, they averaged
between 80 and 110 converts a year, and after the 1890s they averaged nearly 450 converts per year. In all, they preached 1,684 missions and made 5,882 converts by the beginning of 1907—the year
when the Paulists gave up on keeping detailed records because the
missions were too numerous (Figure 6.3).[129] The Paulists were but

one order: for every Paulist mission, there were several Redemptorist, Passionist, or Jesuit missions.[130]

The converts received into the church at Paulist missions represented only a portion of those whom the Paulists persuaded. Since the Paulists were usually at a mission for at most two weeks, the people they received were those who could be prepared for conversion in such a short period of time. For example, at a mission in Wilmington, Delaware, in the spring of 1872, the Paulist Fathers recorded no conversions. But "one negro and seven other persons presented themselves as converts but too late to be instructed and received on the mission."[131] The missionaries were generally reluctant to accept converts quickly unless they could be thoroughly instructed. One woman who had been both an Episcopalian and a Baptist in Newport, New York, was instructed "with great pleasure," but "she desired to be received privately into the church, & to be allowed to conceal her profession of faith." The priests refused to allow a private conversion, so she was conditionally baptized in public. The fathers acknowledged that there was "a danger in receiving one with so short a preparation, but it was felt that to leave her to the necessity of a new struggle, after she had once conquered her difficulties, & opened her heart in confidence would be perilous & cruel."[132] When the Paulists recorded the number of converts they had made, there were many who were left to be carried to conversion by the resident (usually overworked) pastor, as at Holyoke, Massachusetts, where "seven Protestants made application, and five were admitted before the close, by baptism & profession of faith into the bosom of the church."[133] When the Paulists returned for later missions in the same place, they often found that those whom they had preached to earlier had been received into the church.[134] Even those Protestants who did not come forward for instruction still gained an enhanced impression of Catholicism. As the chronicler put it after one mission, "A great many Protestants attended the mission and though only a few were received, yet a vast amount of prejudice was removed and good of soil prepared for the future growth of the Faith in their hearts."[135]

The Paulists not only made more converts and preached to more Protestants, they made them in more places. While the Paulists continued to do most of their missions in the Northeast and Chesapeake—

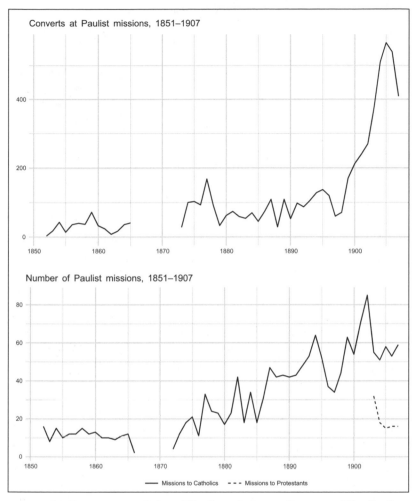

FIGURE 6.3 Summary statistics of Paulist missions, 1851–1907. The Paulists greatly expanded the presence of their missions over the course of the nineteenth century, and they also got better at making converts. Data: *Chronicle of the Missions*, 1:163–66; 2: flyleaf; 5:318–20.

where the majority of Americans lived, after all—they also expanded to the Midwest. Throughout the 1870s and 1880s, Wisconsin, Minnesota, Michigan, Illinois, Indiana, and Ohio all received many visits from the Paulists (Figure 6.4). Reflecting a wider split that would eventually be made apparent in the controversy over "Americanism," the Catholic hierarchy was divided over the value of the Paulist

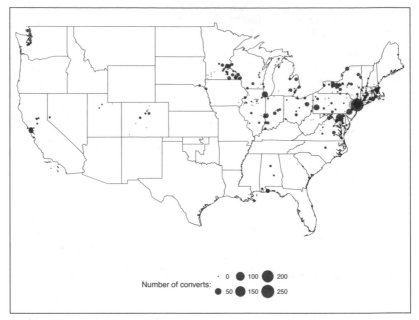

Number of converts: · 0   ● 100   ● 200   ● 50   ● 150   ● 250

FIGURE 6.4 Paulist missions, 1871–1893. After the Civil War, the Paulists held more missions in the West and Midwest, traveling on the railroads rather than coasting vessels. Data: *Chronicle of the Missions*, 1:163–66; 2: flyleaf; 5:318–20.

apostolate. Because the Paulists had to be invited by a bishop, they usually gave missions in dioceses led by Americanist bishops, such as the Minnesota diocese presided over by Archbishop John Ireland, one of the champions of the Paulists.[136] Before the Civil War, the Paulists had traveled up and down the seaboard in coasting vessels; after the war, they traveled east and west on railroads. The railroads let them get to more places more often, and when they got off the train, they preached to the railroad workers, both Catholics and Protestants.[137] But the Paulists reached places where even railroads did not run, places like Fort Fairfield, Maine, on the Canadian border, which they dubbed "Punkindom."[138]

Next the Paulists expanded to the West. In 1875, Father A. L. Rosecrans, the son of the Civil War general and convert William Rosecrans, led a series of missions in California and the western states. At the cathedral in San Francisco, Rosecrans "found a great many converts" already and made several more; in Salt Lake City, there were "several converts from Mormonism found here who were devout Catholics."[139] From his experience with the converts he made himself, Rosecrans thought that "if anything is to convert the Mormons it certainly is the Catholic Religion—for they seem to take to it, so to speak, better than to any other."[140]

Something of the grit of these Paulist missionaries can be seen in Father Edward Brady's missions in Colorado. Brady was diagnosed with a throat problem, perhaps an early stage of the cancer that killed him, and in the winter of 1881–1882 he was ordered to Colorado to recuperate. Brady's definition of allowing his throat to rest was preaching a dozen missions, sometimes in the city of Boulder but other times in small mining camps that he reached by crossing the Continental Divide on snowshoes. With the help of local priests, he heard about 5,000 confessions from Catholics with little connection to the church and made a dozen converts.[141] During the 1890s, the Paulists established another mission band in the West, which made western and southwestern missions a regular part of their work.[142]

The Paulists also made more converts at the turn of the century because they got better at inviting Protestants. They had often lectured on themes such as "Why I Became a Catholic," and Protestants had always come to the missions even if there were not special services for them. But in the first decade of the twentieth century, Paulists began to hold missions specifically for non-Catholics, which increased conversions. These attempts at converting Protestants also had a more general impact on Americans. As Catholic missionary priests barnstormed around the country holding missions, the choice of conversion to Catholicism confronted more and more Americans.

The Paulist expansion across space produced an expansion into the interiority of Protestants and Catholics. Jay Dolan has argued that these missions, functioning like Protestant revivals, were a type of conversion for Catholics who had no connection to their faith. Returning to Catholicism from indifference was not unlike a conversion to Catholicism from Protestantism.[143] The missions put people who had inherited their religious identity and then returned to the church in the same category as someone who had crossed religious boundaries. For everyone, religion was becoming more of a chosen identity, even in a religion marked strongly by ethnicity and inheritance.[144]

✙

In his spiritual diary, William Strachan recorded the pull of that momentous choice. From 1901 to 1904, Strachan penciled thoughts on his religious inclinations and church visits on a legal pad, often mentioning the Paulists. But Strachan didn't keep the diary as a spiritual exercise to lead himself to Catholicism. He kept the diary because it was a spiritual practice recommended by Mary Baker Eddy, the founder of Christian Science.[145] During a period of dissatisfaction with Christian Science in 1903 and 1904, he experimented with different types of Christianity. Manhattan afforded him opportunities to attend two or three churches on Sundays. He heard Congregationalist minister Lyman Abbott preach, sometimes listened to a Methodist preacher, then went to the Paulist home church on Fifty-Ninth Street for catechesis, after which he might shuttle down to Park Avenue to hear a lecture on "the church as a human organization."[146] Of the several churches that he tried out, the Catholic Church had the greatest draw.

By January 1904, Strachan was attending lectures by the Paulist Fathers. These lectures were often doctrinal and sometimes autobiographical on the topic "Why I Am a Catholic."[147] Strachan admired "the courage of the priests who nightly . . . answer questions relating to the catholic faith." Strachan knew the pressure the priests were under, since he was judging them by the standards of Christian Science. But he was determined to give the Catholics a fair chance to persuade him, for he regarded it as "a Christian duty for me now to learn & seek & study all I can of Catholicism as long as I have the opportunity, for the priest the other night wished . . . that protestants should use every chance to learn of the true church."[148] Strachan spent much of his time with the Paulists, listening in their catechism classes, attending masses and solemn vespers, and reading books about church fathers such as Tertullian and Origen. He compiled lists of questions for the priests and recorded arguments for and against Catholicism that he thought up or found in his reading. He discovered that focusing on the altar during Catholic services took away his lust, but he also worried that some of the ceremonies and images might be idolatrous because of the human tendency to "worship the sign."

Strachan did not record which religion he finally settled on; indeed, he may not have settled on any. At the end of his diary, he was perplexed by these questions: "Was my 3 years study of C[hristian] S[cience] the beginning of my coming into Catholicism. Or is my present study of Catholicism the early days of my C.S. career?" He had other choices too, for he recorded that "there are 4 churches I have been thinking of joining": the Christian Scientists, Roman Catholics, Unitarians, and an unidentified denomination labeled "D." The Paulist Fathers, with the help of Mary Baker Eddy and several New York preachers, had caused Strachan to experience on an intensely personal scale what Catholic missions, Protestant revivals, and the immigration from the religions of the world had caused for most Americans: a sense that they were being forced to make a momentous choice between many religions. Strachan, unlike many, never resolved the tension that pressed upon him. He could only declare, "I am sincere! That is the all essential thing."[149]

Conclusion

"MAYBES ARE THE ESSENCE OF THE SITUATION"

WILLIAM STRACHAN GAVE VOICE to his perplexity amid the appeals of the many religious options available to him. Though his inability to decide between them was particular to his own experience, the underlying pattern of religious instability was common to his and earlier generations, extending back at least as far as Hannah Adams's experience in preparing her *Dictionary of All Religions*. Adams had not only experienced the variety of religions; as an Enlightenment scholar, she had also dispassionately cataloged and classified them. Neither Adams nor Strachan were able to go beyond expressing the private doubt they experienced to explain the underlying characteristics and logic of the pattern they shared with so many others. But had Strachan perused the shelves of a bookseller or public library in New York while he was in the throes of writing his diary, alongside Mary Baker Eddy's *Science and Health with Key to the Scriptures* and the Paulist Fathers' collection of conversion narratives, *From the Highways of Life*, he would have found a recently published volume by the popular scholar and speaker, William James.[1]

James, who taught psychology and philosophy at Harvard, had also turned his attention to religion. In 1901 and 1902, James gave the prestigious Gifford Lectures on natural religion at the University of Edinburgh, which were published as *The Varieties of Religious Experience: A Study in Human Nature*. Within the contexts of the new science of psychology and the philosophical debate about what kinds of religious beliefs could be warranted in a scientific age, James offered a framework for understanding religious choice.[2] At issue for James was not so much whether religious beliefs were true, but what it meant to have to choose between them and justify that choice. James's book was a compelling description of the religious dilemmas facing modern Americans not because it was an accurate description of timeless human nature, but because it was grounded in the psychology of lived religious experience at the start of the twentieth century.

James was one of a group of intellectuals who were attempting the scholarly study of religion in the United States. That group included scholars of comparative religion like James Freeman Clarke and James C. Moffat, many of whom were induced to the study of religion, as one historian has put it, "from a felt need to measure Christianity against alternatives."[3] James was also a major contributor to a new philosophy called pragmatism. His friend Charles Sanders Peirce had coined the term to denominate a philosophical system that argued that ideas were true insofar as one could act upon them, not insofar as they accurately described the metaphysical structure of the world. Peirce came to his ideas from his work as an astronomer and statistician, where error and uncertainty were the facts to be reckoned with. Peirce and James were joined by the jurist Oliver Wendell Holmes, whose dictum "the life of the law has not been logic; it has been experience" suggested that the law was no more than an uncertain prediction about how judges might rule.[4] The hallmark of pragmatism for James, as for Peirce and Holmes, was finding a way to act in the face of uncertainty.

For James, religious uncertainty could be studied empirically. James found confirmation of his belief in the importance of empiricism, along with abundant materials for the study of religion, in the research of his former Harvard student and later Stanford colleague, Edwin Diller Starbuck. Starbuck was a Quaker turned (briefly) evangelical turned scientist with a mystical streak. He insisted on mailing detailed, probing questionnaires about religious experience

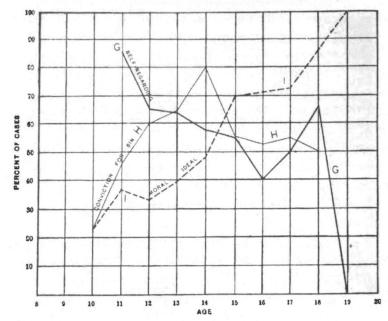

FIGURE C.1 One of Edwin Starbuck's charts from his empirical study of conversion. This chart attempts to correlate gender and age with the motivations for conversion. The three curves (from top to bottom: "self-regarding," "conviction for sin," and "moral ideal") represent the frequency of certain motivations for conversion charted against the age of females in the study. The terminology of the Protestant morphology of conversion has become the categories of scientific study with predictions but uncertainties about cause and effect. Edwin Diller Starbuck, *The Psychology of Religion: An Empirical Study of the Growth of Religious Consciousness* (New York: C. Scribner's Sons, 1899), 56.

over the objection of his mentor James, who thought surveys had "reached the proportions of an incipient nuisance." Those surveyed were hardly a random sample: Starbuck selected at least some of his respondents, such as the Unitarian minister Edward Everett Hale, because they were prominent public figures. Starbuck also gathered "776 cases of conversion from the Drew Theological [Seminary] Alumni record." In 1899, Starbuck published the results of his research, trying to correlate conversions with variables such as age, puberty, gender, and participation in revivals, as well as trying to observe scientifically the relationship between feelings before and after conversion (Figure C.1). When James visited him at Stanford,

Starbuck let him read his raw materials, and James frequently quoted from them in *Varieties*.[5] The empirical, psychological studies of Starbuck and James were followed by studies from James Leuba, Elmer T. Clark, and George Albert Coe, who used the same empirical method but in general did not heed James's warnings and shrank religious experience to biological materialism.[6] The broader intellectual movement of pragmatism, and the specific psychological study of religion by James and his colleagues, shared several convictions: that any kind of knowledge was fundamentally uncertain, but that knowledge of religion could nevertheless be reclaimed from uncertainty, so long as the study of religion was taken as the study of experience.

James always insisted that philosophy had to be rooted in experience. He crafted his explanations of contemporary religious dilemmas through his study of conversion experiences as viewed through his own religious temperament and mystical experiences, though he always denied that he was a mystic. As important as James's work was for succeeding generations of scholars, in his own day it gave voice to the questions of religious identity. To put it in terms that James himself would have used, his description of religion was the fruit, not the root, of nineteenth-century patterns of conversion.[7]

✝

James worked out his ideas about religion in a series of essays and lectures that led to *The Varieties of Religious Experience*. His first sustained attempt to bring the study of psychology to bear on religion was a November 1888 essay on the "Psychology of Belief." In that essay, James defined religious belief as a reaction, driven in part by logic but mostly by the emotions of fear and pleasure, to whatever one paid attention to. Like Jefferson in the Virginia Statute for Religious Freedom more than a century earlier, James recognized that people cannot simply change their beliefs at will: "If belief consists in an emotional reaction of the entire man on an object, how can we believe at will? We cannot control our emotions. Truly enough, a man cannot believe at will abruptly."[8] Unlike Jefferson, James thought one's reactions depended more on emotions rather than reason.

Whether someone believed, and in what he or she believed, was thus in no simple sense a matter of exercising the will but depended at least in part on the options that were propounded and on the reactions that those options raised. James thus began his thinking about religion with a set of principles about options, reactions, habits, and the will that were characteristic of his writings on psychology generally.[9]

To those constant themes, James added the trenchant observation that "the true opposites of belief, psychologically considered, are doubt and inquiry, not disbelief."[10] Disbelief, in other words, was a species of belief; agnosticism, not atheism, was the inverse of faith.[11] These principles provided a method for understanding how religious belief could be destabilized: if belief depended on a mostly nonvolitional, emotional reaction from the focus of one's attention, then competing claims on attention by religious groups changed the terms under which religious belief was formed. And if the opposite of belief was not disbelief but doubt, then the posture of the individual confronted with many options was not certain disbelief but uncertain belief.

James developed these ideas further in his 1881 lecture "Reflex Action and Theism." He took the notion that the actions of human beings depended on reactions and nerve impression and applied that idea to religion. But so far from limiting the nerve impressions to the senses, James wrote that the impression "that confronts us, that knocks on our mental door and asks to be let in, and fixed and decided upon and actively met, is just this whole universe itself and its essence." The universe presented itself in the form of many religious claims:

> The whole flood of faiths and systems here rush in. Philosophies and denials of philosophy, religions and atheisms, skepticisms and mysticisms, confirmed emotional moods and habitual practical biases, jostle one another; for all are alike trials, hasty, prolix or of seemly length, to answer this momentous question. . . . For no one of them is final. They form but the middle segment of the mental curve, [conception, between impression and action] and not its termination.[12]

In other words, James saw people as necessarily deciding on the impressions that the many religious sects and other philosophies made on them. He pushed back against the claim that religion was physiologically determined to argue that the only thing that was determined was that one had to make a choice.

When James included "atheisms, skepticisms" among the "flood of faiths and systems," he mentioned a category toward which he felt involuntarily attracted. Most of his writings on religion are those of a man of science to whom atheism was a live possibility even as he sought to defend the legitimacy of religious faith. James lived at a time when one mode of being irreligious was nearly closed but another was opening. By the late nineteenth century, the possibility of not having a disposition toward religion at all—of simply not having considered religion one way or the other—was becoming less of an option. Americans of the early nineteenth century frequently had no formal religious affiliation; the rates of affiliation to churches went up from initially low levels as the century progressed.[13] At the same time that the United States began to send out missionaries around the world, it was itself experiencing one of the largest Christianization movements in the nineteenth century.[14] It was not uncommon for home missionaries, evangelists, and distributors of tracts to find the recipients of their attention unaware of the claims of religion. This unaffiliated category never went away: social gospel reformers of the late nineteenth century were anxious about the lack of religion among immigrants and the urban poor. But the tremendous labor of missionaries and evangelists—and of the apologists and polemicists who resisted them—meant that space for being a religious "none" was considerably diminished over the course of the century.[15]

The replacement for being passively unaffiliated was the option of being actively disaffiliated. In the United States, the opening wedges for irreligion were Thomas Paine's *Age of Reason* (1794–1807) and Ethan Allen's *Reason the Only Oracle of Man* (1784). Paine and Allen won a few adherents to Deism but stirred a far greater public outrage against their infidelity.[16] By the end of the nineteenth century, irreligious options included groups like Felix Adler's Ethical Culture movement (founded 1877), the Free Religious Association (founded 1867), and the writings and lectures of skeptics like

Robert Owen, Frances Wright, Octavius Brooks Frothingham, and Robert Ingersoll.[17]

But ironically, much of the work of creating conceptual room for infidelity was done by those who argued against them: people who would never have read Bob Ingersoll's books or attended his lectures read denunciations of him, and those denunciations presented irreligion as an option to be reckoned with.[18] Many converts thought that turning to a different religion was the only possible way to avoid infidelity, as when Isaac Hecker concluded that "there is no half way house between Catholicism and infidelity."[19] Other converts took seriously the possibility that they might be atheists in their hearts. When converts came to faith, they saw their conversion as opposed to irreligion, as when Stephen H. Bradley concluded, "I now defy all the Deists and Atheists in the world to shake my faith in Christ."[20] By the late nineteenth century, the conceptual room for infidelity was far larger, so that religion was defined against irreligion.[21]

James reckoned with the momentous choice implied by religious skepticism in his 1895 essay "Is Life Worth Living?" The essay combined two questions of vital importance to him: Could one be certain of ultimate knowledge, especially religious knowledge? And was that knowledge certain enough to stay one's hand from committing suicide? The question of suicide had an edge for James, who in his youth had considered taking his life, as had his sister, Alice. James's depressions, including his dream of a "black haired youth with greenish skin" in an insane asylum, as well as moments of fullness he experienced in Switzerland and the Adirondacks, were the catalyst for his later work on the *Varieties of Religious Experience.* He used his own dream as an anonymous example of melancholy in the Gifford Lectures, and the idea for those lectures seems to have crystallized after a kind of mystical experience.[22] In "Is Life Worth Living?" James took the question of suicide as an extreme but revealing case of human perplexity: "We are of one substance with these suicides, and their life is the life we share"—a life of uncertainty about what disposition one should take to the cosmos. The conditions of existence in his age required that one possess "the plainest intellectual integrity" to come to grips with the instability of ultimate belief.[23]

Though belief was unstable, it was not impossible. "To believe in that [supernatural] world," James argued, "*may* be the most essential function that our lives in this world have to perform." James answered the question of whether life was worth living with a resounding *maybe*. But maybe was a good enough answer for him, despite the arguments of "agnostic positivism" that science had learned (or would learn) all that was necessary to be known and that therefore "we must always wait for sensible evidence for our beliefs; and where such evidence is inaccessible we must frame no hypotheses whatever." This idea James rejected, because inevitably one must act on one's convictions if one can be truly said to have convictions at all. James was far from denying that science had made faith difficult, but the certainty of science was illusionary. James thus exhorted his audience to "believe what is in the line of your needs, for only by the belief is the need fulfilled." As James put it, the conditions of religious life, even of personal existence versus suicide, "is a case of maybe. . . . [M]aybes are the essence of the situation."[24]

⁌✠⁍

James extended his defense of the obligation to believe in his essay "The Will to Believe," first published in 1896 after an address at Yale. James began his talk with a joke about the centuries-old distinction between Yale as "your good old orthodox College" and "Harvard freethinking and indifference." The joke had a point because of the challenge that freethinking and scientific rationalism had brought against the validity of religious belief, so James brought to Yale his "essay in justification *of* faith." The kind of faith that James was willing to defend was "the lawfulness of *voluntarily* adopted faith."[25]

James proceeded to give an acute account of the way that people believe, along with a vocabulary for describing it. He gave "the name of *hypothesis* to anything that may be proposed to our belief" and called "the decision between two hypotheses an *option*." An option he termed (1) "*living* or *dead*," where a living option was one where each hypothesis "makes some appeal, however small, to your belief"; (2) "*forced* or *avoidable*," where a forced option was one with "no possibility of not choosing"; and (3) "*momentous* or *trivial*," placing decisions about religion decidedly into the momentous category.[26]

It is important to note exactly the terms by which James thought that options about religion were forced, a connection he had explained earlier:

> Our only way . . . of doubting, or refusing to believe, that a certain thing *is*, is continuing to act as if it were *not*. . . . And so if I must not believe that the world is divine, I can only express that refusal by declining ever to act distinctively as if it were so, which can only mean acting on certain critical occasions as if it were *not* so, or in an irreligious way. There are, you see, inevitable occasions in life when inaction is a kind of action, and must count as action.[27]

In all his writings, James insisted that ideas necessarily lead to action. Religion was an extreme case, since religion could only be expressed through actions or inaction. The conclusion that he drew was that one could not assume a posture of waiting for evidence when it came to religion.

Having laid the groundwork with his terminology in "The Will to Believe," and his observation that it was "preposterous on the very face of it to talk of our opinions being modifiable at will," James went on to critique two possible approaches to religious belief. He first took up Pascal's famous argument that one should believe in God, because if that belief were true one would gain infinitely, and if the belief were false one would lose nothing. James dismissed this wager out of hand as "the language of the gaming-table" and as religious faith "put to its last trumps." Faith adopted under Pascal's wager could not be a "living option," for "a faith in masses and holy water adopted willfully after such a mechanical calculation would lack the inner soul of faith's reality."[28]

James took more pains in rebutting the arguments of the English mathematician William Kingdon Clifford. Clifford argued that "it is wrong always, everywhere, and for anyone, to believe anything upon insufficient evidence"—even if the belief ended up being true.[29] James responded that "our passional nature not only lawfully may, but must, decide an option between propositions, whenever it is a genuine option that cannot by its nature be decided on intellectual grounds."[30] As a radical empiricist, James thought that it was not possible to achieve certainty on such matters, that "we must go on experiencing and thinking over our experience."[31] People cannot "always wait with impunity till the coercive evidence shall have arrived," for "we *may* wait if we will . . . but if we do so, we do so at our peril as much as if we believed. In either case we *act*, taking our life into our hands."[32]

᛭

While James was working out his thoughts on religion, he was engaged in correspondence with Henry William Rankin, the librarian at Mount Hermon Boys' School in Northfield, Massachusetts. Mount Hermon had been founded in 1881 by evangelist Dwight Lyman Moody. Moody was to the second half of the nineteenth century what Charles Finney had been to the first: an innovator in the techniques of evangelism who brought the message of conversion to increasingly larger audiences. He was heir to Finney's method of bringing sinners to conversion through prayer and, like Finney, he gathered enormous crowds wherever he preached: in his base in Chicago, but also in Brooklyn and New York, Philadelphia, Boston, London, San Francisco, Sacramento, and other cities. Like the pioneers of the American Tract Society, Moody was skilled at using print media, especially newspapers, to spread his message widely.[33] When the 1893 World's Fair was held in Chicago, Moody made his message global, running a six-month-long campaign to evangelize the thousands of people from around the world who came to the fair. Exactly what effect Moody had even his publicist reckoned as "impossible to tabulate," though he noted that "conversions were a daily occurrence, sometimes numbering scores in a single service . . . [T]he vilest from the city slums were gloriously saved, as well as many a wild, reckless visitor from afar."[34] Moody ran his evangelistic campaign at the same time that the World's Parliament of Religions met in Chicago. Jews, Catholics, Orthodox Christians, Protestants (though the Presbyterian General Assembly officially disapproved), Hindus, Confucians, Shintoists, Muslims, Spiritualists, and Christian Scientists—these and other groups were all represented in the parliament by speakers such as Isaac Mayer Wise for Reform Jews and the Paulist priest Augustine Hewit for Catholics.[35] The Parliament of Religions was many things to many people: an opportunity to express the idea that

Christ alone could save, or to extend the idea of Christ to all the world's religions; a claim that all religions were one, or a demonstration of the particulars of one's own religion. The important thing was the juxtaposition of Moody's evangelism and the parliament's pluralism. In 1893, the Parliament of Religions opened the doors to even greater religious pluralism, at the same time that conversions by evangelicals like Moody, but also by Catholics like Hewit, were achieving considerable success.

The stakes of Moody's revival campaign and the Parliament of Religions—the tension between the particular demands of conversion and the pluralistic universe of choices—were replayed in microcosm in the exchange between Rankin, a member of Moody's evangelistic empire, and William James. Like James, Rankin had an interest in extraordinary religious experiences, about which James wished to read widely in preparation for giving the Gifford Lectures. Rankin, who frankly admired James's work, sent him many volumes: Charles Finney, Catherine of Genoa, Catherine of Siena, Teresa of Avila, John Bunyan, David Brainerd, James Brainerd Taylor, Sarah Edwards, John Wesley, George Whitefield, Brother Lawrence, and others who cannot be identified, including a Hindu convert to Christianity and a native of Greenland who converted to Christianity and lost his magical powers, as well as works of philosophy, theology, and demonology.[36]

Rankin also tried to convert James to evangelical Christianity. Besides sending James the books he requested, Rankin sent him clippings from various religious periodicals on the theme of conversion. James turned these to his research on religion: "The clippings that you shower upon me are something useful, less for my own spiritual needs, than for my literary enterprises." James did not regard himself as a Christian and consistently refused Rankin's entreaties. "I doubt whether I ever can be a Christian in the sense which you are one, and yet in some way or other I shall probably come out not incongruously with your specifications," James wrote back to Rankin.[37] Rankin was full of arguments for Christianity that responded in detail to James's own work. In one letter, he quoted the statement in James's essay "The Will to Believe" that "no bell in us tolls to let us know for certain when truth is in our grasp." Rankin took the evangelical view "that *when all the conditions are met the bell tolls;* With the effect of making the Divine Being, his Goodness, and personal relations to the obedient soul, the most vivid realities of consciousness." In response to James's statement "If we take the wrong road we shall be dashed to pieces. We do not certainly know whether there is any right one," Rankin quoted Jesus's words in the Gospel of John: "'I am the Way, the Truth & the Life.' No man was ever led astray by him."[38]

Even though James rejected Rankin's evangelism, he did not brush it off. James confided some of his most personal ideas about religion to Rankin.[39] In 1896, James wrote, "I cannot call myself a Christian, and indeed go with my father in not being able to tolerate the notion of a selective personal relation between God's creatures and God himself as any thing ultimate." In a later letter, he explained that "although religion is the great interest of my life, I am rather hopelessly non-evangelical, and take the whole thing too impersonally." James's reasons were revealing: "I am more interested in religion than in anything else, but with a strange shyness of closing my hand on any definite symbols that might be too restrictive."[40] James felt the dilemma of believing that he had exposited to others, but he was reluctant to settle on any particular faith (especially Christianity) that might restrict his options. Though James told Rankin he did admire the "completeness of your Christian faith, and the *concreteness of association* between your abstract theism and the Christian symbols," James viewed himself as "a mediator between scientific agnosticism and the religious view of the world (Christian or not)."[41]

In short, James's work in *Varieties* depended on reading conversion narratives as sources, but—quite unwillingly—he also had to consider them within the framework of a forced obligation to choose, thanks to Rankin's relentless evangelism.[42] James pointed out Rankin's importance in a letter sent on the eve of delivering the Gifford Lectures: "my 'lectures'—poor things!—will constitute my reaction upon all your letters."[43]

✠

One of the distinctive characteristics of James's Gifford Lectures was their frequent and lengthy quotation from narratives of religious experience drawn from many time periods. James was attempting to be timeless in his analysis; his subtitle, after all, was "A Study in Human Nature." Nevertheless, James was a sharp observer of religion in his own day. He noticed that "in the fully evolved Revivalism of Great Britain and America" there was a "codified and stereotyped procedure of conversion" of the instantaneous, ritualized type, which "assumed that only its own type of religious experience can be perfect."[44] His lectures took in Spiritualism, the Mind Cure, Buddhism, Finney and Edwards and Newman, his father, and even himself.[45] Though he depicted the *Varieties* as an insight into timeless human nature, James actually described the anxieties of religion in his own day.

In defining his topic, James was not interested in people who inherited their religion by habit, but in people with original religious experiences. Thus he passed over the "ordinary religious believer, who follows the conventional observances of his country, whether it be Buddhist, Christian, or Mohammedan. His religion has been made for him by others, communicated to him by tradition, determined to fixed forms by imitation, and retained by habit. It would profit us little to study this second-hand religious life."[46] So strong was this inclination that it defeated James's recurring professional interest in habit and his injunction that "by their fruits ye shall know them, not by their roots."[47] James was well aware of the problem of defining religion, observing that it "cannot stand for any single principle or essence, but is rather a collective name."[48] Still, for the purpose of his lectures, James circumscribed the topic to "personal religion," limited to "the feelings, acts, and experiences of individual men in their solitude, so far as they apprehend themselves to stand in relation to whatever they may consider the divine."[49] This provisional definition was James's effort to get to the problem of choice and experience. We need not share his prejudice against inherited religion or religion practiced by "dull habit" to note that James regarded religion that was chosen as its genuine form.

Much of the *Varieties* is structured around a taxonomy of religious experience. James distinguished between two kinds of religion: "the religion of healthy-mindedness" and the religion of "the sick soul." This idiom fit James's work as a psychologist who was increasingly interested in therapy rather than laboratory work. In support of his classification, James borrowed from Francis Newman (brother of the famous convert to Catholicism John Henry Newman, and himself a convert from evangelicalism to a rational theism) a distinction between "'the once-born and the twice-born.'" The once-born, or healthy-minded, saw God "as the animating Spirit of a beautiful harmonious world; . . . they do not look into themselves."[50] They could be termed once-born because they had no need for a conversion to restore themselves to the religious happiness that they had by birth. In this class, James categorized many Catholics but also liberal Protestants: groups that he thought favored development within a religion rather than stressing the need for conversion.[51] In contrast was the religion of the sick souls, for whom evil was a real problem, and whose lives were inextricably tangled up with it. James termed these people twice-born because they needed a conversion experience to achieve religious happiness.[52] In his category of sick souls, James distinguished between active conversions, for which Charles Finney was his ideal type, and "self-surrender" conversions, in which one gave up one's will to God.[53] James emphasized "the cases of instantaneous conversion," which seemed more important to him than the habitual, and showed how these were connected across religious traditions.[54]

At the start of his final lecture, James promised to be "dryer and less sympathetic" than the "emotionality" of his earlier lectures, but he was anything but dry as he considered the practical implications of his lectures. James observed that after "the science of religions" had "assimilated all the necessary historical material and distilled out of it as its essence the same conclusions which I myself a few moments ago pronounced . . . she has now to exert her critical activity, and to decide how far, in the light of other sciences and in that of general philosophy, such beliefs can be considered *true*."[55] In offering his response, James disclaimed the method of "the scientist, so-called" whose profession was too "materialistic" to give him a fair shot at answering the question. James further disclaimed the "survival theory" of religion—that is, the idea that religion was a mere vestige of primitive thought in an enlightened, scientific age.[56] Rather, James saw the problem of religious choice as a real one that he and his listeners faced: "However particular questions [as opposed to scientific generalizations] connected with our individual destinies may be answered, it is only by acknowledging them as genuine questions, and living in the sphere of thought which they open up, that we become profound." In James's view each person had to live with such questions of salvation as matters of genuine choice, "but to live thus is to be religious."[57]

James's personal answer to the question of which religion was true tried "to reduce religion to its lowest admissible terms, to that minimum . . . on which it may be hoped all religious persons may agree."[58] He thought this was necessary because the student of religions "has to become acquainted with so many groveling and horrible superstitions," so that "a presumption easily arises in his mind that any belief that is religious probably is false."[59] James thought that the "warring gods and formulas of the various religions do indeed cancel each other, but there is a certain uniform deliverance in which religions all appear to meet."[60] James's solution (which in a way created yet another competing kind of religious belief) was only one out of many possible options. Determining perfectly between them was impossible, even though one was obligated to choose between them. Yet an uncertain choice was sufficient. As James concluded in a postscript: "For practical life at any rate, the *chance* of salvation is enough."[61]

✠

James thought that the universe had laid on him the necessity of making religious choices in the face of uncertainty, but that burden came as much from the conditions of modern American religion. No one had chosen the conditions of obligatory religious choice, though the condition was the accretion of many small choices by converts who moved from one religion to the next, and sometimes back again; who invented their own religious traditions and convinced others to join them; who passed out tracts or joined missionary orders to make new converts, or who wrote and preached so that their co-religionists would not convert; who attacked all religions as irrational; or who claimed their religion as the basis of civil society and the hope of salvation. Those individual choices to convert were pregnant with potential losses and potential gains. Converts stood to lose the religious identity and practices they had learned from family and even their families themselves, to lose their position in society and their credibility with their neighbors; converts stood to gain a new sense of self, a new community of fellow believers, and even to gain truth, God, and eternal life. What converts gave up and what they received became not only part of individual biography but also part of the history of the nation. Nevertheless, reckoning what the nation gave up and what it won is harder to gauge, since no group was in a position to say which change was for the good, which for the ill. Still, because of more than a century's worth of conversion, the nation gave up the possibility of an inherited and stable faith that could go unchallenged, and it gained every possible religious option except the option of not choosing at all. For converts, for the nation, their history was a story of loss and gain.

Note on Sources

THE HISTORY OF conversions can be found in several kinds of sources. The largest group of sources are the print conversion narratives that were published frequently by almost every religious group. In most cases, these narratives were retrospective constructs by their authors put into service of wider polemical battles between religious groups. As such, they should be treated skeptically whenever possible. Whatever skepticism these narratives deserve as biographical sources for the lives of their individual authors, in the aggregate they nevertheless testify to the patterns of conversion and the pressures to convert. Above all, it must be remembered that these narratives were told by people who actually did cross religious lines despite the consequences for family, social position, and interior stability.

These printed conversions often functioned as a kind of typology. A few prominent conversions provided the pattern (types) that other people then lived out in their own conversions (antitypes).[1] Some conversions more nearly embodied the theology of conversion favored by a particular group. The messiness of human life scarcely ever lined up with the precision of theology, and even narratives that selected and arranged facts to give them spiritual meaning found it difficult to match theology with events. Yet religious communities treated some narratives more than others as exemplars. Furthermore, some conversion narratives occupied a central role in networks of print and thus influenced many more people. For example, *The Life of David Brainerd* was theologically significant because Jonathan Edwards edited it, and it was widely reprinted and excerpted long after its original publication.[2] A sure sign that one narrative was a training manual for others is that later converts cited that narrative as a model for their own conversion.[3]

Manuscript conversion narratives are another set of sources. These manuscript narratives often proved to be not so very different from printed ones. They were often constructed just like print narratives, albeit for circulation among family rather than among the public, and they seldom contained a decidedly different account of the reasons for and meaning of a conversion than the more public printed narratives.[4] The similarity between manuscript narratives and printed narratives suggests that printed accounts of conversion were not simply public performances but convey as much about the interior, personal experience of conversion as we are likely to know. The manuscript accounts do occasionally reveal people who were brought to the brink of conversion and felt all its pressures but who did not actually convert.

Finally, there is a mass of nineteenth-century material contributing to and interpreting conversions. Whether it was a hand press, a stereotype, or an offset press, the printing press piled volume upon volume urging people to convert from one religion to another, and then more volumes giving them reasons not to convert. Converts frequently mentioned key texts. These tracts, pamphlets, periodicals, and books usually describe the ideals of conversion and sometimes recount actual conversions. The correspondence of bishops, ministers, and rabbis provide background about their dealings with converts and descriptions of the rituals by which they made them. Especially helpful in this regard are the records and reminiscences of missionaries. Clerics and scholars often reflected on the meaning and nature of conversion with great insight.

The difficulty is not in finding evidence, but in figuring out what it all adds up to.

Notes

Introduction

1. Samuel Hill, ms. autobiography, Samuel Hill papers (MssCol 1397), Manuscripts and Archives, The New York Public Library, Astor, Lenox and Tilden Foundations, New York, pp. 1, 25. The only treatment of Hill's life is Mary Malloy, *Devil on the Deep Blue Sea: The Notorious Career of Captain Samuel Hill of Boston* (Jersey Shore, PA: Bullbrier Press, 2006). On Deism in the early republic, see Eric R. Schlereth, *An Age of Infidels: The Politics of Religious Controversy in the Early United States* (Philadelphia: University of Pennsylvania Press, 2013); Amanda Porterfield, *Conceived in Doubt: Religion and Politics in the New American Nation* (Chicago: University of Chicago Press, 2012).

2. Hill, ms. autobiography, 5, 7, 11, 15, 26–28. Malloy, *Devil on the Deep Blue Sea*, 130–33.

3. Hill, ms. autobiography, 24–25. David Bogue, *An Essay on the Divine Authority of the New Testament*, 4th ed. (Malacca, 1817); Doddridge's book was printed in scores of editions. On Morrison, see Eliza Armstrong Morrison, *Memoirs of the Life and Labours of Robert Morrison*, 2 vols. (London: Longman, Orme, Brown, Green, and Longmans, 1839). On early American missionary Christianity, see Emily Conroy-Krutz, *Christian Imperialism: Converting the World in the Early American Republic* (Ithaca, NY: Cornell University Press, 2015).

4. Hill, ms. autobiography, 31–42. Hill wrote the location and the date (June 14, 1819) after his account. He added, "The preceding form of a solemn dedication, I transcribed from Dr Doddridge's Rise and Progress of Religion in the Soul, as after a full & fair perusal of it, and having attentively considered the subject I was convinced that I could not compose a form so well adopted to the occasion." The prayer, "an example of Self-Dedication, or a solemn form of renewing our Covenant with God," appears in chapter 14 of Doddridge's work, e.g., Philip Doddridge, *The Rise and Progress of Religion in the Soul* (Montrose, Scotland: David Buchanan, 1790), 161–62.

5. The United States looks more typical compared to the rest of world, especially the global South. Mark Noll, *The New Shape of World Christianity* (Downers Grove, IL: InterVarsity Press, 2007), 109–25, 189.

6. Pew Research Center, "Faith in Flux" (April 2009): http://www.pewforum.org/2009/04/27/faith-in-flux/; Pew Research Center, " 'Nones' on the Rise: One-in-Five Adults Have No Religious Affiliation" (October 9, 2012): http://www.pewforum.org/2012/10/09/nones-on-the-rise/; cf. Robert N. Bellah, et al., *Habits of the Heart: Individualism and Commitment in American Life*, updated ed. (Berkeley: University of California Press, 1996), 221, 235; Elizabeth Drescher, *Choosing Our Religion: The Spiritual Lives of America's Nones* (New York: Oxford University Press, 2016): 37–38, 56, 61–62. The patterns in the 2009 Pew study are all confirmed in Pew Research Center, "America's Changing Religious Landscape" (May 12, 2015): http://www.pewforum.org/2015/05/12/americas-changing-religious-landscape/#factors-behind-the-changes-in-americans-religious-identification, pp. 33–47.

7. Robert Prichard, *A History of the Episcopal Church*, rev. ed. (Harrisburg, PA: Morehouse Publishing, 1999), 250.

8. Pew Research Center, "U.S. Catholics Open to Non-traditional Families" (September 2, 2015): http://www.pewforum.org/2015/09/02/u-s-catholics-open-to-non-traditional-families/.

9. Pew Research Center, "A Portrait of Jewish Americans" (October 1, 2013): http://www.pewforum.org/2013/10/01/jewish-american-beliefs-attitudes-culture-survey/.

10. Lee Hale, " 'Cultural Mormons' Adjust the Lifestyle but Keep the Label," *NPR* (August 28, 2016): http://www.npr.org/2016/08/28/490116191/cultural-mormons-adjust-the-lifestyle-but-keep-the-label. Cf. Pew Research Center, "A Portrait of Mormons in the U.S." (July 24, 2009): http://www.pewforum.org/2009/07/24/a-portrait-of-mormons-in-the-us/; Rick Philipps and Ryan T. Cragun, "Mormons in the United States 1990–2008: Socio-demographic Trends and Regional Differences" (2011): http://commons.trincoll.edu/aris/files/2011/12/Mormons2008.pdf.

11. Religious studies scholars have long pointed out that the term *religion* is not an obvious or natural category, but rather one deployed as part of an Enlightenment project of comparing and lumping disparate practices and groups within a single class. I am arguing something analogous: within that category, the term *religion* in the United States came to denote the part of one's identity that one has chosen. On this point, see Michael J. Altman, "Constructed in Doubt: The Evangelical Invention of Religion in Early America," *Fides et Historia* 46, no. 2 (2014): 60–63.

12. Robert Barro, Jason Hwang, and Rachel McCleary, "Religious Conversion in 40 Countries," *Journal for the Scientific Study of Religion* 49, no. 1 (2010): 15–36, doi:10.1111/j.1468-5906.2009.01490.x. See especially table 3. These figures are reported for years ranging from 1991 to 2001. The highest rate of conversion reported for the United States is 15.9 percent; they use a narrower definition of conversion than the Pew reports cited above.

13. Thomas A. Tweed, *Crossing and Dwelling: A Theory of Religion* (Cambridge, MA: Harvard University Press, 2006), esp. 73–77.

14. Northwest Ordinance (1787), art. 1; U.S. Const. amend. I.

15. Lyman Beecher, *Autobiography, Correspondence, &c. of Lyman Beecher*, ed. Charles Beecher, 2 vols. (London: Sampson Low, Son, and Marston, 1863), 2:304.

16. Cf. Sarah Barringer Gordon, *The Spirit of the Law: Religious Voices and the Constitution in Modern America* (Cambridge, MA: Belknap Press of Harvard University Press, 2010), 1–14.

17. Virginia Statue for Religious Freedom, in Julian P. Boyd, ed., *Papers of Thomas Jefferson* (Princeton, NJ: Princeton University Press, 1950–), 2:545–57. Thomas E. Buckley, *Establishing Religious Freedom: Jefferson's Statute in Virginia* (Charlottesville: University of Virginia Press, 2013), 55–81; Thomas E. Buckley, *Church and State in Revolutionary Virginia, 1776–1787* (Charlottesville: University Press of Virginia, 1977), 74–165; Merrill D. Peterson and Robert C. Vaughan, eds., *The Virginia Statute for Religious Freedom: Its Evolution and Consequences in American History* (Cambridge: Cambridge University Press, 1988).

18. The characterization of the American religious system as one that provided freedom of religion within a voluntary, denominational system is one of the oldest ideas in American religious history. The classic expression of the idea is Sidney E. Mead, *The Lively Experiment: The Shaping of Christianity in America* (New York: Harper and Row, 1963), and Sydney E. Ahlstrom, *A Religious History of the American People* (New Haven: Yale University Press, 1972), but the idea informs almost all American religious history.

19. David Yamane, *Becoming Catholic: Finding Rome in the American Religious Landscape* (New York: Oxford University Press, 2014), 2, quoting Phillip Hammond, *Religion and Personal Autonomy: The Third Disestablishment in America* (Columbia: University of South Carolina Press, 1992), 9–11; Diana L. Eck, *A New Religious America: How a "Christian Country" Has Become the World's Most Religiously Diverse Nation* (San Francisco: HarperSanFrancisco, 2002); Wade Clark Roof, *A Generation of Seekers: The Spiritual Journeys of the Baby Boom Generation* (San Francisco: HarperSanFrancisco, 1993); Wade Clark Roof, *Spiritual Marketplace: Baby Boomers and the Remaking of American Religion* (Princeton, NJ: Princeton University Press, 1999). On the 1950s, see Amanda Porterfield, *The Transformation of American Religion: The Story of a Late-Twentieth-Century Awakening* (New York: Oxford University Press, 2001).

20. Bellah, *Habits of the Heart*, 221.

21. Register of Congregation Shearith Israel, volume for 1834–1857, transcript, Records of Congregation Shearith Israel (I-4), box 1, folder 15, American Jewish Historical Society, New York and Boston, MA.

22. Historians of American religion have long called for work that encompasses multiple religious traditions within a single study. Thomas A. Tweed, ed., *Retelling U.S. Religious History* (Berkeley: University of California Press, 1997); Harry S. Stout and D. G. Hart, eds., *New Directions in American Religious History* (New York: Oxford University Press, 1997); Randall J. Stephens, ed., *Recent Themes in American Religious History: Historians in Conversation* (Columbia: University of South Carolina Press, 2009).

23. Sidney E. Mead, *The Lively Experiment: The Shaping of Christianity in America* (New York: Harper and Row, 1963); Sidney E. Mead, *The Nation with the Soul of a Church* (New York: Harper and Row, 1975).

24. Ahlstrom, *Religious History of the American People*. James O'Toole, "Religious History in the Post-Ahlstrom Era," in Stephens, *Recent Themes*, 13–18.

On the reasons historians turned to shorter time periods, see Jo Guldi and David Armitage, *The History Manifesto* (Cambridge: Cambridge University Press, 2014), http://dx.doi.org/10.1017/9781139923880, pp. 38–60.

25. Stout and Hart, *New Directions*, 5.

26. Thomas A. Tweed, "An American Pioneer in the Study of Religion: Hannah Adams (1755–1831) and Her Dictionary of All Religions," *Journal of the American Academy of Religion* 60, no. 5 (1992): 437–64; M. W. Vella, "Theology, Genre and Gender: The Precarious Place of Hannah Adams in American Literary History," *Early American Literature* 28, no. 1 (1993): 21–41; Leigh Eric Schmidt, "A History of All Religions," in *Whither the Early Republic: A Forum on the Future of the Field*, ed. John Lauritz Larson and Michael A. Morrison (Philadelphia: University of Pennsylvania Press, 2005), 177–84; James Turner, *Religion Enters the Academy: The Origins of the Scholarly Study of Religion in America* (Athens: University of Georgia Press, 2011), 24–31; Gary D. Schmidt, *A Passionate Usefulness: The Life and Literary Labors of Hannah Adams* (Charlottesville: University of Virginia Press, 2004).

27. Hannah Adams and Hannah Farnham Sawyer Lee, *A Memoir of Miss Hannah Adams* (Boston: Gray and Bowen, 1832), 13–15.

28. Adams, *Memoir*, 42–43.

29. Adams, *Memoir*, 14–15.

30. Adams, *Memoir*, 42–43.

31. Porterfield, *Conceived in Doubt*, 14–47.

32. Hannah Adams, *The History of the Jews*, 2 vols. (Boston: John Eliot Jr., 1812); cf. Dan Judson, "The Mercies of a Benign Judge: A Letter from Gershom Seixas to Hannah Adams, 1810," *American Jewish Archives Journal* 56 (2004): 179–189.

33. Stephen Cleveland Blythe, *An Apology for the Conversion of Stephen Cleveland Blythe, to the Faith of the Catholic, Apostolic, and Roman Church* (Montreal: Nahum Mower, 1815), 48–49.

34. Joseph Smith History, circa Summer 1832, p. 2, *The Joseph Smith Papers*, online edition, http://www.josephsmithpapers.org/paper-summary/history-circa-summer-1832/; cf. Richard L. Bushman, *Joseph Smith: Rough Stone Rolling* (New York: Alfred A. Knopf, 2005), 39–40.

35. Journal, 1835–1836, p. 23, *The Joseph Smith Papers*, online edition, http://www.josephsmithpapers.org/paper-summary/journal-1835-1836/. I have not retained deletions from the manuscript.

36. Stephen J. Stein, *Communities of Dissent: A History of Alternative Religions in America* (New York: Oxford University Press, 2003).

37. Anthony Trollope, *North America* (New York: Harper and Brothers, 1862), 273–74, 277.

38. *New-York Freeman's Journal and Catholic Register*, March 22, 1845, 302. On the connection between proselytism, pluralism, and civility, see Martin E. Marty and Frederick E. Greenspahn, eds., *Pushing the Faith: Proselytism and Civility in a Pluralistic World* (New York: Crossroad, 1988).

39. On Baptists versus Methodists, see, for example, Peter Cartwright, *Autobiography of Peter Cartwright: The Backwoods Preacher* (New York: Carlton & Porter, 1857), 69, 108–9, 118, 219, 226–27.

40. Charles Comfort Tiffany, *A History of the Protestant Episcopal Church in the United States of America*, 3rd ed. (New York: Charles Scribner's Sons, 1903), vii.

41. Max Lilienthal, "The Jews in Russia under Nicolai I," *Asmonean*, June 30, 1854, 84; *Asmonean*, July 7, 1854, 93–94; *Asmonean*, July 14, 1854, 101.

42. Patrick Carey, *Orestes A. Brownson: American Religious Weathervane* (Grand Rapids, MI: William B. Eerdmans, 2004), 142; Henry F. Brownson, *Orestes A. Brownson's . . . Life*, 3 vols. (Detroit: Henry F. Brownson, 1898–1900), 1:485. On families and conversion, see Anne C. Rose, "Some Private Roads to Rome: The Role of Families in American Victorian Conversions to Catholicism," *Catholic Historical Review* 85, no. 1 (January 1999): 35; Anne C. Rose, *Beloved Strangers: Interfaith Families in Nineteenth-Century America* (Cambridge, MA: Harvard University Press, 2001).

43. Thomas Wentworth Higginson, *The Sympathy of Religions* (Boston: Free Religious Association, 1876), 6; Leigh Eric Schmidt, "Cosmopolitan Piety: Sympathy, Comparative Religions, and Nineteenth-Century Liberalism," in *Practicing Protestants: Histories of the Christian Life in America, 1630–1965*, ed. Laurie F. Maffly-Kipp, Leigh Eric Schmidt, and Mark R. Valeri (Baltimore: Johns Hopkins University Press, 2006), 199–221. See also Leigh Eric Schmidt, *Restless Souls: The Making of American Spirituality* (San Francisco: HarperOne, 2005), 106–15. The other exception was layered religious belief, such as the possibility of practicing Spiritualism at the same time that one was a Protestant, or the continued belief in magic. Ann Braude, *Radical Spirits: Spiritualism and Women's Rights in Nineteenth-Century America* (Boston: Beacon Press, 1989); Jon Butler, *Awash in a Sea of Faith: Christianizing the American People* (Cambridge, MA: Harvard University Press, 1990), 67–96.

44. Matthew Bowman, *The Urban Pulpit: New York City and the Fate of Liberal Evangelicalism* (New York: Oxford University Press, 2014), 4–12, 124–25, 133, 198–99.

45. Kathryn Gin Lum, *Damned Nation: Hell in America from the Revolution to Reconstruction* (New York: Oxford University Press, 2014).

46. E.g., *The Substance of Leslie's Method with the Deists; and, The Truth of Christianity Demonstrated* (New York: American Tract Society, between 1827 and 1830); Andrew Fuller, *Three Queries to the Rejectors of Christianity* (New York: American Tract Society, 1832); *Infidelity Refuted: Dialogue between Pastor Reichenbach and an Infidel Peasant* (New York: Tract Society of the Methodist Episcopal Church, after 1833); A. W. Burnham, *The Infidel Reclaimed* (New York: American Tract Society, between 1835 and 1848); William Wisner, *"I am an Infidel!": An Authentic Narrative* (New York: American Tract Society, 1832); Elihu W. Baldwin, *Universalism Exposed* (Andover, MA: New England Tract Society, 1823); Andrew Fuller, *Reasons from the Bible, for Believing That the Future Punishment of the Wicked Will Be Endless* (New York: American Tract Society, between 1827 and 1832); Joel Hawes, *Reasons for Not Embracing the Doctrine of Universal Salvation* (New York: American Tract Society, 1829); Archibald Alexander, *Future Punishment; or, The Universalist Refuted* (New York: American Tract Society, 1836).

47. Charles Coupe, "Indifferentism," *Publications of the Catholic Truth Society* 37 (1898): 5–7. The Paulists, for example, preached against "indifferentism" in their missions to non-Catholics. *Chronicle of the Missions Given by the Congregation of Missionary Priests of St. Paul the Apostle*, six manuscript volumes, Office of Paulist History and Archives, North American Paulist Center, Washington, DC, 6:244. John J. Keane, "Father Hecker," *Catholic World* 49, no. 289 (April 1889): 5.

48. George Marsden, *Jonathan Edwards: A Life* (New Haven, CT: Yale University Press, 2003), 8. On the idea of religious pluralism, see William R. Hutchison, *Religious Pluralism in America: The Contentious History of a Founding Ideal* (New Haven, CT: Yale University Press, 2003); David Mislin, *Saving Faith: Making Religious Pluralism an American Value at the Dawn of the Secular Age* (Ithaca, NY: Cornell University Press, 2015); Charles H. Lippy, *Pluralism Comes of Age: American Religious Culture in the Twentieth Century* (Armonk, NY: M. E. Sharpe, 2000), 3–17.

49. Charles Taylor, *A Secular Age* (Cambridge, MA: Belknap Press of Harvard University Press, 2007). For reactions to Taylor, see Michael Warner, Jonathan VanAntwerpen, and Craig Calhoun, eds., *Varieties of Secularism in a Secular Age* (Cambridge, MA: Harvard University Press, 2013); James K. A. Smith, *How (Not) to Be Secular: Reading Charles Taylor* (Grand Rapids, MI: William B. Eerdmans, 2014); Edward J. Blum, "Slaves, Slavery, and the Secular Age: Or, Tales of Haunted Scholars, Liberating Prisons, Exorcised Divinities, and Immanent Devils," in *Race and Secularism in America*, ed. Jonathon S. Kahn and Vincent W. Lloyd (New York: Columbia University Press, 2016), 77–98. For a similar argument, see Peter Berger and Anton Zijderveld, *In Praise of Doubt* (New York: HarperOne, 2009); Gregor Thuswaldner, "A Conversation with Peter L. Berger: 'How My Views Have Changed,'" *The Cresset* 78, no. 3: 16–21, http://thecresset.org/2014/Lent/Thuswaldner_L14.html; David Martin, *Pentecostalism: The World Their Parish* (Malden, MA: Wiley-Blackwell, 2001), 23–24.

50. William James, *The Will to Believe, and Other Essays*, in *Writings, 1878–1899*, ed. Gerald E. Myers (New York: Library of America, 1992), 457–59.

51. Taylor, *Secular Age*, 1–3.

52. Taylor, *Secular Age*, 2.

53. Taylor, *Secular Age*, 3.

54. Cf. Charles Taylor, *Varieties of Religion Today: William James Revisited* (Cambridge, MA: Harvard University Press, 2002).

55. Taylor, *Secular Age*, 27, 36–37.

56. Taylor, *Secular Age*, 540.

57. Taylor, *Secular Age*, 768–69.

58. Taylor, *Secular Age*, 10–11.

59. E.g., Linford D. Fisher, *The Indian Great Awakening* (New York: Oxford University Press, 2012), 84–106.

60. Lewis Rambo, *Understanding Religious Conversion* (New Haven, CT: Yale University Press, 1993) is a standard work on theories of conversion. Rambo offers a description of the multiplicity of meanings of conversion, which he then attempts to fit within a "holistic model" that is useful as a work of theory, but

that suffers from being trans-historical and trans-geographical. See pp. 2, 5, 7–19, which lay out the possible meanings of the term and describe the model.

61. Taylor, *Secular Age*, 5; William James, *The Varieties of Religious Experience*, in *Writings 1902–1910*, ed. Bruce Kuklick (New York: Library of America, 1987), 36. On James's provisional definition, cf. Tweed, *Crossing and Dwelling*, 34–35, 49–50.

62. A. R. (Ammi Ruhamah) Bradbury, Diary, 1872–1874, Mss. Octavo Vols. B, American Antiquarian Society, Worcester, MA. Cf. John Leland, *The Writings of the Late Elder John Leland: Including Some Events in His Life* (New York, 1845), 9–15.

63. There are more conversions of interest than can be discussed here. For related studies see Derek Chang, *Citizens of a Christian Nation: Evangelical Missions and the Problem of Race in the Nineteenth Century* (Philadelphia: University of Pennsylvania Press, 2010); D. Oliver Herbel, *Turning to Tradition: Converts and the Making of an American Orthodox Church* (New York: Oxford University Press, 2013); Patrick D. Bowen, *A History of Conversion to Islam in the United States*, vol. 1, *White American Muslims before 1975* (Boston: Brill, 2015).

1 · Prayer

1. On Presbyterianism, see George M. Marsden, *The Evangelical Mind and the New School Presbyterian Experience: A Case Study of Thought and Theology in Nineteenth-Century America* (New Haven, CT: Yale University Press, 1970); Randall Herbert Balmer and John R. Fitzmier, *The Presbyterians* (Westport, CT: Greenwood Press, 1993); Leonard J. Trinterud, *The Forming of an American Tradition: A Re-examination of Colonial Presbyterianism* (Freeport, NY: Books for Libraries Press, 1970); Paul C. Gutjahr, *Charles Hodge: Guardian of American Orthodoxy* (New York: Oxford University Press, 2011), 38–43, 66, 70–71, 202, 265, 273–74; Mark A. Noll, *America's God: From Jonathan Edwards to Abraham Lincoln* (New York: Oxford University Press, 2002), 5, 20–21, 162, 164, 166–68, 175–76, 179, 413–15, especially pp. 253–329 on Calvinist theology.

2. These statistics are for the Presbyterian groups that were part of the Presbyterian Church in the U.S.A. in 1926. Herman Carl Weber, *Presbyterian Statistics through One Hundred Years, 1826–1926* (Philadelphia: Presbyterian Church in the U.S.A., 1927), 11–37. Cf. Edwin S. Gaustad, Philip L. Barlow, and Richard W. Dishno, *New Historical Atlas of Religion in America* (New York: Oxford University Press, 2001), 131–38; Noll, *America's God*, 166.

3. For an amusing anecdote on infant baptism versus believer's baptism, see the Baptist minister John Leland's account of his baptism as a child in John Leland, *The Writings of the Late Elder John Leland: Including Some Events in His Life* (New York, 1845), 9–10.

4. The category of being received on examination is more difficult to interpret. It probably includes people who converted as adults but who had been baptized by infants and so were not rebaptized (as, for example, the Baptists would have done), but it probably also includes people who switched denominations but could not obtain a certificate or letter. Adult baptism likely refers to anyone who was too old to be baptized as an infant—that is, someone whom

the church judged to have the ability to take the baptismal vows for him- or herself.

5. Charles G. Finney, *The Memoirs of Charles G. Finney: The Complete Restored Text*, ed. Garth Rosell and Richard A. G. Dupuis (Grand Rapids, MI: Academie Books, 1989), 356–82. For Finney, see Charles E. Hambrick-Stowe, *Charles G. Finney and the Spirit of American Evangelicalism* (Grand Rapids, MI: Eerdmans, 1996).

6. See Marsden, *Evangelical Mind*, 250–51, for an argument that the real issue in the 1837 schism was doctrine and that slavery was, at that time, a wedge issue; for later denominational schisms over slavery, see Mark A. Noll, *The Civil War as a Theological Crisis* (Chapel Hill: University of North Carolina Press, 2006); Gutjahr, *Charles Hodge*, 168–85. For the New Haven theology, see Oliver Crisp and Douglas A Sweeney, eds., *After Jonathan Edwards: The Courses of the New England Theology* (New York: Oxford University Press, 2012), 63–77, 130–41, 178–196.

7. On the origins of evangelicals, see W. R. Ward, *The Protestant Evangelical Awakening* (New York: Cambridge University Press, 1992); W. R. Ward, *Early Evangelicalism: A Global Intellectual History, 1670–1789* (New York: Cambridge University Press, 2006); Mark A. Noll, *The Rise of Evangelicalism: The Age of Edwards, Whitefield, and the Wesleys*, A History of Evangelicalism: People, Movements, and Ideas in the English-Speaking World (Downers Grove, IL: InterVarsity Press, 2003); John Wolffe, *The Expansion of Evangelicalism: The Age of Wilberforce, More, Chalmers, and Finney*, A History of Evangelicalism: People, Movements, and Ideas in the English-Speaking World (Downers Grove, IL: InterVarsity Press, 2007).

8. On evangelical models of conversion, see D. Bruce Hindmarsh, *The Evangelical Conversion Narrative: Spiritual Autobiography in Early Modern England* (Oxford: Oxford University Press, 2005); Susan Juster, "'In a Different Voice': Male and Female Narratives of Religious Conversion in Post-Revolutionary America," *American Quarterly* 41, no. 1 (March 1989): 34–62, http://www.jstor .org/stable/2713192; Kyle Roberts, *Evangelical Gotham: Religion and the Making of New York City, 1783–1860* (Chicago: University of Chicago Press, 2016), 19–26.

9. Finney, *Memoirs*, 365–66.

10. Finney, *Memoirs*, 27.

11. On the Rochester revivals, see Paul E. Johnson, *A Shopkeeper's Millennium: Society and Revivals in Rochester, New York, 1815–1837* (New York: Hill and Wang, 1991); Marianne Perciaccante, *Calling Down Fire: Charles Grandison Finney and Revivalism in Jefferson County, New York, 1800–1840* (Albany: State University of New York Press, 2003); Whitney R. Cross, *The Burned-Over District: The Social and Intellectual History of Enthusiastic Religion in Western New York, 1800–1850*, rev. ed. (New York: Octagon Books, 1981).

12. Roberts, *Evangelical Gotham*, 268–72.

13. Charles G. Finney, *Lectures on Revivals of Religion*, ed. William G. McLoughlin (Cambridge, MA: Belknap Press of Harvard University Press, 1960), 167.

14. For the long historiography on conversion relations, see, *inter alia*, Edmund S. Morgan, *Visible Saints: The History of a Puritan Idea* (New York: New

York University Press, 1963); David D. Hall, *The Faithful Shepherd: A History of the New England Ministry in the Seventeenth Century* (Chapel Hill: University of North Carolina Press, 1972), ch. 5; Patricia Caldwell, *The Puritan Conversion Narrative: The Beginnings of American Expression* (Cambridge: Cambridge University Press, 1983); Charles Lloyd Cohen, *God's Caress: The Psychology of Puritan Religious Experience* (New York: Oxford University Press, 1986); Norman Pettit, *The Heart Prepared: Grace and Conversion in Puritan Spiritual Life* (New Haven, CT: Yale University Press, 1966); Erik R. Seeman, *Pious Persuasions: Laity and Clergy in Eighteenth-Century New England* (Baltimore: Johns Hopkins University Press, 1999), 147–79; Douglas Winiarski, "Souls Filled with Ravishing Transport: Heavenly Visions and the Radical Awakening in New England, 1742," *William and Mary Quarterly*, 3rd ser., 61 (2004): 3–46; Sarah Rivett, *The Science of the Soul in Colonial New England* (Chapel Hill: University of North Carolina Press, 2011). In comparing the nineteenth-century relations to the eighteenth- and seventeenth-century relations, I am drawing on the relations published or described in George Selement and Bruce Woolley, eds., *Thomas Shepard's "Confessions,"* Publications of the Colonial Society of Massachusetts 58 (Boston: Colonial Society of Massachusetts, 1981); Thomas Shepard, *God's Plot; the Paradoxes of Puritan Piety; Being the Autobiography & Journal of Thomas Shepard* (Amherst: University of Massachusetts Press, 1972); Douglas L. Winiarski, "Gendered 'Relations' in Haverhill, Massachusetts, 1719–1742," in *In Our Own Words: New England Diaries, 1600 to the Present*, ed. Peter Benes, The Dublin Seminar for New England Folklife, Annual Proceedings 2006 (Boston: Boston University Press, 2008), 58–78; Kenneth P. Minkema, "The Lynn End 'Earthquake' Relations of 1727," *New England Quarterly* 69, no. 3 (September 1996): 473–99; Kenneth P. Minkema, "The East Windsor Conversion Relations, 1700–1725," *Connecticut Historical Society Bulletin* 51, no. 1 (1986): 7–63; Kenneth P. Minkema, "A Great Awakening Conversion: The Relation of Samuel Belcher," *William and Mary Quarterly*, 3rd ser., 44, no. 1 (1987): 121–26.

15. Finney, *Lectures*, 173.

16. This kind of warning dated back to the colonial evangelical awakenings—e.g., in Gilbert Tennent, *The Danger of an Unconverted Ministry* (Boston, 1742).

17. Finney, *Lectures*, 339–40.

18. Finney, *Lectures*, 173.

19. Finney, *Lectures*, 338–39.

20. Finney, *Lectures*, 380.

21. Finney, *Lectures*, 197.

22. Leigh Eric Schmidt, *Holy Fairs: Scotland and the Making of American Revivalism*, 2nd ed. (Grand Rapids, MI: Eerdmans, 2001); E. Brooks Holifield, *The Covenant Sealed: The Development of Puritan Sacramental Theology in Old and New England, 1570–1720* (New Haven, CT: Yale University Press, 1974); Charles E. Hambrick-Stowe, *The Practice of Piety: Puritan Devotional Disciplines in Seventeenth-Century New England* (Chapel Hill: University of North Carolina Press, 1982); Paul Keith Conkin, *Cane Ridge, America's Pentecost* (Madison: University of Wisconsin Press, 1990).

23. Finney, *Lectures*, 268–69.

24. Finney, *Lectures*, 89–106, 124–139. Cf. John Williamson Nevin, *The Anxious Bench* (Chambersburg, PA, 1843).

25. Jonathan Edwards, *The Life of David Brainerd*, in *Works of Jonathan Edwards Online*, vol. 7, ed. Norman Pettit, p. 134 (originally published 1749). Rivett, *Science of the Soul*, 336–46, points out the importance of Brainerd's narrative.

26. *Herald of Truth*, October 24, 1835, 338; Ted A. Smith, *The New Measures: A Theological History of Democratic Practice* (New York: Cambridge University Press, 2007), 1, quoting *Burchardism vs. Christianity* (Poughkeepsie, NY: Plott and Ramey, 1837); Russell Streeter, *Mirror of Calvinistic Fanatical Revivals; or, Jedediah Burchard & Co. during a Protracted Meeting of Twenty-Six Days*, 2nd ed. (Woodstock, VT: N. Haskell, 1835), 51–52, 55; C. G. Eastman, *Sermons, Addresses, and Exhortations by Rev. Jedediah Burchard* (Burlington, VT: Chauncey Goodrich, 1836). On the broad implications of the new measures, see in particular Smith, *New Measures*, pp. 69–72 on prayer and pp. 106–39 on choice; Richard Rabinowitz, *The Spiritual Self in Everyday Life: The Transformation of Personal Religious Experience in Nineteenth-Century New England* (Boston: Northeastern University Press, 1989), 97–101, emphasizing the techniques for hastening conversions, also significant for emphasizing the importance of the social setting for these personal experiences.

27. Kathryn Teresa Long, *The Revival of 1857–58: Interpreting an American Religious Awakening* (New York: Oxford University Press, 1998), 18; Samuel Irenaeus Prime, *The Power of Prayer, Illustrated in the Wonderful Displays of Divine Grace at the Fulton Street and Other Meetings* (New York: Scribner, 1858); Samuel Irenaeus Prime, *Five Years of Prayer, with the Answers* (London: James Nisbet, 1864), 35–60.

28. Finney later made a further systematization of his thought in a systematic theology that tried to base the entirety of Christian theology on his method of revivalism. Charles Grandison Finney, *Lectures on Systematic Theology: Embracing Ability (Natural, Moral and Gracious) Repentance, Impenitance, Faith and Unbelief* (Oberlin, OH: James M. Fitch, 1847).

29. *A Brief History of the American Tract Society, Instituted at Boston, 1814, and Its Relation to the American Tract Society at New York, Instituted 1825* (Boston: T. R. Marvin, 1857); *Sketch of the Origin and Character of the Principal Series of Tracts of the American Tract Society* (New York: American Tract Society, 1849). I have also consulted the first through sixteenth *Annual Reports of the American Tract Society* (New York, 1825–1841). Descriptions of the publication history of the tracts are drawn from my computational examination of the ATS tracts in the catalog of the American Antiquarian Society, explained in more detail in Lincoln Mullen, "Quantifying the American Tract Society: Using Library Catalog Data for Historical Research," *Religion in American History*, August 1, 2013, http://usreligion.blogspot.com/2013/08/quantifying-american-tract-society.html.

30. For the benevolence movement, see Lori Ginzberg, *Women and the Work of Benevolence* (New Haven, CT: Yale University Press, 1992); William G. McLoughlin, *Revivals, Awakenings, and Reform: An Essay on Religion and Social Change in America, 1607–1977* (Chicago: University of Chicago Press, 1980); Charles I. Foster, *An Errand of Mercy: The Evangelical United Front, 1790–1837*

(Chapel Hill: University of North Carolina Press, 1960); Wolffe, *Expansion of Evangelicalism*, 159–92; Michael P. Young, *Bearing Witness against Sin: The Evangelical Birth of the American Social Movement* (Chicago: University of Chicago Press, 2006).

31. Besides institutional histories, Candy Gunther Brown and Paul Nord have both written books about the ATS and the economics and functions of nineteenth-century evangelical publishing. Most recently John Lardas Modern in his *Secularism in Antebellum America* studied the reach of the ATS's distribution of tracts. Kyle Roberts wrote an article on the ATS's most popular tract, *The Dairyman's Daughter*. Candy Gunther Brown, *The Word in the World: Evangelical Writing, Publishing, and Reading in America, 1789–1880* (Chapel Hill: University of North Carolina Press, 2004), 49–50, 62–65; David Paul Nord, *Faith in Reading: Religious Publishing and the Birth of Mass Media in America* (New York: Oxford University Press, 2004); John Lardas Modern, *Secularism in Antebellum America* (Chicago: University of Chicago Press, 2011), 49–118; Kyle B. Roberts, "Locating Popular Religion in the Evangelical Tract: The Roots and Routes of *The Dairyman's Daughter*," *Early American Studies* 4, no. 1 (2006): 233–70. Also important on American religious publishing are John Fea, *The Bible Cause: A History of the American Bible Society* (New York: Oxford University Press, 2016); Paul C. Gutjahr, *An American Bible: A History of the Good Book in the United States, 1777–1880* (Palo Alto, CA: Stanford University Press, 1999); Nathan O. Hatch and Mark A. Noll, eds., *The Bible in America: Essays in Cultural History* (New York: Oxford University Press, 1982); Monica L. Mercado, "'Have You Ever Read?': Imagining Women, Bibles, and Religious Print in Nineteenth-Century America," *U.S. Catholic Historian* 31, no. 3 (2013): 1–21, doi:10.1353/cht.2013.0023.

32. On Anglophone evangelicalism, see Mark A. Noll, *The Rise of Evangelicalism: The Age of Edwards, Whitefield, and the Wesleys*, A History of Evangelicalism: People, Movements, and Ideas in the English-Speaking World (Downers Grove, IL: InterVarsity Press, 2003); John Wolffe, *The Expansion of Evangelicalism: The Age of Wilberforce, More, Chalmers, and Finney*, A History of Evangelicalism: People, Movements, and Ideas in the English-Speaking World (Downers Grove, IL: InterVarsity Press, 2007).

33. Roberts, "Locating Popular Religion," 236. Figures for tracts in the aggregate were published in the ATS annual reports cited above. For the antebellum communication revolution more generally, see Daniel Walker Howe, *What Hath God Wrought: The Transformation of America, 1815–1848* (Oxford: Oxford University Press, 2007), 5–7, 222–35, 690–98.

34. *An Adventure in Vermont; or, The Story of Mr. Anderson* (Andover, MA, between 1826 and 1829); William Newman, *To a Youth at School* (Andover, MA, between 1823 and 1826); David Bogue, *Instruction of the Rising Generation* (New York, between 1827 and 1832); *To Children and Youth, on the Importance of Prayer* (Andover, MA, 1825), among many other tracts intended for or discussing children.

35. The term *sinner's prayer* was common in twentieth-century evangelicalism. The best-known sinner's prayer was found in Bill Bright's 1965 tract *Four Spiritual Laws* (http://www.campuscrusade.com/fourlawseng.htm), explicated in

John G. Turner, *Bill Bright and the Campus Crusade for Christ: The Renewal of Evangelicalism in Postwar America* (Chapel Hill: University of North Carolina Press, 2009), 99–103, and David Harrington Watt, *A Transforming Faith: Explorations of Twentieth-Century American Evangelicalism* (New Brunswick, NJ: Rutgers University Press, 1991), 15–32.

36. *Constitution of the American Tract Society, with Addresses to Christians Recommending the Distribution of Religious Tracts, and Anecdotes Illustrating Their Beneficial Effects* (New York: American Tract Society, 1826), 5.

37. Cf. Martin E. Marty, *The Infidel: Freethought and American Religion* (Cleveland: Meridian Books, 1961) on the imaginative place of "the infidel" in Protestant print culture.

38. Dating the tracts requires comparing the address listed on the tracts with the changing headquarters of the ATS, and sometimes comparing typefaces. This work has been done by S. J. Wolfe, "Dating American Tract Society Publications through 1876 from External Evidences: A Series of Tables," website of the American Antiquarian Society, http://www.americanantiquarian.org /node/6693.

39. Thomas Goodwin, *Growth in Grace* (New York, between 1827 and 1832).

40. Luke 18:13–14 (AV).

41. Luke 23:42–43 (AV).

42. Legh Richmond, *The African Servant* (New York, between 1827 and 1832), 7.

43. *A Voice from Heaven* (New York, 1830).

44. *Solemn Inquiries, and Counsel to Careless Sinners* (New York, between 1827 and 1832), 3.

45. Daniel Tyerman, *The Dairyman* (New York, between 1827 and 1832). The wrappers of tracts usually contained supplementary materials that augmented the theme of the tract itself and that sometimes functioned as a short, four-page tract in its own right.

46. *The One Thing Needful: A Dialogue* (New York, 1825), 1, quoting Mark 9.

47. Solomon Carpenter, *Children of the Forest* (New York, 1831 or 1832), 9–10. Here and elsewhere, I have identified the biblical references in brackets.

48. Hebrews 3:15, 4:7; which itself quotes Psalm 95.

49. 2 Corinthians 6:2, quoted in John Campbell, *The Danger of Delay* (New York, between 1827 and 1832).

50. Richard Baxter, *Now or Never* (New York, 1831). Cf. Richard Baxter, *A Call to the Unconverted; Now or Never* (Glasgow: Chalmers and Collins, 1825). This text, like many of Baxter's works, was printed in scores of editions.

51. Herman Norton, *Convictions Stifled: A Narrative of Facts* (New York, 1838).

52. Eliakim Phelps, *Lydia Sturtevant; or, The Fatal Resolution: An Authentic Narrative* (New York, 1833).

53. Henry A. Boardman, *The Almost Christian* (New York, 1833), 15; cf. Acts 26:28.

54. Campbell, *Danger of Delay*, 1–7.

55. William Nevins, *What Must I Do to Be Saved* (New York, 1835), 6–7.

56. Hannah More, *The Ring-Leader* (New York, between 1832 and 1853).

57. Martha Crafts Lee, *Some Memorials of Edward Lee: An Authentic Record* (New York, 1838), 2.

58. Campbell, *Danger of Delay*, 12.

59. Philip Doddridge, *The Rise and Progress of Religion in the Soul* (Leeds: J. Binns, 1795), 89–96.

60. Nord, *Faith in Reading*, 113–50; Brown, *Word in the World*, 115–39.

61. Roberts, "Locating Popular Religion," 234.

62. Not every tract was fictionalized, however. *The Story of Mr. Anderson*, for example, recounts details of hearing George Whitfield and of fighting in the Revolutionary War against the army of John Burgoyne that seem as reliable as any other narrative.

63. Roberts, "Locating Popular Religion," 233–70; Legh Richmond, *The Dairyman's Daughter: An Authentic Narrative* (New York, between 1827 and 1832).

64. This attempt, however, failed; Walworth became a Catholic. See Chapter 6. Clarence Walworth, *The Oxford Movement in America; or, Glimpses of Life in an Anglican Seminary* (New York: Catholic Book Exchange, 1895), 15–16.

65. From the copy at the American Antiquarian Society. Robert Hall, *The Work of the Holy Spirit* (New York, between 1825 and 1827).

66. Nord, *Faith in Reading*, 41–60. These details can also be found repeatedly in the ATS annual reports.

67. *General View of Colportage: As Conducted by the American Tract Society in the United States* (New York: Daniel Fanshaw, 1845); Charles Peabody, *Twenty Years among the Colporteurs* (New York: American Tract Society, 1865), http://hdl .handle.net/2027/njp. 32101065973289; "The American Colporteur System" (New York: American Tract Society, 1836), 20, reprinted in *American Tract Society Documents, 1824–1925* (New York: Arno Press, 1972); Nord, *Faith in Reading*, 89–112; Brown, *Word in the World*, 46–78; the fullest discussion of the cultural effects of colportage is John Lardas Modern, "Evangelical Secularism and the Measure of Leviathan," *Church History: Studies in Christianity and Culture* 77, no. 4 (2008): 801–76, doi:10.1017/S0009640708001613; also in Modern, *Secularism in Antebellum America*, 49–118. I'm especially indebted to Modern's idea of "evangelical secularism."

68. *Colporteur Reports of the American Tract Society, 1841–1846* (Newark, NJ: New Jersey Historical Records Survey Project, 1940).

69. *Colporteur Reports*, 4–5, 11, 20, 29.

70. Cf. David Paul Nord, "Religious Reading and Readers in Antebellum America," *Journal of the Early Republic* 15, no. 2 (July 1, 1995): 241–72, doi:10.2307/3123909.

71. *Constitution of the ATS*, 20–24. *The Address of the Executive Committee of the American Tract Society, to the Christian Public* (New York: American Tract Society, 1825), quotations about number of conversions from page 5, narratives on 13–24.

72. *Colporteur Reports*, 65.

73. Rivett, *Science of the Soul*, 336–46; John A. Grigg, *The Lives of David Brainerd: The Making of an American Evangelical Icon* (New York: Oxford University Press, 2009).

74. John Newton, *The Life of the Rev. John Newton* (New York: American Tract Society, 1832).

75. In his *Treatise concerning Religious Affections*, Jonathan Edwards described how this process worked: "A scheme of what is necessary, and according to a rule already received and established by common opinion, has a vast (though to many a very insensible) influence in forming persons' notions of the steps and method of their own experiences. I know very well what their way is; for I have had much opportunity to observe it. Very often, at first, their experiences appear like a confused chaos, as Mr. Shepard expresses it: but then those passages of their experience are picked out, that have most of the appearance of such particular steps that are insisted on; and these are dwelt upon in the thoughts, and these are told of from time to time, in the relation they give: these parts grow brighter and brighter in their view; and others, being neglected, grow more and more obscure: and what they have experienced is insensibly strained to bring all to an exact conformity to the scheme that is established." Jonathan Edwards, *Religious Affections*, in *Works of Jonathan Edwards Online*, vol. 2, ed. Paul Ramsey, p. 160.

76. Max Louis Rossvally, *A Short Sketch of the Life and Conversion of a Jew* (New York: James Huggins, 1876), 19. See Chapter 5 for discussion of conversions from Judaism.

77. There are actually 88 narratives, assuming that the Darius Goff of 1856 is the same person as the Darius Goff of 1858. These relations are in an unprocessed archival collection, so I have cited the collection here and identified each quotation below by the writer's name. Pawtucket Congregational Church Records, folder labeled "Religious Experiences 1856–1866, 1868," Congregational Library, Boston, MA.

78. Cf. *Obstacles to Conversion* (New York, 1837).

79. Nehemiah Adams, *Instantaneous Conversion, and Its Connection with Piety* (Boston: Gould and Lincoln, 1858), 5–8; for the argument against instantaneous conversion, see "The Revival," *Boston Courier*, April 15, 1858. For the businessmen's revival, see John Corrigan, *Business of the Heart: Religion and Emotion in the Nineteenth Century* (Berkeley: University of California Press, 2002); Kathryn Long, *The Revival of 1857–58: Interpreting an American Religious Awakening* (New York: Oxford University Press, 1998).

80. William C. Conant, *Narrative of Remarkable Conversions and Revival Incidents: Including . . . an Account of the Rise and Progress of the Great Awakening of 1857–58* (New York: Derby and Jackson, 1858), xviii, 442, 310, 149, 376. In the introduction Beecher was clearly uncomfortable with the demand for instantaneous conversions and tried to suggest ways that people might be converted without a sudden experience; he was nevertheless obligated to argue that conversion was by definition instantaneous.

81. Augustus Hopkins Strong, *Systematic Theology: A Compendium and Commonplace-Book Designed for the Use of Theological Students* (Rochester, NY, 1886), 436–37.

82. Roberts, *Evangelical Gotham*, 186–87, 201–2.

83. Anne S. Brown and David D. Hall, "Family Strategies and Religious Practice: Baptism and the Lord's Supper in Early New England," in *Lived Religion in America: Toward a History of Practice*, ed. David D. Hall (Princeton, NJ: Princeton University Press, 1997), 53; Jonathan Edwards, "An Humble Inquiry . . . Concerning the Qualifications Requisite to a Complete Standing and Full Communion in the Visible Christian Church," in vol. 12, *Ecclesiastical Writings*, ed. David D. Hall, *Works of Jonathan Edwards* (New Haven, CT: Yale University Press, 1994), 213.

84. The ages of East Windsor converts can be found in Minkema, "East Windsor Conversion Relations," 7–63. Cf. Eleanor Emerson, *Memoirs of Mrs. Eleanor Emerson* (n.p.: Lincoln & Edmands, 1809), 37: "Many . . . elderly men and women, and also children, have been lately converted."

85. James Bennet, *Duties to Relatives* (New York, between 1827 and 1832); H. N. Brinsmade, *Address to Mothers* (Andover, MA, 1825).

86. Andrew Fuller, *Three Queries to the Rejectors of Christianity* (New York, 1832); John Owen, *The Decay of Spiritual Affections* (New York, not before 1831).

87. Nehemiah Adams, *The Baptized Child* (Boston, 1836), 76, 79, http://hdl .handle.net/2027/hvd.ah4fx4.

88. E.g., Philip Doddridge, *Family Worship* (New York, 1825); David Bogue, *The Instruction of the Rising Generation in the Principles of the Christian Religion Recommended* (New York, between 1827 and 1832); William Craig Brownlee, *The Spoiled Child* (New York, between 1844 and 1846); Isaac Watts, *To Children and Youth, on the Importance of Prayer* (Andover, MA, 1825); *A New Heart the Child's Best Portion* (New York, 1823); Daniel Dana, *Address to Youth* (New York, between 1825 and 1827); William Newman, *To a Youth at School* (Andover, MA, between 1823 and 1826); *To the Parents of Sabbath School Children* (New York, not before 1833); Horatio Nelson Brinsmade, *Address to Mothers* (Andover, MA, 1824 or 1825).

89. William Scribner, *Pray for Your Children; or, An Appeal to the Parents to Pray Continually for the Welfare and Salvation of Their Children* (Philadelphia: Presbyterian Board of Publication, 1873), 7, http://hdl.handle.net/2027/loc .ark:/13960/t6k087953.

90. Daniel Huntington, *Hints on Early Religious Education* (Andover, MA, 1825), 16.

91. Ebenezer Dickey, *To Parents* (New York, 1828), inside cover.

92. Samuel Miller, *The Christian Education of the Children and Youth in the Presbyterian Church* (Philadelphia, 1840), 20–21, 24–25, 31, http://hdl.handle.net /2027/njp. 32101076422961.

93. Cf. Diana Pasulka, "A Somber Pedagogy: A History of the Child Death Bed Scene in Early American Children's Religious Literature, 1674–1840," *Journal of the History of Childhood and Youth* 2, no. 2 (2009): 171–97.

94. William S. Plumer, *Thoughts on Religious Education and Early Piety* (New York, 1836), 7–8, 27, 72–73, 82–84, 91, http://hdl.handle.net/2027/hvd.3204409 6983895. On Plumer, see *American National Biography Online*, s.v. "Plumer, William Swan," http://www.anb.org/articles/08/08-01193.html.

95. *[Brandon] Vermont Telegraph*, April 18, 1838, Chronicling America: Historic American Newspapers, Library of Congress, http://chroniclingamerica .loc.gov/lccn/sn83025661/1838–04–18/ed-1/seq-2/.

96. Anne M. Boylan, *Sunday School: The Formation of an American Institution, 1790–1880* (New Haven, CT: Yale University Press, 1988), 14–15. I have depended also on Elise Leal, "'Bringing Little Ones to Christ': The Evangelical Transformation of American Sunday Schools and Changing Attitudes toward Childhood Conversion, 1790–1824," paper presented at the American Society of Church History, Atlanta, GA, January 2016.

97. For a collection of these texts, see *Sunday School Books in 19th Century America* (East Lansing: Michigan State University Libraries Special Collections), https://www.lib.msu.edu/ssbdata/.

98. Charlotte Elizabeth, *The Glory of Israel; or, Letters to Jewish Children on the Early History of Their Nation* (Philadelphia: American Sunday-School Union, 1843), 46.

99. Boylan, *Sunday School*, 1–6.

100. Edwin Wilbur Rice, *The Sunday-School Movement, 1780–1917, and the American Sunday-School Union, 1817–1917* (American Sunday-School Union, 1917), 52, 444–45.

101. Boylan, *Sunday School*, 138, 141, 143.

102. Boylan, *Sunday School*, 14–16, estimates in table 1 on page 11.

103. Quoted in Rice, *Sunday School Movement*, 161.

104. Rice, *Sunday-School Movement*, 263–65; Anne M. Boylan, "The Role of Conversion in Nineteenth-Century Sunday Schools," *American Studies* 20, no. 1 (April 1, 1979): 35–48.

105. *[Brandon] Vermont Telegraph*, July 11, 1838, Chronicling America: Historic American Newspapers, Library of Congress, http://chroniclingamerica .loc.gov/lccn/sn83025661/1838-07-11/ed-1/seq-2/.

106. Rice, *Sunday-School Movement*, 420.

107. Horace Bushnell, *Discourses on Christian Nurture* (Boston: Massachusetts Sabbath School Society, 1847), 6–7, http://catalog.hathitrust.org /Record/011530767. This early edition was suppressed. For the longer version, see Horace Bushnell, *Views of Christian Nurture, and of Subjects Adjacent Thereto* (Hartford, CT: E. Hunt, 1848), http://hdl.handle.net/2027/mdp . 39015011568923?urlappend=%3Bseq=7.

108. Boylan, *Sunday School*, 149.

109. For example, the theological consensus among Episcopalians on baptism and adult renewal as "two pillars of assurance" had fractured by the last quarter of the nineteenth century. Robert W. Prichard, *The Nature of Salvation: Theological Consensus in the Episcopal Church, 1801–73*, Studies in Anglican History (Urbana: University of Illinois Press, 1997), 1–35, 171–208.

110. Modern, *Secularism in Antebellum America*, ch. 1.

111. *The New Birth* (New York, between 1827 and 1830), 11.

112. Matthew Bowman has demonstrated that conversion was as much a part of "liberal evangelicalism" as it was evangelicalism proper. The difference was that liberal evangelicalism came to regard worship and the personal experience of Christ rather than an encounter with the Word as the means of conversion. See Matthew Bowman, *The Urban Pulpit: New York City and the Fate of Liberal Evangelicalism* (New York: Oxford University Press, 2014), 2–4, 10–11, 96–97, 117–18.

113. John Newton, "Nay, I cannot let thee go," from *Olney Hymns* (London, 1779), number 10, quoted in Jacob Ten Eyck Field, *John de Long; or, The Prodigal of Fifty Years* (New York, 1834), 8–10.

114. Lyman Beecher, *A Comparison of the Apostolic Age with the Present*, 4th ed. (Boston: American Board of Commissioners for Foreign Missions, 1833), 7.

2 · Gift

1. John Howard Payne, *The Payne-Butrick Papers*, 2 vols., ed. William L. Anderson, Jane L. Brown, and Anne F. Rogers (Lincoln: University of Nebraska Press, 2010), 1:263; Luke 18:1–8 (AV).

2. John Huss, "Ordination Sermon of John Huss," *Missionary Herald* 30, no. 3 (1834): 98.

3. In a profound essay that has not had the full impact on the field that it deserves, Leigh Schmidt has pointed out the need to look for "practices of exchange" in addition to "supply-side" models of the "voluntaristic marketplace." He points out that thinking of American religion in terms of a gift economy does not take away from thinking of it in terms of a market, but it does open up possibilities for considering it in terms of reception. Leigh Eric Schmidt, "Practices of Exchange: From Market Culture to Gift Economy in the Interpretation of American Religion," in *Lived Religion in America: Toward a History of Practice*, ed. David D. Hall (Princeton, NJ: Princeton University Press, 1997), 71–73. Schmidt's argument is parallel to the argument of the historian of missions Lamin O. Sanneh, who critiques much of the historiography of missions because its "attention was directed to the priority of foreign transmission rather than local reception." Lamin O. Sanneh, *Disciples of All Nations: Pillars of World Christianity* (Oxford: Oxford University Press, 2008), 131. See also Lamin O. Sanneh and Grant Wacker, "Christianity Appropriated: Conversion and the Intercultural Process," *Church History* 68, no. 4 (1999): 954–61, doi: 10.2307/3170211; Lamin O. Sanneh, *Translating the Message: The Missionary Impact on Culture*, 2nd ed. (Maryknoll, NY: Orbis Books, 2009); Andrew F. Walls, *The Cross-Cultural Process in Christian History: Studies in the Transmission and Appropriation of Faith* (Maryknoll, NY: Orbis Books, 2002).

4. Alexander Keith Johnston, "Moral and Statistical Chart Showing the Geographical Distribution of Man according to Religious Belief, with the Principal Protestant Mission Stations in the Middle of the Nineteenth Century," in *The Physical Atlas of Natural Phenomena*, 2nd ed. (Edinburgh: William Blackwood and Sons, 1856), plate 34. Courtesy of the David Rumsey Map Collection, Cartography Associates, http://www.davidrumsey.com/luna/servlet/s/8vjr7u.

5. Edwin S. Gaustad, Philip L. Barlow, and Richard W. Dishno, *New Historical Atlas of Religion in America* (New York: Oxford University Press, 2001), 116–17.

6. Kenneth Morrison and Michael D. McNally question whether the term *conversion* is adequate for the Indian experience of Christianity. Morrison prefers the term *religious change* as it relates to power and changing cosmologies. While I retain the term *conversion* because of the specificity of having a

conversion experience recognizable to white Christians and to undergoing rituals especially baptism, by explaining these conversions as a complex of choices and by paying attention below to cosmology rather than religion itself, I in essence adopt their method without adopting their concern over the term. Kenneth M. Morrison, *The Solidarity of Kin: Ethnohistory, Religious Studies, and the Algonkian-French Religious Encounter* (Albany: State University of New York Press, 2002), 131, 145; Michael D. McNally, "The Practices of Native American Christianities," in *American Christianities: A History of Dominance and Diversity*, ed. Catherine A. Brekus and W. Clark Gilpin (Chapel Hill: University of North Carolina Press, 2011), 66; Michael D. McNally, "The Practice of Native American Christianity," *Church History* 69, no. 4 (December 1, 2000): 834–59, doi:10.2307/3169333.

7. William G. McLoughlin, *Cherokees and Missionaries, 1789–1839* (New Haven, CT: Yale University Press, 1984).

8. McLoughlin, *Cherokees and Missionaries*, 332–33.

9. Payne, *Payne-Butrick Papers*, 1:28. Payne's notes would later be used by E. G. Squier, an amateur ethnologist interested in the mounds in the Ohio and Mississippi River valleys. Squier made marginal notes on Payne's manuscript, comparing the Cherokee religion to other world religions. For example, about the Cherokee divining crystals he wrote, "Similar chrystals sacred among the Australians. See Gray's Australia, vol. 2 P." And on the worship of thunder on the mountain he wrote, "The same worship existent in Peru—see McCulloh & LaVega. E. G. S." Payne, *Payne-Butrick Papers*, pp. 1:28, 344n69, 22, 343n61. Both Payne and Squier were amateurs who, whatever their personal religious beliefs might have been, approached religion from a comparative perspective. For other ethnographic reports of Cherokee traditions, see Samuel Worcester, "Cherokee Traditions," *New Echota Letters: Contributions of Samuel A. Worcester to the Cherokee Phoenix*, ed. Jack Frederick Kilpatrick and Anna Gritts Kilpatrick (Dallas: Southern Methodist University Press, 1968), 43–52, reproducing *Cherokee Phoenix*, April 1, 1829, and April 29, 1829.

10. Payne, *Payne-Butrick Papers*, 1:131–32.

11. Payne, *Payne-Butrick Papers*, 1:20–21, 1:129–30.

12. The Christian view is sometimes called monogenesis. Scientific racism, and in particular the scientific idea of polygenesis, were later developments. Cf. Colin Kidd, *The Forging of Races: Race and Scripture in the Protestant Atlantic World, 1600–2000* (Cambridge: Cambridge University Press, 2006).The idea that religious tolerance can be based on the recognition that different religious traditions pertain to different groups is sometimes regarded as a modern, even a contemporary, phenomenon. But Stuart B. Schwartz, *All Can Be Saved: Religious Tolerance and Salvation in the Iberian Atlantic World* (New Haven, CT: Yale University Press, 2008), has convincingly shown that such an idea was common in early modern Iberia.

13. Rufus Anderson, *Memoir of Catharine Brown, a Christian Indian of the Cherokee Nation* (Boston: S. T. Armstrong and Crocker and Brewster, 1825), 22. For a scholarly edition of this text, along with Catherine Brown's own writings, see Theresa Strouth Gaul, ed., *Cherokee Sister: The Collected Writings of Catherine Brown, 1818–1823* (Lincoln: University of Nebraska Press, 2014).

14. Anderson, *Memoir of Catharine Brown*, 154. The quotation is from Acts 17:26.

15. Cf. the essays on "The Nineteenth-Century Missionary as Scholar" and "Humane Learning and the Missionary Movement" in Andrew F. Walls, *The Missionary Movement in Christian History: Studies in the Transmission of Faith* (Maryknoll, NY: Orbis Books, 1996), 187–210.

16. E. Brooks Holifield, *Theology in America: Christian Thought from the Age of the Puritans to the Civil War* (New Haven, CT: Yale University Press, 2003); Mark A. Noll, *America's God: From Jonathan Edwards to Abraham Lincoln* (Oxford: Oxford University Press, 2002); Samuel Colcord Bartlett, *Historical Sketches of the Missions of the American Board* (New York: Arno Press, 1972).

17. Payne, *Payne-Butrick Papers*, 1:5–17, 1:21, 1:28–31, 1:129, 2:112, 2:119.

18. Anderson, *Memoir of Catharine Brown*; John Arch, *Memoir of John Arch, a Cherokee Young Man*, 3rd ed. (Boston: Massachusetts Sabbath School Society, 1836).

19. Arch, *Memoir*, 10, 12.

20. Anderson, *Memoir of Catharine Brown*, 22.

21. Anderson, *Memoir of Catharine Brown*, 11–13, 22; Arch, *Memoir*, 12.

22. Katherine Carté Engel, *Religion and Profit: Moravians in Early America* (Philadelphia: University of Pennsylvania Press, 2011).

23. Rowena McClinton, ed., *The Moravian Springplace Mission to the Cherokees* (Lincoln: University of Nebraska Press, 2007); Adelaide L. Fries et al., eds., *Records of the Moravians in North Carolina* (Raleigh, NC: Edwards and Broughton, 1922).

24. Meg Devlin O'Sullivan, "A Family Affair: Cherokee Conversion to American Board Churches, 1817–1839," *Tennessee Historical Quarterly* 64, no. 4 (December 2005): 264–83.

25. Schmidt, "Practices of Exchange," 69–91.

26. McClinton, ed., *Moravian Springplace Mission*, 1:420–21; Joyce B. Phillips and Paul Gary Phillips, eds., *The Brainerd Journal: A Mission to the Cherokees, 1817–1823*, Indians of the Southeast (Lincoln: University of Nebraska Press, 1998), 108–110, 123, 196. The foundational work on gift economies is Marcel Mauss, *The Gift: The Form and Reason for Exchange in Archaic Societies*, trans. W. D. Halls (New York: W. W. Norton, 2000), which points out that giving a gift placed a reciprocal obligation on the recipient.

27. McClinton, ed., *Moravian Springplace Mission*, 1:37; for the conversion of Margaret Vann, see Edmund Schwarze, *History of the Moravian Missions among Southern Indian Tribes of the United States* (Bethlehem, PA: Times Publishing Co., 1923), 83–127.

28. McClinton, ed., *Moravian Springplace Mission*, 1:66–68.

29. Payne, *Payne-Butrick Papers*, 1:116.

30. McClinton, ed., *Moravian Springplace Mission*, 1:57. The journal further recorded, "She must be suffering greatly physically."

31. McClinton, ed., *Moravian Springplace Mission*, 1:57–58.

32. McClinton, ed., *Moravian Springplace Mission*, 1:176–77.

33. The sermon's text was 2 Cor. 5:10. McClinton, ed., *Moravian Springplace Mission*, 1:68.

34. McClinton, ed., *Moravian Springplace Mission*, 1:284, 289; on deathbed scenes, see David Hempton, *Methodism: Empire of the Spirit* (New Haven: Yale University Press, 2005), 60–68.

35. McClinton, ed., *Moravian Springplace Mission*, 1:284.

36. This account of Peggy Vann's conversion is drawn from a journal, not a published conversion narrative. The Moravians were certainly writing for an audience, for the journals were distributed among the other Moravian missionaries for their edification. (The ABCFM missionaries had an even stronger sense of audience, for their journals were sometimes published in the ABCFM annual reports and sometimes in the *Missionary Herald*.) But the journal was written day by day, which meant that it was more difficult for the missionaries to craft a coherent narrative over time. To be sure, the missionaries did read the events in their converts' lives within their theologies and their narrative genres of conversion. But whatever their lens, they were still recording day-to-day observations of actual events in the converts' lives.

37. McClinton, ed., *Moravian Springplace Mission*, 1:354.

38. McClinton, ed., *Moravian Springplace Mission*, 1:355–56.

39. McClinton, ed., *Moravian Springplace Mission*, 1:364.

40. McClinton, ed., *Moravian Springplace Mission*, 1:365; August Gottlieb Spangenberg, *An Exposition of Christian Doctrine, as Taught in the Protestant Church of the United Brethren; or, Unitas Fratrum* (London: W. & A. Strahan, 1784).

41. McClinton, ed., *Moravian Springplace Mission*, 1:406.

42. McClinton, ed., *Moravian Springplace Mission*, 1:375.

43. McClinton, ed., *Moravian Springplace Mission*, 1:20–22, 37, 529; Fries et al., eds., *Records of the Moravians*.

44. McClinton, ed., *Moravian Springplace Mission*, 1:441, 491. Hicks also read *Idea Fidei Fratrum* after he desired to be converted. He reported that "while reading . . . he enjoyed a great blessing for his heart. . . . He asked to be allowed to keep this book longer to become even more familiar with its contents."

45. McClinton, ed., *Moravian Springplace Mission*, 1:484.

46. Conevery Bolton Valencius, *The Lost History of the New Madrid Earthquakes* (Chicago: University of Chicago Press, 2013), 106–44.

47. William G. McLoughlin, ed., *The Cherokee Ghost Dance: Essays on the Southeastern Indians, 1789–1861* (Macon, GA: Mercer, 1984); McLoughlin, *Cherokees and Missionaries*, 95; Payne, *Payne-Butrick Papers*, 1:23–27, 1:128; McClinton, ed., *Moravian Springplace Mission*, 1:38–39.

48. McClinton, ed., *Moravian Springplace Mission*, 1:486, 2:503.

49. McClinton, ed., *Moravian Springplace Mission*, 1:529, 1:539.

50. McLoughlin, *Cherokees and Missionaries*, 51–53.

51. Phillips and Phillips, eds., *Brainerd Journal*, 80, 86, 135, 213, 448, 486.

52. Phillips and Phillips, eds., *Brainerd Journal*, 407–23. Original manuscripts consulted ABC 18.3.1, 2:159–61, 2:189, 2:205–7,3:9–10, North American Indian Mission Records, American Board of Commissioners for Foreign Missions, Houghton Library, Harvard University, Cambridge, MA (hereafter cited by call number).

53. Anderson, *Memoir of Catharine Brown*, 32. The ABCFM records contain a list of the books. Thomas Scott, *The Holy Bible . . . with Explanatory*

Notes, Practical Observations, and Copious Marginal References, stereotype ed. (Boston: S. T. Armstrong, 1830). This Samuel was one of the founders of the ABCFM, not his nephew the translator discussed below. William Buell Sprague, ed., *Annals of the American Pulpit*, 9 vols., reprint ed. (New York: Arno Press, 1969), 2:398–402.

54. Phillips and Phillips, eds., *Brainerd Journal*, 407–23.

55. Leonard Woods, *A Sermon Preached at Haverhill (Mass.), in Remembrance of Mrs. Harriet Newell* (Boston: Samuel T. Armstrong, 1814); Moses Waddel, *Memoirs of the Life of Miss Caroline Elizabeth Smelt* (New York: Daniel Fanshaw, 1818).

56. Phillips and Phillips, eds., *Brainerd Journal*, 132, 182, 185, 196.

57. Phillips and Phillips, eds., *Brainerd Journal*, 144, 128.

58. Anderson, *Memoir of Catharine Brown*, 11–12, 60–61.

59. Arch, *Memoir*, 14; Anderson, *Memoir of Catharine Brown*, 27, 37–38; Phillips and Phillips, eds., *Brainerd Journal*, 150, 178.

60. The ABCFM was officially nondenominational at its founding, but as denominations founded their own mission boards, it became more and more Congregationalist. For the purposes of ecclesiastical oversight, the Congregationalist ABCFM missionaries usually put themselves under the authority of the Southern presbyteries, so they frequently referred to themselves as Presbyterians.

61. The term "national evangelism" comes from Sam Haselby, *The Origins of American Religious Nationalism* (New York: Oxford University Press, 2015), 2–3. See ch. 3 and ch. 6 in particular for these competing visions as described by Haselby.

62. Phillips and Phillips, eds., *Brainerd Journal*, 137.

63. Daniel Butrick to Jeremiah Evarts, August 20, 1829; ABC 18.3.1, vol. 5, no. 391.

64. *Cherokee Phoenix*, June 4, 1828.

65. Elizur Butler to Jeremiah Evarts, September 22, 1830, ABC 18.3.1, vol. 6, no. 74. Also quoted in Henry Thompson Malone, *Cherokees of the Old South: A People in Transition* (Athens: University of Georgia Press, 1956), 113–14.

66. Malone, *Cherokees*, 113–14.

67. Phillips and Phillips, eds., *Brainerd Journal*, 161–62; Articles of Faith and Covenant, ABC 18.3.1, 2:98.

68. McClinton, ed., *Moravian Springplace Mission*, 37–38; Payne, *Payne-Butrick Papers*, 1:29–30. A guide to the distinctive practices of the Moravians is Adelaide L. Fries, *Customs and Practices of the Moravian Church*, rev. ed. (Winston-Salem, NC: Board of Christian Education and Evangelism, 1973).

69. Malone, *Cherokees*, 115–16, quoting William Chamberlin to Jeremiah Evarts, July 8, 1824, in ABC 18.3.1 vol. 3, no. 24; Daniel Butrick to Jeremiah Evarts, August 20, 1829, in ABC 18.3.1, vol. 5, no. 391.

70. Phillips and Phillips, eds., *Brainerd Journal*, 406, 424.

71. Arch, *Memoir*, 7–9, 11; Anderson, *Memoir of Catharine Brown*; McClinton, ed., *Moravian Springplace Mission*, 1:544.

72. McClinton, ed., *Moravian Springplace Mission*, 1:122.

73. McClinton, ed., *Moravian Springplace Mission*, 1:107, 161.

74. McClinton, ed., *Moravian Springplace Mission,* 1:200.

75. Althea Bass, ed., *Cherokee Messenger* (Norman: University of Oklahoma Press, 1936).

76. McClinton, ed., *Moravian Springplace Mission,* 1:196–97.

77. Phillips and Phillips, eds., *Brainerd Journal,* 198.

78. James Mooney, "Myths of the Cherokee," in *Nineteenth Annual Report of the Bureau of American Ethnology, 1897–98* (Washington, DC: Government Printing Office, 1900), part 1, pp. 15–17.

79. Anderson, *Memoir of Catharine Brown,* 14.

80. Samuel Worcester, "Explanation of the Sequoyah Syllabary," *New Echota Letters,* 5–9, cf. 14–33, reproducing *Cherokee Phoenix,* February 21, 1828.

81. Willard Walker and James Sarbaugh, "The Early History of the Cherokee Syllabary," *Ethnohistory* 40, no. 1 (January 1993): 70–94, doi:10.2307/482159; Ellen Cushman, "The Cherokee Syllabary from Script to Print," *Ethnohistory* 57, no. 4 (2010): 625–49, doi:10.1215/00141801–2010–039; McLoughlin, *Cherokees and Missionaries,* 218, 229.

82. Arch, *Memoir,* 21, 29.

83. For a history of the mission school, see John Demos, *The Heathen School: A Story of Hope and Betrayal in the Age of the Early Republic* (New York: Vintage, 2014).

84. Joseph Tracy, *History of the American Board of Commissioners for Foreign Missions,* 2nd ed. (New York: M. W. Dodd, 1842), 167; McLoughlin, *Cherokees and Missionaries;* Anderson, *Memoir of Catharine Brown,* 63–64; Phillips and Phillips, eds., *Brainerd Journal,* 172, 524n48.

85. William G. McLoughlin, *The Cherokees and Christianity, 1794–1870: Essays on Acculturation and Cultural Persistence,* ed. Walter H. Conser (Athens: University of Georgia Press, 1994), 74–77. The ABCFM missionaries, who were all paedobaptists who baptized by sprinkling, wished to make the translation of *baptizo* ambiguous enough to mean "wash" by any mode, while the Baptists, who baptized only professing adult converts by immersion, wished to make the word unambiguously mean "to immerse." See John Wright, *Early Bibles of America: Being a Descriptive Account of Bibles Published in the United States, Mexico and Canada* (T. Whittaker, 1894), 277–79.

86. John Lardas Modern, *Secularism in Antebellum America* (Chicago: University of Chicago Press, 2011), 84–88.

87. "Resolutions by Missionaries," *New Echota Letters,* 82–92, reproducing *Cherokee Phoenix,* January 1, 1831.

88. *Worcester v. Georgia,* 31 U.S. (6 Pet.) 515 (1832); William G. McLoughlin, *Champions of the Cherokees: Evan and John B. Jones* (Princeton, NJ: Princeton University Press, 1990).

89. Modern, *Secularism,* 88.

90. Daniel Sabin Butrick, *Antiquities of the Cherokee Indians* (Vinita, Indian Territory [OK]: Indian Chieftain, 1884), 10.

91. Butrick, *Antiquities,* 11, 15.

92. Butrick, *Antiquities,* 10–11. Butrick continued to blame whites many other places in his journal, among them a long historical narrative on pp. 14–20.

93. As McLoughlin writes, "By 1830 the very terms in which the spiritual problems were formulated and answered by the *adonisgi* were Christian, not Cherokee." McLoughlin, *Champions of the Cherokees*, 77.

94. McLoughlin, *Cherokees and Missionaries*, 337–38. McLoughlin himself thinks that the numbers were very low and quotes numerous mission agencies to that effect. My reading is, in one sense, going against the grain of McLoughlin's analysis. Russell Thornton, C. Matthew Snipp, and Nancy Breen, *The Cherokees: A Population History* (Lincoln: University of Nebraska Press, 1990). Malone, citing denominational sources, sums up the number of Cherokee converts as 1,028 Methodist converts in 1829; 192 Cherokee communicants (a much higher bar) for the ABCFM in 1831; 120 Baptist church members; and 74 Moravian converts. Malone, *Cherokees*, 117.

95. "Resolutions by Missionaries," *New Echota Letters*, 88, reproducing *Cherokee Phoenix*, January 1, 1831.

96. McLoughlin, *Cherokees and Christianity*, 193.

97. "The story of Native Christianity is not only irreducible to missionary history; it often meaningfully begins only after the missionaries (not to mention their prodigious correspondence) have left, and along with them the historical record." McNally, "Practices," 61.

3 · Hope

1. Leviticus 25:10 (AV).

2. Steven Hahn, *A Nation under Our Feet: Black Political Struggles in the Rural South, from Slavery to the Great Migration* (Cambridge, MA: Belknap Press of Harvard University Press, 2003), 112–16, 128, 136–37, 143.

3. J. B. T. Marsh, *The Story of the Jubilee Singers, with Their Songs*, rev. ed. (New York: S. W. Green's Son, 1883), 26; *Jubilee and Plantation Songs . . . as Sung by the Hampton Students, Jubilee Singers, Fisk University Students, and Other Companies* (Boston: Oliver Diston, 1887); *Jubilee Songs as Sung by the Jubilee Singers, of Fisk University* (New York: Bigelow and Main, n.d.); William Francis Allen, Charles Pickard Ware, and Lucy McKim Garrison, *Slave Songs of the United States* (1867; reprint, New York: Peter Smith, 1951). On spirituals, see Lawrence W. Levine, *Black Culture and Black Consciousness: Afro-American Folk Thought from Slavery to Freedom*, anniversary ed. (New York: Oxford University Press, 2007), 5–14, 30–54; Lawrence W. Levine, "Slave Songs and Slave Consciousness: An Exploration in Neglected Sources," in *African-American Religion: Interpretive Essays in History and Culture*, ed. Timothy Earl Fulop and Albert J. Raboteau (New York: Routledge, 1997), 57–88.

4. "O Sinner, You'd Better Get Ready," *Jubilee and Plantation Songs*, 46.

5. "Children, You'll Be Called On," *Jubilee and Plantation Songs*, 29.

6. "Come, Let Us All Go Down," *Jubilee and Plantation Songs*, 33.

7. "Hard Trials," *Jubilee and Plantation Songs*, 39.

8. "Chilly Water," *Jubilee and Plantation Songs*, 38–39; cf. "In the River of Jordan," *Jubilee and Plantation Songs*, 43–44, and "Wade in the Water," *New Jubilee Songs: As Sung by the Fisk Jubilee Singers of Fisk University*, 2nd ed. (Nashville, TN: Fisk University, 1904), 8–9.

9. "Peter, Go Ring Them Bells," *Jubilee and Plantation Songs*, 77.

10. "Hard Trials," *Jubilee and Plantation Songs*, 39.

11. "Reign, Master Jesus," *Jubilee and Plantation Songs*, 36.

12. "March On," *Jubilee and Plantation Songs*, 28.

13. "In That Great Getting Up Morning," *Jubilee and Plantation Songs*, 68.

14. "Without doubt, the Exodus story was the most significant myth for American black identity, whether slave or free." Albert J. Raboteau, "The Black Experience in American Evangelicalism: The Meaning of Slavery," in *African-American Religion: Interpretive Essays in History and Culture*, ed. Timothy Earl Fulop and Albert J. Raboteau (New York: Routledge, 1997), 101; Eddie S. Glaude, *Exodus!: Religion, Race, and Nation in Early Nineteenth-Century Black America* (Chicago: University of Chicago Press, 2000), 1–103; John Coffey, *Exodus and Liberation: Deliverance Politics from John Calvin to Martin Luther King Jr.* (New York: Oxford University Press, 2014), 79–180; Eugene Genovese, *Roll, Jordan, Roll: The World the Slaves Made* (New York: Random House, 2011), 280–81. On Moses, see Paul Harvey, *Moses, Jesus, and the Trickster in the Evangelical South* (Athens: University of Georgia Press, 2012), 6–95. Albert Raboteau has pointed out the prevalence of references to the book of Revelation in conversion narratives, and their eschatological language. Albert J. Raboteau, *A Fire in the Bones: Reflections on African-American Religious History* (Boston: Beacon Press, 1995), 152–65; cf. Genovese, *Roll, Jordan, Roll*, 183–93. Besides those cited above, these spirituals from *Jubilee and Plantation Songs* contain eschatological imagery: "Children, We All Shall Be Free" (8); "I'll Hear the Trumpet Sound" (10); "From Every Graveyard" (11); "Going to Ride Up in the Chariot" (12–13); "Religion Is a Fortune" (24); "Steal Away" (34); "Zion's Children" (36); "Shine, Shine" (41); "I'm Going to Live with Jesus" (45); "O Sinner, You'd Better Get Ready" (46); "Rise and Shine" (47); "Humble Yourself" (48); "Is Master Going to Sell Us To-morrow" (51); "Hold the Light" (52); "Some of These Mornings" (54–55); "When the Bridegroom Comes" (55); "Didn't My Lord Deliver Daniel" (56); "Over There" (57); "I Must Go" (59); "I'm Going to Sing All the Way" (61); "Sweet Canaan" (62); "Getting Ready to Die" (63); "Zion, Weep A-Low" (70); "I Want to Be Ready" (74); "Going Up" (75).

15. David Levering Lewis, *W. E. B. Du Bois: A Biography* (New York: John MacRae Books, 2009), 55. On Du Bois and religion, see in particular Edward J. Blum, *W. E. B. Du Bois, American Prophet* (Philadelphia: University of Pennsylvania Press, 2011).

16. W. E. B. Du Bois, *The Souls of Black Folk*, 3rd ed. (Chicago: A. C. McClurg, 1903), 199, 201.

17. Andrew Walls, *The Missionary Movement in Christian History: Studies in the Transmission of Faith* (Maryknoll, NY: Orbis Books, 1996), 221–40.

18. *Kambiz GhaneaBassiri, A History of Islam in America: From the New World to the New World Order* (Cambridge: Cambridge University Press, 2010), 59–94; Richard Brent Turner, *Islam in the African American Experience*, 2nd ed. (Bloomington: Indiana University Press, 2003), 11–46. Yvonne P. Chireau, *Black Magic: Religion and the African American Conjuring Tradition* (Berkeley: University of California Press, 2003), 11–34; Jeffrey E. Anderson, *Conjure in African American Society* (Baton Rouge: Louisiana State University Press, 2005).

19. Mark A. Noll, *The Civil War as a Theological Crisis* (Chapel Hill: University of North Carolina Press, 2006), 31–52, 75–94.

20. The historian Daniel L. Fountain has argued that the Civil War was a decisive turning point for African Americans toward Christianity. His argument is based in part on the quantitative evidence he has gathered from 381 WPA narratives. Of those narratives, "38.8% of those surveyed converted to Christianity while they were slaves. . . . A clear majority, 61.2% of the slaves within this survey, were not Christians before gaining their freedom." Fountain also points to an eschatological interpretation of emancipation as a reason for conversions of freedpeople. Daniel L. Fountain, *Slavery, Civil War, and Salvation: African American Slaves and Christianity, 1830–1870* (Baton Rouge: Louisiana State University Press, 2010), esp. 16–18, 32. Fountain's quantitative evidence and methodology are not definitive, especially because of the timing of when the WPA interviews occurred, but they do seem to point to increased conversions to Christianity after the Civil War.

21. One interpretative problem in American religion is whether black Christianity and white evangelicalism, which share similar theologies but have different and often entirely separate social experiences, should be considered part of the same movement. For the most part, the historiography on evangelicalism and black Christianity has not considered the two together.

22. Clifton H. Johnson, ed., *God Struck Me Dead: Religious Conversion Experiences and Autobiographies of Ex-Slaves*, 2nd ed. (Cleveland: Pilgrim Press, 1993), viii–ix. The narratives in this collection "were gathered by A. P. Watson, a graduate student in anthropology in the years 1927–29" (p. xxix). Offhand references in the narratives show that they must have been conducted mostly in Tennessee, though the narrators had lived in many other places.

23. Raboteau, *Fire in the Bones*, 27; cf. Albert J. Raboteau, *Slave Religion: The "Invisible Institution" in the Antebellum South*, updated ed. (New York: Oxford University Press, 2004), 289–318.

24. Eddie S. Glaude Jr., *African American Religion: A Very Short Introduction* (New York: Oxford University Press, 2014), 6. African American Christianity produced one of the original religious traditions of the United States, with profound implications, via Pentecostalism, for world Christianity. Here I am modifying Paul Conkin's argument, though attempting to incorporate his larger point: "It makes good sense to talk about African influences on various Christian confessions in America, but no sense at all to classify black Christians, who are present in every denomination, as constituting a separate form of Christianity, at least so long as one defines a religious tradition in terms of scriptures, doctrines, polities, and moral standards." Paul K. Conkin, *American Originals: Homemade Varieties of Christianity* (Chapel Hill: University of North Carolina Press, 1997), ix. On African American missionaries to Africa, see Walter L. Williams, *Black Americans and the Evangelization of Africa, 1877–1900* (Madison: University of Wisconsin Press, 1982). On the importance of Pentecostalism, see Randall J. Stephens, *The Fire Spreads: Holiness and Pentecostalism in the American South* (Cambridge, MA: Harvard University Press, 2008). And on the importance of Pentecostalism for world Christianity, see Philip Jenkins, *The Next Christendom: The Coming of Global Christianity*, 3rd ed. (Oxford: Oxford University Press, 2011); Philip Jenkins, *The New Faces of Christianity:*

Believing the Bible in the Global South (New York: Oxford University Press, 2006); cf. Walls, *Missionary Movement in Christian History*, 235–57.

25. The Christian theological virtues, after Paul's formulation in 1 Corinthians 13:13, are faith, hope, and love. Protestant Christianity, especially its evangelical forms, has emphasized faith in conversion (*sola fide*); it is my contention that African American Christianity, at least as understood through conversion, emphasized hope.

26. Nat Turner, *The Confessions of Nat Turner, the Leader of the Last Insurrection in Southampton, Va.* (Baltimore: Thomas R. Gray, 1831), 11, http://docsouth.unc.edu/neh/turner/turner.html.

27. Charles Taylor argues that time has become secular. Charles Taylor, *A Secular Age* (Cambridge, MA: Belknap Press of Harvard University Press, 2007), 54–61, 195–96, 207–9, 712–20. Mark M. Smith, *Mastered by the Clock: Time, Slavery, and Freedom in the American South* (Chapel Hill: University of North Carolina Press, 1997), points out how masters used secular clock time as a tool for exploitation.

28. Among the questions that some Works Progress Administration (WPA) interviewers asked were questions about Christianity: "Did the slaves have a church on your plantation? Did they read the Bible? Who was your favorite preacher? Your favorite spirituals? Tell about the baptizing; baptizing songs. Funerals and funeral songs. . . . Tell why you joined a church and why you think all people should be religious." But the interviewers also asked about conjuring, asking whether the interviewees knew about "Charms? Stories about 'Raw Head and Bloody Bones' or other 'hants' of ghosts? . . . What do you think of voodoo? . . . What charms did they wear and to keep off what diseases?" *Born in Slavery: Slave Narratives from the Federal Writers' Project, 1936–1938*, Library of Congress, American Memory, http://memory.loc.gov/ammem/snhtml/snhome .html (hereafter WPA Narratives, cited by narrator), 1:xxi–xxii.

29. On African American conversion narratives and traditions of Bible reading that contributed to it, see Yolanda Pierce, *Hell without Fires: Slavery, Christianity, and the Antebellum Spiritual Narrative* (Gainesville: University Press of Florida, 2005); Laurie F. Maffly-Kipp, *Setting Down the Sacred Past: African-American Race Histories* (Cambridge, MA: Belknap Press of Harvard University Press, 2010); Joanna Brooks, *American Lazarus: Religion and the Rise of African-American and Native American Literatures* (New York: Oxford University Press, 2003); Katherine Clay Bassard, *Transforming Scriptures: African American Women Writers and the Bible* (Athens: University of Georgia Press, 2010); Allen Dwight Callahan, *The Talking Book: African Americans and the Bible* (New Haven, CT: Yale University Press, 2006); Ann Taves, *Fits, Trances, and Visions: Experiencing Religion and Explaining Experience from Wesley to James* (Princeton, NJ: Princeton University Press, 1999); Kimberly Rae Connor, *Conversions and Visions in the Writings of African-American Women* (Knoxville: University of Tennessee Press, 1994).

30. One of Taylor's key arguments is that the modern self has became "buffered," that is, not porous to the influences of external supernatural powers. Taylor, *Secular Age*, 37–42, 134–42, 262–64, 300–7, 548. As Edward Blum points out, slaves' bodies were not buffered from the control of their owners, and their

souls were not buffered from transcendent experiences. Edward J. Blum, "Slaves, Slavery, and the Secular Age; or, Tales of Haunted Scholars, Liberating Prisons, Exorcised Divinities, and Immanent Devils" in *Race and Secularism in America*, ed. Jonathon S. Kahn and Vincent W. Lloyd (New York: Columbia University Press, 2016), 77–98.

31. Paul Harvey, *Through the Storm, through the Night: A History of African American Christianity* (Lanham, MD: Rowman and Littlefield, 2011), 21.

32. Rebecca Anne Goetz, *The Baptism of Early Virginia: How Christianity Created Race* (Baltimore: Johns Hopkins University Press, 2012), 1–12; Edmund S. Morgan, *American Slavery, American Freedom: The Ordeal of Colonial Virginia* (New York: Norton, 1975); see the essays in Craig R. Prentiss, ed., *Religion and the Creation of Race and Ethnicity: An Introduction* (New York: New York University, 2003), but especially 13–27, 112–23; Colin Kidd, *The Forging of Races: Race and Scripture in the Protestant Atlantic World, 1600–2000* (Cambridge: Cambridge University Press, 2006), 79–167.

33. Robert Lewis Dabney, *A Defence of Virginia: And through Her, of the South, in Recent and Pending Contests against the Sectional Party* (New York: E. J. Hale, 1867), 94–208, quotations from 279, 281; Elizabeth Fox-Genovese and Eugene D. Genovese, *The Mind of the Master Class: History and Faith in the Southern Slaveholders' Worldview* (Cambridge: Cambridge University Press, 2005), 473–527.

34. On conversions of slaves and freedpeople in the First Great Awakening, see Thomas S. Kidd, *The Great Awakening: The Roots of Evangelical Christianity in Colonial America* (New Haven, CT: Yale University Press, 2007), 213–33; Mechal Sobel, *Trabelin' On: The Slave Journey to an Afro-Baptist Faith* (Westport, CT: Greenwood Press, 1979), 58–76; Jon F. Sensbach, *A Separate Canaan: The Making of an Afro-Moravian World in North Carolina, 1763–1840* (Chapel Hill: University of North Carolina Press, 1998); Jon F. Sensbach, *Rebecca's Revival: Creating Black Christianity in the Atlantic World* (Cambridge, MA: Harvard University Press, 2005); Sylvia R. Frey and Betty Wood, *Come Shouting to Zion: African American Protestantism in the American South and British Caribbean to 1830* (Chapel Hill: University of North Carolina Press, 1998), 63–117.

35. Colossians 3:22.

36. Edward J. Blum and Paul Harvey, *The Color of Christ: The Son of God and the Saga of Race in America* (Chapel Hill: University of North Carolina, 2012), 95–98.

37. Henry Box Brown and Charles Stearns, *Narrative of Henry Box Brown, Who Escaped from Slavery, Enclosed in a Box 3 Feet Long and 2 Wide* (Boston: Brown and Stearns, 1849), 16–18, ix. All of the slave narratives published in North America are available from William L. Andrews and Patricia Buck Dominguez, eds., "North American Slave Narratives," *Documenting the American South* (Chapel Hill: University of North Carolina, 2004–14), http://docsouth.unc.edu/neh/index.html.

38. Leonard Black, *The Life and Sufferings of Leonard Black, a Fugitive from Slavery* (New Bedford, MA: Benjamin Lindsey, 1847), 20–22, http://docsouth.unc.edu/neh/black/black.html. It was rare that a slave received support as did Mahommah Baquaqua when he escaped from Brazil to Haiti and was supported

by a missionary. Samuel Moore, *Biography of Mahommah G. Baquaqua . . . A Convert to Christianity* (Detroit: Samuel Moore, 1854), 59, http://docsouth.unc .edu/neh/baquaqua/baquaqua.html.

39. On how the patrols restricted religion, see Sally E. Hadden, *Slave Patrols: Law and Violence in Virginia and the Carolinas* (Cambridge, MA: Harvard University Press, 2001), 74, 81, 108–9, 113, 118, 125–27, 140–41, 146–48. On the effects on slave religion, see Raboteau, *Slave Religion*, 217, 293.

40. Thomas Anderson, *Interesting Account of Thomas Anderson, a Slave*, ed. J. P. Clark (n.p., 1854), 1–4, http://docsouth.unc.edu/neh/anderson/anderson .html.

41. Anderson, *Interesting Account*, 11.

42. Charles Emery Stevens, *Anthony Burns: A History* (Boston: John P. Jewett, 1856), 162–64, http://docsouth.unc.edu/neh/stevens/stevens.html; *American National Biography Online*, s.v. "Burns, Anthony," http://www.anb.org /articles/20/20-00129.html.

43. Bethany Veney, *The Narrative of Bethany Veney, a Slave Woman* (Worcester, MA, 1889), 15–16, http://docsouth.unc.edu/fpn/veney/veney.html.

44. *Memoir of Old Elizabeth, a Coloured Woman* (Philadelphia: Collins, 1863), 3–10, http://docsouth.unc.edu/neh/eliza1/eliza1.html; *Elizabeth, a Colored Minister of the Gospel Born in Slavery* (Philadelphia: Tract Association of Friends, 1889), 2–4, http://docsouth.unc.edu/neh/eliza2/eliza2.html. One "Uncle Johnson" was remarkable in the eyes of a white Protestant for his faith in a future heaven. Gustavus Lemuel Foster, *Uncle Johnson, the Pilgrim of Six Score Years* (Philadelphia: Presbyterian Board of Publication, 1867), 70–71, http://docsouth .unc.edu/neh/foster/foster.html.

45. Thomas Jones, *Experience and Personal Narrative of Uncle Tom Jones* (Boston: H. B. Skinner, n.d.), 18–21, http://docsouth.unc.edu/neh/jonestom /jones.html; Thomas H. Jones, *The Experience of Thomas H. Jones, Who Was a Slave for Forty-Three Years* (Boston: Bazin and Chandler, 1862), 25–26, http:// docsouth.unc.edu/fpn/jones/jones.html.

46. James Watkins, *Struggles for Freedom; or, The Life of James Watkins, Formerly a Slave in Maryland* (Manchester, England, 1860), 18–20.

47. Steven Deyle, *Carry Me Back: The Domestic Slave Trade in American Life* (New York: Oxford University Press, 2005), 289. On the conditions of slavery in the Mississippi, see Walter Johnson, *River of Dark Dreams: Slavery and Empire in the Cotton Kingdom* (Cambridge, MA: Belknap Press of Harvard University Press, 2013); Edward E. Baptist, *The Half Has Never Been Told: Slavery and the Making of American Capitalism* (New York: Basic Books, 2014).

48. Henry Cheatam, in WPA Narratives, 1:69.

49. Octavia V. Rogers Albert, *The House of Bondage* (New York: Hunt and Eaton, 1890), 11–13.

50. For all the complexities of the interaction between slaves and masters, see Erskine Clarke, *Dwelling Place: A Plantation Epic* (New Haven, CT: Yale University Press, 2005), 50–51, 86–90, 95, 125–39, 140–51, 169–72, 250–54, 407.

51. Frederick Douglass, *Narrative of the Life of Frederick Douglass, an American Slave* (Boston: Anti-Slavery Office, 1845), 122, http://docsouth.unc.edu /neh/douglass/douglass.html.

52. Douglass, *Narrative*, 53–54.

53. Douglass, *Narrative*, 55, quoting Luke 12:47.

54. Douglass, *Narrative*, 57.

55. Douglass, *Narrative*, 61–62.

56. Douglass, *Narrative*, 78–79.

57. Douglass, *Narrative*, 118.

58. David Walker, *Walker's Appeal . . . to the Coloured Citizens of the World*, 3rd ed. (Boston: David Walker, 1830), 2, 42, esp. 39–49, http://docsouth.unc .edu/nc/walker/walker.html.

59. Brown, *Narrative of Henry Box Brown*, 18–19.

60. C. James Trotman, *Frederick Douglass: A Biography* (Santa Barbara, CA: Greenwood, 2011), 140–41. Even allowing a wide latitude for exaggeration, Ottilie Assing, a confidant of Douglass's, reported that he had become an admirer of Feuerbach. Ottilie Assing to Ludwig Feuerbach, May 15, 1871, in Maria Diedrich, *Love across Color Lines: Ottilie Assing and Frederick Douglass* (New York: Hill and Wang, 1999), 259–60.

61. Though Douglass thought the Emancipation Proclamation was the turning point in the meaning of the war, he was nevertheless disappointed that its limited scope meant that "it was not a proclamation of 'liberty throughout all the land, unto all the inhabitants thereof.'" Frederick Douglass, *The Life and Times of Frederick Douglass* (Hartford, CT: Park, 1882), 429–30; David W. Blight, *Frederick Douglass' Civil War: Keeping Faith in Jubilee* (Baton Rouge: Louisiana State University Press, 1991), 101–21: "The Civil War provided the central event in Douglass' life that reinforced his providential view of history."

62. Sara Colquitt, WPA Narratives, 1:88.

63. Siney Bonner, WPA Narratives, 1:39–40.

64. Amy Chapman, WPA Narratives, 1:59–60.

65. Josiah Henson, *Truth Stranger Than Fiction: Father Henson's Story of His Own Life* (Boston: John P. Jewett, 1858), 25–29, http://docsouth.unc.edu/neh /henson58/henson58.html; Josiah Henson, *The Life of Josiah Henson, Formerly a Slave, Now an Inhabitant of Canada, as Narrated by Himself* (Boston: Arthur D. Phelps, 1849), 26, http://docsouth.unc.edu/neh/henson49/henson49.html.

66. Johnson, ed., *God Struck Me Dead*, 128.

67. Charity Anderson, WPA Narratives, 1:14.

68. Johnson, ed., *God Struck Me Dead*, 115.

69. Johnson, ed., *God Struck Me Dead*, 144.

70. Johnson, ed., *God Struck Me Dead*, 172.

71. Noah Davis, *A Narrative of the Life of Rev. Noah Davis, a Colored Man* (Baltimore: John F. Weishampel Jr., 1859), 19–25.

72. Jarena Lee, *Religious Experience and Journal of Mrs. Jarena Lee, Giving an Account of Her Call to Preach the Gospel* (Philadelphia: Jarena Lee, 1849), 3.

73. Protestant Christianity was not the only option for African Americans. Slaves owned by Jewish masters sometimes converted to Judaism and, in the years after the Civil War, converted to Judaism or created their own forms of "black Israelite" religions. Lauren F. Winner, "Taking Up the Cross: Conversion among Black and White Jews in the Civil War South," in *Southern Families at War: Loyalty and Conflict in the Civil War South*, ed. Catherine Clinton (New York: Oxford

University Press, 2000), 193–209; Jacob S. Dorman, *Chosen People: The Rise of American Black Israelite Religions* (New York: Oxford University Press, 2013). For the conversion of the African American attorney Rufus Perry to Judaism in New York, see the *New-York Tribune*, August 5, 1912, in *Chronicling America: Historic American Newspapers*, Library of Congress, http://chroniclingamerica.loc.gov /lccn/sn83030214/1912—08—05/ed-1/seq-5/. Catholicism, especially in Louisiana but elsewhere as well, was an option for some African Americans. Cyprian Davis, *The History of Black Catholics in the United States* (New York: Crossroad, 1990); Cecilia A. Moore, "Conversion Narratives: The Dual Experiences and Voices of African American Catholic Converts," *U.S. Catholic Historian* 28, no. 1 (January 1, 2010): 27–40, http://www.jstor.org/stable/40731252. By the 1920s, Muslims had a missionary movement among African Americans. Edward E. Curtis IV, "African-American Islamization Reconsidered: Black History Narratives and Muslim Identity," *Journal of the American Academy of Religion* 73, no. 3 (September 2005): 659–84, http://www.jstor.org/stable/4139915.

74. On female preaching in the antebellum period, see Catherine A. Brekus, *Strangers and Pilgrims: Female Preaching in America, 1740–1845* (Chapel Hill: University of North Carolina Press, 1998), 117–266.

75. David Hempton, *Methodism: Empire of the Spirit* (New Haven, CT: Yale University Press, 2005), 55–85, 115, 140.

76. William J. Allinson, *Memoir of Quamino Buccau, a Pious Methodist* (Philadelphia: Henry Longstreth, 1851), 7, http://docsouth.unc.edu/neh/allinson /allinson.html?. For other antebellum published slave conversion narratives, see William Grimes, *Life of William Grimes, the Runaway Slave* (New York, 1825), 28, http://docsouth.unc.edu/neh/grimes25/grimes25.html; L. C. Capehart, *Reminiscences of Isaac and Sukey* (Raleigh, NC: Edwards and Broughton, 1907), 11, http://docsouth.unc.edu/neh/capehart/capehart.html; Thomas Lewis Johnson, *Twenty-Eight Years a Slave; or, The Story of My Life in Three Continents* (London: Christian Workers' Depot, 1909), 9–11, 13–19, http://docsouth.unc .edu/neh/johnson1/johnson.html; Friday Jones, *Days of Bondage; Autobiography of Friday Jones; Being a Brief Narrative of His Trials and Tribulations in Slavery* (Washington, DC: Commercial Publishing, 1883), 1–3, http://docsouth.unc .edu/neh/fjones/jones.html; Elijah P. Marrs, *Life and History of the Rev. Elijah P. Marrs* (Louisville, KY: Bradley and Gilbert, 1885), 13–15, http://docsouth.unc .edu/neh/marrs/marrs.html; S. J. McCray, *Life of Mary F. McCray* (Lima, OH, 1898), 10–13, http://docsouth.unc.edu/neh/mccray/mary.html; *Biography of London Ferrill* (Lexington, KY: A. W. Elder, 1854), 1–3, http://docsouth.unc.edu /neh/ferrill/ferrill.html; Peter Randolph, *Sketches of Slave Life* (Boston: Peter Randolph, 1855), 25–26, http://docsouth.unc.edu/neh/randol55/randol55.html; William H. Robinson, *From Log Cabin to the Pulpit; or, Fifteen Years in Slavery* (Eau Claire, WI: James H. Tifft, 1913), 137–42, http://docsouth.unc.edu/fpn /robinson/robinson.html; James Lindsay Smith, *Autobiography of James L. Smith* (Norwich: Bulletin, 1881), 26, http://docsouth.unc.edu/neh/smithj/smithj.html; Isaac Williams, *Aunt Sally; or, The Cross the Way of Freedom* (Cincinnati: American Reform Tract and Book Society, 1858), 44–45, http://docsouth.unc.edu /neh/sally/sally.html.

77. Johnson, ed., *God Struck Me Dead*, 73.

78. Johnson, ed., *God Struck Me Dead*, 141.

79. Johnson, ed., *God Struck Me Dead*, 126.

80. Johnson, ed., *God Struck Me Dead*, 172.

81. Johnson, ed., *God Struck Me Dead*, 141.

82. Raboteau, *Fire in the Bones*, 141–51.

83. Johnson, ed., *God Struck Me Dead*, 128.

84. Johnson, ed., *God Struck Me Dead*, 88. In her vision she "heard a voice saying, 'Rise, Mary,' but since the interviewer generally replaced names with initials, that may have been an allusion to Jesus's words in the garden to Mary after his resurrection, especially since several other African American converts heard variations on the same phrase.

85. Johnson, ed., *God Struck Me Dead*, 148–49. The six wings are also imagery from the Book of Revelation.

86. Johnson, ed., *God Struck Me Dead*, 15.

87. Johnson, ed., *God Struck Me Dead*, 17, quoting Ephesians 2:8.

88. Johnson, ed., *God Struck Me Dead*, 22.

89. Johnson, ed., *God Struck Me Dead*, 62.

90. Johnson, ed., *God Struck Me Dead*, 110; cf. Blum and Harvey, *Color of Christ*, 76–104.

91. Johnson, ed., *God Struck Me Dead*, 64. It is possible that, in the language of a "natural man" or like language, some conversion narratives preserve symbolism or ideas from African animist religious traditions. Certainly, the resonance of certain Christian symbols, most notably baptism, with African animist meanings is well documented. See, e.g., Harvey, *Through the Storm*, 51–54. Yvonne P. Chireau, *Black Magic: Religion and the African American Conjuring Tradition* (Berkeley: University of California Press, 2003). I have found little evidence of such syncretism in the conversion narratives, however.

92. Johnson, ed., *God Struck Me Dead*, 8–9.

93. Johnson, ed., *God Struck Me Dead*, 71.

94. Johnson, ed., *God Struck Me Dead*, 73.

95. Johnson, ed., *God Struck Me Dead*, 114.

96. George C. Rable, *God's Almost Chosen People: A Religious History of the Civil War* (Chapel Hill: University of North Carolina Press, 2010), 88, 291–93; Ben Wright and Zachary W. Dresser, eds., *Apocalypse and the Millennium in the American Civil War Era* (Baton Rouge: Louisiana State University Press, 2013).

97. One difficulty with the WPA narratives as a source in this regard is that they all were produced in a compressed number of years long after the Civil War. Because of this, the people were rather old and thus were mostly adolescents or young adults when they were slaves.

98. Hahn, *A Nation under Our Feet*, 45–46. Hahn also writes, "But this may simultaneously understate the number whose spiritual sensibilities and activities were influenced by Christianity and exaggerate the social and cultural impact of denominational faiths." Fountain, *Slavery, Civil War, and Salvation*, 16–18, 32, concurs in the general assessment of how many enslaved African Americans adopted Christianity.

99. Edward J. Blum, *Reforging the White Republic: Race, Religion, and American Nationalism, 1865–1898* (Baton Rouge: Louisiana State University Press,

2005), 59–60; Joe Martin Richardson, *Christian Reconstruction: The American Missionary Association and Southern Blacks, 1861–1890* (Athens: University of Georgia Press, 1986; reprint, Tuscaloosa: University of Alabama Press, 2008), 143–59. For other, generally less optimistic, studies of the Reconstruction missionaries, see Derek Chang, "Women, Empire, and the Home Mission Project in Late Nineteenth-Century America," in *Competing Kingdoms: Women, Mission, Nation, and the American Protestant Empire, 1812–1960,* ed. Barbara Reeves-Ellington, Kathryn Kish Sklar, and Connie A. Shemo (Durham: Duke University Press, 2010), 269–92; Jacqueline Jones, *Soldiers of Light and Love: Northern Teachers and Georgia Blacks, 1865–1873* (Chapel Hill: University of North Carolina Press, 1980).

    100. Katherine L. Dvorak, *An African-American Exodus: The Segregation of the Southern Churches* (Brooklyn, NY: Carlson, 1991), 69–120.

    101. Anthony Abercrombie, WPA Narratives, 1:2.

    102. Oliver Bell, WPA Narratives, 1:27–28.

    103. Jennie Bowen, WPA Narratives, 1:42–43.

    104. Emma Crockett, WPA Narratives, 1:93.

    105. Johnson, ed., *God Struck Me Dead*, 37.

    106. Johnson, ed., *God Struck Me Dead*, 37.

    107. Johnson, ed., *God Struck Me Dead*, 59.

    108. Johnson, ed., *God Struck Me Dead*, 99.

    109. Johnson, ed., *God Struck Me Dead*, 111.

    110. Johnson, ed., *God Struck Me Dead*, 59.

    111. Johnson, ed., *God Struck Me Dead*, 111.

    112. Johnson, ed., *God Struck Me Dead*, 66–67.

    113. Scott Nesbit and Edward L. Ayers, *Visualizing Emancipation* (Richmond, VA: Digital Scholarship Lab, University of Richmond), http://dsl.richmond.edu/emancipation/; Edward L. Ayers and Scott Nesbit, "Seeing Emancipation: Scale and Freedom in the American South," *Journal of the Civil War Era* 1, no. 1 (March 2011): 3–24.

    114. Hahn, *A Nation under Our Feet*, 45–46.

    115. Roger Finke and Rodney Stark, *The Churching of America, 1776–2005: Winners and Losers in Our Religious Economy*, 2nd ed. (New Brunswick, NJ: Rutgers University Press, 2005), p. 191, figure 5.5.

    116. *Census of Religious Bodies: 1926* (U.S. Census Bureau, 1926), 70, https://www2.census.gov/prod2/decennial/documents/13949806v1ch1.pdf. Cf. Rodney Stark, "The Reliability of Historical United States Census Data on Religion," *Sociology of Religion* 53, no. 1 (1992): 91–95, doi:10.2307/3711631.

4 · Kingdom

    1. *A Debate between Rev. A. Campbell and Rev. N. L. Rice, on the Action, Subject, Design, and Administrator of Christian Baptism* (Lexington, KY: A. T. Skillman & Son, 1844); E. Brooks Holifield, "Theology as Entertainment: Oral Debate in American Religion," *Church History* 67, no. 3 (September 1998): 499–520. Public debates about religion can be found everywhere in nineteenth-century sources; to cite another example, Robert Owen and Alexander Campbell, *The Evidences of*

Christianity: A Debate between Robert Owen . . . and Alexander Campbell . . . Held in the City of Cincinnati, Ohio, in April 1829, 4th ed. (Cincinnati: E. Morgan, 1852).

2. Rice went on to hold a number of other published debates and ended his career as a professor of polemical theology. *A Debate on the Doctrine of Universal Salvation . . . between Rev. E. M. Pingree and Rev. N. L. Rice* (Cincinnati: J. A. James, 1845); *A Debate on Slavery . . . between Rev. J. Blanchard and N. L. Rice* (Cincinnati: Wm. H. Moore, 1846).

3. Alexander Campbell, *The Christian Baptist*, vol. 3 (Buffalo, NY: Alexander Campbell, 1825–1826), 208; *A Debate on the Roman Catholic Religion . . . between Alexander Campbell and John B. Purcell* (Cincinnati: H. S. Bosworth, 1865).

4. *Debate between Campbell and Rice*, 790.

5. *Debate between Campbell and Rice*, 829, 834.

6. Alexander Campbell, *Delusions: An Analysis of the Book of Mormon* (Boston: Benjamin H. Greene, 1832), 13. This text reprinted Campbell's 1831 review of the Book of Mormon first published in Alexander Campbell's magazine, *The Millennial Harbinger.*

7. *Debate between Campbell and Rice*, 829, 834.

8. *Minutes of the Annual Conferences of the Methodist Episcopal Church, for the Years 1773 to 1828* (New York: T. Mason and G. Lane, 1840), http://hdl .handle.net/2027/nyp.33433069134967.

9. Jan Shipps, *Mormonism: The Story of a New Religious Tradition* (Urbana: University of Illinois Press, 1985). While these groups are sometimes called "new religious movements," Paul Conkin has more helpfully called them "American originals," pointing out their connection to historical Christianity. Paul Keith Conkin, *American Originals: Homemade Varieties of Christianity* (Chapel Hill: University of North Carolina Press, 1997). Stephen J. Stein, *Communities of Dissent: A History of Alternative Religions in America* (New York: Oxford University Press, 2003).

10. Paul Johnson and Sean Wilentz, *The Kingdom of Matthias* (New York: Oxford University Press, 1994).

11. Lawrence Foster, *Women, Family, and Utopia: Communal Experiments of the Shakers, the Oneida Community, and the Mormons*, Utopianism and Communitarianism (Syracuse, NY: Syracuse University Press, 1991).

12. Priscilla Brewer, *Shaker Communities, Shaker Lives* (Hanover, NH: University Press of New England, 1986); Stephen J. Stein, *The Shaker Experience in America* (New Haven, CT: Yale University Press, 1992). The estimate of twenty thousand conversions is Brewer's, p. xx.

13. Jacob Dorman, *Chosen People: The Rise of American Black Israelite Religions* (New York: Oxford University Press, 2013).

14. On the earlier histories of primitivism, see Theodore Dwight Bozeman, *To Live Ancient Lives: The Primitivist Dimension in Puritanism* (Chapel Hill: University of North Carolina Press, 1988); and on biblicism, see Mark A. Noll, *In the Beginning Was the Word: The Bible in American Public Life, 1492–1783* (New York: Oxford University Press, 2016), 2–3, 9, 17, 41, 45–47, passim.

15. Sylvester Bliss, *Memoirs of William Miller: Generally Known as a Lecturer on the Prophecies and the Second Coming of Christ* (Boston: Joshua V. Himes, 1853); Ernest R. Sandeen, *The Roots of Fundamentalism: British and American Millenarianism, 1800–1930* (Chicago: University of Chicago Press, 1970); Matthew Avery Sutton, *American Apocalypse: A History of Modern Evangelicalism* (Cambridge, MA: Belknap Press of Harvard University Press, 2014).

16. Parley Parker Pratt, *The Autobiography of Parley Parker Pratt, One of the Twelve Apostles of the Church of Jesus Christ of Latter-Day Saints* (New York, 1874), 159.

17. On Campbellite baptismal practices see Alexander Campbell, "Dialogue on Re-Immersion," *Millennial Harbinger* 3, no. 3 (March 5, 1832): 118–23. In general, Baptists and Campbellites did not think of themselves as rebaptizing, since they tended to consider baptisms that did not follow after faith or that were performed in some mode other than immersion as not being baptisms at all.

18. Lucy Mack Smith, *Lucy's Book: A Critical Edition of Lucy Mack Smith's Family Memoir*, ed. Lavina Fielding Anderson and Irene M. Bates (Salt Lake City, UT: Signature Books, 2001), 7.

19. Whitney R. Cross, *The Burned-Over District: The Social and Intellectual History of Enthusiastic Religion in Western New York, 1800–1850*, rev. ed. (New York: Octagon Books, 1981).

20. Joseph Smith History, 1838–1856, vol. A-1, p. 2, *The Joseph Smith Papers*, online edition, http://www.josephsmithpapers.org/paper-summary/history -1838-1856-volume-a-1-23-december-1805-30-august-1834/(hereafter Joseph Smith History, 1838–1856).

21. John Matzko, "The Encounter of the Young Joseph Smith with Presbyterianism," *Dialogue: A Journal of Mormon Thought* 40, no. 3 (2007): 68–84; Richard L. Bushman, *Joseph Smith: Rough Stone Rolling* (New York: Alfred A. Knopf, 2005), 30–126.

22. The 1832 account was never published in Smith's lifetime, while the 1838 account was published as part of Joseph Smith's official history of the church. There are also versions of the story told by Smith's contemporary followers. For details about the various accounts of the first vision, see Bushman, *Rough Stone Rolling*, 570n34; Marvin S. Hill, "The First Vision Controversy: A Critique and Reconciliation," *Dialogue: A Journal of Mormon Thought* 34, no. 1/2 (2001): 35–54; and the historical introductions to the two histories written by Joseph Smith, cited in notes 20 and 25.

23. Joseph Smith History, 1838–1856, 2–4.

24. Joseph Smith History, 1838–1856, 3.

25. Joseph Smith History, circa Summer 1832, p. 3, *The Joseph Smith Papers*, online edition, http://www.josephsmithpapers.org/paper-summary/history -circa-summer-1832/ (hereafter Joseph Smith History, 1832). On this account as a conversion relation, cf. Bushman, *Rough Stone Rolling*, 39–41.

26. Joseph Smith History, 1832, 3. With minor variations, the vision quotes or is structured similarly to 1 John 5:19; Rom. 3:12; 2 Tim. 4:4.

27. Joseph Smith History, 1838–1856, 2–4.

28. Joseph Smith History, 1838–1856, 34. This 1838 version of his first vision was printed in *The Pearl of Great Price* in 1851 and eventually canonized by

the Church of Jesus Christ of Latter-day Saints in 1880. *The Pearl of Great Price: Being a Choice Selection from the Revelations, Translations, and Narrations of Joseph Smith* (Liverpool: F. D. Richards, 1851), 36–48.

29. Joseph Smith History, 1838–1856, 23–24.

30. Smith, *Lucy's Book*, 258.

31. Smith, *Lucy's Book*, 281, 291, 294, 331–32.

32. Joseph Smith History, 1838–1856, 38.

33. The Articles and Covenants were published as the second section in the 1835 edition of Doctrine and Covenants. *Doctrine and Covenants of the Church of the Latter-day Saints: Carefully Selected from the Revelations of God* (Kirtland, OH: F. G. Williams, 1835), 77–82, in *The Joseph Smith Papers*, online edition, http://www.josephsmithpapers.org/paper-summary/doctrine-and-covenants -1835/. In the current canon of the LDS Church, this document is Doctrine and Covenants, 20.

34. Joseph Smith History, 1838–1856, 38.

35. Val Dean Rust, *Radical Origins: Early Mormon Converts and Their Colonial Ancestors* (Urbana: University of Illinois Press, 2004), 10, table 1.

36. *History of the Church, BYU Studies Quarterly* website, 7:472, https:// byustudies.byu.edu/hc/hcpgs/hc.aspx. On Brigham Young, see John G. Turner, *Brigham Young, Pioneer Prophet* (Cambridge, MA: Belknap Press of Harvard University Press, 2012).

37. Smith, *Lucy's Book*, 220.

38. Smith, *Lucy's Book*, 230–31; Solomon Mack, *Narrative of the Life of Solomon Mack* (New York, 1810).

39. Pratt, *Autobiography*, 21.

40. Pratt, *Autobiography*, 22–23

41. Pratt, *Autobiography* 24, 31, 37, 42–43.

42. Mary Brown Pulsipher, "History of Mary Brown Pulsipher," microfilm of manuscript, MSS MFilm 00095 item 02, Huntington Library, http://hdl .huntington.org/cdm/ref/collection/p16003coll15/id/25132. For this citation I am grateful to John G. Turner, *The Mormon Jesus: A Biography* (Cambridge, MA: Belknap Press of Harvard University Press, 2016), 39–40.

43. Pratt, *Autobiography*, 74–76.

44. Mark 16:17.

45. Pratt, *Autobiography*, 74–76.

46. William E. McLellin, *The Journals of William E. McLellin, 1831–1836*, ed. Jan Shipps and John W. Welch (Urbana: University of Illinois Press, 1994), 29.

47. McLellin, *Journals*, 33; cf. 1 Cor. 12:10; 1 John 4:1.

48. McLellin, *Journals*, 33–35.

49. Doctrine and Covenants, 10:53, 10:63; Joseph Smith History, 1838–1856, 16, 17, 19, 20.

50. Joseph Smith History, 1838–1856, 37, 39, 42.

51. *History of the Church*, 1:37, 39.

52. On the role of the Book of Mormon in conversions, see Terryl L. Givens, *By the Hand of Mormon: The American Scriptures that Launched a New World Religion* (New York: Oxford University Press, 2002), 235–39; Turner, *Mormon Jesus*, 37–43.

53. Candy Gunther Brown, *The Word in the World: Evangelical Writing, Publishing, and Reading in America, 1789–1880* (Chapel Hill: University of North Carolina Press, 2004); Paul C. Gutjahr, *An American Bible: A History of the Good Book in the United States, 1777–1880* (Stanford, CA: Stanford University Press, 1999); Paul C. Gutjahr, *The Book of Mormon: A Biography* (Princeton, NJ: Princeton University Press, 2012). On the Bible's importance for politics, see James P. Byrd, *Sacred Scripture, Sacred War: The Bible and the American Revolution* (New York: Oxford University Press, 2013).

54. 1 Nephi 13:34.

55. Alma 30:7–9. Cf. Alma 31:5: "The preaching of the word had a great tendency to lead the people to do what was just—yea, it had a more powerful effect upon the minds of the people than the sword."

56. Mosiah 3:16.

57. Alma 36:6–9, 18–20; cf. the same story in Mosiah 27:8–37.

58. Enos 1:3–5.

59. Alma 5:12–13.

60. 1 Nephi 11–12.

61. Alma 30:58.

62. Alma 31.

63. Alma 32:21–42, 34:33.

64. Elizabeth Cannon Porter, *The Cities of the Sun: Stories of Ancient America Founded on Historical Incidents in the Book of Mormon* (Salt Lake City, UT: Deseret News, 1910), 21.

65. Unless one is obliged to practice an uncritically critical approach, one might even think that converts who had learned more about their faith and reflected more about their experiences would be able to offer accounts that understood their motives *better* than a spontaneous account.

66. Horace Cowan, missionary report, 1834, MS 6104, Church History Library, Church of Jesus Christ of Latter-Day Saints, Salt Lake City, UT, https://eadview.lds.org/findingaid/MS%206104/.

67. Joseph Coe, missionary report, 1832, Church History Library, Church of Jesus Christ of Latter-Day Saints, Salt Lake City, UT, https://eadview.lds.org/findingaid/MS%206104/.

68. McLellin, *Journals*, 46.

69. On anticlericalism, see Nathan O. Hatch, *The Democratization of American Christianity* (New Haven, CT: Yale University Press, 1989), 44, 120, 163, 174–76, 227ff.

70. Elam Luddington, missionary report, 1845, Church History Library, Church of Jesus Christ of Latter-Day Saints, Salt Lake City, UT, https://eadview.lds.org/findingaid/MS%206104/.

71. Hazen Aldrich, missionary report, 1835, Church History Library, Church of Jesus Christ of Latter-Day Saints, Salt Lake City, UT, https://eadview.lds.org/findingaid/MS%206104/.

72. McLellin, *Journals*, 62–64, 39.

73. Cowan, missionary report.

74. McLellin, *Journals*, 31, 36.

75. McLellin, *Journals*, 29.

76. McLellin, *Journals*, 112.

77. McLellin, *Journals*, 39, 43.

78. On the "plan of salvation," see Douglas James Davies, *An Introduction to Mormonism* (New York: Cambridge University Press, 2003), 3–28, 135–36.

79. McLellin, *Journals*, 83–84.

80. Pratt, *Autobiography*, 139, 141. On visions, see Turner, *Mormon Jesus*, 59–61, 65–88.

81. Nathan West, missionary report, circa 1835, Church History Library, Church of Jesus Christ of Latter-Day Saints, Salt Lake City, UT, https://eadview.lds.org/findingaid/MS%206104/.

82. Benjamin L. Clapp, missionary report, 1845, Church History Library, Church of Jesus Christ of Latter-Day Saints, Salt Lake City, UT, https://eadview.lds.org/findingaid/MS%206104/.

83. Edward Partridge, missionary report, 1835, Church History Library, Church of Jesus Christ of Latter-Day Saints, Salt Lake City, UT, https://eadview.lds.org/findingaid/MS%206104/.

84. Cowan, missionary report.

85. Cowan, missionary report.

86. Elam Luddington, missionary report, 1845, Church History Library, Church of Jesus Christ of Latter-Day Saints, Salt Lake City, UT, https://eadview.lds.org/findingaid/MS%206104/.

87. Patrick Q. Mason, *The Mormon Menace: Violence and Anti-Mormonism in the Postbellum South* (New York: Oxford University Press, 2011).

88. Samuel H. Smith, missionary report, circa 1831, Church History Library, Church of Jesus Christ of Latter-Day Saints, Salt Lake City, UT, https://eadview.lds.org/findingaid/MS%206104/.

89. Coe, missionary report.

90. Truman Waite, missionary report, 1833, Church History Library, Church of Jesus Christ of Latter-Day Saints, Salt Lake City, UT, https://eadview.lds.org/findingaid/MS%206104/.

91. Samuel H. Smith, missionary report, circa 1831, Church History Library, Church of Jesus Christ of Latter-Day Saints, Salt Lake City, UT, https://eadview.lds.org/findingaid/MS%206104/.

92. Coe, missionary report.

93. McLellin, *Journals*, 137.

94. Cowan, missionary report.

95. Daniel Stephens, missionary report, 1835, Church History Library, Church of Jesus Christ of Latter-Day Saints, Salt Lake City, UT, https://eadview.lds.org/findingaid/MS%206104/.

96. Charles Dalton, missionary report, 1845, Church History Library, Church of Jesus Christ of Latter-Day Saints, Salt Lake City, UT, https://eadview.lds.org/findingaid/MS%206104/.

97. McLellin, *Journal*, 71.

98. Pratt, *Autobiography*, 150.

99. Samuel Morris Brown, *In Heaven as It Is on Earth: Joseph Smith and the Early Mormon Conquest of Death* (New York: Oxford University Press, 2012), 44–45.

100. McLellin, *Journals*, 83–84.

101. Partridge, missionary report.

102. Lewis Robbins, missionary report, 1835, Church History Library, Church of Jesus Christ of Latter-Day Saints, Salt Lake City, UT, https:// eadview.lds.org/findingaid/MS%206104/.

103. Cowan, missionary report.

104. Smith, missionary report.

105. Leonard J. Arrington, *Great Basin Kingdom: An Economic History of the Latter-Day Saints, 1830–1900*, new ed. (Urbana: University of Illinois Press, 2004).

106. LeRoy R. Hafen and Ann W. Hafen, *Handcarts to Zion: The Story of a Unique Western Migration, 1856–1860* (Lincoln: University of Nebraska Press, 1992).

107. Richard L. Jensen and William G. Hartley, "Immigration and Emigration," *Encyclopedia of Mormonism* (Provo, UT: Brigham Young University, 2007), quoting Brigham Young to A. Lyman, et al., Brigham Young Letterbooks, Aug. 2, 1860, LDS Church Archives, http://eom.byu.edu/.

108. William Adams, autobiography for the period 1822–1849, MS 8039, Church History Library, Church of Jesus Christ of Latter-Day Saints, Salt Lake City, UT.

109. Richard Ballantyne, journal, vol. 1, September 28, 1852–March 13, 1853, Church History Library, Church of Jesus Christ of Latter-Day Saints, Salt Lake City, UT, https://eadview.lds.org/dcbrowser/002290968/.

110. Ballantyne, "Autobiography of Richard Ballantyne, Written on the Oregon Short Line Railroad," 1861, Church History Library, Church of Jesus Christ of Latter-Day Saints, Salt Lake City, UT, https://eadview.lds.org/dcbrowser /002290968/.

111. Hannah Thompson, autobiographical sketch, circa 1910, Church History Library, Church of Jesus Christ of Latter-Day Saints, Salt Lake City, UT, https://eadview.lds.org/dcbrowser/002290968/.

112. On anti-Mormonism, see J. Spencer Fluhman, *"A Peculiar People": Anti-Mormonism and the Making of Religion in Nineteenth-Century America* (Chapel Hill: University of North Carolina Press, 2012).

113. Sarah Barringer Gordon, *The Mormon Question: Polygamy and Constitutional Conflict in Nineteenth-Century America*, Studies in Legal History (Chapel Hill: University of North Carolina Press, 2002); Mason, *Mormon Menace*; Kathleen Flake, *The Politics of American Religious Identity: The Seating of Senator Reed Smoot, Mormon Apostle* (Chapel Hill: University of North Carolina Press, 2004).

114. Polly Aird, *Mormon Convert, Mormon Defector: A Scottish Immigrant in the American West, 1848–1861* (Norman, OK: Arthur H. Clark, 2009).

115. John D. Nutting and Frank S. Johnson, *Mormon Morals* (Cleveland, OH: Utah Gospel Mission, 1906), 14–16.

116. D. J. Claiborne, *The Story of a Mormon Convert: How He Was Lured into Mormonism, and How He Found the Light Again, as Told by Himself* (Cleveland, OH: Utah Gospel Mission, 1922).

117. Dean May, "A Demographic Portrait of the Mormons, 1830–1980," in *The New Mormon History: Revisionist Essays on the Past*, ed. D. Michael Quinn (Salt Lake City, UT: Signature Books, 1992), ch. 7.

5 · Sincerity

1. S. Jane Picken Cohen, *Henry Luria; or, The Little Jewish Convert: Being Contained in the Memoir of Mrs. S. J. Cohen* (New York: John F. Trow, 1860), 44–45, 49–52.

2. Cohen, *Henry Luria*, 52–53.

3. Cohen, *Henry Luria*, 54–55.

4. Cohen, *Henry Luria*, 56; Henry Samuel Morais, *The Jews of Philadelphia* (Philadelphia: Levytype, 1894), 18.

5. The *beth din* (rabbinical court) of three Jewish leaders that assembled for her conversion cannot have been comprised of rabbis, since the first permanent rabbi in America, Abraham Rice, did not settle in the United States until 1840. Jonathan D. Sarna, *American Judaism: A History* (New Haven, CT: Yale University Press, 2004), 91.

6. Cohen, *Henry Luria*, 63–64. My guides to the ritual and halakhic aspects of conversion to Judaism have been Menachem Finkelstein, *Conversion: Halakhah and Practice* (Ramat Gan, Israel: Bar-Ilan University Press, 2006); Lawrence J. Epstein, *The Theory and Practice of Welcoming Converts to Judaism: Jewish Universalism* (Lewiston, NY: E. Mellen Press, 1992); Lawrence J. Epstein, *Conversion to Judaism: A Guidebook* (Northvale, NJ: Jason Aronson, 1994).

7. Raphael Jacob Moses, *Last Order of the Lost Cause: The Civil War Memoirs of a Jewish Family in the Old South*, ed. Mel Young (Lanham, MD: University Press of America, 1995), 24–25.

8. Cohen, *Henry Luria*, 56.

9. Moses, *Last Order*, 24–25.

10. Cohen, *Henry Luria*, 55, 60, 57; Abraham H. Cohen to Hyman Marks, Philadelphia, July 9, 1815, MS-552 Mikveh Israel Records, box 1, folder 2 (item 246), American Jewish Archives, Cincinnati, OH.

11. Cohen, *Henry Luria*, 72, 74.

12. Cohen, *Henry Luria*, 85, quoting Isaiah 1:18.

13. Cohen, *Henry Luria*, 85, emphasis added.

14. Cohen, *Henry Luria*, 91.

15. Cohen, *Henry Luria*, 105–51.

16. Cohen, *Henry Luria*, 90, 101–2.

17. Anne C. Rose, *Beloved Strangers: Interfaith Families in Nineteenth-Century America* (Cambridge, MA: Harvard University Press, 2001), 146–83.

18. Kevin Michael Schultz, *Tri-faith America: How Catholics and Jews Held Postwar America to Its Protestant Promise* (New York: Oxford University Press, 2011); Will Herberg, *Protestant-Catholic-Jew: An Essay in American Religious Sociology* (Garden City, NJ: Doubleday, 1955); Lila Corwin Berman, *Speaking of Jews: Rabbis, Intellectuals, and the Creation of an American Public Identity* (Berkeley: University of California Press, 2009).

19. Sarna, *American Judaism*, 375–76.

20. For the most comprehensive comparative history of Jewish conversion, see Todd Endelman, *Leaving the Jewish Fold: Conversion and Radical Assimilation in Modern Jewish History* (Princeton, NJ: Princeton University Press, 2015), especially ch. 6. Endelman argues that the United States, though freer than

many states in Europe, still puts Jews under significant pressure to assimilate via conversion.

21. Max Lilienthal, "The Jews in Russia under Nicolai I," *Asmonean*, June 30, 1854, 84; *Asmonean*, July 7, 1854, 93–94; *Asmonean*, July 14, 1854, 101. Bruce Ruben, *Max Lilienthal: The Making of the American Rabbinate* (Detroit: Wayne State University Press, 2011), 122, attributes these articles to Lilienthal. Cf. Michael A. Meyer, *Response to Modernity: A History of the Reform Movement in Judaism* (New York: Oxford University Press, 1988), 238, 241–43.

22. Bertram W. Korn, *The American Reaction to the Mortara Case: 1858–1859* (Cincinnati: American Jewish Archives, 1957); Josef L. Altholz, "A Note on the English Catholic Reaction to the Mortara Case," *Jewish Social Studies* 23, no. 2 (1961): 111–18, http://www.jstor.org/stable/4465859; David I. Kertzer, *The Kidnapping of Edgardo Mortara* (New York: Alfred Knopf, 1997).

23. Augusta Ellis Johnson to Alvin P. Horey, January 6, 1869, box 1, folder 2; Johnson to Horey, January 9, 1869, box 1, folder 3; Horey to Johnson, January 8, 1869, box 1, folder 4; Johnson to Horey, January 13, 1869, box 1, folder 5, Augusta Ellis Johnson Papers, American Jewish Historical Society, New York and Boston, MA (hereafter AJHS).

24. Dan Judson, "The Mercies of a Benign Judge: A Letter from Gershom Seixas to Hannah Adams, 1810," *American Jewish Archives Journal* 56 (2004): 187.

25. Federal Constitution, article 6, section 3; South Carolina Constitution of 1778, article 12; Pennsylvania Constitution of 1776, section 45; reproduced in Edwin Gaustad, *Neither King nor Prelate: Religion and the New Nation, 1776–1826*, rev. ed. (Grand Rapids, MI: Eerdmans, 1993), 170–71.

26. Sarah Barringer Gordon, *The Spirit of the Law: Religious Voices and the Constitution in Modern America* (Cambridge, MA: Belknap Press of Harvard University Press, 2010), 1–14. The term *popular constitutionalism* comes from Larry D. Kramer, *The People Themselves: Popular Constitutionalism and Judicial Review* (New York: Oxford University Press, 2005).

27. Isaac Leeser, "The Jewish Chronicle and the Occident," *Occident* 3, no. 1 (1845): 41–43. Leeser also noted that he had made converts to Judaism as sincere as any converts that Christians could claim. The anonymous pamphleteer Honestus made much the same argument. *A Critical Review of the Claims Presented by Christianity for Inducing Apostacy in Israel* (New York: Frere and Bellew, 1852).

28. A number of historians, among them Eric L. Goldstein, *The Price of Whiteness: Jews, Race, and American Identity* (Princeton, NJ: Princeton University Press, 2006), 16, have pointed out that in the United States Jews were not "the Other" against which the dominant culture defined itself. In Europe, the division was often between "Aryan" and "Semite"; in the United States it was between "black" and "white."

29. Richard W. Cogley, *John Eliot's Mission to the Indians before King Philip's War* (Cambridge, MA: Harvard University Press, 1999), 9–22.

30. Judah Monis, *The Whole Truth* (Boston, 1722); Benjamin Colman, *A Discourse Had in the College-Hall at Cambridge, March 27, 1722. Before the baptism of R. Judah Monis* (Boston, 1722). Milton M. Klein, "A Jew at Harvard in the 18th Century," *Proceedings of the Massachusetts Historical Society*, 3rd ser., 97 (1985): 135–45, http://www.jstor.org/stable/25080947.

31. Hannah Adams, *A Memoir of Miss Hannah Adams*, ed. Hannah Farnham Sawyer Lee (Boston: Gray and Bowen, 1832), 32–37, 75–77; Hannah Adams, *The History of the Jews from the Destruction of Jerusalem to the Nineteenth Century* (Boston: John Eliot Jr., 1812), 1:335, 1:338–52, 2:57–58, 2:67, 2:211, 2:220. Adams based her history primarily on Jacques Basnage's 1706 *History of the Jews*, though she also corresponded with Gershom Seixas about American Jewry. Judson, "Mercies of a Benign Judge," 179–89. See also David Max Eichhorn, *Evangelizing the American Jew* (Middle Village, NY: Jonathan David, 1978), 9–12, 28–31.

32. Adams, *Memoir*, 49.

33. Adams, *History of the Jews*, 2:67, 2:296–98. The text she read was *A Short Account of Mr. Frey, a Converted Jew* (Hartford, CT: Lincoln and Gleason, 1807). She also read the likely fictionalized account of the conversion of a "Mr. Lapidoth" and his family. *The Converted Jew; or, An Account of the Conversion to Christianity of Mr. Lapidoth and Family and of the Baptism of Himself, His Wife, and Thirteen Children . . . at Vianen, in Holland, March 18, 1805* (Hartford, CT: Lincoln and Gleason, 1807).

34. C. S. Hawtrey to Hannah Adams, n.d., box 1, folder 2; Hannah More to Hannah Adams, January 26, 1816, box 1, folder 2, Hannah Adams Papers, AJHS.

35. Adams, *Memoir*, 42–43.

36. *Christian Herald*, September 17, 1816, 369; November 9, 1816, 102; March 22, 1817, 414; August 1, 1818, 272.

37. The narrative of the incorporation of the American Society for Meliorating the Condition of the Jews is told at greater length in Eichhorn, *Evangelizing the American Jew*, 33–44.

38. Pauline Maier, "The Revolutionary Origins of the American Corporation," *William and Mary Quarterly*, 3rd ser., 50, no. 1 (1993): 51–84, doi:10.2307/2947236: 53–54. New York passed a general incorporation statute in 1811, "Act Relative to Incorporations for Manufacturing Purposes," but it was limited to business and not charitable organizations. A 1784 law allowed for general incorporation of religious societies, but not charitable organizations. New York did not enact a general incorporation statute for charitable organizations until 1848. *Constitution of the American Society for Meliorating the Condition of the Jews: . . . And the Act of Incorporation Granted by the Legislature of the State of New-York* (New York: Abraham Paul, 1820).

39. *Universalist Magazine*, July 22, 1826, 19. On Noah, see Jonathan D. Sarna, *Jacksonian Jew: The Two Worlds of Mordecai Noah* (New York: Holmes and Meier, 1980).

40. New York Constitution of 1777, article 38; reaffirmed more concisely in the New York Constitution of 1821, article 7, section 3. Cf. Susanna Linsley, "Saving the Jews: Religious Toleration and the American Society for Meliorating the Condition of the Jews," *Journal of the Early Republic* 34, no. 4 (2014): 638, doi:10.1353/jer.2014.0075.

41. *Universalist Magazine*, July 22, 1826, 19.

42. *The First Report of the American Society for Meliorating the Condition of the Jews, Presented May 9, 1823* (New York, 1823); *The Second Report of the American Society for Meliorating the Condition of the Jews, Presented May 14, 1824* (New York, 1824); *The Third Report of the American Society for Meliorating the Condition*

of the Jews, May 13, 1825 (New York, 1825); *Report of the American Society for Meliorating the Condition of the Jews* (New York, 1843); *The Twenty-Fifth Report of the American Society for Meliorating the Condition of the Jews* (New York, 1848); *Dusselthal Abbey: Count von Der Recke's Institution for Destitute Orphans and Jewish Proselytes* (London: James Nisbet, 1836). For benevolent institutions, see Lori Ginzberg, *Women and the Work of Benevolence* (New Haven, CT: Yale University Press, 1992); David Sehat, *The Myth of American Religious Freedom* (New York: Oxford University Press, 2011), 51–71.

43. William B. Sprague, *The Annual Sermon, Preached before the American Society for Meliorating the Condition of the Jews, on May 9, 1847* (New York, 1847); William Ramsay, *The Annual Sermon Preached before the American Society for Meliorating the Condition of the Jews, May 9, 1852* (New York, 1852). George L. Berlin, "Joseph S. C. F. Frey, the Jews, and Early Nineteenth Century Millenarianism," *Journal of the Early Republic* 1, no. 1 (1981): 27–49, doi:10.2307/3122773, argues that Jewish missions were motivated early by millenarian concerns; Yaakov Ariel emphasizes that millenarian concerns were especially prevalent among Christian missionaries from the 1880s through the twentieth century. Yaakov S. Ariel, *Evangelizing the Chosen People: Missions to the Jews in America, 1880–2000* (Chapel Hill: University of North Carolina, 2000); Yaakov S. Ariel, *On Behalf of Israel: American Fundamentalist Attitudes toward Jews, Judaism, and Zionism, 1865–1945* (Brooklyn, NY: Carlson, 1991). On the origins of dispensationalism, see George M. Marsden, *Fundamentalism and American Culture: The Shaping of Twentieth Century Evangelicalism, 1870–1925* (New York: Oxford University Press, 1980), 43–62; Matthew Avery Sutton, *American Apocalypse: A History of Modern Evangelicalism* (Cambridge, MA: Belknap Press of Harvard University Press, 2014), 15–22.

44. Linsley, "Saving the Jews," 625–51.

45. Zadig studied at Princeton with Robert Baird, the author of the well-known history of *Religion in America* (New York, 1844).

46. *Report of the American Society for Meliorating the Condition of the Jews* (1843), 6–11, 40–48.

47. Joseph S. C. F. Frey, *The Converted Jew; or, Memoirs of the Life of Joseph Samuel C. F. Frey* (Boston: Samuel T. Armstrong, 1815), 19, 23.

48. Frey, *Converted Jew*, 13–15, also published in several other British and American editions. For example, J. S. C. F. Frey, *Narrative of the Rev. Joseph Samuel C. F. Frey* (New York, 1834), was bound together (at least in the AJHS copy) with the third edition of Frey, *Essays on Christian Baptism* (New York, 1834), likely to explain his changed views on baptism since he had become a Baptist.

49. Frey, *Converted Jew*, 27, 30.

50. Frey, *Converted Jew*, 31–33.

51. Frey, *Converted Jew*, 34–41. Frey's name in English was pronounced "free" after the meaning and not the spelling of his name.

52. Adams, *History of the Jews*, 2:305.

53. *Tobit's Letters to Levi; or, A Reply to the Narrative of Joseph Samuel C. F. Frey* (New York, 1816). Cf. George L. Berlin, *Defending the Faith: Nineteenth-Century American Jewish Writings on Christianity and Jesus* (Albany: State University of New York Press, 1989), 7–24; Jonathan D. Sarna, "The Freethinker, the Jews,

and the Missionaries: George Houston and the Mystery of 'Israel Vindicated,' " *AJS Review* 5 (January 1, 1980): 101–14, http://www.jstor.org/stable/1486455; Jonathan D. Sarna, "The American Jewish Response to Nineteenth-Century Christian Missions," *Journal of American History* 68, no. 1 (June 1981): 35–51, doi:10.2307/1890901.

54. Isaac Leeser, "The American Society for Meliorating the Condition of the Jews, and Its Organ, the Jewish Chronicle," *Occident* 1, no. 1 (April 1843): 43–47; Isaac Leeser, "The American Society for Meliorating the Condition of the Jews," *Occident* 1, no. 2 (May 1843): 100–104.

55. Frey published a number of polemical works: J. S. C. F. Frey, *Essays on Christian Baptism* (Newark, NJ, 1830); Joseph S. Frey, *Judah und Israel: or, The Restoration and Conversion of the Jews and Ten Tribes: To Which Is Added Essays on the Passover* (London: Ward, 1837); Joseph S. C. F. Frey, *Joseph and Benjamin: A Series of Letters on the Controversy between Jews and Christians: Comprising the Most Important Doctrines of the Christian Religion* (London: Hill, 1837); Joseph S. C. F. Frey, *The Scripture Types: A Course of Lectures* (Philadelphia: American Baptist Publication Society, 1841); Joseph S. C. F. Frey, *A Course of Lectures on the Messiahship of Christ* (New York: Joseph Samuel C. F. Frey, 1844).

56. Frey, *Judah und Israel,* 156–59.

57. John Oxlee, *Three Letters Humbly Submitted to the Consideration of His Grace the Most Reverend the Lord Archbishop of Canterbury . . . on the Inexpediency and Futility of Any Attempt to Convert the Jews to the Christian Faith,* first American edition (Philadelphia: Abraham Collins, 1843), 95.

58. Isaac Mayer Wise, "The American Synagog [*sic*] as It Is," *Asmonean,* October 8, 1852, 246–47.

59. Isaac Mayer Wise, "The Messiah," *Occident* 7, no. 7 (August 1849): 229–44.

60. Even Warder Cresson, a Protestant who had converted to Judaism, complained that missionaries were paid, citing specific facts and figures. Warder Cresson, *The Key of David; David the True Messiah; or, The Anointed of the God of Jacob* (Philadelphia, 1852), 281–87.

61. Wise, "The American Synagog," 246–48.

62. Isaac Mayer Wise, *A Defense of Judaism versus Proselytizing Christianity* (Cincinnati: American Israelite, 1889), 55–57.

63. Sarna, *American Judaism,* 375–76.

64. Jonathan D. Sarna, "The 'Mythical Jew' and the 'Jew Next Door' in Nineteenth-Century America," in *Anti-Semitism in American History,* ed. David A. Gerber (Urbana: University of Illinois Press, 1986), 57–78.

65. On conversion narratives as a genre, see Stuart A. Federow, "Convert Autobiographies as a Genre of Literature" (rabbinic thesis, Hebrew Union College–Jewish Institute of Religion, 1982).

66. See, for example, Walt Whitman's reports of synagogue attendance. Walt Whitman, "A Peep at the Israelites," *Aurora,* March 28, 1842, and "Doings at the Synagogue," *Aurora,* March 29, 1842, in *Walt Whitman of the New York Aurora,* ed. Joseph Jay Rubin and Charles H. Brown (State College, PA: Bald Eagle Press, 1950), 31–34. Thanks to Shari Rabin for pointing me to the Whitman references and to the Leeser articles cited below. See Shari L. Rabin, "Manifest

Jews: Mobility and the Making of American Judaism, 1820–1877" (PhD thesis, Yale University, 2015). Emily Bingham, *Mordecai: An Early American Family* (New York: Hill and Wang, 2003), 132–36, 154–58, describes the Mordecai family's interactions with Episcopalians. Joseph Simpson, *The Missionary Scape-Goat, Employed by Brutal Convert-Hunting Nimrods, Riding on a Beastly Crowing Rooster* (Baltimore: Hanzsche, 1853), 1–34, also describes a Christian visitor to a Yom Kippur service.

67. Isaac Leeser, "The Prospect," *Occident* 6, no. 8 (November 1848): 377.

68. Isaac Leeser, "Intercourse with Missionaries," *Occident* 16, no. 9 (December 1858): 442.

69. A common concern among the Reform movement was "decorum." Jews who were willing to attend Christian services seem to have sought out this kind of decorum, which would also have left them free from inquiries into the state of their souls. Meyer, *Response*, 24–25, 102, 197, 57.

70. Berlin, *Defending the Faith*, 45–74.

71. Bingham, *Mordecai*, 132–36. Many other members of the Mordecai family converted, as detailed in Bingham's work. For the diary of another Southern Jewish young man who had doubts about his faith but who did not convert to Christianity, see Joseph Lyons, *The Diary of Joseph Lyons, 1833–1835*, ed. Marie Ferrara et al. (Charleston, SC: College of Charleston Library, 2005). For Southern converts between Judaism and Christianity, including some slaves, see Lauren F. Winner, "Taking Up the Cross: Conversion among Black and White Jews in the Civil War South," in *Southern Families at War: Loyalty and Conflict in the Civil War South*, ed. Catherine Clinton (New York: Oxford University Press, 2000), 193–209.

72. See *Glory of Israel* 1, no. 1 (January 1903), 1–3. Ariel, *Evangelizing*, 55–68.

73. *Oxford English Dictionary Online*, s.v. "pervert," http://www.oed.com /view/Entry/141683.

74. Jonathan D. Sarna and Karla Goldman, "From Synagogue-Community to Citadel of Reform: The History of K. K. Bene Israel (Rockdale Temple) in Cincinnati, Ohio," in *American Congregations*, ed. James P. Wind and James Welborn Lewis, 2 vols. (Chicago: University of Chicago Press, 1994), 1:178.

75. Max Louis Rossvally, *A Short Sketch of the Life and Conversion of a Jew* (New York: J. Huggins, 1876), 17–19. David Stern to Bernhard Felsenthal, October 7, 1884; Stern to Felsenthal, October 13, 1884, Bernhard Felsenthal Papers, box 1, folder 2, AJHS.

76. For two excellent works of scholarship on intermarriage, see Rose, *Beloved Strangers*; Bingham, *Mordecai*.

77. Malcolm H. Stern, "The Function of Genealogy in American Jewish History," in *Essays in American Jewish History* (Cincinnati: American Jewish Archives, 1958), 84; Jonathan D. Sarna, "Intermarriage in America: The Jewish Experience in Historical Context," in *Ambivalent Jew: Charles Liebman in Memoriam*, ed. Stuart Cohen and Bernard Susser (New York: Jewish Theological Seminary of America, 2007), 125–33.

78. The Babylonian Talmud does make exceptional provisions for the conversion of women captured in war who are to be married, but this is an exception that proves the rule.

79. David B. Nones to Benjamin Nones, letter to parents, May 27, 1810; David B. Nones to Benjamin Nones, June 1, 1810, box 1, folder 2, Nones Family Papers, AJHS. See Abigaill Franks to Naphtali Franks, June 7, 1743, in Abigaill Levy Franks, *The Letters of Abigaill Levy Franks, 1733–1748,* ed. Edith B. Gelles (New Haven, CT: Yale University Press, 2004), 123–24, for another colonial family in New York whose children intermarried.

80. Saul Jacob Rubin, *Third to None: The Saga of Savannah Jewry* (Savannah, GA: privately printed, 1983), 203, 376n105; Dana Evan Kaplan, "The Determination of Jewish Identity below the Mason-Dixon Line: Crossing the Boundary from Gentile to Jew in the Nineteenth Century South," *Journal of Jewish Studies* 52, no. 1 (2001): 118.

81. Nathan Marcus Adler to Isaac Leeser, March 22, 5615 [=1855], box 1, folder 4; Simeon Abrahams to Isaac Leeser, May 27, 5615 [=1855], box 1, folder 2, Isaac Leeser Papers, AJHS.

82. Petition of Benjamin Jacobs to Hayman Levy to marry a non-Jew, Jacques Judah Lyons Collection, AJHS; *Publications of the American Jewish Historical Society* 26, no. 1 (1918): 29–30.

83. Benjamin Nones to Beth Din of K. K. Shagnar a Shamaïm, August 7, 1793, in *The American Jewish Woman: A Documentary History,* ed. Jacob Rader Marcus (Cincinnati: American Jewish Archives, 1981), 52–53.

84. Marcus, ed., *American Jewish Woman,* 53–54.

85. *American Israelite,* January 16, 1880, 6.

86. *American Israelite,* October 1, 1875, 7. The converts in this paragraph are discussed in Kaplan, "Determination," 114–16, from which I have taken the biographical details.

87. *American Israelite,* April 23, 1875, 6; Kaplan, "Determination," 115.

88. Conversion certificate of Marie Berthelot, quoted in Kaplan, "Determination," 109. Kaplan does mention several lifelong converts who were denied Jewish burials, 105–7.

89. Register of Congregation Shearith Israel, volume for 1834–1857, transcript, box 1, folder 15, Records of Congregation Shearith Israel, AJHS.

90. Kirkas certificate. For the similar conversion of Jacob Bar Abraham Abinu, see *Publications of the American Jewish Historical Society* 27 (1920–21): 231–32. For a much later conversion certificate of a convert to Judaism, see David Meir Rabinowitz conversion certificate, Boston 1909, box 1, folder 1, David Meir Rabinowitz Papers, AJHS. Not every applicant for conversion was received, however. In 1788, a man named James Foster came to New York, applied to Congregation Shearith Israel to be converted to Judaism, but was apparently turned down. He wrote a letter to the trustees of the congregation, requesting letters of recommendation so that he could be converted in Amsterdam. James Foster to trustees of K. K. Shearith Israel, June 5, 1788, Jacques Judah Lyons Collection, AJHS.

91. Yevamos 47b. All quotations from the Babylonian Talmud are from the Schottstein edition. David Harry Ellenson and Daniel Gordis, *Pledges of Jewish Allegiance: Conversion, Law, and Policymaking in Nineteenth- and Twentieth-Century Orthodox Responsa* (Stanford, CA: Stanford University Press, 2012), 13–37.

92. Yevamos 48b.

93. Niddah 13b; Yevamos 48b; Bava Metzia 58b–59b.

94. Sarna, *American Judaism*, 52–61.

95. Frank Fox, "Quaker, Shaker, Rabbi: Warder Cresson, the Story of a Philadelphia Mystic," *Pennsylvania Magazine of History and Biography* 95, no. 2 (April 11, 1971): 147–94, http://www.jstor.org/stable/20090539; Stuart Schoffman, "'Insane on the Subject of Judaism': Pursuing the Ghost of Warder Cresson," *Jewish Quarterly Review*, n.s., 94, no. 2 (April 1, 2004): 318–60, http://www.jstor.org/stable/1455430. Though Cresson never became or claimed to be a rabbi, the otherwise sober scholarship of Frank Fox replicates one of the features of nineteenth-century conversion narratives in making any Jew involved in conversion a rabbi. Herbert Friedenwald, "Warder Cresson: Zionist and Convert to Judaism," *Jewish Comment* 12, no. 7 (November 30, 1900): 1ff.

96. Gwynedd meeting records, cited in Fox, "Quaker, Shaker, Rabbi," 152.

97. *Babylon the Great Is Falling! The Morning Star; or, Light from on High Written in Defence of the Rights of the Poor and Oppressed* (Philadelphia: Garden and Thompson, 1830).

98. Fox, "Quaker, Shaker, Rabbi," 156.

99. Ruth Kark, *American Consuls in the Holy Land, 1832–1914* (Detroit: Wayne State University Press, 1994), 307–10.

100. *Encyclopedia Judaica*, 2nd ed., s.v. "Jerusalem." Philadelphia, by contrast, had a population of 258,037 in the 1840 census. Historical Census Browser, University of Virginia Library, http://mapserver.lib.virginia.edu/php/county .php.

101. Warder Cresson, *Jerusalem, the Centre and Joy of the Whole Earth, and the Jew, the Recipient of the Glory of God* (Philadelphia: J. Harding, 1844); Cresson, *Key of David*. Cf. Henry Smith, *The Protestant Bishopric in Jerusalem: Its Origin and Progress* (London: B. Wertheim, 1847), 35–36, 67–70; Daniel Huntington, *The Duty of Christians to Jews: A Sermon [to] the Palestine Missionary Society, in Halifax* (Boston, 1823), 12–13; Joseph Wolff, *Missionary Journal and Memoir of the Rev. Joseph Wolf: Missionary to the Jews* (New York: E. Bliss and E. White, 1824); Donald M. Lewis, *The Origins of Christian Zionism: Lord Shaftesbury and Evangelical Support for a Jewish Homeland* (Cambridge: Cambridge University Press, 2010), 213–23, 271–98.The establishment of the Anglican bishopric in Jerusalem in collaboration with German Protestants, which he called the "Jerusalem 'abomination,'" was one of the decisive factors in convincing John Henry Newman to convert to Roman Catholicism. John Henry Newman, *Apologia Pro Vita Sua: The Two Versions of 1864 and 1865* (London: Oxford University Press, 1913), 202, 246–47, 249, 253, 260, 26–66, 274, 352.

102. William Makepeace Thackeray, *Notes of a Journey from Cornhill to Grand Cairo, by Way of Lisbon, Athens, Constantinople, and Jerusalem* (New York: Wiley and Putnam, 1846), 109, 130–31.

103. Cresson, *Key of David*, 17, 19.

104. Cresson, *Key of David*, 205.

105. Cresson, *Jerusalem*, 206. Warder Cresson, "The Tub; or, The House Turned Upside Down," *Occident* 6, no. 10 (January 1849).

106. Cresson, *Key of David*, 203.

107. Cresson, *Key of David*, 216; *Occident* 21, nos. 5, 6, 7 (1863).

108. "The Lunacy Trial of Warder Cresson," published serially in *Occident* 21, no. 5 (August 1863): 203–13 (quotation from 206); *Occident* 21, no. 6 (September 1863): 248–55; and *Occident* 21, no. 7 (October 1863): 301–9. Cresson, *Key of David*, 243. Thomas Jefferson, *Notes on the State of Virginia* (London, 1787), 265.

109. "The Lunacy Trial of Warder Cresson," *Occident* 21, no. 6 (September 1863): 249.

110. Fox, "Quaker, Shaker, Rabbi," 180–81.

111. Cresson, *Key of David*, 223–44.

112. "The Lunacy Trial of Warder Cresson," *Occident* 21, no. 5 (August 1863): 203.

113. "The Holy Land," *Occident* 10, no. 7 (October 1852): 361. Michael Boaz Israel, "Relief by Agriculture for Palestine," *Occident* 12, no. 7 (October 1854): 351–55; Michael Boaz Israel, "A Few Practical Observations before Commencing Agriculture in the East," *Occident* 13, no. 3 (June 1855): 133–37.

114. Herman Melville, *Clarel: A Poem and Pilgrimage in the Holy Land* (New York, 1876); Herman Melville, *Journals*, ed. Howard C. Horsford and Lynn Horsford (Chicago: Northwestern University Press, 1989); William Potter, *Melville's "Clarel" and the Intersympathy of Creeds* (Kent, OH: Kent State University Press, 2004).

115. *The Conversion of a Jew by Reading the New Testament in Prison* (Philadelphia: Sunday and Adult School Union, 1815).

116. Lew Wallace, *Ben-Hur: A Tale of the Christ* (New York: Harper and Brothers, 1880).

117. Mrs. Pogson Smith, *Zerah, the Believing Jew* (New York: Protestant Episcopal Press, 1837).

118. Lloyd, *Thirza; or, The Attractive Power of the Cross*, 2nd American ed. (Boston: Massachusetts Sabbath School Society, 1848). These novels owe some of their appeal to the nineteenth-century fascination with the "historical Jesus." See the discussion of Renan below. They also drew on semifictional or even fantastical accounts of the conversion of Jews published in North America since the colonial era, e.g., Samuel Brett, *A True Relation of the Proceedings of the Great Council of the Jews* (Keene, NH: Amos Taylor, 1795).

119. Many converts granted themselves the title "rabbi" after their conversions, or were at least called rabbis by Christians. The impulse toward calling converts rabbis was polemical: the conversion of a rabbi was deemed a more powerful argument for the truth of Christianity than the conversion of a Jew who did not practice his own religion when he converted, which was how Jews described former Jews. Converted Jews also had a large and curious audience when they spoke about the Jewish practice, which encouraged inflating their credentials. And finally, most conversion narratives described the converts' Jewish education, which may have struck Christian readers as rabbinical.

120. Albert Edward Thompson, *A Century of Jewish Missions* (Chicago: Fleming H. Revell, 1902), 265.

121. On the popularity of Rossvally, see Aaron Bernstein, *Some Jewish Witnesses for Christ* (London: Operative Jewish Converts' Institution, 1909).

122. The first such organization in New York was the Jewish Christian Brotherhood in New York and Chicago under W. W. Harschaw. The next most important was Jacob Freshman's Hebrew Christian Mission. Thompson, *Century of Jewish Missions*, 232, 237.

123. Rossvally, *Short Sketch*, 52.

124. Stern does not appear in Jacob Rader Marcus and Judith M. Daniels, eds., *The Concise Dictionary of American Jewish Biography* (Brooklyn, NY: Carlson, 1994).

125. David Stern to Bernhard Felsenthal, April 24, 1884, Bernhard Felsenthal Papers, box 1, folder 2, AJHS. Ezra Spicehandler and Theodore Wiener, eds., "Bernhard Felsenthal's Letters to Osias Schorr," in *Essays in American Jewish History* (Cincinnati: American Jewish Archives, 1958), 379–406.

126. *American Israelite*, August 1, 1879.

127. Tobias Brinkmann, *Sundays at Sinai: A Jewish Congregation in Chicago* (Chicago: University of Chicago Press, 2012). William J. Potter to Bernhard Felsenthal, July 8, 1879, box 2, folder 3, Bernhard Felsenthal Papers, AJHS.

128. *American Israelite*, May 1, 1885, 4. *New York Times*, April 19, 1885. *Chicago Tribune*, April 20, 1885. In the *American Israelite*, Wise seemed to question whether Stern was a rabbi, but he had been received as such by his congregation and by Felsenthal. David Stern to Bernhard Felsenthal, April 1885; A. B. Weil to Bernhard Felsenthal, April 22, 1885, Felsenthal Papers, AJHS.

129. Trustees of Congregation Temple Israel to Bernhard Felsenthal, box 1, folder 15, Bernhard Felsenthal Papers, AJHS. Another well-known convert who returned to Judaism was Arnold B. Ehrlich. See Jacob Kabakoff, "New Light on Arnold Bogomil Ehrlich," *American Jewish Archives* 36 (1984): 202–24. Sonneschein was discredited in part because he was compared to an earlier convert, Henry Gersoni. Gersoni had been born in Vilna, then converted to Russian Orthodox Christianity in St. Petersburg. He repented of his conversion publicly in a Jewish newspaper, *Ha-Maggid*, but on his emigration to England, he was accused of living in a Christian mission house. On Sonneschein, see Benny Kraut, "Judaism Triumphant: Isaac Mayer Wise on Unitarianism and Liberal Christianity," *AJS Review* 7/8 (January 1982): 219–22.

130. David Stern to Bernhard Felsenthal, April 24, 1884, Bernhard Felsenthal Papers, box 1, folder 2, AJHS.

131. Ernest Renan, *The Life of Jesus*, first English ed. (London: Trübner, 1864), 309; Halvor Moxnes, "Renan's Vie de Jésus as Representation of the Orient," in *Jews, Antiquity, and the Nineteenth-Century Imagination*, ed. Hayim Lapin and Dale B. Martin (Bethesda: University Press of Maryland, 2003), 85–108; Lisa Moses Leff, "Self-Definition and Self-Defense: Jewish Racial Identity in Nineteenth-Century France," *Jewish History* 19, no. 1 (2005): 7–28, http://www.jstor.org/stable/20100943; Alan Pitt, "The Cultural Impact of Science in France: Ernest Renan and the Vie de Jésus," *Historical Journal* 43, no. 1 (2000): 79–101, http://www.jstor.org/stable/3021014.

132. Goldstein, *Price of Whiteness*; Matthew Frye Jacobson, *Whiteness of a Different Color: European Immigrants and the Alchemy of Race* (Cambridge, MA: Harvard University Press, 1998).

133. Joseph Krauskopf, *Jewish Converts, Perverts and Dissenters* (Philadelphia: Oscar Klonower, 1891), 13–14; Kraut, "Judaism Triumphant," 179.

134. Dana Evan Kaplan, "W. E. Todd's Attempt to Convert to Judaism and Study for the Reform Rabbinate in 1896," *American Jewish History* 83, no. 4 (1995): 429.

135. David Stern to Bernfard Felsenthal, October 7, 1884, Bernhard Felsenthal Papers, box 1, folder 2, AJHS.

136. David Stern to Bernfard Felsenthal, October 13, 1884, Bernhard Felsenthal Papers, box 1, folder 2, AJHS.

137. Henry Berkowitz circular to Bernhard Felsenthal, received August 19, 1890, Bernhard Felsenthal Papers, AJHS; also published in *CCAR Yearbook for 5652* (Cincinnati: Bloch, 1892), 84–85.

138. *CCAR Yearbook for 5651* (Cincinnati: Bloch, 1891), 1:80–82; *CCAR Yearbook for 5652* (Cincinnati: Bloch, 1892), 25, 66–128. At stake was both the question of what ritual observances were binding for Reform Jews and what power rabbis or rabbinic organizations had to impose those regulations. The *CCAR Yearbooks* gather many newspaper articles by rabbis on the questions, as well as papers written by rabbis for the annual meeting. Isaac Mayer Wise had a substantial correspondence on these questions. On the proper ritual, see Wise to Julius L. Mayerberg, February 20, 1891, Isaac Mayer Wise Digital Archive, American Jewish Archives, Cincinnati. On receiving "renegades" back to Judaism, see Wise to L. Weiss, October 30, 1891.

139. Genesis 34.

140. David L. Gollaher, "From Ritual to Science: The Medical Transformation of Circumcision in America," *Journal of Social History* 28, no. 1 (1994): 5–36, http://www.jstor.org/stable/3788341.

141. Bernard Felsenthal, *Zur Proselytenfrage im Judenthum* (Chicago: E. Rubovits, 1878), also published in Breslau; Spicehandler and Wiener, eds., "Bernhard Felsenthal's Letters."

142. Samuel Freuder, *A Missionary's Return to Judaism: The Truth about the Christian Missions to the Jews* (New York: Sinai, 1915), 20–33.

143. Freuder may have been granted his diploma on the basis of his one year of study plus his study in Berlin, but his name does not appear in the Hebrew Union College yearbook as a graduate. See *Annual Report of the Union of American Hebrew Congregations* (Cincinnati: Block, 1891), 3:2800. The fullest discussion of whether Freuder actually received rabbinical ordination from Hebrew Union College is in Dana Evan Kaplan, "Rabbi Samuel Freuder as a Christian Missionary: American Protestant Premillennialism and an Apostate Returner, 1891–1924," *American Jewish Archives* 50, no. 1 (January 1998): 42–43. It is clear that Freuder was regarded as a rabbi by both Jews and Christians throughout his life.

144. Freuder's conversion was reported widely in newspapers as well, such as the Mormon paper *Deseret Weekly* 43 (September 26, 1891), 439.

145. Freuder, *Missionary's Return*, 17; Krauskopf, *Jewish Converts*, 12–14. Cf. Richard Wightman Fox, *Jesus in America: Personal Savior, Cultural Hero, National Obsession* (New York: HarperOne, 2005), 159–306; Stephen Prothero, *American Jesus: How the Son of God Became a National Icon* (New York: Farrar, Strauss and Giroux, 2004).

146. Freuder, *Missionary's Return*, 41, 40–43.

147. Freuder, *Missionary's Return*, 38.

148. Freuder, *Missionary's Return*; Samuel Freuder, *My Return to Judaism*, 3rd ed. (New York: Bloch, 1924); "Jew Quits Christianity," *New York Times*, June 5, 1908; *New York Times*, January 14, 1916. For Freuder, see Kaplan, "Rabbi Samuel Freuder," 41–74.

149. Freuder, *Missionary's Return*, 12.

150. Freuder, *Missionary's Return*, 84–85.

151. J. F. de Le Roi, *Geschichte der Evangelischen Judenmissen seit Entstehung des neurenen Judentums* (Leipzig, 1899). Henry Einspruch, *Jewish Confessors of the Faith* (Jewish Missions Committee, United Lutheran Church of America, 1925), 5–6, misstates de Le Roi's estimate as 204,500 but is inclined to think that it is low. On de Le Roi, see Thompson, *Century of Jewish Missions*, 136.

152. Thompson, *Century of Jewish Missions*, 263–64.

153. *The American Jew*, pamphlet in the possession of AJHS, pp. 897–900.

154. Thompson, *Century of Jewish Missions*, appendix 2; Freuder, *Missionary's Return*, 65. Thomas Wentworth Higginson cited a similar calculation that "Christendom converts annually three or four Jews in Jerusalem, at a cost of $20,000 each." Thomas Wentworth Higginson, *The Sympathy of Religions* (Boston: Free Religious Association, 1876), 32.

155. A. E. Thompson writing in *Glory of Israel* 1, no. 1 (January 1903): 4–5. Thompson repeated and revised some of these estimates in Thompson, *Century of Jewish Missions*, 263.

156. Rossvally, *Short Sketch*, 60.

6 · Repose

1. John Thayer, *An Account of the Conversion of the Reverend Mr. John Thayer . . . Who Embraced the Roman Catholic Religion at Rome*, 5th ed. (Baltimore: William Goddard, 1788), 1.

2. In 1890, Catholics were 192,313 of 254,627 religious adherents in Suffolk County, Massachusetts. *Census of 1890*, "Religious Bodies Data, Number of Communicants or Members by Type of Church Organization," Minnesota Population Center, National Historical Geographic Information System: Version 2.0 (Minneapolis, MN: University of Minnesota, 2011), http://nhgis.org.

3. On anti-Catholicism in the Revolutionary period, see James P. Byrd, *Sacred Scripture, Sacred War: The Bible and the American Revolution* (New York: Oxford University Press, 2013), 5, 25, 129, 131; Maura Jane Farrelly, *Papist Patriots: The Making of an American Catholic Identity* (New York: Oxford University Press, 2012), 188–218. Thomas Edward Bridgett, *A New England Convert; or, The Story of the Rev. John Thayer* (London, 1897), 39, thinks that Thayer had French Huguenot ancestry. Thayer's fluency with French and his access to an abandoned Huguenot church in Boston, which he turned into a Catholic chapel, seem to corroborate that guess.

4. Thayer, *Account*, 10–13; letter from Abbé de Lunel, July 16, 1783, in Giuseppe Loreto Marconi, *The Life of the Venerable Benedict Joseph Labre*, trans. J. Barnard (Wigan, England, 1786), 209–10.

5. Thayer, *Account*, 14–15; Bridgett, *New England Convert*, 23–39.

6. See letter dated August 16, 1787, from a woman who converted, in Thayer, *Account*, 28. John Gilmary Shea, *Life and Times of the Most Rev. John Carroll* (New York: J. G. Shea, 1888), 386–92, 416, 453–54.

7. For lists of converts, see, among many others, John Gilmary Shea, "Converts, Their Influence and Work in This Country," *American Catholic Quarterly Review* 8, no. 31 (July 1883): 509–28; Richard H. Clarke, "Our Converts [Part I]," *American Catholic Quarterly Review* 18, no. 71 (1893): 539–61; Richard H. Clarke, "Our Converts [Part II]," *American Catholic Quarterly Review* 19, no. 73 (1894): 112–38; Alfred Young, *Catholic and Protestant Countries Compared in Civilization, Popular Happiness, General Intelligence, and Morality* (New York: Catholic Book Exchange, 1895), 592–611; D. J. Scannell-O'Neill, *Distinguished Converts to Rome in America* (St. Louis: B. Herder, 1907); Georgina Peel Curtis, ed., *Some Roads to Rome in America* (St. Louis: B. Herder, 1909); Georgina Peel Curtis, ed., *Beyond the Road to Rome in America* (St. Louis: B. Herder, 1914).

8. *Chronicle of the English Missions Given by the Redemptorist Fathers in the United States of N. America* and *Chronicle of the Missions Given by the Congregation of Missionary Priests of St. Paul the Apostle*, six manuscript volumes, Paulist Fathers Archives, New York (hereafter Paulist Mission Chronicles). For the converts mentioned, see 1:25–26. For summary statistics of the Paulist missions, see 1:163–66; 2: flyleaf; 5:318–20; Paulist Mission Chronicles. Jay Dolan, *Catholic Revivalism: The American Experience, 1830–1900* (South Bend, IN: University of Notre Dame Press, 1978), offers the fullest treatment of Catholic missions; see also the journal *Hecker Studies*, published by the Paulists. Data for historic state boundaries comes from the National Historical Geographic Information System (cited above); data for railroad maps below comes from William G. Thomas III, Richard Healey, et al., *Railroads and the Making of Modern America*, http://railroads.unl.edu.

9. E. Rameur, "The Progress of the Church in the United States," *Catholic World* 1, no. 1 (1865): 4.

10. Clarke, "Our Converts [Part I]," 541–42, makes the unfounded guess about the "convert element," compounding it with an error in arithmetic. George K. Malone, *The True Church: A Study in the Apologetics of Orestes Brownson* (Mundelein, IL: Saint Mary of the Lake Seminary, 1957), 2, correctly cites Clarke's estimate as converts and their descendants. But Sydney Ahlstrom, *A Religious History of the American People* (New Haven, CT: Yale University Press, 1972), 548, mistakenly cites the 700,000 number from Malone as referring to converts alone. Jenny Franchot, *Roads to Rome: The Antebellum Protestant Encounter with Catholicism* (Berkeley: University of California Press, 1994), xx, repeats the error, citing Ahlstrom and (without page number) Gaustad's *Atlas*. Edwin Scott Gaustad and Philip L. Barlow, with Richard W. Dishno, *New Historical Atlas of Religion in America* (New York: Oxford University Press, 2001), 155–62, 309–20, offer no estimate of Catholic conversions.

11. Rameur, "Progress of the Church," 13.

12. *New-York Freeman's Journal and Catholic Register*, July 6, 1844, 4; July 20, 1844, 21; October 26, 1844. For example, D. C. Johnston and Mr. Briggs were confirmed at the same time as Orestes Brownson, along with most of Brownson's

large family. Jack Larkin, "What He Did for Love: David Claypoole Johnston and the Boston Irish, 1825–1865," *Common-place* 13, no. 3 (spring 2013), http://www.common-place.org/vol-13/no-03/larkin/.

13. Patrick Allitt, *Catholic Converts: British and American Intellectuals Turn to Rome* (Ithaca, NY: Cornell University Press, 1997).

14. D. Oliver Herbel makes a similar argument about the reason for conversions to Eastern Orthodoxy in the United States from the late nineteenth century through the twentieth century. Herbel notes that converts to Eastern Orthodoxy exercised a paradoxical choice: they exercised the freedom of American religion to choose a traditional religion. He writes that "these intra-Christian American conversions to Orthodoxy can be best understood as a turn to tradition. . . . Their cases show that non-Orthodox Christians are using the very American context of religious choosing and religious novelty-creation to make what might seem a very un-American choice in favor of an unbroken tradition, which they find in Orthodox Christianity, in a very American way." D. Oliver Herbel, *Turning to Tradition: Converts and the Making of an American Orthodox Church* (New York: Oxford University Press, 2013); D. Oliver Herbel, "A Catholic, Presbyterian, and Orthodox Journey: The Changing Church Affiliation and Enduring Social Vision of Nicholas Bjerring," *Journal for the History of Modern Theology* 14, no. 1 (2007), 49–80. In contrast, Joel Brady argues that Greek Catholics who became Russian Orthodox usually saw their movement between churches as a continuity of practice and identity. Joel Brady, "Becoming What We Always Were: 'Conversion' of U.S. Greek Catholics to Russian Orthodoxy, 1890–1914." *U.S. Catholic Historian* 32, no. 1 (2014): 23–48.

15. While emphasizing that the institutional "jump was immense" for Catholic converts, Allitt also argues that "intellectually . . . conversion was often incremental" and that for many intellectuals, "the continuities in [their] thought before and after conversion are in many ways more striking than the discontinuities." Allitt, *Catholic Converts*, 3.

16. Ray Allen Billington, *The Protestant Crusade, 1800–1860: A Study of the Origins of American Nativism* (New York: Rinehart, 1952); Steven K. Green, *The Bible, the School, and the Constitution: The Clash That Shaped Modern Church-State Doctrine* (New York: Oxford University Press, 2012); Jon Gjerde, *Catholicism and the Shaping of 19th Century America*, ed. S. Deborah Kang (New York: Cambridge University Press, 2012).

17. Stephen Cleveland Blythe, *An Apology for the Conversion of Stephen Cleveland Blythe, to the Faith of the Catholic, Apostolic, and Roman Church* (Montreal: Nahum Mower, 1815), 48–49.

18. Orestes A. Brownson, "Sparks on Episcopacy," *Brownson's Quarterly Review* 1 (July 1844): 386–96; "Nature and Office of the Church," *Brownson's Quarterly Review* 1 (April 1855): 247; "Bishop Hopkins on Novelties," *Brownson's Quarterly Review* 1 (July 1844): 366; Orestes A. Brownson, *The Convert; or, Leaves from My Experience* (New York: E. Dunigan and Brother, 1857); Patrick W. Carey, *Orestes A. Brownson: American Religious Weathervane* (Grand Rapids, MI: William B. Eerdmans, 2004).

19. Francis Xavier Weninger, *Catholicity, Protestantism and Infidelity: An Appeal to Candid Americans* (New York: Sadlier, 1869); Fanny Maria Pittar, *A Protestant Converted to Catholicity by Her Bible and Prayer-Book: And the Strug-*

gles of a Soul in Search of Truth (Buffalo, NY: Catholic Publication Company, 1884).

20. Martin John Spalding, *Lectures on the Evidences of Catholicity: Delivered in the Cathedral of Louisville*, 5th ed. (Baltimore: John Murphy, 1870). Spalding's quotation is from the Nicene Creed, with similar wording in the Apostles' Creed. The essential structure of Spalding's arguments, especially the explication of the clause about the church in the Nicene or Apostles' Creed, is replicated in most Catholic apologetics from the nineteenth century, especially the works by John Milner and John Adam Moehler discussed below. For the argument about the new kind of evidential apologetics, see E. Brooks Holifield, *Theology in America: Christian Thought from the Age of the Puritans to the Civil War* (New Haven, CT: Yale University Press, 2003), 1–24, 173–96; cf. Mark A. Noll, *America's God: From Jonathan Edwards to Abraham Lincoln* (New York: Oxford University Press, 2002), 93–113.

21. Gaustad and Barlow, *New Historical Atlas*, 155–59.

22. Pierce Connelly, *A Letter and a Farewell Sermon* (Natchez, MS: Stanton and Besançon, 1835), 17–22.

23. Clarke, "Our Converts [Part 1]," 542.

24. Quoted in Walter Elliott, *The Life of Father Hecker* (New York: Columbus Press, 1891), 409–10.

25. John Henry Newman, *Tracts for the Times, No. 90: Remarks on Certain Passages in the Thirty-Nine Articles*, 1st American ed. (New York: J. A. Sparks, 1841).

26. Clarence Walworth, *The Oxford Movement in America; or, Glimpses of Life in an Anglican Seminary* (New York: Catholic Book Exchange, 1895). Elliott, *Life of Father Hecker*, 194–201; *The Journal of the . . . General Convention [1901]* (Printed for the Convention, 1902), 17–20, 193–94, 225–26, https://books.google.com/books?id=nthCAQAAMAAJ; Robert W. Prichard, *A History of the Episcopal Church* (New York: Morehouse, 2014), ch. 6.

27. John Gatta, "The Anglican Aspect of Harriet Beecher Stowe," *New England Quarterly* 73, no. 3 (September 1, 2000): 412–33, doi:10.2307/366685.

28. Philip Schaff, *The Principle of Protestantism as Related to the Present State of the Church*, trans. John Williamson Nevin (Chambersburg, PA: German Reformed Church, 1845); Philip Schaff, *America: A Sketch of the Political, Social, and Religious Character of the United States of North America* (New York: Scribner, 1855); John B. Payne, "Schaff and Nevin, Colleagues at Mercersburg: The Church Question," *Church History* 61, no. 2 (1992): 169–90; Stephen Ray Graham, *Cosmos in the Chaos: Philip Schaff's Interpretation of Nineteenth-Century American Religion* (Grand Rapids, MI: Eerdmans, 1995). Cf. Schaff and Nevin to John Henry Newman, *An Essay on the Development of Christian Doctrine* (London: J. Toovey, 1845).

29. John Williamson Nevin, "The Sect System," *Mercersburg Review* 1 (1849): 537, 539. See D. G. Hart, *John Williamson Nevin: High-Church Calvinist* (Philipsburg, NJ: P. & R. Publishing, 2005).

30. *New-York Freeman's Journal and Catholic Register*, August 14, August 21, 1852. Also quoted in James Hastings Nichols, *Romanticism in American Theology: Nevin and Schaff at Mercersburg* (Chicago: University of Chicago Press, 1961), 211, see also pp. 192–217.

31. *The Late Defections to the Roman Catholic Church from the Reformed Church in the United States* (Pottstown, PA, 1871).

32. Allitt, *Catholic Converts;* Patrick Allitt, "American Women Converts and Catholic Intellectual Life," *U.S. Catholic Historian* 13, no. 1 (January 1, 1995): 57–79; Franchot, *Roads to Rome;* Anne C. Rose, "Some Private Roads to Rome: The Role of Families in American Victorian Conversions to Catholicism," *Catholic Historical Review* 85, no. 1 (January 1999): 35; Anne C. Rose, *Beloved Strangers: Interfaith Families in Nineteenth-Century America* (Cambridge, MA: Harvard University Press, 2001).

33. Paulist Mission Chronicles, 1:232; Isaac Thomas Hecker, *Questions of the Soul* (New York: D. Appleton, 1855), 5, 123.

34. John Baptist Purcell to Francis Patrick Kenrick, September 17, 1853 (31-B-10); Martin John Spalding to Francis Patrick Kenrick, March 12, 1856 (32A-N-23); Francis Patrick Kenrick to Marin John Spalding, April 29, 1854 (34-J-20), all in Archbishop Kenrick Papers, Archives of the Archdiocese of Baltimore, Associated Archives at St. Mary's Seminary and University, Baltimore, MD (hereafter AAB). Patrick Allitt writes, "It is difficult to find any example of an intellectual who derived either social or monetary gain from conversion" to Catholicism. Allitt, *Catholic Converts,* 6.

35. T. J. Jackson Lears, *No Place of Grace: Antimodernism and the Transformation of American Culture, 1880–1920* (New York: Pantheon, 1981), 183–214.

36. Stephanie A. T. Jacobe, "Thomas Fortune Ryan and the Issue of Identity in Catholic Biography," *U.S. Catholic Historian* 29, no. 3 (2011): 35–41, doi:10.1353/cht.2011.0041; Stephanie A. T. Jacobe, "'Whatever They Considered Would Be Most Conductive to His Glory': The Religious Conversion of Thomas Fortune Ryan," *U.S. Catholic Historian* 32, no. 2 (2014): 51–66, doi:10.1353/cht .2014.0009. Bliss is discussed below.

37. Isaac Thomas Hecker, *Isaac T. Hecker, the Diary: Romantic Religion in Ante-bellum America,* ed. John Farina (New York: Paulist Press, 1988), 13, 135–36, 321; Elliott, *Life of Father Hecker,* 76, 80, 91, 102, 229, 243.

38. Hecker, *Questions of the Soul,* 153–55.

39. For the idea of a religious gift economy, see Leigh Eric Schmidt, "Practices of Exchange: From Market Culture to Gift Economy in the Interpretation of American Religion," in *Lived Religion in America: Toward a History of Practice,* ed. David D. Hall (Princeton, NJ: Princeton University Press, 1997), 69–91. Gjerde, *Catholicism,* 220–56.

40. Mark Noll, "Protestant Reasoning about Money and the Economy, 1790–1860: A Preliminary Probe," in *God and Mammon: Protestants, Money, and the Market, 1790–1860,* ed. Mark Noll (New York: Oxford University Press, 2002), 265–95; Stewart Davenport, *Friends of the Unrighteous Mammon: Northern Christians and Market Capitalism, 1815—1860* (Chicago: University of Chicago Press, 2008); Gjerde, *Catholicism,* 220–56.

41. Lyman Beecher, *A Plea for the West* (Cincinnati: Truman and Smith, 1835), 10, 12. Gjerde, *Catholicism,* 96–137, is only the most recent work to take up the question of politics and conversion.

42. Brownson, *Convert,* 163–79; Carey, *Brownson,* 92–94.

43. The Americanism that brought Pope Leo XIII's rebuke was precipitated by a French translation of Walter Elliott's *Life of Father Hecker,* which

the French Abbé Charles Maignen attacked as heretical. Charles Maignen, *Le Père Hecker, Est-il Un Saint?* (Paris: V. Retaux, 1899); Thomas Timothy McAvoy, *The Americanist Heresy in Roman Catholicism, 1895–1900* (South Bend, IN: University of Notre Dame Press, 1963).

44. Robert Baird, *Religion in America; or, An Account of the Origin, Relation to the State, and Present Condition of the Evangelical Churches in the United States, with Notices of the Unevangelical Denominations* (New York: Harper and Brothers, 1844), 269–70.

45. Payne, "Schaff and Nevin," 174.

46. *The Catechism of the Council of Trent* (Baltimore: F. Lucas, 1829), 118–20; Canons of the Council of Trent, seventh session, canons on baptism, canon 4, in *The Canons and Decrees of the Council of Trent*, trans. H. J. Schroeder (Charlotte, NC: TAN Books, 1971), 53. I am grateful to Govind Sreenivasan for tracing the recognition of baptism by pagans back to Thomas Aquinas, *Summa Theologica*, III, q. 67. a. 3–5, and Gratian, *Decretum*, Pars III, Distinctio IV, Canones 20, 21–23, 28, 31–32.

47. Samuel Eccleston to Francis Patrick Kenrick, October 25, 1835 (27A-L-10); Francis Patrick Kenrick to Samuel Eccleston, October 26, 1835 (25-F-5), Archbishop Kenrick Papers, AAB.

48. Philip Schaff, ed., *The Creeds of Christendom* (Grand Rapids, MI: Baker Book House, 1983), 2:207–11.

49. Clarke, "Our Converts [Part 1]," 539.

50. Levi Silliman Ives, *The Trials of a Mind in Its Progress to Catholicism: A Letter to His Old Friends* (London: Thomas Richardson, 1854), 11. The book he read was John Adam Moehler, *Exposition of the Doctrinal Differences between Catholics and Protestants, as Evidenced by the Symbolical Writings*, trans. James Burton Robertson (New York: Edward Dunigan, 1844), usually referred to as Moehler's *Symbolism*.

51. H. H. Wyman, "Out of Calvinism into Truth," in *From the Highways of Life : . . . Stories of Conversions by the Converts Themselves* (New York: Paulist Press, 1893), 45.

52. Elliott, *Life of Father Hecker*, 10.

53. Augustine Francis Hewit, "How I Became a Catholic," in *From the Highways of Life: . . . Stories of Conversions by the Converts Themselves* (New York: Paulist Press, 1893), 13–14; Nathaniel Augustus Hewit to Nathaniel Hewit, n.d. [1832], Augustine F. Hewit Papers, Paulist Fathers Archives, New York (hereafter Hewit Papers).

54. Hewit to his mother, September 1840; Hewit to Nathaniel Hewit, October 7, 1840; Hewit to Nathaniel Hewit, October 29, 1840; Hewit to Nathaniel Hewit, November 8, 1840; Hewit to Nathaniel Hewit, January 19, 1841, all in Hewit Papers.

55. Hewit to Nathaniel Hewit, January 24, 1841; Hewit to Nathaniel Hewit, October 7, 1844, both in Hewit Papers.

56. Hewit to Nathaniel Hewit, May 16, 1844; Hewit to Nathaniel Hewit, October 7, 1844; both in Hewit Papers.

57. Hewit, "How I Became a Catholic," 13–14; Hewit to Nathaniel Hewit, August 31, 1845, Hewit Papers; cf. *Catholic Encyclopedia*, s.v. Augustine Francis Hewit.

58. Francis A. Baker to Dwight E. Lyman, September 18, 1844, Francis A. Baker Papers, Paulist Fathers Archives, New York.

59. Paulist Mission Chronicles, 1:82, and undated newspaper clippings opposite that page. *From the Highways of Life: . . . Stories of Conversions by the Converts Themselves* (New York: Paulist Press, 1893).

60. Paulist Mission Chronicles, 1:41.

61. Paulist Mission Chronicles, 1:152.

62. Paulist Mission Chronicles, 2:21.

63. Paulist Mission Chronicles, 1:175.

64. Dolan, *Catholic Revivalism*, xix–xx, 1–24, 91–112.

65. Paulist Mission Chronicles, 1:150, 147. Many more examples of this usage could be cited.

66. Paul Curtis, letter to unnamed former parishioner, April 20, 1872, in Visitation Nuns, *The Life and Characteristics of the Right Reverend Alfred A. Curtis* (New York: P. J. Kennedy and Sons, 1913), 49–50.

67. Thomas Paine, *The Age of Reason* (London: R. Carlile, 1818); Ethan Allen, *Reason the Only Oracle of Man; or, A Compendious System of Natural Religion* (Bennington, VT: Haswell and Russell, 1784); Amanda Porterfield, *Conceived in Doubt: Religion and Politics in the New American Nation* (Chicago: University of Chicago Press, 2012); Eric R. Schlereth, *An Age of Infidels: The Politics of Religious Controversy in the Early United States* (Philadelphia: University of Pennsylvania Press, 2013).

68. Charles Wharton, *Letter to the Roman Catholics of Worcester* (Philadelphia, 1784); Charles Wharton, *A Reply to an Address to the Roman Catholics of the United States of America* (Philadelphia, 1785); Charles Henry Wharton, *The Remains of the Rev. Charles Henry Wharton, D.D., with a Memoir of His Life*, ed. George Washington Doane (Philadelphia: William Stavely, 1834); John Carroll, *An Address to the Roman Catholics of the United States of America by a Catholic Clergyman* (Annapolis, 1784), in *The John Carroll Papers*, 3 vols., ed. Thomas O'Brien Hanley (Notre Dame, IN: University of Notre Dame Press, 1976), 1:82–144; John Carroll to Charles Plowden, September 18, 1784, and February 27, 1785, in *The John Carroll Papers*, 3 vols., ed. Thomas O'Brien Hanley (Notre Dame, IN: University of Notre Dame Press, 1976), 1:150, 167–68; Shea, *Life of Carroll*, 225–36.

69. Carroll, *Address*, 1:85–86, 89.

70. Blythe, *Apology*, 51; George J. Mountain, *A Letter to Mr. S. C. Blythe, Occasioned by the Recent Publication of the Narrative of His Conversion to the Romish Faith* (Montreal: Nahum Mower, 1822), 11.

71. Connelly, *Letter*, 20, 23. On the imagined place of the "infidel," see Martin E. Marty, *The Infidel: Freethought and American Religion* (Cleveland: Meridian Books, 1961).

72. Louis de Goesbriand, *Catholic Memoirs of Vermont and New Hampshire* (Burlington, VT, 1886), 14, 18–20. The Hotel-Dieu convent was the subject of Maria Monk's infamous exposé. A number of female converts to Catholicism entered religious orders, among them Elizabeth Ann Bayley Seton (Mother Seton, canonized as the first U.S. saint and founder of the Sisters of Charity) and Rose Hawthorne Lathrop (Mother Mary Alphonsa, founder of the Domin-

ican Sisters of Hawthorne). Charles I. White, *Life of Mrs. Eliza A. Seton, Foundress and First Superior of the Sisters or Daughters of Charity in the United States of America*, 2nd rev. ed. (Baltimore: J. Murphy, 1856).

73. De Goesbriand, *Memoirs*, 33. Daniel Barber, *Catholic Worship and Piety, Explained and Recommended* (Washington, DC: E. De Krafft, 1821), 28–37.

74. Daniel Barber, *The History of My Own Times*, 3 vols. (Washington, DC: S. C. Ustick, 1827); de Goesbriand, *Memoirs*, 29–67.

75. Information about the controversial Ffrench is scarce; see Lawrence A. Desmond and Donna M. Norell, *The Case for Fr. Charles Dominic Ffrench (1775–1851)* (Yorkton, Saskatchewan: Laverdure, 2004).

76. Barber, *History*, 4, 17; de Goesbriand, *Memoirs*, 61–67.

77. Daniel Barber, *Catholic Worship and Piety*. It was rare, but not unheard of, for most of a congregation to follow their minister when he converted. Many people in his Illinois parish followed the ex-Catholic and former Quebec priest Charles Chiniquy when he was excommunicated in 1856–1858 and became a Protestant. Charles Chiniquy, *The Life and Labours of the Rev. Father Chiniquy* (Glasgow: Religious Tract and Book Society of Scotland, 1861); Charles Chiniquy, *Fifty Years in the Church of Rome* (New York: Fleming H. Revell, 1886). See Richard Lougheed, *The Controversial Conversion of Charles Chiniquy* (Toronto: Clements, 2008), 100–111; Caroline B. Brettell, *Following Father Chiniquy: Immigration, Religious Schism, and Social Change in Nineteenth-Century Illinois* (Carbondale: Southern Illinois University Press, 2015).

78. Daniel Barber to Miss A. S., December 24, 1819, in Barber, *Catholic Worship and Piety*, 36.

79. James O'Toole, *The Faithful: A History of Catholics in America* (Cambridge, MA: Belknap Press of Harvard University Press, 2009), 11–48, 50–93.

80. Gjerde, *Catholicism*, 16.

81. Augustine Francis Hewit, *The King's Highway; or, The Catholic Church in the Way of Salvation as Revealed in the Holy Scriptures* (New York: Catholic Publication Society, 1874), iii.

82. Hewit, "How I Became a Catholic"; John Farina, *An American Experience of God: The Spirituality of Isaac Hecker* (New York: Paulist Press, 1981), 16–17.

83. Rameur, "Progress of the Church," 11.

84. Joseph Bernard Code, *Dictionary of the American Hierarchy (1789–1964)* (New York: Joseph F. Wagner, 1964), 425–26.

85. Patrick W. Carey, *Catholics in America: A History* (Westport, CT: Praeger, 2004), 45; Sebastian Bach Smith, *Notes on the Second Plenary Council of Baltimore* (New York: P. O'Shea, 1874); Peter Guilday, *A History of the Councils of Baltimore* (New York: Macmillan, 1932).

86. Among other Catholic Publication Society narratives, not to mention instructional books and apologetics, see Count de Falloux, *The Life and Letters of Madame Swetchine*, trans. H. W. Preston (New York: Catholic Publication Society, 1867); Joshua Huntington, *Gropings after Truth: A Life Journey from New England Congregationalism to the One Catholic and Apostolic Church* (New York: Catholic Publication Society, 1868); Augustine Francis Hewit, *Memoir*

of the Life of the Rev. Francis A. Baker, Priest of the Congregation of St. Paul, 7th ed. (New York: Catholic Publication Society, 1889); Sarah M. Brownson, *Life of Demetrius Augustine Gallitzin, Prince and Priest* (New York: Catholic Publication Society, 1873); John Henry Newman, *Apologia Pro Vita Sua* (New York: Catholic Publication Society, n.d.); Demetrius Augustine Gallitzin, *A Defense of Catholic Principles* (New York: Catholic Publication Society, n.d.); Demetrius Augustine Gallitzin, *Letters to a Protestant Friend on the Holy Scriptures* (New York: Catholic Publication Society, n.d.). Other publishers also brought out convert biographies: Clarence A. Walworth, *Reminiscences of Edgar P. Wadhams, First Bishop of Ogdensburg* (New York: Benziger, 1893); Ellen H. Walworth, *Life Sketches of Father Walworth, with Notes and Letters* (Albany, NY: J. B. Lyon, 1907); J[ulia] C. Smalley, *The Young Converts; or, Memoirs of the Three Sisters, Debbie, Helen and Anna Barlow,* ed. Isaac T. Hecker (New York: P. O'Shea, 1861).

87. The biblical passage at issue was Hebrews 6:4–6. The Authorized (King James) Version used by Protestants translated the relevant phrase as "to renew them again unto repentance," the Douay-Rheims versions used by Catholics translated it as "to be renewed again to penance," and Clarence Walworth translated it as "to be renewed again by penance." Walworth, *Oxford Movement,* 25.

88. Gaustad and Barlow, *New Historical Atlas,* 99–101. The Episcopal Church also had missions to the West, as did the Catholics, but the Episcopal Church was far less successful in the West and in nonurban areas. Prichard, *History of the Episcopal Church,* chs. 5–6.

89. *A Full and True Statement of the Examination and Ordination of Mr. Arthur Carey* (New York: James A. Sparks, 1843).

90. Walworth, *Oxford Movement,* 31. Most Christian denominations recoil from rebaptism. If there is any question about someone's baptism, Episcopalians, like Catholics, performed a conditional baptism. Though trine baptism was an ancient practice, it was unusual in the modern church. The rubrics of the 1789 American *Book of Common Prayer,* as revised in 1841, state, "Then shall the minister take each person to be baptized by the right hand; and placing him conveniently by the Font, according to his discretion, . . . then shall dip him in the water, or pour water upon him." *The Book of Common Prayer and Administration of the Sacraments and Other Rites and Ceremonies of the Church: According to the Use of the Protestant Episcopal Church in the United States of America* (New York: H. and S. Raynor, 1842), 166. The first prayer book of Edward VI prescribed trine baptism, but the requirement was left out of all subsequent English and American prayer books. The American prayer book did contain rubrics for conditional baptism.

91. Walworth, *Oxford Movement,* 13.

92. Walworth, *Oxford Movement,* 9. The students had difficulty finding the text because two passages in Acts refer to the apostle Paul's baptism. Acts 9:18 is the first recounting, but it does not mention regeneration. When Paul later gives a speech in Jerusalem about his conversion, he mentions that Ananias told him, "Arise, and be baptized, and wash away thy sins" (Acts 22:16 KJV).

93. Walworth, *Oxford Movement,* 10.

94. Walworth, *Oxford Movement,* 31. *New York Times,* September 20, 1900; Walworth, *Life Sketches of Father Walworth;* Walter Elliott, "Father Walworth: A Character Sketch," *Catholic World* 73 (June 1901): 320–37.

95. Barclay A. Smith to Charles West Thomson, January 27, 1844, and November 5, 1844, box 1, folder 1, Charles West Thomson Papers (MS 625), New-York Historical Society, New York.

96. Levi Silliman Ives, *The Priestly Office: A Pastoral Letter to the Clergy of North Carolina* (New York: Stanford and Swords, 1849); Michael Taylor Malone, "Levi Silliman Ives: Priest Bishop, Tractarian, and Roman Catholic Convert" (PhD dissertation, Duke University, 1970).

97. Farina, *American Experience*, 16–17. On Hecker, see Katherine Burton, *Celestial Homespun* (London: Longmans, Green, 1943); Joseph McSorley, *Father Hecker and His Friends: Studies and Reminiscences* (St. Louis: B. Herder, 1952); Vincent F. Holden, *The Yankee Paul: Isaac Thomas Hecker* (Milwaukee: Bruce Publishing, 1958); Vincent F. Holden, *The Early Years of Isaac Thomas Hecker (1819–1844)* (New York: AMS Press, 1974); John Farina, ed., *Hecker Studies: Essays on the Thought of Isaac Hecker* (New York: Paulist Press, 1983); William L. Portier, *Isaac Hecker and the First Vatican Council* (Lewiston, NY: E. Mellen Press, 1985); Martin J. Kirk, *The Spirituality of Isaac Thomas Hecker: Reconciling the American Character and the Catholic Faith* (New York: Garland, 1988); David J. O'Brien, *Isaac Hecker: An American Catholic* (New York: Paulist Press, 1992); Larry Hostetter, *The Ecclesial Dimension of Personal and Social Reform in the Writings of Isaac Thomas Hecker* (Lewiston, NY: Edwin Mellen Press, 2001); Boniface Hanley, *Paulist Father, Isaac Hecker: An American Saint* (Mahwah, NJ: Paulist Press, 2008).

98. Hecker, *Diary*, 63; Anne C. Rose, *Transcendentalism as a Social Movement, 1830–1850* (New Haven, CT: Yale University Press, 1981).

99. Charles Dana to Isaac Hecker, January 2, 1844; James Kay Jr. to Isaac Hecker, April 14, 1844, both in Isaac Hecker Papers, Paulist Fathers Archives, New York (hereafter Hecker Papers).

100. Quoted in Elliott, *Life of Father Hecker*, 72, 150.

101. Hecker to Brownson, March 28, 1844, in Joseph F. Gower and Richard M. Leliaert, eds., *The Brownson-Hecker Correspondence* (Notre Dame, IN: University of Notre Dame Press, 1979), 88–90.

102. Hecker to Brownson, March 15, 1844, in Gower and Leliaert, eds., *Correspondence*, 86.

103. Hecker to Brownson, April 7, 1844, in Gower and Leliaert, eds., *Correspondence*, 93–94; Hecker to his brothers, April 19, 1844, Hecker Papers. Hecker gave many details of his searching for the Catholic Church in letters to his brothers, June 11, 1844; June 14, 1844; June 19, 1844. This Samuel Seabury is not to be confused with his more famous grandfather, the first Episcopal bishop in the United States.

104. Isaac Hecker to his brothers, April 24, 1844, Hecker Papers.

105. Brownson to Hecker, June 6, 1844; Hecker to Brownson, June 24, 1844, both in Gower and Leliaert, eds., *Correspondence*, 103, 106.

106. Hecker to Brownson, August 2, 1844, in Gower and Leliaert, eds., *Correspondence*, 109.

107. Jenny Franchot has demonstrated how Catholic themes appear in the literature of other Concord authors writing at the same time as Thoreau. Franchot, *Roads to Rome*, chs. 10–13, 16.

108. Isaac Hecker to Henry David Thoreau, July 31, 1844; Thoreau to Hecker, August 14, 1844; Hecker to Thoreau, August 15, 1844; Thoreau to Hecker, n.d., all in E. Harlow Russell, ed., *A Bit of Unpublished Correspondence between Henry D. Thoreau and Isaac T. Hecker* (Worcester, MA: Charles Hamilton, 1902), 5–10.

109. Hecker to Brownson, September 5, 1844, in Gower and Leliaert, eds., *Correspondence*, 114.

110. Hecker to Mon. T. R. Père [Michael Heilig], May 30, 1848, Hecker Papers; also quoted in Gower and Leliaert, eds., *Correspondence*, 20.

111. Dolan, *Catholic Revivalism*, 25–90. Paulist Mission Chronicles, 1:6.

112. Paulist Mission Chronicles, 1:93.

113. Isaac Thomas Hecker, *Aspirations of Nature* (New York: J. B. Kirker, 1857).

114. Isaac Hecker to Redemptorists, April 1858, Hecker Papers.

115. Paulist Mission Chronicles, 1:175.

116. Gerald P. Fogarty, *The Vatican and the American Hierarchy from 1870 to 1965* (Stuttgart: Hiersemann, 1982).

117. Paulist Mission Chronicles, 2:405, 3:95. Carey, *Catholics*, 45; Cyprian Davis, *The History of Black Catholics in the United States* (New York: Crossroad, 1990); cf. Matthew Cressler, "Black Catholic Conversion and the Burden of Black Religion," *Journal of Africana Religions* 2, no. 2 (2014): 280–87.

118. *Sermons Delivered during the Second Plenary Council of Baltimore, October 1866* (Baltimore: Kelly and Piet, 1866), 66–86.

119. James Kent Stone, *The Invitation Heeded: Reasons for a Return to Catholic Unity* (New York: Catholic Publication Society, 1870), 5–13.

120. Stone, *Invitation Heeded*, 30–31. Stone received a rejoinder in Leonard Woolsey Bacon, *How the Rev. Dr. Stone Bettered His Situation: An Examination of the Assurance of Salvation, and the Certainty of Belief to Which We Are Affectionately Invited by His Holiness the Pope* (New York: American and Foreign Christian Union, 1870). Bacon objected to Stone's relying on baptism rather than faith in Christ, and in particular mocked his "hypothetical [i.e., conditional] baptism" (pp. 1–16).

121. Roll of Paulist members, typescript, Paulist Archives. Paulist Mission Chronicles, 2:43. Stone, *Invitation Heeded*, 7, 24, 30–31.

122. George Bliss, autobiography, typescript, 1:34–36, 1:51–53, in George Bliss Papers (MS 951), New-York Historical Society, New York (hereafter Bliss autobiography).

123. David McAdam et al., eds., *History of the Bench and Bar of New York* (New York: New York History Company, 1897), 2:48–51; Bliss autobiography, 1:104–5, 1:202–7. Bliss's father was president of several railroads.

124. Bliss autobiography, 2:253–482. George Bliss to Sarah Walker, May 2, 1895, Bliss Papers.

125. Correspondence with Mary Langtree, box 32, folder 1; correspondence with Mary O'Sullivan, box 32, folder 4, both in Jane Minot Sedgwick II Papers, Sedgwick Family Papers, Massachusetts Historical Society, Boston, MA (hereafter Sedgwick Papers). See Erin Bartram, "Jane Minot Sedgwick II and the World of American Catholic Converts, 1820–1890" (PhD thesis, University of

Connecticut, 2015); Erin Bartram, "'Jane Will Be Useful, and Because Useful, Happy': An Elite New England Family Confronts Conversion in the 1850s," *U.S. Catholic Historian* 32, no. 2 (August 14, 2014): 29–49, doi:10.1353/cht.2014.0008.

126. Religious notebooks, only some with titles, e.g., "One or two extracts Dr Wiseman on Transubstantiation," box 32, folders 9–11, Sedgwick Papers.

127. Religious notebooks; S. E. W. R. to Jane Sedgwick, June 15, 1854, box 32, folder 26, Sedgwick Papers.

128. Mary O'Sullivan to Jane Sedgwick, July 3, 1853, and Mary O'Sullivan to Jane Sedgwick, [July 1853], box 32, folder 26, Sedgwick Papers; Diary 1, 1815, box 30, folder 24, Jane Minot Sedgwick I Diaries, Sedgwick Papers.

129. Paulist Mission Chronicles, 1:163–66; 2: flyleaf; 5:318–20.

130. Dolan, *Catholic Revivalism*, 21.

131. Paulist Mission Chronicles, 2:55.

132. Paulist Mission Chronicles, 1:289.

133. Paulist Mission Chronicles, 1:283.

134. A Protestant lawyer was left under instruction and a few months later was received into the church. Paulist Mission Chronicles, 2:65.

135. Paulist Mission Chronicles, 3:135–36.

136. Marvin Richard O'Connell, *John Ireland and the American Catholic Church* (St. Paul: Minnesota Historical Society Press, 1988), 287–89.

137. Paulist Mission Chronicles, 3:140.

138. Paulist Mission Chronicles, 3:36.

139. Paulist Mission Chronicles, 2:108.

140. Paulist Mission Chronicles, 2:124.

141. Paulist Mission Chronicles, 2:454–59.

142. Jay Dolan provides a rich reading of individual mission chronicles combined with quantitative analysis of class in the New York City missions. I have extended his analysis across space by using the data the Paulists recorded about their missions. Dolan, *Catholic Revivalism*, 113–37.

143. Dolan, *Catholic Revivalism*, 168.

144. Paulist Mission Chronicles, 1:175.

145. The New York Public Library lists the diary under the name William Stratch, but I believe the name was misread and is actually William Strachan. The catalog entry also lists Strachan or Stratch as a convert to Roman Catholicism, though there is nothing in the diary itself that demonstrates that he converted, only that he was interested. William Stratch diary (MssCol 2902), Manuscripts and Archives, The New York Public Library, Astor, Lennox, and Tilden Foundations, New York. Leigh Schmidt has described this kind of seeker in *Restless Souls: The Making of American Spirituality* (San Francisco: Harper, 2005).

146. Stratch diary, entries for April 1900; entry for January 17, 1904.

147. From a later period, James F. Cunningham, *Why I Am a Catholic* (New York: Paulist Press, 1938), but Hecker and Walworth also gave lectures with this title.

148. Stratch diary, entries for January 16–17, 1904.

149. Stratch diary, entries through January 1904.

Conclusion

1. This is merely suggestive, but in December 1905, William James's *Psychology: A Shorter Course* was among the most checked out books from the New York Public Library. "Books People Are Reading," *New-York Tribune*, December 4, 1905, 5, Chronicling America: Historic American Newspapers, Library of Congress, http://chroniclingamerica.loc.gov/lccn/sn83030214/1905-12-04/ed-1/seq-5/. On the spread of James's ideas about religion, see Matthew S. Hedstrom, *The Rise of Liberal Religion: Book Culture and American Spirituality in the Twentieth Century* (New York: Oxford University Press, 2013), 4–5, 8–9, 19–20, 192–93, passim.

2. In American theology, there was an increasing emphasis on rational arguments for religious belief, drawing on the Enlightenment in the beginning of the century and on science in the latter part. This trend in theology had a symbiotic relationship with the trend in personal identity, functioning as both cause and effect. E. Brooks Holifield, *Theology in America: Christian Thought from the Age of the Puritans to the Civil War* (New Haven, CT: Yale University Press, 2003), 173–96; George M. Marsden, *Fundamentalism and American Culture: The Shaping of Twentieth Century Evangelicalism, 1870–1925* (New York: Oxford University Press, 1980), 16–17, 20, 26, 57, 121, 219.

3. James Turner, *Religion Enters the Academy: The Origins of the Scholarly Study of Religion in America* (Athens: University of Georgia Press, 2011), 56.

4. Louis Menand, *The Metaphysical Club* (New York: Farrar, Straus, and Giroux, 2001), 227–29, 339–47, 347–58.

5. Edwin Diller Starbuck, *The Psychology of Religion: An Empirical Study of the Growth of Religious Consciousness* (New York: C. Scribner's Sons, 1899), vii, 31. See Christopher White, "A Measured Faith: Edwin Starbuck, William James, and the Scientific Reform of Religious Experience," *Harvard Theological Review* 101, no. 3/4 (July 1, 2008): 431–50.

6. James Henry Leuba, *The Psychological Origin and the Nature of Religion* (London: A. Constable, 1909); James Henry Leuba, *The Belief in God and Immortality: A Psychological, Anthropological and Statistical Study* (Boston: Sherman, French, 1916); James Henry Leuba, *The Psychology of Religious Mysticism* (New York: Harcourt, Brace, 1925); Elmer Talmage Clark, *The Psychology of Religious Awakening* (New York: Macmillan, 1929); George Albert Coe, *The Psychology of Religion* (Chicago: University of Chicago Press, 1916).

7. James himself used this biblical allusion several times, including William James, *The Varieties of Religious Experience*, in *Writings, 1902–1910*, ed. Bruce Kuklick (New York: Library of America, 1987), 26. I am indebted throughout this discussion to Robert D. Richardson, *William James: In the Maelstrom of American Modernism* (Boston: Mariner Books, 2007), 287–416. Of the large literature on James's work and life, I have found these works especially helpful: White, "Measured Faith," 431–50; Charles Taylor, *Varieties of Religion Today: William James Revisited* (Cambridge, MA: Harvard University Press, 2002); Wayne Proudfoot, ed., *William James and a Science of Religions: Reexperiencing "The Varieties of Religious Experience"* (New York: Columbia University Press, 2004); Ann Taves, *Fits, Trances, and Visions: Experiencing Religion and Explaining Expe-*

rience from Wesley to James (Princeton, NJ: Princeton University Press, 1999), 308–47.

8. William James, "The Psychology of Belief," in *Writings, 1878–1899*, ed. Gerald E. Myers (New York: Library of America, 1992), 1021–56. This quotation is from the revised version of the essay included as the chapter "The Perception of Reality" in William James, *The Principles of Psychology*, 2 vols. (London: Macmillan, 1891), 2:321.

9. On reaction, habit, and will, see William James, "Reflex Action and Theism," in *Writings, 1878–1899*, 540–65. These themes run throughout all of James's works on psychology, including *Principles of Psychology* and especially *Talks to Teachers on Psychology*, in *Writings, 1878–1899*, 707–822.

10. James, "Psychology of Belief," 1022.

11. Many freethinkers did take the posture of agnosticism instead of atheism, chief among them Robert Ingersoll. Robert G. Ingersoll, "Why I Am an Agnostic," in *Works of Robert G. Ingersoll*, 12 vols. (New York: Dresden, 1902), 4:5–67. Susan Jacoby, *The Great Agnostic: Robert Ingersoll and American Freethought* (New Haven, CT: Yale University Press, 2013), 17, thinks that "Ingersoll himself made no distinction between atheists and agnostics," but the distinction was meaningful in Ingersoll's day, and Jacoby has a presentist ax to grind.

12. James, "Reflex Action and Theism," 99.

13. Roger Finke and Rodney Stark, *The Churching of America, 1776–2005: Winners and Losers in Our Religious Economy*, 2nd ed. (New Brunswick, NJ: Rutgers University Press, 2005), 23.

14. Andrew Walls, *The Missionary Movement in Christian History: Studies in the Transmission of Faith* (Maryknoll, NY: Orbis Books, 1996), 221–40.

15. The American Tract Society colporteur reports and the Paulist missionary records cited in earlier chapters often mention people who had never seriously encountered religion before. In the contemporary United States, the "rise of the nones" has been tracked as a significant trend, but it seems plausible that the nones are not so much rising as returning, as rates of religious affiliation decline from the very high levels of the mid-twentieth century. Pew Forum on Religion and Public Life, " 'Nones' on the Rise: One-in-Five Adults Have No Religious Affiliation" (Pew Research Center, October 9, 2012), http://www.pewforum.org/2012/10/09/nones-on-the-rise/.

16. On early American irreligion, see Eric R. Schlereth, *An Age of Infidels: The Politics of Religious Controversy in the Early United States* (Philadelphia: University of Pennsylvania Press, 2013).

17. Howard B. Radest, *Toward Common Ground: The Story of the Ethical Societies in the United States* (New York: Ungar, 1969); James Turner, *Without God, without Creed: The Origins of Unbelief in America* (Baltimore: Johns Hopkins University Press, 1985); Susan Jacoby, *Freethinkers: A History of American Secularism* (New York: Metropolitan Books, 2004); Leigh Eric Schmidt, *Village Atheists: How America's Unbelievers Made Their Way in a Godly Nation* (Princeton, NJ: Princeton University Press, 2016).

18. Martin E. Marty, *The Infidel: Freethought and American Religion* (Cleveland: Meridian Books, 1961).

19. Isaac Thomas Hecker, *Isaac T. Hecker, the Diary: Romantic Religion in Ante-bellum America*, ed. John Farina (New York: Paulist Press, 1988), 281.

20. Stephen H. Bradley, *A Sketch of the Life of Stephen H. Bradley . . . Including His Remarkable Experience of the Power of the Holy Spirit* (Madison, CT, 1830), 11.

21. Peter Watson, *The Age of Atheists: How We Have Sought to Live Since the Death of God* (New York: Simon and Schuster, 2014), deals mostly with Europe but tracks the development of atheism as a lived possibility since Nietzsche.

22. Richardson, *William James*, 82–83, 120–21, 193–94, 354–56, 372–76, 398–400; cf. James, *Varieties of Religious Experience*, 149–51.

23. James, "Is Life Worth Living?," in *Writings, 1878–1899*, 484.

24. James, "Is Life Worth Living?," 502. This attitude James gave the title "radical empiricism," defined in the preface to *The Will to Believe and Other Essays in Popular Philosophy*, in *Writings, 1878–1899*, 447–48.

25. James, "Will to Believe," in *Writings, 1878–1899*, 457, emphasis added.

26. James, "Will to Believe," 457–59.

27. James, "Is Life Worth Living?," 497.

28. James, "Will to Believe," 460. James was somewhat unjust to Pascal, who was also trying to deal with the problem of faith within an uncertain universe, as well as to William Clifford. See David A. Hollinger, *After Cloven Tongues of Fire: Protestant Liberalism in Modern American History* (Princeton, NJ: Princeton University Press, 2013), 103–16.

29. James was refuting Clifford's 1877 essay "The Ethics of Belief." James, "Will to Believe," 462.

30. James, "Will to Believe," 464.

31. James, "Will to Believe," 466.

32. James, "Will to Believe," 478.

33. On Moody's media techniques, see Bruce J. Evensen, *God's Man for the Gilded Age: D. L. Moody and the Rise of Modern Mass Evangelism* (New York: Oxford University Press, 2003).

34. H. B. Hartzler, *Moody in Chicago; or, The World's Fair Gospel Campaign* (New York: Fleming H. Revell, 1894), 254.

35. John Henry Barrows, ed., *The World's Parliament of Religions: An Illustrated and Popular Story of the World's First Parliament of Religions, Held in Chicago in Connection with the Columbian Exposition of 1893*, 2 vols. (Chicago: Parliament, 1893), http://catalog.hathitrust.org/Record/006688051.

36. William James to Henry William Rankin, June 12, 1897, in Ignas K. Skrupskelis and Elizabeth M Berkeley, eds., *The Correspondence of William James*, 12 vols. (Charlottesville: University Press of Virginia, 1992), 8:274–76; James to Rankin, June 17, 1897, in *Correspondence*, 8:599 (calendared); James to Rankin, December 21, 1895, in *Correspondence* 8:575 (calendared).

37. James to Rankin, September 30, 1898, in *Correspondence*, 8:438–39. In a later letter, after acknowledging the receipt of volumes he requested, James wrote, "The rest of your letters, the religious reflections, go to the place in my mind where I keep all such things till the day for final reaction comes. So far, my religion is much less acute and personal than yours." James to Rankin, January 16, 1899, in *Correspondence*, 8:488. And again: "I have found your long

letters interesting enough. What a real scholar you are! and what a believer!" James to Rankin, February 22, 1899, in *Correspondence*, 8:499.

38. Rankin to James, May 25, 1897, in *Correspondence*, 8:268; see also James to Rankin, June 12, 1897, in *Correspondence*, 8:274–76.

39. Richardson, *William James*, 365.

40. James to Rankin, January 19, 1896, in *Correspondence*, 8:122; James to Rankin, February 1, 1897, in *Correspondence*, 8:228.

41. James to Rankin, June 21, 1896, in *Correspondence*, 8:155.

42. Richardson, *William James*, 379, 421.

43. James to Rankin, July 8, 1902, in *Correspondence*, 10:81.

44. James, *Varieties of Religious Experience*, 211.

45. Toward the end of his life, James grew more definitive in his ideas when explaining mysticism. He expressed something of this idea in *Varieties of Religious Experience*, 433, but more forcefully in a 1910 essay on mysticism: "States of mystical intuition may be only very sudden and great extensions of the 'field of consciousness.'" James, "A Suggestion about Mysticism" in *Writings, 1902–1910*, 1272; cf. "The Energies of Men," in *Writings, 1902–1910*, 1223–41.

46. James, *Varieties of Religious Experience*, 15.

47. James, *Varieties of Religious Experience*, 26.

48. James, *Varieties of Religious Experience*, 32.

49. James, *Varieties of Religious Experience*, 36

50. James, *Varieties of Religious Experience*, 79. Newman wrote his own de-conversion narrative. Francis William Newman, *Phases of Faith; or, Passages from the History of My Creed* (London: Trubner, 1870). See the biographical sketch of Newman in David Hempton, *Evangelical Disenchantment: Nine Portraits of Faith and Doubt* (New Haven, CT: Yale University Press, 2008), 41–69. It is worth noting that in his autobiography, Newman also had a model of choice as forced reaction (albeit more rationalist than emotional) like James's: "He [meaning, Newman] has had *no choice* but to adopt the intellectual conclusions which offend them."

51. James, *Varieties of Religious Experience*, 80.

52. James, *Varieties of Religious Experience*, 121–76.

53. James, *Varieties of Religious Experience*, 196.

54. These kinds of experiences are akin to what I have been calling inherited and chosen religion. Charles Taylor, on whom I have depended for these categories as indicated in the introduction, likewise moves from James to those categories; see Taylor, *Varieties of Religion Today*, esp. 31–60.

55. James, *Varieties of Religious Experience*, 438–39.

56. James, *Varieties of Religious Experience*, 439–46.

57. James, *Varieties of Religious Experience*, 448.

58. James, *Varieties of Religious Experience*, 450–51.

59. James, *Varieties of Religious Experience*, 439.

60. James, *Varieties of Religious Experience*, 454.

61. James, *Varieties of Religious Experience*, 469.

Note on Sources

1. In writing about American conversions to Eastern Orthodoxy, Oliver Herbel has used a similar method. He prefers a different but compatible terminology (suiting his Orthodox subject), writing that the conversions of the leaders he studies "have been seen as iconic and theologically normative in America." D. Oliver Herbel, *Turning to Tradition: Converts and the Making of an American Orthodox Church* (New York: Oxford University Press, 2013), 2.

2. On the biography of Brainerd, see John A. Grigg, *The Lives of David Brainerd: The Making of an American Evangelical Icon* (New York: Oxford University Press, 2009); Sarah Rivett's *The Science of the Soul in Colonial New England* (Chapel Hill: University of North Carolina Press, 2011), 336–346.

3. On conversion as a genre, see D. Bruce Hindmarsh, *The Evangelical Conversion Narrative: Spiritual Autobiography in Early Modern England* (New York: Oxford University Press, 2005); John Owen King, *The Iron of Melancholy: Structures of Spiritual Conversion in America from the Puritan Conscience to Victorian Neurosis* (Middletown, CT: Wesleyan University Press, 1983); Stuart A. Federow, "Convert Autobiographies as a Genre of Literature" (rabbinic thesis, Hebrew Union College—Jewish Institute of Religion, 1982); Rodger M. Payne, *The Self and the Sacred: Conversion and Autobiography in Early American Protestantism* (Knoxville: University of Tennessee Press, 1998); John D. Barbour, *Versions of Deconversion: Autobiography and the Loss of Faith* (Charlottesville: University Press of Virginia, 1994).

4. For example, Simeon Crowell's narrative of becoming a Baptist was intended for circulation among his family. Simeon Crowell commonplace-book, 1790–1824, manuscript, Massachusetts Historical Society, Boston, MA. These manuscript conversion narratives intended for an audience are similar to the practices of authors' manuscripts circulated like published texts in an earlier period, as described in David D. Hall, *Ways of Writing: The Practice and Politics of Text-Making in Seventeenth-Century New England* (Philadelphia: University of Pennsylvania Press, 2008), 29–80.

Acknowledgments

THIS BOOK BEGAN in the collegial Department of History at Brandeis University. I could not imagine a wiser or more unfailingly generous adviser than Jonathan Sarna. I would not have attempted this study without being able to lean on the depth of his knowledge of one tradition and the breadth of his knowledge of others. Among several ways that Jane Kamensky has been my teacher, she improved my writing; in reading her comments, I often realized that she understood what I was trying to say better than I did. Readers will recognize how much David Hackett Fischer has shaped my thinking whenever they encounter terms such as *primary synthesis* or *deep change*. Govind Sreenivasan introduced me to the work of Charles Taylor in an informal reading group on *Sources of the Self*. I am grateful to Yoni Appelbaum, Cassandra Berman, Ian Campbell, Zev Eleff, Maura Jane Farrelly, April French, Geraldine Gudefin, John Hannigan, Allison Lange, Matt Linton, Anne Marie Reardon, and Emily Sigalow for critiquing parts of the manuscript. Craig and Tiffany Smith were faithful friends and guides throughout graduate school.

The book was finished thanks to my colleagues in the Department of History and Art History at George Mason University, who have done everything possible to support my scholarly work. I am especially grateful to those with whom I have worked most closely and who helped me with this project, directly or indirectly: Sheila Brennan, Cindy Kierner, Sam Lebovic, Sharon Leon, Sun-Young Park, Brian Platt, Stephen Robertson, and Rosie Zagarri. John Turner not only offered helpful comments on many parts of the manuscript, especially the introduction and Chapter 4; he did as much as anyone to help the manuscript become a book.

Some aspects of Chapter 6 are informed by my article "The Contours of Conversion to Catholicism in the Nineteenth Century," *U.S. Catholic Historian* 32, no. 2 (Spring 2014): 1–27.

Mark Noll generously offered detailed comments on a draft, which proved invaluable for revision. Jack Matzko taught me how to write when I was an undergraduate, and he line-edited this entire manuscript. I am thankful to him for being my teacher all these years.

For financial support, I am grateful to have received an Irving and Rose Crown Fellowship from Brandeis University, along with a research grant from the Andrew W. Mellon Foundation. A grant for Gerardo Marti's "Congregations and Social Change" seminar at Calvin College gave me a profitable summer in the company of sociologists and historians while I was beginning work. The Ruth B. Fein Prize from the American Jewish Historical Society let me research Chapter 5 at the Center for Jewish History in New York. The Kate B. and Hall J. Peterson Fellowship from the American Antiquarian Society provided for the research for most of Chapter 1 and part of Chapter 6. A junior faculty leave from George Mason University in fall 2015 let me complete most of the revisions for the book.

For permission to use images or cite unpublished archival material, I acknowledge the courtesy of the New-York Historical Society (archival collections in Chapter 6); the Massachusetts Historical Society (archival collections in Chapter 6); Manuscripts and Archives at the New York Public Library (archival collections in the introduction and Chapter 6); the Congregational Library (archival collections in Chapter 1); the Houghton Library at Harvard University and Wider Church Ministries of the United Church of Christ (archival collections in Chapter 2); the American Antiquarian Society (Figures 1.2 and 1.3); the American Jewish Historical Society (Figure 5.1 and archival material in Chapter 5); Special Collections at the University of Tennessee at Chattanooga (Figure 2.1); North Carolina Collection Photographic Archives, Wilson Library, UNC-Chapel Hill (Figure 3.1); Church History Library, the Church of Jesus Christ of Latter-day Saints (Figure 4.2); the Paulist Fathers Archives (archival material in Chapter 6); the Archives of the Archdiocese of Baltimore at the Associated Archives at St. Mary's Seminary and

University (archival material in Chapter 6); Fort Bend County Libraries and the Portal to Texas History (cover image).

Many librarians and archivists contributed their expertise and help, but I am especially grateful to Paul Erickson, Lauren Hewes, and Laura Wasowicz at the American Antiquarian Society; David Rosenberg at the Center for Jewish History; Cristina Prochilo, Claudette Newhall, and Peggy Bendroth at the Congregational Library; Tricia Pyne and Alison Foley of the Associated Archives at St. Mary's Seminary and University; Denise Eggers and Father Paul Robichaud of the Paulist Fathers Archives; and George Oberle at George Mason University. Thanks to Joyce Seltzer of Harvard University Press for her support for the manuscript and for her guidance on how to improve it. The anonymous peer reviewers for the Press also provided many valuable suggestions.

Two churches provided the framework of my family's life while I worked on this book: Evangelical Baptist Church in Newton, Massachusetts, and Truro Anglican Church in Fairfax, Virginia. Keith and Sharon Jones are friends who took us into their family. Kellen and Anna Beth Funk have been our friends and companions in college, graduate school, marriage, and child-rearing. No one has been readier to read over the manuscript than Kellen, who has a gift for improving my work. (He gave the book its title, too.) Since we met as undergraduates, Kellen has been the other half of my intellectual and spiritual life.

My father and mother, Paul and Tammy Mullen, have made everything possible with their love, not least by giving me an education. I hope that they will see this book as an attempt to understand the history of what they taught me about Christianity. My wife, Abby, is a historian in her own right. She has made innumerable corrections to everything I have ever written, all while enduring my refusal to show her anything that I was working on until I thought it was done enough. I hope that I can repay those debts to her while she writes her dissertation. The other debts I do not see how I could ever repay. My daughter, Margaret, was born just as I began work on the book; my son, Paul, was born while I was completing it. I have often thought of what Jonathan Sarna told me: "People will remember your children longer than they will remember your books." This book is dedicated to the memory of my grandmother, Elizabeth Mae Mullen, who passed down the faith to her children's children.

Index

Abercrombie, Anthony, 127–128
Adams, Hannah, 9, 11–13, 181, 182, 184, 188, 270
Adams, Nehemiah, 53, 56
Adams, William, 166–167
Adler, Felix, 210, 275
Adler, Nathan Marcus, 197
African American Christians, 103–131; and ecstatic experience, 120–121, 123–127; and emancipation, 121–123, 125, 127, 134, 137, 142–144, 146–147; and eschatology, 104–109, 108, 111, 113, 118, 120–121, 126–131; and exodus motif, 105; and hope, 104–106, 120, 126
African Methodist Episcopal Church, 118–119, 122–123, 131
African Methodist Episcopal Church Zion, 118
agnostics. *See* irreligion
Ahlstrom, Sidney, 10
Aldrich, Hazen, 158
Allen, Ethan, 241, 243, 275
Allen, Fanny, 243–244, 246
American Bible Society (ABS), 45, 47, 159, 228, 252
American Board of Commissioners for Foreign Missions (ABCFM), 2, 65, 67–68, 72, 76–77, 83, 86–101, 308n36, 309n60, 310n85
American Missionary Association (AMA), 127
American Society for Meliorating the Condition of the Jews (ASMCJ), 183–186, 188–190, 206–207

American Sunday School Union (ASSU), 60–61
American Tract Society (ATS), 18, 32–48, 52–53, 62, 87, 228; colporteurs of, 46–48
Anderson, Charity, 120
Anderson, Rufus, 74, 89, 95, 101
Anderson, Thomas, 111–112
Anglicans. *See* Episcopalians
Arch, John (Atsee), 73–74, 85, 87, 89, 93, 96–97
atheism, 4–5, 15, 35, 56, 154, 227, 240–243, 274–276. *See also* irreligion

Baird, Robert, 233–234
Baker, Francis A., 248, 253
Ballantyne, Richard, 167–168
baptism, 31, 50, 87–88, 104, 115, 171, 211; conditional baptism, 235, 240, 256, 264, 346n90, 348n120; instances of, 2, 17, 22, 64–65, 81–85, 92, 118, 128–129, 146, 149–150, 160–168, 187–188, 194, 216–217, 237–244, 250–252; forced baptism, 179–180; and justifications of slavery, 110; rates of, 23–26, 219; and Mormons, 145–147, 149–151, 154–156, 160–168; rebaptism, 139, 160, 188, 234–235, 250, 322n17, 346n90; theology of, 56–58, 61–62, 132, 134, 137–138, 143, 226, 234–237, 250–252. *See also* conversion: naming practices of
Baptists, 14, 22, 47, 54–55, 67–68, 89–93, 97–99, 101, 112–113, 131, 132, 137–138, 146, 157–158, 170, 188, 193, 264
Barber family, 243–246

359